HEGEL, NIETZSCHE, AND PHILOSOPHY

This challenging study explores the theme of freedom in the philosophy of Hegel and Nietzsche. In the first half of the book, Will Dudley sets Hegel's *Philosophy of Right* within a larger systematic account and innovatively deploys the *Logic* to interpret it. The author shows that freedom involves not only the establishment of certain social and political institutions but also the practice of philosophy itself. In the second half, Dudley reveals how Nietzsche's discussions of decadence, nobility, and tragedy map onto an analysis of freedom that critiques heteronomous choice and Kantian autonomy, and ultimately issues in a positive conception of liberation. In a provocative conclusion, Hegel and Nietzsche are portrayed as complementary, emphasizing different aspects of freedom and modes of philosophical thought, but concurring in the view that freedom is in part attained through philosophical thinking.

In boldly bringing Hegel and Nietzsche together into a conversation, something that is rarely attempted, Dudley has developed a set of original interpretations that will be of considerable importance to students of these philosophers, and more generally to political theorists and historians of ideas.

Will Dudley is Assistant Professor of Philosophy, Williams College.

MODERN EUROPEAN PHILOSOPHY

General Editor

Robert B. Pippin, *University of Chicago*

Advisory Board

Gary Gutting, *University of Notre Dame*
Rolf-Peter Horstmann, *Humboldt University, Berlin*
Mark Sacks, *University of Essex*

Some Recent Titles

Daniel W. Conway: *Nietzsche's Dangerous Game*
John P. McCormick: *Carl Schmitt's Critique of Liberalism*
Frederick A. Olafson: *Heidegger and the Ground of Ethics*
Günter Zöller: *Fichte's Transcendental Philosophy*
Warren Breckman: *Marx, the Young Hegelians, and the Origins of Radical Social Theory*
William Blattner: *Heidegger's Temporal Idealism*
Charles Griswold: *Adam Smith and the Virtues of the Enlightenment*
Gary Gutting: *Pragmatic Liberalism and the Critique of Modernity*
Allen Wood: *Kant's Ethical Thought*
Karl Ameriks: *Kant and the Fate of Autonomy*
Alfredo Ferrarin: *Hegel and Aristotle*
Cristina Lafont: *Heidegger, Language and World-Discourse*
Nicholas Wolsterstorff: *Thomas Reid and the Story of Epistemology*
Daniel Dahlstrom: *Heidegger's Concept of Truth*
Michelle Grier: *Kant's Doctrine of Transcendental Illusion*
Henry Allison: *Kant's Theory of Taste*
Allen Speight: *Hegel, Literature and the Problem of Agency*
J. M. Bernstein: *Adorno*

HEGEL, NIETZSCHE, AND PHILOSOPHY

Thinking Freedom

WILL DUDLEY
Williams College

CAMBRIDGE
UNIVERSITY PRESS

CAMBRIDGE UNIVERSITY PRESS
Cambridge, New York, Melbourne, Madrid, Cape Town, Singapore, São Paulo

Cambridge University Press
The Edinburgh Building, Cambridge CB2 8RU, UK

Published in the United States of America by Cambridge University Press, New York

www.cambridge.org
Information on this title: www.cambridge.org/9780521812504

First published 2002
This digitally printed version 2007

A catalogue record for this publication is available from the British Library

Library of Congress Cataloguing in Publication data
Dudley, Will, 1967–
Hegel, Nietzsche, and philosophy : thinking freedom / Will Dudley.
p.   cm.
Includes bibliographical references and index.
ISBN 0-521-81250-X
1. Hegel, Georg Wilhelm Friedrich, 1770–1831.   2. Nietzsche, Friedrich Wilhelm,
1844–1900.   3. Liberty.   I. Title.
B2949.L5 .D83   2002
123′.5′092243 – dc21   2001052693

ISBN 978-0-521-81250-4 hardback
ISBN 978-0-521-03886-7 paperback

For Earl and Louise Dudley,
my first and best teachers

CONTENTS

ACKNOWLEDGMENTS

I would not have been capable of completing this book were it not for the people who prepared, inspired, and guided me along the way, only a few of whom I can mention here. My parents taught me to read and write with care and to pursue all challenges, including those of the intellect, to the utmost of my ability. Alan White introduced me to philosophy when I was an undergraduate, provided the example that first led me to consider devoting myself to it, and offered generous comments on two drafts of this book. John McCumber introduced me to Hegel, showed me how philosophical scholarship should be done, and gave sage advice at every stage of this project. Stephen Houlgate planted the seeds that became the idea for this book, and set a standard for reading Hegel to which I will always aspire. Peter Fenves helped me to understand how my interpretations of Hegel and Nietzsche could be connected, and gave me invaluable feedback on my attempts to articulate that connection. Kevin Hill assisted me in finding my way through Nietzsche's texts and the vast secondary literature that has grown up around them. Ardis Collins, David Kolb, Robert Pippin, Jana Sawicki, and several anonymous reviewers read drafts of all or part of the book; their encouragement sustained my effort, and their criticisms improved the result. Terence Moore, Stephanie Achard, and Russell Hahn provided expert editing and guidance throughout the production process. Isaac Dietzel, my former student, proofread the final manuscript. Donna Chocal handled many administrative details and lent much-needed sanity and perspective to the enterprise. Williams College hired me, making the continued pursuit of philosophy possible, and has surrounded me with colleagues and students who make that pursuit enjoyable and stimulating.

The conversation and companionship of many friends have been a source of pleasure and support throughout the development of this book, and I am grateful to all of them. Finally, and most importantly, Janette Kessler Dudley has joined me for the last ten years in working to build a home in which we can both become who we are; Nicholas Kessler Dudley and Elizabeth Kessler Dudley have, more recently, done their best to ensure that our home is never dull.

   This book incorporates, in modified form, portions of several previously published articles. I would like to thank the editors and publishers of those articles for their permission to reprint material from the following: "Freedom in and through Hegel's Philosophy," *Dialogue: Canadian Philosophical Review* 39 (2000): 683–703; "A Limited Kind of Freedom: Hegel's Logical Analysis of the Finitude of the Will," *The Owl of Minerva* 31.2 (Spring 2000): 173–198; "A Case of Bad Judgment: The Logical Failure of the Moral Will," *Review of Metaphysics* 51 (December 1997): 379–404; and "Freedom and the Need for Protection from Myself," *The Owl of Minerva* 29.1 (Fall 1997): 39–67.

TEXTS, TRANSLATIONS, AND ABBREVIATIONS

I have used the Suhrkamp edition of Hegel's *Werke*, ed. Eva Moldenhauer and Karl Markus Michel, 20 vols. (Frankfurt: Suhrkamp, 1970–1).

I have used the following translations (which I have often modified) of various volumes of the Suhrkamp *Werke*:

A = Vol. 13, *Aesthetics: Lectures on Fine Art*, tr. T. M. Knox, vol. 1 (of 2) (Oxford: Clarendon, 1975).

EG = Vol. 10, *Hegel's Philosophy of Mind*, tr. A. V. Miller (Oxford: Clarendon, 1971).

EL = Vol. 8, *The Encyclopaedia Logic*, tr. T. F. Geraets, W. A. Suchting, and H. S. Harris (Indianapolis, Ind.: Hackett, 1991).

EN = Vol. 9, *Hegel's Philosophy of Nature*, tr. A. V. Miller (Oxford: Clarendon, 1970).

GP = Vols. 18–20, *Lectures on the History of Philosophy*, tr. E. S. Haldane and Frances H. Simson, vols. 1–3 (Atlantic Highlands, N.J.: Humanities Press, 1974).

PG = Vol. 12, *Introduction to the Philosophy of History*, tr. Leo Rauch (Indianapolis, Ind.: Hackett, 1988).

PhG = Vol. 3, *Hegel's Phenomenology of Spirit*, tr. A. V. Miller (Oxford: Oxford University Press, 1977).

PR = Vol. 7, *Elements of the Philosophy of Right*, ed. Allen W. Wood, tr. H. B. Nisbet (Cambridge: Cambridge University Press, 1991).

R = Vol. 16, *Lectures on the Philosophy of Religion*, tr. E. B. Speirs and J. Burdon Sanderson, vol. 1 (of 3) (Atlantic Highlands, N.J.: Humanities Press, 1974).

WL (vols. 1 and 2) = Vols. 5 and 6, *Hegel's Science of Logic*, tr. A. V. Miller (Atlantic, Highlands, N.J.: Humanities Press, 1969).

I have also made use of and reference to:

K = "Kolleg 1825/26," in *Vorlesungen: Ausgewählte Nachschriften und Manuskripte*, ed. Walter Jaeschke, vol. 6 (Hamburg: Felix Meiner,

1983–94), pp. 205–276; translated by Quentin Lauer as "Hegel's Introduction to the History of Philosophy," in his *Hegel's Idea of Philosophy* (New York: Fordham University Press, 1983), pp. 67–142.

PdR = *Philosophie des Rechts: Die Vorlesung von 1819/20 in einer Nachschrift*, ed. Dieter Henrich (Frankfurt am Main: Suhrkamp, 1983).

VG = *Die Vernunft in der Geschichte*, ed. J. Hoffmeister (Hamburg: Felix Meiner, 1955); translated by H. B. Nisbet as *Lectures on the Philosophy of World History: Introduction, Reason in History* (Cambridge: Cambridge University Press, 1975).

VGP = *Vorlesungen über die Geschichte der Philosophie*, ed. J. Hoffmeister (Hamburg: Felix Meiner, 1940); translated by T. M. Knox and A. V. Miller as *Introduction to the Lectures on the History of Philosophy* (Oxford: Oxford University Press, 1985).

VPR = *Vorlesungen über die Philosophie der Religion*, in *Vorlesungen*, ed. W. Jaeschke, vols. 3–5; translated by R. F. Brown, Peter C. Hodgson, and J. M. Stewart, assisted by J. P Fitzer and H. S. Harris, as *Lectures on the Philosophy of Religion*, ed. Peter C. Hodgson, 3 vols. (Berkeley: University of California Press, 1984–7).

VRP = *Vorlesungen über Rechtsphilosophie, 1818–1831*, ed. K-H. Ilting, 4 vols. (Stuttgart: Frommann-Holzboog, 1973).

Numbered sections, which are the same in the German and English editions, are referred to whenever possible. In these cases, an "A" (for *Anmerkung*) following the paragraph number indicates one of Hegel's own remarks on the paragraph, and a "Z" (for *Zusatz*) indicates material, usually taken from notes on Hegel's lectures, appended by earlier editors. When no paragraph numbers are available, I refer to page numbers, giving both the German and the English pagination, separated by a slash.

All citations of Nietzsche are from *Sämtliche Werke: Kritische Studienausgabe in 15 Bänden* (abbreviated *KSA*), ed. Giorgio Colli and Mazzino Montinari, 15 vols. (Berlin: de Gruyter, 1980).

I have used the following translations (which I have often modified) of various volumes of the *Sämtliche Werke*:

A = *The Antichristian*, translated by Walter Kaufmann as *The Antichrist*, in *PN* (see below).

BW = *Basic Writings of Nietzsche*, ed. Walter Kaufmann (New York: Modern Library, 1968).

DS = "David Strauss, the Confessor and the Writer," tr. R. J. Hollingdale, in *UB* (see below).

EH = *Ecce Homo*, tr. Walter Kaufmann, in *BW*.

FW = The Joyful Science, translated by Walter Kaufmann as *The Gay Science* (New York: Vintage Books, 1974).

FWag = The Case of Wagner, tr. Walter Kaufmann, in *BW.*

GD = Twilight of the Idols, tr. Walter Kaufmann, in *PN* (see below).

GM = On the Genealogy of Morals, tr. Walter Kaufmann, in *BW.*

GT = The Birth of Tragedy, tr. Walter Kaufmann, in *BW. SK* indicates the "Attempt at a Self-Criticism" added by Nietzsche to the second edition.

JGB = Beyond Good and Evil, tr. Walter Kaufmann, in *BW.*

M = Dawn, translated by R. J. Hollingdale as *Daybreak* (Cambridge: Cambridge University Press, 1982).

MA = Human, All Too Human, tr. R. J. Hollingdale (Cambridge: Cambridge University Press, 1986).

NN = "On the Uses and Disadvantages of History for Life," tr. R. J. Hollingdale, in *UB* (see below).

PN = The Portable Nietzsche, ed. Walter Kaufmann (New York: Viking Press, 1954).

RL = Friedrich Nietzsche on Rhetoric and Language, ed. and tr. Sander L. Gilman, Carole Blair, and David J. Parent (Oxford: Oxford University Press, 1989).

SE = "Schopenhauer as Educator," tr. R. J. Hollingdale, in *UB* (see below).

UB = Untimely Meditations, tr. R. J. Hollingdale (Cambridge: Cambridge University Press, 1983).

WB = "Richard Wagner in Bayreuth," tr. R. J. Hollingdale, in *UB.*

WM = The Will to Power, ed. Walter Kaufmann, tr. Walter Kaufmann and R. J. Hollingdale (New York: Vintage, 1968).

Z = Thus Spoke Zarathustra, tr. Walter Kaufmann, in *PN.*

Numbered sections, which are the same in the German and English editions, are referred to whenever possible. References to *KSA* provide the volume followed by the page number.

INTRODUCTION: FREEDOM AND PHILOSOPHY

No idea is so generally recognized as indefinite, ambiguous, and open to
the greatest misconceptions (to which therefore it actually falls a victim) as
the idea of freedom : none in common currency with so little appreciation
of its meaning.

Hegel[1]

1. The Significance of Freedom: From Politics to Philosophy

Hegel's remark is as true today as it was 170 years ago: freedom, one of our
most common and powerful concepts, is used (and misused) with extraor-
dinarily little appreciation of its significance. Worse, Hegel is wrong to
say that freedom's openness to misconception is "generally recognized."
Not only is freedom poorly understood, but we are falsely confident
that we do understand it. This doubly unfortunate condition dissuades
people from undertaking needed investigations into the meaning of
freedom.

Such investigations are needed because, across much of the world,
the concept of freedom plays an important role in the organization of
people's lives. People strongly desire freedom, and therefore support
governments, programs, policies, and candidates that they perceive to
advance its cause. But what people perceive to advance the cause of freedom depends upon what they understand freedom to be. And thus what
people understand freedom to be, even if their understanding is not explicitly articulated, matters a great deal to the way they live. As Robert
Pippin has put it:

> Modern agents can be said to be by and large committed to the right, truly
> authoritative modern norm, freedom, and so an equal entitlement to a
> free life, but suffer from the indeterminacy that the mere notion of free-
> dom leaves us with. (As the twentieth century has made clear, libertarian,
> welfarist, socialist and totalitarian projects all claim a commitment to the
> supreme principle of freedom.)[2]

1

Philosophers who think about freedom therefore have an opportunity to make a contribution not only to, but also beyond, their discipline. Most of the time, the analysis of abstract concepts is far removed from the concerns of anyone but professional academics. With freedom it is otherwise. Because developments in the understanding of the concept of freedom have an impact not only on the discipline of philosophy, but also on the ways in which individuals and communities structure their lives, freedom is a topic on which philosophers may do professionally respectable work while also entertaining the hope that their labor may be of some relevance to the wider world. If philosophers think about the meaning of freedom, and if such thinking improves our understanding of the conditions of our social and political liberation, then we all have a better chance of living more freely.

Of course, philosophers do not have a monopoly on thinking about freedom. Freedom is at issue across the humanities and the social sciences. To take but two preeminent examples from recent scholarship: the sociologist Orlando Patterson (in his two-volume study, *Freedom in the Making of Western Culture* and *Freedom in the Modern World*) and the historian Eric Foner (in *The Story of American Freedom*) have both explored the importance of the concept of freedom in the lives of nonacademics.[3] But whereas such sociological and historical studies tend to focus on how freedom has in fact been understood, and on how such understandings have in fact shaped the world, a distinctly philosophical investigation must determine how freedom *ought* to be understood, and how the world *must* be shaped if freedom is to be realized in it.

The concept of freedom is thus one of the most important points of intersection between the traditional branches of theoretical and practical philosophy. Freedom is of theoretical interest because we can wonder what freedom is, and whether or not we are capable of being free. And it is of practical interest because, given that we are capable of being free, and that being free is desirable, we can wonder how to live in such a way that this capability is most fully realized.

If philosophers think about the meaning of freedom, however, they will discover an even deeper connection between freedom and philosophy. Thinking about freedom reveals that its conditions of realization include not only certain social and political developments but also the practice of philosophy itself. In other words, philosophy is directly as well as indirectly liberating: philosophy contributes indirectly to freedom by articulating the social and political conditions of its realization; but philosophy also contributes directly to freedom because freedom is not only something about which philosophers think, but also something that is produced through philosophical thinking.

2. Competing Conceptions of Freedom

The claim that philosophy is a liberating activity is likely to be met with skepticism, if not outright derision. One of my main goals in this book, therefore, is to explain and defend it. In order to do so, I will have to argue that freedom ought to be understood or conceived in a certain way, and that other conceptions of freedom are deficient by comparison. Making such an argument requires a standard by which to judge competing conceptions of freedom. The standard I will use is that of *comprehensiveness.*

One conception of freedom (A) is more comprehensive than another (B) if, and only if, two criteria are met: first, A must include and expand upon the freedoms included in B; and second, the newfound freedoms included in A must rectify a specific limitation or dependence from which the supposedly free subject can be shown to suffer in B, and thus serve as the condition of the freedoms included in B, without which the latter would prove to be illusory.

In moving from one conception of freedom to another that is more comprehensive, nothing is lost and something is gained. Nothing is lost because the more comprehensive conception retains the freedoms included in the less comprehensive conception. Something is gained because the more comprehensive conception expands and improves upon the less comprehensive conception by recognizing that the freedoms included in the latter are necessary but not sufficient conditions of freedom.

We therefore ought to understand freedom as comprehensively as we can. It is my contention that we are able to do so by drawing on and bringing together the work of Hegel and Nietzsche. The interpretations of their work that form the bulk of this book will show that freedom, most comprehensively understood, requires not only the development of certain social and political structures, but also the activity of philosophy itself.

In preparation for these interpretations, I want to consider very briefly the two most important conceptions of freedom on which Hegel and Nietzsche build, but which they also criticize for being insufficiently comprehensive. The first and less comprehensive of these two is that of liberalism. The second, which is more comprehensive than that of liberalism but still less comprehensive than those of Hegel and Nietzsche, is that of Kant.[4]

LIBERAL FREEDOM

> A free-man is he, that in those things, which by his strength and wit he is able to do, is not hindered to do what he has a will to.
>
> Hobbes[5]

Liberalism understands freedom as the ability of a person to do what she chooses to do, with as few external impediments as possible. Such freedom has come to be called "negative" liberty: it is freedom *from* the interference of others, a *lack* of external constraint.[6]

Negative liberty is represented in the common expression, "free as a bird." Animals are taken to enjoy an enviable degree of negative liberty because they are unconstrained by the social ties, conventions, and laws to which humans are subject. Among animals, birds represent the paradigm of negative liberation because they can fly, and so are less constrained by geography and even gravity than other animals. Thus animals in general, and birds in particular, are thought to be free in this sense because they can do what they choose to do, with fewer constraints than humans experience.

The liberal conception of freedom is remarkably simple and, not coincidentally, remarkably powerful. It is likely the response most people would give if asked for a definition of freedom. And, therefore, it has enormous political significance.

This significance was recently demonstrated in American politics by the dramatic ascent of the Republican Party to its first congressional majority in nearly half a century, a development that was explicitly billed by its leaders and proponents as "the freedom revolution."[7] Intellectually, this revolution turned on two ideas that are at the core of liberalism: first, that government exists to secure the freedom of its people; and second, that freedom consists of individuals' ability to act on their choices with a minimum of external constraint. These ideas were conjoined with a belief that the government of the United States, by expanding the public sphere to encompass matters that should have been left to private choice, had itself become a hindrance to, rather than the protector of, the freedom of its citizens. Given this belief, and their commitment to and particular understanding of freedom, Republican leaders drew the logical conclusion that the government of the United States should be scaled back – its budget cut and its programs reduced – and then redirected to what they understood to be its core functions: the protection of freedom from international threats through the provision of a national defense, and the protection of freedom from domestic threats through the provision of police and prisons. Running on this platform, the Republican Party enjoyed a spectacular electoral triumph in 1994, one that illustrates the importance of freedom to voters, the connection between a theoretical conception of freedom and a practical political program, and the intuitive appeal of the liberal conception of freedom.

KANTIAN FREEDOM

Will is a kind of causality of living beings insofar as they are rational, and freedom would be that property of such causality that it can be efficient

independently of alien causes *determining* it . . . What, then, can freedom of
the will be other than autonomy, that is, the will's property of being a law
to itself? . . . Hence a free will and a will under moral laws are one and the
same.

Kant[8]

Kant criticizes liberalism on the ground that the ability to act on one's
choices with minimal external constraint is a necessary but not a sufficient
condition of freedom. Freedom, Kant argues, requires not only that individuals be allowed to act in accordance with their choices (which is all
that liberalism's understanding of freedom involves), but also that they
be genuinely responsible for those choices themselves. And the capacity
for such responsibility requires that individuals be endowed with free will:
at least some choices must be determined not by causes external to the
will (which include, for Kant, an individual's own desires), but rather by
the will's respect for the universal moral law that it gives to itself. In short,
whereas liberalism understands freedom as the person's unfettered ability to do what she chooses, Kant insists that freedom must be understood
as the will's ability to determine autonomously what the person chooses
to do.

On Kant's view, then, animals are not free at all. Animals, and most
especially birds, may well experience fewer constraints on the execution
of their chosen actions than humans do. But to call their actions "chosen,"
Kant argues, is seriously misleading. Animals lack rationality, and consequently lack autonomy. The causes of all of their actions are external to
them, originating not in choices determined by autonomous willing but
rather in heteronomous instincts. There is nothing for humans to envy,
therefore, in the negative liberty enjoyed by animals, for without rational
and autonomous willing, such negative liberty fails to be freedom.

Kant's view might seem to have several obvious disadvantages in comparison to that of liberalism. First, it is notoriously complicated: the liberal understanding of freedom can be presented in a few pages, but
a good explication of Kantian freedom requires a book-length study.[9]
Second, it confounds common sense: liberal freedom involves doing what
one chooses, but Kantian freedom involves subjecting oneself to moral
laws even in the absence of any desire to do so, and thus doing what is
required simply because it is required. To ordinary ears this sounds not
like freedom, but rather its opposite. Third, it is metaphysical: the subject
of liberal freedom is the person, but the subject of Kantian freedom is
the will, a mysterious kind of noumenal causality that can never be experienced but that must be effective if moral agency is to be possible.[10]
Fourth, and finally, the link between this metaphysical freedom of the
will and the social and political freedom of the person is deeply problematic. In particular, for Kant a rational agent's freedom, since it resides in the noumenal will, is independent of the agent's physical and

political situation; though he would grant that starvation or slavery makes it harder to ignore heteronomous motives, there is still no phenomenal situation that a noumenally free agent is not obligated, and therefore able, to overcome. The most Kant might say (and not without difficulty) is that some political systems and cultures are more conducive than others to their citizens' being able to ignore phenomenal motives; but social and political arrangements can never be essential to human freedom for him.[11]

Nonetheless, the Kantian conception of freedom is superior to that of liberalism, and for the reason Kant himself provides: one may meet the liberal standard and yet fail to be free. Although independence from constraint or interference is an indispensable element of freedom, upon reflection it is shown to be incomplete: I may, like an animal, be free to do what I choose while it is still the case that my choices, and so my actions, are not truly my own. I may choose to smoke because I am addicted, I may choose to attend college because I have been raised in a particular way, or I may choose to eat because I am hungry. In each of these cases, even if my ability to act is unconstrained, my "choice" is driven by factors over which I have little or no control, and I therefore remain dependent in a significant sense. Kant thus shows that the acting and choosing of persons is truly free only if such actions and choices are determined by autonomous willing.

In other words, the Kantian conception of freedom is more comprehensive than the liberal conception. First, Kantian freedom includes liberal freedom, because the agent whose choices are determined by autonomous willing is not considered free unless it is also the case that her attempts to act on those choices are subject to minimal external constraint. Second, the Kantian conception expands upon that of liberalism by providing for freedom of the will, which the liberal conception does not include. And third, such freedom of the will is the condition of genuine freedom of choice: even if the liberal subject is free to act upon her choices without constraint, her choosing itself remains externally determined, a limitation that is rectified only if she is capable of autonomous willing.

Thus nothing is lost and something is gained in moving from conceiving of freedom as the person's unfettered action to conceiving of freedom as the will's autonomy or self-determination. Nothing is lost because the idea that freedom requires negative liberty is preserved. But something is gained because the conception of freedom as the autonomy of the will recognizes and responds to the fact that negative liberty is a necessary but not a sufficient condition of freedom. Freedom requires autonomous willing *and* unconstrained acting; the latter fails to be free without the former, and *both* are contained in the Kantian conception.

3. Hegel and Nietzsche

Although the Kantian conception of freedom is more comprehensive than that of liberalism, it is still not comprehensive enough. In the same way that reflection upon freedom of action reveals its limitations and its reliance on freedom of the will, reflection upon freedom of the will shows that it too is limited and depends upon yet another kind of freedom. Such reflection, and the development of a sufficiently comprehensive conception of freedom that rectifies the limitations of willing, are the work of this book. More accurately, the work of this book is to examine the reflections of Hegel and Nietzsche upon freedom of the will, and to show that they independently produce complementary results, which can be brought together to yield a conception of freedom more comprehensive than that of Kant.[12]

Hegel and Nietzsche, I will argue, both adopt Kant's strategic move against liberalism, whereby he shows that its particular understanding of freedom depends upon a further kind of freedom for which it is unable to account. But they then turn this move against Kant himself. In the same way that Kant shows that acting persons are truly free only if their choices are determined by a free will, Hegel and Nietzsche show that willing can be truly free only in virtue of an activity other than itself. That is, although self-determination of the will is a more comprehensive conception of freedom than unfettered action, it rests on yet another kind of freedom, without which willing fails to be genuinely self-determining.

It is this conclusion that produces the deep connection between freedom and philosophy, for the liberating activity that Hegel and Nietzsche identify as the condition of free willing is the practice of philosophy itself. Thus Hegel and Nietzsche ultimately show us not only that freedom is a central topic of consideration *in* philosophy, but also that the most comprehensive freedom is achieved *through* philosophical practice.

Philosophy is liberating in two distinct senses. First, it is indirectly liberating because it is by means of philosophy that we are able to determine what it is to be free, and thus to determine the conditions of living freely. In other words, philosophical thinking is a condition of genuinely free willing, because freedom cannot be willed in the absence of a philosophical determination of what freedom is; philosophy yields theoretical results that must be applied practically in extra-philosophical spheres, the social and political spheres in which we live and act. Second, philosophy is also directly liberating, because one of the theoretical results it yields is the idea that an important part of being free is living philosophically. In other words, it is not only the social and political applications of philosophy's theoretical results that are liberating, but the practice of philosophy itself.

This much, I will argue, Hegel and Nietzsche agree upon. But they also disagree in several important respects. First, although they share the view that Kantian autonomy is not a sufficiently comprehensive conception of freedom, their reflections expose different limitations to which willing is subject. Second, because they expose different limitations of willing, Hegel and Nietzsche identify different ways in which the Kantian conception of freedom must be modified and enlarged. Third and finally, although these modifications and enlargements result, in both cases, in an understanding that freedom involves philosophy, Hegel and Nietzsche do not understand philosophical practice in the same way, and so have different understandings of the ways in which this practice is liberating.

My conclusion will be that the different responses of Hegel and Nietzsche to Kant prove to be complementary. Their central point of agreement – that Kantian autonomy is an insufficiently comprehensive conception of freedom – teaches us that freedom involves not only acting and willing, but also practicing philosophy. But the different ways in which they arrive at this result, and the different interpretations that they give to it, teach us that our conception of freedom as philosophical practice must be still more comprehensive than that provided by either Hegel or Nietzsche alone. We need a theoretical understanding of freedom that incorporates the insights of both Hegel and Nietzsche into what the activity of philosophy involves, and a philosophical practice that incorporates the complementary models of philosophical activity that the texts of Hegel and Nietzsche exemplify.

4. Goals and Structure of the Book

With this book I hope to make a contribution both to the project of understanding freedom, and to the project of understanding the texts of Hegel and Nietzsche. If I am right, the two tasks are interrelated: our understanding of Hegel and Nietzsche is helpfully guided by attending to their attention to the problem of freedom, and our understanding of freedom is furthered by the insights gained from that exegetical work.

To the extent that I am successful, this book should contribute to philosophical scholarship in several ways. First and foremost, it should draw attention to the fact that a comprehensive treatment of the problem of freedom cannot be provided by liberal political theory or by Kantian moral philosophy. Instead, I hope to show, the freedoms these discourses treat are dependent upon the more comprehensive freedom of philosophical thinking. The primary consequence of this is that "practical" discussions of politics and morality must be connected to "theoretical" work on the nature of thought.

Second, since this more comprehensive conception of freedom and my conclusions about its consequences will be produced by bringing Hegel and Nietzsche together, this book should also contribute to the history of philosophy. Although interest in both Hegel and Nietzsche continues to increase in the English-speaking world, there is still relatively little work that relates the two.[13]

Third, my interpretation of Hegel's conception of freedom is importantly different from other treatments of the topic. I do not confine myself to the *Philosophy of Right*, but instead argue that Hegel's account of objective spirit needs to be read within the context of his philosophy of spirit as a whole – in particular, we must understand the limitations to the freedom of willing that Hegel identifies, and the role that he envisions for art, religion, and philosophy in overcoming them.[14] Moreover, in reading the *Philosophy of Right* and the other parts of the philosophy of spirit I make use of the *Logic*, and try to show how the introduction of logical considerations leads to an improved understanding of Hegel's conception of freedom.[15]

Fourth and finally, my interpretation of Nietzsche as continuing the efforts of Kant and Hegel to determine the conditions of freedom brings him into direct engagement with German Idealism. I argue that Nietzsche's discussions of decadence, nobility, and tragedy can be mapped onto an analysis of the conditions of freedom that offers critiques of both heteronomous choice and Kantian autonomy, and that ultimately issues in a positive conception of liberation.

The structure of the book has been determined by its goals. Following this introduction, the body of the work is divided into two parts, the first devoted to an interpretation of Hegel, the second to an interpretation of Nietzsche. These interpretations are followed by a conclusion, in which I attempt to show how the insights of the two parts can and must be thought together.

The structures of the two parts are quite similar. Each is composed of four chapters. The opening chapters of both Part I and Part II locate the concept of freedom in the texts of Hegel and Nietzsche, respectively, and present my approach to reading those texts. Hegel's works, of course, comprise a system, so Chapter 1 identifies the places where freedom appears in that system, and explains both how those occurrences relate to each other, and how their systematic interrelation bears on my interpretation of them.[16] Nietzsche's works, of course, are unsystematic, so Chapter 5 (the opening chapter of Part II) explains both how I have reconstructed an account of freedom from them, and how their lack of systematicity bears on that account.

The second chapters of both parts are concerned with freedom of the will: Chapter 2 presents Hegel's analysis; Chapter 6 presents Nietzsche's. Both of these analyses produce positive results by negative means: they determine the conditions of freedom of the will by identifying the limitations of various types of willing that fail to achieve it. In Hegel, this analysis takes the shape of a critique of what he calls the moral will, and results in the conclusion that a truly free will is an ethical one, one belonging to a citizen of a rational political state. In Nietzsche, the subject of critique is what he calls the decadent will, and the conclusion drawn is that the possessor of a free will is one who is a member of a noble community.

Whereas the second chapters of the two parts determine the conditions of freedom of the will by identifying the limitations that incompletely free types of willing cannot overcome, the third chapters determine the limits to which even a free will is subject. This negative work again provides positive rewards, this time in the form of a determination of the requirements of freedom that willing cannot meet. Chapter 3, which presents Hegel's analysis, demonstrates that although ethical citizenship in a rational state is the most complete freedom that willing can provide, this political activity has limitations that only the activities Hegel discusses in absolute spirit – art, religion, and philosophy – can overcome. Chapter 7, which presents Nietzsche's analysis of the limits of free willing, demonstrates that freedom requires the transformation of noble individuals and communities into what he calls tragic ones, in which liberation is increased by forsaking noble autonomy in favor of an openness to being affected by that which is external and alien.

The concluding chapters of Parts I and II examine the roles that philosophy, as Hegel and Nietzsche understand and practice it, has to play in overcoming the limitations of willing and leading us toward the most comprehensive possible freedom. Chapter 4 presents Hegel's understanding of philosophy as conceptual systematization, illuminates it by reflecting on the systematic conceptual development that we have seen Hegel perform in Chapters 2 and 3, and considers the senses in which this systematic practice may be said to be liberating. Chapter 8 presents Nietzsche's understanding of philosophy as the genealogical destabilization and transformation of established conceptual systems, illuminates it by reflecting on the philosophical genealogy that we have seen Nietzsche perform in Chapters 6 and 7, and considers the senses in which this genealogical practice may be said to be liberating.

These concluding chapters thus attend not only to the differences between Hegel's and Nietzsche's understandings of philosophy, but also to the differences between the ways in which their own philosophical practices exemplify these understandings. Because *what* Hegel and Nietzsche say is that the practice of philosophy is liberating, *how* each of them practices philosophy is revealing of what they understand freedom to be. In other words, the different philosophical styles of Hegel and Nietzsche amount to differences of philosophical substance as well, and an explication of their substantive views cannot ignore the styles in which those views are expressed.[17]

The stylistic differences between Hegel and Nietzsche bear not only on the substance of the question of freedom, but also on the styles in which the two parts of this book have been composed. Although my discussions of Hegel and Nietzsche are structured quite similarly, they are noticeably different in style. These differences are mandated by the exegetical goal of producing adequate interpretations of both Hegel and Nietzsche. Given that Hegel and Nietzsche differ so markedly in style, and given that these differences are not merely stylistic, there is no single interpretive style adequate to the work of both thinkers. Rather than force one style onto both interpretations, then, I have tried instead to find for each interpretation the style best suited to it. As a result, my interpretation of Hegel is recognizably Hegelian, with respect to both its conceptual vocabulary and its internal organization and subdivision. By contrast, my interpretation of Nietzsche is, if not recognizably Nietzschean (for such a style is not particularly well suited to the kind of careful exegesis and analysis that I aim to produce), at least not Hegelian. I have provided it with an organization that is intended to be faithful to Nietzsche's texts and vocabulary while also illuminating the question of freedom, which is one of the things I think those texts and that vocabulary are best able to do.

The book's conclusion brings together the complementary results of Parts I and II to produce a conception of freedom that is more comprehensive than either Hegel or Nietzsche, when read without reference to the other, is able to provide. This conception, like those of Hegel and Nietzsche, retains the understanding that freedom involves free willing and unfettered acting, but recognizes that the possibility of both of these activities ultimately depends upon the practice of philosophy. This liberating practice is now understood, however, to encompass both Hegelian conceptual systematization and Nietzschean genealogical destabilization of established conceptual systems. The conclusion, and the book, ends by suggesting briefly how the liberation afforded by such philosophical practices relates back to the liberation of the social and political sphere with which our interest in freedom begins.

I

FREEDOM IN AND THROUGH HEGEL'S PHILOSOPHY

THE PLACE OF FREEDOM IN HEGEL'S PHILOSOPHY

Hegel thinks that there is nothing more important for us to understand, and nothing that we understand more poorly, than freedom. In fact, his whole philosophical system, in all its incredible breadth and detail, can be understood as a single extended demonstration of the importance and meaning of freedom. Moreover, Hegel's philosophy is not only *about* freedom, but also claims to be productive *of* it: in the course of his philosophical investigation of what it means to be free, Hegel arrives at the view that freedom depends upon the practice of philosophy.

Understanding this view, which is the central aim of Part I of this book, requires us to examine what Hegel has to say about freedom, philosophy, and their interconnection. This chapter prepares for that examination by locating freedom within Hegel's system. Section 1 provides a brief overview of the three main parts of Hegel's system: logic, the philosophy of nature, and the philosophy of spirit. Section 2 explicates the concept of freedom developed in the *Logic*. Section 3 then draws on that logical concept to explain why the entirety of the philosophy of spirit should be understood as an account of freedom. It also briefly discusses the parts of the philosophy of spirit, and the place of the *Philosophy of Right* within it. Section 4 concludes the chapter with some remarks on the structure and method of the rest of Part I, which interprets Hegel's account of freedom, both within and beyond the *Philosophy of Right*, in order ultimately to understand why and how Hegel considers the practice of philosophy to be liberating.

1. The Parts of Hegel's System: Logic, Nature, Spirit

Freedom makes its first appearance in Hegel's philosophy before his system proper even begins: the *Phenomenology of Spirit*, which serves as an introduction to the system, is an account of the elevation of consciousness to a standpoint that Hegel characterizes as free, the standpoint of the speculative philosopher. The speculative philosopher engages in conceptual thinking, and Hegel claims that in virtue of such thinking she is free.[1]

The attainment of the standpoint of the speculative philosopher marks the transition from the introduction to the system proper; the *Phenomenology* prepares the way for the free conceptual thinking that transpires in the logic, the philosophy of nature, and the philosophy of spirit. These three main parts of Hegel's system are distinguished from each other by the kind of thing they endeavor to think or comprehend. Logic seeks the conceptual comprehension of thought itself: it studies the pure concepts with which thinking beings think.[2] In contrast to logic, the philosophies of nature and spirit seek the conceptual comprehension of beings that have an existence external to thought, a real existence in space and time. Together they thus comprise what Hegel calls *Realphilosophie*. The philosophy of nature attempts to comprehend those beings that can justifiably be called natural, and the philosophy of spirit attempts to comprehend those beings that can justifiably be called spiritual.

Freedom not only describes the condition of the speculative philosopher, but is also one of the concepts that she comes to think as she moves through philosophy. Freedom first arises in the *Logic*, where it marks the important transition from the logic of essence to the logic of the concept.[3] This logical concept of freedom is then assumed by the speculative philosopher throughout the *Realphilosophie*, in the course of her attempts to comprehend natural and spiritual beings. In virtue of the very meanings of "nature" and "freedom," natural beings prove to be those that are incapable of being free; the purview of the philosophy of nature is limited to that which "exhibits no freedom in its existence, but only necessity and contingency."[4] And in virtue of "spirit" being defined as that which is not merely natural, spiritual beings and free beings then prove to be one and the same; the philosophy of spirit proclaims at its outset that "the essential . . . feature of spirit is freedom."[5]

Freedom thus enjoys extraordinary prominence in Hegel's system: it is the condition attained by the speculative philosopher at the end of the *Phenomenology*; it is one of the crucial concepts that such a philosopher thinks in the *Logic*; it defines the philosophy of nature, as that which is conceptually excluded from it; and it defines the philosophy of spirit, as that which it is concerned to comprehend.

But identifying the prominence of freedom in Hegel's system is not the same thing as understanding it. To do so, we have to turn to the *Logic*, which provides the concept of freedom that is assumed throughout the *Realphilosophie*. The *Logic* is relevant to the philosophy of spirit (and to the philosophy of nature) because Hegel understands the concepts it studies to be the conditions of all thinking whatsoever: we cannot help using them whenever we think about anything at all. This means that Hegel's attempt to think about or conceptually comprehend spiritual beings in the philosophy of spirit employs concepts developed in his *Logic*. In particular, Hegel's attempt to comprehend the freedom of spiritual beings employs the concept of freedom developed in the *Logic*. So to understand his account of what it is to be a free being with a real existence – that is, a spiritual being – we must first understand his account, found in the *Logic*, of what it is to be free *simpliciter*. Although this discussion may seem abstract and difficult to readers unfamiliar with Hegel's *Logic*, it is indispensable to Hegel's entire account of freedom, and so to my entire interpretation of that account, and therefore cannot be avoided. I have endeavored, however, to make it as brief and clear as possible, and to provide examples that illuminate the conceptual distinctions at issue.

2. The Logical Concept of Freedom

Freedom is determined in the *Logic* as the overcoming of necessity. Necessity itself is determined as "the merely internal, and for that reason merely external, connection of mutually independent existences."[6] That the connection between two things is merely internal means that although being connected to the other is constitutive of what each thing is, this fact is not evident: "The identity of the two things that appear bound in necessity, and which, for that reason, lose their independence, is at first only an inner identity that is not yet present to those who are subject to necessity."[7] This makes the connection merely external in the sense that it is not understood to be an intrinsic feature of the things it connects.[8] Rather, the connection is understood to be an accidental relation obtaining between "mutually independent existences." Plainly put, a thing is unfree, or subject to necessity, when it is bound to something that is external to itself and thus irrelevant to making it what it is. Such an external bond prevents the thing from being self-determining, and so from being free.

One of Hegel's examples is the planets: all are connected in a system of orbits, but at the same time this connection does not make them what they are; each planet is the planet that it is, all by itself, and its participation in a system with other planets is an additional feature, external to that which makes it what it is.[9] Mars would still be Mars, in other words, even if Venus did not exist, and thus the bond between their orbits involves the two in a relationship of necessity and external determination that restricts the independence of both.

If necessity is a relationship in which mutually independent or external things are bound to and determined by each other, and freedom is the overcoming of necessity, then freedom would seem to be achievable in one of two ways: either the bonds between the mutually external things could be cut, so that the things no longer restrict each other; or the externality could be overcome (internalized), so that the things remain bound but understand that being bound to each other is constitutive of what they are. In the latter case, freedom would be achieved because a thing's independence cannot be threatened by that which makes it what it is; in fact, if a thing can be what it is only in virtue of being bound in a particular way, then that bond actually makes possible its independent existence as the thing that it is.

But the former option – the cutting of the bonds – which might appear to be the more intuitive, fails to solve the problem. As long as the relata continue to exist, they must remain related, even if their relation is only that of things trying to escape, or unwilling to acknowledge, any relation between themselves. Thus the attempt to sever all connection fails, leaving the two things both bound and external to each other, and so unfree.

Whereas the planets are bound together in necessity, which they can never overcome, an example of the failed attempt to achieve such overcoming through the cutting of bonds can be found in the inveterate bachelor who avoids all long-term relationships. Such a person understands his identity to be what it is independent of other people, and thus views long-term relationships as restrictive and limiting. Although he may enter into them for various reasons – out of loneliness or sexual desire, perhaps – he can never experience them as constitutive of a union that creates and sustains his identity and thus makes possible his liberation. On the contrary, he necessarily experiences long-term relationships as diminishing his freedom, which he therefore believes he can find only through their dissolution. But such dissolution is always imperfect: it transforms the bachelor's relationship to his former partner but cannot eradicate it. As Hegel puts it: "the person who flees is not yet free, for in fleeing, he is still determined by the very thing from which he is fleeing."[10]

Since the cutting of the bonds fails to liberate, freedom can be produced only through a demonstration that the bound elements are not truly external to each other, through making manifest the fact that their identities are reciprocally constitutive. Necessity becomes freedom not by severing bonds, but by developing a different understanding of the character of the things bound. They must come to be seen not as entities independent of one another, external to and restrictive of one another, but as distinct parts internal to a larger, self-determining whole that encompasses them and their interconnections.

In this new understanding, both the whole and its parts are seen to be free. The whole is free because in being bound to its parts it is bound only to itself. The parts are free because, even though they are bound to other parts and to the whole, these bonds are now understood to be internal to the nature of the parts themselves; it is understood that each part is what it is only in virtue of being a part of the whole. This means that the parts could not even be themselves without being bound to the other parts of the whole, which means that, instead of constituting external restrictions on each other, the parts actually constitute the other parts themselves.[11]

The ultimate difference, then, between a necessary relation and a free one is that in the latter the bonds of the former have been comprehended as internal to the very nature of the things bound, which means that the things bound have been comprehended as internal to each other.[12] Thus Hegel writes that

> the process of necessity is the overcoming of what is present at first as rigid externality, so that its inwardness is revealed. What this process shows is that the terms that appear initially to be bound together are not in fact alien to one another; instead, they are only moments of one whole, each of which, being related to the other, is at home with itself (*bei sich selbst*), and goes together with itself (*mit sich selbst*). This is the transfiguration of necessity into freedom.[13]

Whereas the planets and inveterate bachelors are bound in necessity (no matter how desperately the latter try to escape it or how loudly they proclaim that they have), Hegel considers the entry into a loving marriage to be an example of the transformation of a necessary bond into a free one. Partners who enter into such a marriage, according to Hegel, change their self-understanding: they come to understand themselves not as individuals with preestablished and separate identities who are accidentally connected to each other, but as members of a union in which their very identity as individuals is constituted. Marriage gives one "self-consciousness of one's individuality *within this unity* . . . so that one is present in it not as an independent person but as a *member*."[14] This transformation of self-consciousness internalizes the bond between the partners, by making explicit the fact that their bond is intrinsic to what they are: "the *union* of the natural sexes, which was merely *inward* [prior to marriage]...and whose existence was for this very reason merely external, is transformed into a *spiritual* union, into self-conscious love."[15] Because this internalization of an external bond is the logical criterion for the transformation of necessity into freedom, the entry into a loving marital union allows partners to experience themselves as freely bound together.

The internalization of the external that marks the movement from necessity to freedom also amounts, for Hegel, to the transfiguration of the finite into the infinite. He defines the finite as "whatever comes to an end, what *is*, but ceases to be where it connects with its other, and is thus restricted by it. Hence the finite subsists in its relation to its other, which is its negation and presents itself as its limit."[16]

Given this definition, it is immediately apparent that any two finite things are mutually external in the sense already discussed. The fact that each serves as the other's limit means that the character of each is understood to be fundamentally independent of that of the other. Consequently, the connection between the two can only function as a restriction on both. Finite things are bound to and determined by each other in necessity, not in freedom.

Since finite things are bound in necessity through being connected to other finite things that lie beyond their limits, the transfiguration from finitude to infinity could be sought in two ways. These alternatives correspond precisely to those previously considered as ways of overcoming necessity: either the connection could be severed; or it could be internalized, through the recognition that it constitutes the things that it connects in virtue of constituting the limits that make them what they are.

As before, the first option fails to solve the problem. Disconnecting two finite things may shift the limits of each, but it cannot help but leave both limited. And, Hegel points out, this is true no matter how often the operation is performed; at best, the repetition of disconnection can produce an infinite series of altered relations between things that remain perpetually finite. Famously, Hegel writes that "this *infinity* is *spurious* or *negative* infinity, since it is nothing but the negation of the finite, but the finite arises again in the same way, so that it is no more sublated than not. In other words, this infinity expresses only the requirement that the finite *ought* to be sublated."[17]

It is therefore only the second option, a finite thing's internalization of its connection to its other, and thereby its recognition that it and its other are reciprocally constitutive, that produces genuine, rather than spurious, infinity. In a genuine infinity there are no longer any strictly finite elements that limit and restrict each other, but only elements that are moments of the whole, and therefore are what they are only in that self-determining whole and in their relations to its other moments. Using phraseology identical to that which marks the passage from necessity to freedom, Hegel says that "the genuine infinite . . . consists in remaining at home with itself (*bei sich selbst*) in its other, or, when it is expressed as a process, in coming to itself (*zu sich selbst*) in its other."[18]

Returning to our examples, we can see that the mutually external planets are irredeemably finite, the inveterate bachelor achieves only negative or spurious infinity, and the marriage partners achieve a genuine infinity. The infinitude of the bachelor is negative or spurious because even if he were to abandon or deny his connection to an infinite number of partners, he would never alter the fundamental finitude of his situation. Unable to find himself at home in a union with another person, he clings to his independent identity and thus continues to experience human relationships as the imposition of necessity rather than as the condition of freedom. But the marriage partners, in transforming their understanding of their relationship, from that of an arrangement in which they happen to have joined their independent identities to that of a union within which their shared identities as members are created and sustained, cease to experience each other as restrictive or limiting. Instead, they experience themselves as mutually constitutive of the whole that makes them who they are, and within which they are thus at home.

The conclusion to draw from this brief investigation of the *Logic* is this: for Hegel, freedom results from the transfiguration of the finite into the infinite, and this transfiguration takes place through an internalization of the external. By means of this process, one being discovers that its identity lies in being a member of a union with another being that it once experienced as alien and restrictive. A being is liberated, that is, not by fleeing from what seems to be foreign to it, but through a reconciliation with its other that demonstrates that their mutual estrangement is not insuperable. Freedom thus requires attaining self-determining individuality by renouncing independence: in Hegel's terms, it requires achieving identity-in-difference, the contradiction embodied in genuine love that the bachelor's understanding cannot grasp.[19]

3. The Philosophy of Spirit as an Account of Freedom

Hegel's logical discussion of freedom, and the examples used to illustrate it, show that freedom is available only to certain kinds of beings. Only a being capable of internalizing its external limitations, of achieving a genuine infinity by overcoming the apparent finitude of both itself and its other through a demonstration that the two are members of a larger, self-determining unity, can be free.

For Hegel, this means that no merely natural being is capable of freedom. Natural beings, on his account, "are more or less mutually independent existences; true, through their original unity they stand in mutual connection, so that none can be comprehended without the others; but this connection is in a greater or less degree external to them."[20] Hegel's contention is that "in a greater or less degree" all merely natural beings are like the planets: interconnected and bound together as elements of a whole (the universe, and various smaller wholes within it), yet mutually external at the same time. He expresses this contention in the claim that "even in the most perfect form to which nature raises itself . . . [it] does not attain. . . to complete victory over the externality and finitude of its existence."[21] This claim that natural beings are perpetually finite and subject to externality, together with his analysis of these concepts in the logic, allows Hegel to conclude that "not freedom but necessity reigns in nature."[22]

If externality, finitude, and therefore necessity are the definitive characteristics of natural beings, then freedom is available only to those beings that are not merely natural. Hegel calls such beings spiritual, and his account of them in the philosophy of spirit begins, as we have already seen, with the claim that "the essential . . . feature of spirit is freedom."

This claim should not be taken to mean that Hegel believes in the existence of a mysterious and free being, which he calls "spirit." Rather, his claim is that of the perfectly ordinary beings with which we are familiar, all and only those that can justifiably be called "spiritual" can justifiably be called "free." Of course, this does not tell us when we are justified in calling an ordinary being "spiritual." But it does at least indicate that the project of understanding Hegel's account of freedom coincides with the project of understanding his account of spirit: the entirety of Hegel's philosophy of spirit is an attempt to develop an adequate understanding of the conditions under which a being can justifiably be called spiritual, and thus free.

The philosophy of spirit begins by conceiving of spiritual beings as simply as possible: spiritual beings are those that are not merely natural.[23] This should not be taken to mean that spiritual beings are supernatural, for on Hegel's account everything spiritual is also natural. For example, human beings (who are spiritual in Hegel's sense) are also animals (which are natural). But our animality cannot account for our freedom. On the contrary, in Hegel's view it is the fact that humans are not merely natural, but also spiritual, that gives us the freedom that animals lack.

Since the definitive characteristic of natural beings is the insuperability of their mutual externality, the implication of understanding spiritual beings as not merely natural is that spiritual beings are those that are capable of internalizing their connections to everything that initially seems to be alien to them, and therefore those for which nothing is irreducibly external:

> We must designate as the distinctive determinateness of the concept of spirit, *ideality*, that is . . . the process of turning back (*Zurückkehren*) – and the accomplished turning back (*Zurückgekehrtsein*) – into itself from its other . . . What we have called the ideality of spirit [is] this triumph (*Aufhebung*) over externality . . . Every activity of spirit is nothing but a distinct mode of leading back (*Zurückfuhrung*) what is external to the inwardness which spirit itself is, and it is only by this leading back, by this idealization or assimilation, of what is external that it becomes and is spirit.[24]

Thus Hegel claims that, although "not freedom but necessity reigns in nature," "the substance of spirit is freedom, that is, the absence of dependence on an other, the relating of self to self."[25]

This initial understanding of the spiritual, however, immediately issues in a conceptual contradiction: spiritual beings are conceived as free in virtue of being not merely natural, but as long as spiritual beings are conceived as merely not-natural they cannot be free. To be not-natural is to be related to what is natural as to something external and independent, which is to be finite and connected to nature in necessity rather than in freedom. As Hegel puts it: "At first, spirit stands in relationship to nature as to something external, and in this mode it is finite consciousness; it knows the finite and stands over against nature as an other – for, to begin with, spirit exists as finite spirit. But . . . as finite [spirit] is conceived in contradiction with itself. Spirit is free."[26]

Spiritual beings must therefore be reconceived in a way adequate to their freedom. On the one hand, spiritual beings must continue to be conceived as not merely natural, so that their difference from natural beings, in virtue of which they are capable of overcoming necessity, is preserved. But on the other hand, spiritual beings must not be conceived as merely not-natural, in virtue of which they would be finite and subject to necessity. Taken together, these two requirements entail that spiritual beings must be conceived in such a way that they internalize their connection to the natural world and thus come to be at home within it, but without lapsing back into a merely natural existence. Spiritual beings must be conceived in such a way that they achieve freedom through a positive reconciliation with the merely natural world from which they differ, rather than through a negative flight from it.[27]

The process of revising the conception of the spiritual until spiritual beings are understood to be reconciled with the natural world while preserving their difference from it comprises the entire philosophy of spirit.[28] At each stage in this process, spiritual beings are conceived in a way that is thought to be adequate to their freedom. But reflection shows each of these conceptions, except for the last, to be contradictory: spiritual beings are thought both to be free, and to be subject to externalities that limit their freedom. Such contradictions force further revisions that overcome the specific externalities to which spiritual beings have been thought to be subject. This process, and with it the philosophy of spirit, ends only when a conception of spirit has been developed in which spiritual beings are no longer subject to externality, and so are truly self-determining and free: "The entire development of the concept of spirit presents only spirit's freeing of itself from all its existential forms that do not accord with its concept, a liberation which is brought about by the transformation of these forms into an actuality perfectly adequate to the concept of spirit."[29]

The conceptual development that comprises the philosophy of spirit takes place in three parts, which Hegel calls subjective, objective, and absolute spirit. All three are presented in condensed form in the final third of the *Encyclopedia*. More detailed expositions of the last two are also available. Objective spirit is presented in the *Philosophy of Right* and the lectures on the philosophy of history. Absolute spirit is presented in the lectures on aesthetics, religion, and the history of philosophy.

Subjective, objective, and absolute spirit thus present a series of attempts to conceive spiritual beings in a way that is adequate to their freedom.[30] Subjective, objective, and absolute spirit appear in a determinate order because the conception each presents internalizes the externality to which spiritual beings are subject in the preceding conception. This sequence of conceptions is thus a sequence of progressive internalizations, through which spiritual beings are ultimately conceived in a way that is adequate to their freedom.

Because the freedom of spiritual beings is adequately conceived only at the end of the philosophy of spirit, and because the philosophy of spirit ends with absolute spirit, we can conclude that Hegel understands spiritual beings to be most fully free in the activities that absolute spirit considers: the activities of art, religion, and philosophy. Moreover, because philosophy is the last of these activities to be considered, we can conclude that it is through the practice of philosophy that Hegel considers the liberation of spiritual beings to be complete. Hegel thus claims that philosophy is "the highest, the *freest*, and the wisest configuration of spirit."[31]

But knowing that Hegel believes the practice of philosophy to complete the liberation of spiritual beings is not the same thing as understanding why he holds this belief. Part I of this book provides an interpretation of Hegel's account of the freedom of spiritual beings that ultimately explains why and how Hegel believes the practice of philosophy to contribute to and complete our liberation. The final section of this chapter explains how that interpretation will be carried out.

4. Structure and Method of Part I

We can now see that to understand Hegel's account of freedom we need to understand his account of absolute spirit and the activities it presents. But in order to understand how spiritual beings are liberated by art, religion, and especially by philosophy, we need to determine the specific kinds of externality that these activities overcome. This amounts to determining the externalities to which spiritual beings remain subject at the highest stage of objective spirit. Objective spirit, which considers spiritual beings as willing beings, itself has three main parts: abstract right, morality, and ethical life. To determine the externalities that remain at the end of ethical life, we need to understand the liberation that ethical life does in fact afford. And finally, in order to understand this, we need to determine the specific kinds of externality that ethical life overcomes, which amounts to determining the externalities that remain at the end of morality and the reasons that the willing subject as conceived in morality, or the moral will, necessarily fails to overcome them.[32]

Part I addresses these problems in the order in which they arise in the course of the development of Hegel's philosophy of spirit. Chapter 2 analyzes Hegel's account of the freedom of willing in the *Philosophy of Right*. This analysis centers on morality, and shows that the moral will is internally contradictory: the very features in virtue of which the will is supposed to be free in morality prevent it from being so by ensuring that it remains plagued by externality. Specifically, it shows that the content of the moral will is inevitably external to its form. A by-product of this analysis is thus an understanding of Hegel's famous criticism that the Kantian conception of the autonomous will, which Hegel takes to be a moral one, is "empty" or "formal" and therefore provides an insufficiently comprehensive conception of freedom. By negative implication, this analysis also demonstrates how the will must be reconceived in ethical life if it is to liberate itself by internalizing the limitations to which it is subject in morality.

Chapter 3 picks up where Chapter 2 leaves off, with the assumption that at the highest stage of ethical life, that of the rational state, the spiritual subject is conceived in such a way that it is as free as the activity of willing can possibly make it. It then analyzes the limitations of willing, to show that even at the highest stage of objective spirit the spiritual subject is conceived in a way that remains internally contradictory: the activity of willing, through which the spiritual subject is supposed to overcome the externality of nature, actually ensures that this externality persists. Again negatively, this analysis indicates how the spiritual subject must be reconceived in absolute spirit if it is to be liberated from the externality endemic to all willing.

Chapter 4, with which Part I concludes, explores the ways in which the activities of absolute spirit, and especially philosophy, overcome the externalities that remain at the end of objective spirit. This exploration finally shows us how Hegel understands the most comprehensive freedom of spiritual beings, and how he understands the practice of philosophy to contribute to and complete this liberation.

At this point readers might benefit from referring to the accompanying figure, which provides a skeletal drawing of Hegel's system. The figure identifies both the location of Hegel's account of freedom within his system, and the elements of that account on which Part I focuses.

The analyses in Part I make sense of the sections of the philosophy of spirit with which they are concerned by employing the conceptual determinations found in Hegel's *Logic*. Although this approach requires engaging in a number of abstract and difficult logical discussions, such engagement is both necessary and rewarding. It is necessary because, whether or not Hegel is right that the concepts developed in his *Logic* must be used to comprehend spiritual beings, he does in fact so use them; and it is rewarding because, given that Hegel's philosophy of spirit

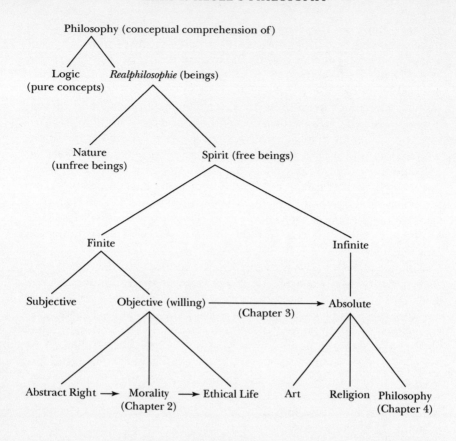

Philosophy (conceptual comprehension of)

Logic (pure concepts)   *Realphilosophie* (beings)

Nature (unfree beings)   Spirit (free beings)

Finite   Infinite

Subjective   Objective (willing) ⎯⎯⎯⎯⎯⎯⎯→ Absolute
                                    (Chapter 3)

Abstract Right ⎯→ Morality ⎯→ Ethical Life   Art   Religion   Philosophy
                        (Chapter 2)   (Chapter 4)

Increasingly comprehensive conceptions of the freedom of spiritual beings

Freedom in Hegel's system

does use those logical concepts, our grasp of the philosophy of spirit is improved when we attend to that use.

The first step in such analyses is to identify the logical concepts most relevant to understanding the section of the philosophy of spirit being analyzed. This identification cannot be made by seeking (or imposing) a formal pattern of correspondence (one-to-one, or otherwise) between the developments in the *Logic* and those in the philosophy of spirit. Rather, one must attend quite carefully to the details of Hegel's texts: in the passages of the philosophy of spirit with which one is concerned, it is often possible to find pointers (both explicit and implicit) to relevant sections of the *Logic*; and in passages of the *Logic*, it is possible to find clues to the interpretation of various parts of the philosophy of spirit.

Once this work is done, the second step is to use the identified logical concepts to understand both the externalities to which spiritual beings remain subject in the conception under consideration, and the reconceptions that are necessary to overcome those externalities and increase their freedom.[33]

I have tried to make my discussions of the *Logic* as clear and concise as possible, and to illustrate them with helpful examples. Where I have not provided examples in the course of these logical discussions it is because I take the subsequent discussions of the relevant portions of the philosophy of spirit to serve as the most helpful illustrations.

THE FREEDOM OF WILLING: HEGEL'S
PHILOSOPHY OF RIGHT

The goal of this chapter is to understand Hegel's conception of the freedom of willing. Understanding this conception requires understanding its development out of Hegel's criticisms of two other conceptions of the freedom of willing, that of liberalism and that of Kant, which he deems insufficiently comprehensive.

Hegel's criticisms of liberal choice and Kantian autonomy, and his own more comprehensive conception of the freedom of willing, are presented most fully in his *Philosophy of Right*. The Introduction develops and criticizes the liberal conception of freedom as choice; the second main section, on morality, develops and criticizes the Kantian conception of autonomy; and the third and final main section, on ethical life, incorporates choice and morality into Hegel's own conception of the freedom of willing as participatory citizenship in a rational state.

The heart of this chapter therefore consists of an analysis of these crucial sections of the *Philosophy of Right*. Morality is the particular focus, because it is the penultimate stage of objective spirit. For this reason, understanding the externalities that limit the freedom of willing subjects in morality is the key to understanding the liberation of those subjects in ethical life. Ethical life, as the final stage of objective spirit, provides the most comprehensive conception of the freedom available to the willing subject.

Understanding the finitude or incomplete freedom of the moral will, and its liberating reconception in ethical life, requires understanding parts of Hegel's discussion of the concept of judgment in the *Logic*. Section 1 therefore provides a brief account of the logical concept of judgment. Section 2 turns to the *Philosophy of Right* to consider the development of the moral conception of the will out of the conceptions presented in the Introduction and abstract right. Section 3 identifies the defining features of the moral will and compares them to those of judgment. Section 4 shows how the finitude of the moral will is related to the finitude of judgment, and then examines three separate attempts of the moral will to overcome its finitude, again using relevant sections of the *Logic* to help understand their failures. This allows us to conclude that the moral will is insuperably finite; specifically, as long as the willing subject is conceived as having the features distinctive to judgment, its content is necessarily external to itself. The section ends with a brief look at how the concept of judgment develops into that of syllogism, and how this development illuminates the one that takes place in the transition from morality to ethical life. Section 5 concludes the chapter by examining the institutions of ethical life – the family, civil society, and the state – that complete the liberation of the willing subject.[1]

1. The Logical Concept of Judgment

Judgment appears in the last of the three main sections of Hegel's *Logic*, the subjective logic, or the doctrine of the concept. The subjective logic is itself divided into three sections – subjectivity, objectivity, and the idea – each of which is further subdivided. Our concern is with subjectivity, of which the judgment (*das Urteil*) is the second moment. The first moment of subjectivity is the concept (*der Begriff*), and the third moment is the syllogism (*der Schluss*).

The most basic form of judgment, with which we are all familiar, is the judgment of identity: "S is P." Hegel points out that such a judgment has two essential, and mutually contradictory, features. First, it is divided into two parts, the subject and the predicate, which are held to be independent of and therefore external to each other; second, and at the same time, those parts are asserted by the judgment to be implicitly identical or mutually internal.

In addition to being a two-part relation of subject and predicate, the judgment is also, Hegel suggests, a three-part relation of universality, particularity, and individuality. This is what it shares with the concept and the syllogism, which are also composed of these three moments. The concept, the judgment, and the syllogism are differentiated by the distinct ways in which these three moments are interrelated in each of them.[2]

In the concept, universality, particularity, and individuality are understood as being immediately identical to each other. As immediately identical, these "moments of the concept cannot be separated."[3] This means that they must be thought as a single unity, that none of the three can be understood apart from the others: "since in the concept their *identity* is *posited*, each of its moments can only be grasped immediately on the basis of and together with the others."[4]

The interrelation of universality, particularity, and individuality is otherwise in judgment. Hegel calls judgment the particular moment of subjectivity, by which he means two things. First, in judgment universality, particularity, and individuality are understood to be separate from each other. Each of the three is now understood to be what it is independent of the character of the others; they are not understood to be immediately identical.[5] Second, and at the same time, the three moments are understood to be related to each other in judgment in such a way that they are inseparable; they are understood to be implicitly identical.[6]

The link between thinking of judgment in terms of subject and predicate, and thinking of it in terms of universality, particularity, and individuality, lies in the fact that the subject of a judgment is an individual, and the predicate is a universal. More specifically, the subject is a concrete unity of particular determinations (which makes it an individual), and the predicate is a universal determinacy attributed to the subject, in virtue of which their identity is posited in the copula, the *is*.[7]

Consider, for example, the following judgment: "This is a tree." *This* is an individual subject, with a number of particular features (it is tall, wide, old, brown and green, living, composed of wood and leaves, and so forth). *Tree* is a universal, a determinate predicate that applies to more than one individual (not only to *this*, but also to that, that, that, and so forth). *Is* links the two, identifying the universal determination "tree" with the individual thing in question.

But if the subject is the moment of individuality, and the predicate is the moment of universality, nothing in the judgment explicitly represents the moment of particularity. Although it is understood that the subject and predicate are linked in virtue of the former having the particular features that define the latter, these particulars are not specified or expressed in the judgment itself. Instead, their place is taken by the copula, the *is*, which links the subject and predicate as the particulars would, but without reference to the particulars themselves.

This makes the copula the key to judgment, because it produces both the inseparability and the separation of the subject and the predicate, the individual and the universal, that define this logical form. It produces inseparability more obviously, because in asserting that each half of the judgment *is* the other it identifies the two. But it also produces separation, because its assertion of the identity of the subject and the predicate is merely an assertion. That is, the copula's promise that the judgment's subject and predicate are identical is not fulfilled within the judgment itself. Such fulfillment would depend on a demonstration that the particular features defining the universal predicate do indeed belong to the individual subject. But the judgment, in replacing the moment of particularity with the empty copula, provides no such demonstration. Judgment thus links its subject and predicate in a way that leaves them separated; instead of identifying a determinate, internal connection of subject and predicate, judgment simply implies the existence of such a connection through an indeterminate *is*. The indeterminacy of the *is*, therefore, leaves the individual subject and the universal predicate, and the particulars that should unite them, all mutually external, and the promise of their implicit identity as yet unredeemed: "Subject and predicate are considered to be complete, each on its own account, apart from the other: the subject as an object that would exist even if it did not possess this predicate; the predicate as a universal determination that would exist even if it did not belong to this subject."[8]

Consequently, as initially conceived, judgment is a self-contradictory logical form, asserting the identity of its moments in a way that produces their separation. This means that the subject and the predicate of the judgment are mutually external, and so are finite and bound in necessity, rather than in freedom. Overcoming this finitude, we have seen, requires a demonstration that the elements of the judgment are not truly external to each other. Overcoming the lack of freedom built into the structure of judgment thus requires making good on the promise of judgment: the claim that its elements are implicitly identical. The development of the concept of judgment in the *Logic* therefore amounts to a sequence of attempts to overcome this contradiction in the initial conception of judgment by replacing the external and indeterminate copula with a particular bond internal to both the universal and the individual moment: "To restore [the] *identity* of the concept, or rather to *posit* it, is the goal of the movement of judgment."[9]

With this basic understanding of the relations between universal, particular, and individual that define the initial conception of judgment, and of the process of transforming these relations that defines the development of this conception, we can now turn our attention to the concept of the will and its development in the *Philosophy of Right*.

2. The Initial Conception of the Will and Its Development

The *Philosophy of Right* presents a series of conceptions of the will that develops in the course of Hegel's attempt to think the will as truly free. The series contains four main conceptions of the will, which are presented and developed in the four main sections of the book: the introduction, abstract right, morality, and ethical life. Each conception of the will is initially thought to be adequate to the concept of the free will, but upon examination is shown to suffer from limitations built into the very features that define it. This situation, which Hegel calls a contradiction (since what the thing is contradicts what it is supposed to be), forces a reconception of the will. Specifically, the will must be reconceived in a way that preserves the freedom of the prior conception while overcoming its limitations. The new conception is then defined by those features that allow it to overcome the limitations of the preceding conception (and that ultimately determine its own limitations).[10]

The moral will is thus defined by the features that allow it to overcome the limitations of the conception of the will presented in abstract right. Identifying its defining features therefore requires understanding the limitations inherent in abstract right, and the features of abstract right that produce those limitations. Those features of abstract right, however, develop specifically in response to the limitations built into the features of the concept of the will presented in the Introduction. Understanding abstract right in order to understand morality thus requires understanding the Introduction as well.

Fortunately, our study of the Introduction and abstract right need not be comprehensive. Most important is to pay attention to the shifting relations among the universal, particular, and individual moments of the will in the course of its development. This is because judgment, as we have just seen, is defined by a specific kind of relation of universality, particularity, and individuality. We will therefore identify the connection between judgment and the moral will by recognizing this specific relation of universality, particularity, and individuality as constitutive of the moral will. In the following discussion of the Introduction and abstract right, then, we will emphasize the evolving relations between the universal, particular, and individual moments of the will that define its ongoing development, and that ultimately issue in the conception of the will that defines morality.

In the Introduction to the *Philosophy of Right*, the will is conceived as the faculty of choice. As such, it is understood to have three basic moments or aspects. First, there is the moment of abstraction, or indeterminacy: the will is free because it can abstract from any particular choice, because it is not bound to pursue any particular interest. Second, there is the moment of determination: the will is free because it can determine itself to a particular choice, because it can choose to pursue a particular interest. Third, there is the moment of remaining abstract in determination: the will is free because even when it has determined itself to a particular choice it can again abstract from it. This last moment means that even though every determination or choice that the will makes belongs to it, the will is never defined by any particular choice that it makes; an important part of this freedom is the realization that the will has an identity that persists through an ongoing temporal process of determining itself to, and abstracting itself from, particular choices and interests. Thus freedom of the will, understood here as freedom of choice, is essentially freedom as possibility: the will is free because it is possible for it to pursue, or not to pursue, any of its chosen interests.

Hegel also describes these three moments of the choosing will in terms of universality, particularity, and individuality.[11] The first moment is the moment of universality, because in it the will is understood as a persistent entity that remains the same as it distinguishes itself from a variety of particular contents by abstracting from them.[12] The second moment is that of particularity, in which the will renounces its empty universality by identifying itself with a particular content. The third moment is that of individuality, which Hegel understands as the unity of universality and particularity. The will is an individual precisely because it is both particular and universal, both capable of identifying with a particular content (which is essential to individuality because it distinguishes this will from other wills) and aware that it has a universal identity that is independent of any particular content with which it happens to identify (without which it would be permanently defined as the particular content it happened to have, and would fail to achieve an individuality independent of it).[13]

In the conception of the will as the faculty of choice, the universal and particular moments are immediately identified with each other to yield the will's individuality. That is, the universality of the individual choosing will is defined as the sum of its particular contents, and each of those particular contents is defined as belonging to the individual in virtue of its being included in the universal sum. Consequently, it is impossible for the contents of the universal and individual moments of the choosing will to diverge. Such divergence could occur if the individual will attempted to determine the particular contents that *should* belong to the universal, on the basis of some nontrivial criteria, and then compared those contents to the particular contents it actually had chosen to place within it. But in the choosing will, the only criterion for determining that a particular content *should* belong to the universal is that it actually *does*, that it actually *has* been chosen for inclusion. This trivial criterion produces the immediate and undivorceable identity of universality, particularity, and individuality that defines the choosing will.[14]

The immediacy of the connection between the universal will and its particular contents, which defines and makes possible freedom of choice, also explains one of the two significant limitations of this form of the will: the choosing will is formal, in one of the two senses in which Hegel uses the term. This sense of "formality" signifies that there is no particular content intrinsic to the will, which follows from the fact that the universal will is merely immediately connected to the particulars it subsumes; rather than specifying which particulars necessarily belong to it, the universal will must simply accept particular contents that come to it externally.

In other words, even though the will is free to pursue its chosen interests, it is not responsible for what those interests are. At this level, its interests are merely "the *drives, desires, and inclinations* by which the will finds itself naturally determined."[15] Thus freedom of choice consists in the will's ability to resolve itself to satisfy a particular drive in a particular way, but does not entail that it satisfy one drive rather than another. As a result, the "free" choices of the will are actually determined by the relative strengths of natural inclinations, over which the will has no control. Freedom requires that the content of the choice, as well as the formal ability to choose, be a product of the will. As long as the will's content is external to its form, the will is dependent on something other than itself, not fully independent, and not fully free.

The second limitation of freedom of choice, which Hegel also calls formality, is its dependence upon the objects from which it is given to choose. In other words, the will that exercises freedom of choice has no control over whether or not the external objects necessary to satisfy its particular drives are available to it. The choosing will is thus formal in the second sense that it is merely subjective.[16]

These two limitations make the faculty of choice an inadequate and self-contradictory conception of the will, which is supposed to be un- limited and free. The will must therefore be reconceived in a way that overcomes its dual formality or dual externality, its limitation by given, external content and by given (or not given) external objects. The will's freedom depends upon internalizing, making a part of itself, anything upon which it is dependent.[17]

In abstract right, therefore, the will is conceived as being committed to willing its own freedom; it knows that it must have its own freedom for its content or object if it is to overcome its formality.[18] It also knows that the first step in willing its own freedom and overcoming its formality is the overcoming of its subjectivity, its dependence on a world of natural objects that it experiences as external and limiting.

The will of abstract right thus seeks its freedom by trying to claim some aspect of the external world as its own. The first stage of its effort is the ownership of property, in which the will identifies itself not only with its ability to choose, but also with an object of its choice, with a small piece of the natural world.[19] This location of its freedom in an external object, which overcomes the mere subjectivity of the choosing will, is the primary feature that characterizes the will in abstract right.[20] That is, in all stages of abstract right, the individual will identifies its freedom with something external to itself. The development from stage to stage within abstract right represents the progressive reconception of the will as it tries to overcome the limitations that arise from its initial identification of its freedom with a particular piece of property.

This development toward freedom in abstract right, as we will see, leads to a reconception of the relationship among the universal, particular, and individual moments of the will. Specifically, the universal and individual moments, which are immediately identified in the choosing will, become separated and mutually external in abstract right. Morality, as we will also see, ultimately arises because although the will of abstract right overcomes the subjectivity of freedom as choice, its logical structure prevents it from ever overcoming its formality. The separation of universal and individual means that in none of its stages is the will of abstract right able to develop a content intrinsic to itself; abstract right is never able to overcome the externality of the individual will's particular content from its universal form.

The first stage of abstract right, freedom as the right to own property, clearly remains formal in this sense of being without intrinsic content. Property does represent a development beyond choice in that it objectifies the will by subordinating a concrete thing in the world to the purposes of the willing subject. But property remains an inadequate existence for freedom, because the choice to own *this* piece of property is still not a product of the will. It is essential to the free will that it own property, but it is not essential that it own any particular piece of property, so the preference for one piece of property over another cannot come from the will itself, and therefore no piece of property that the will happens to identify with can be a truly sufficient objectification of its freedom. That is, although the will's identification with a piece of property internalizes an object that was external to the will, the decision to make this particular identification remains external. Still plagued with external dependence, the property-owning will remains unfree.

This is why the third moment of property is alienation (*Entäusserung*): just as in the third moment of freedom as choice the will has to be able to abstract itself from any determination it makes, in the third moment of freedom as the right to own property it has to be able to abstract itself from any property it owns. Thus, "it is not only *possible* for me to dispose of an item of property as an external thing – I am also *compelled* by the concept to dispose of it as property in order that *my* will, as *existent*, may become objective to me."[21] This is not to say that I must renounce all of my property, but rather that I must renounce some of it if I am to become conscious of the persistent identity of my will. Freedom requires that I be able to, and sometimes do, alienate my property; failing to do so, I would become permanently identified with a decision that did not stem from my will, and could not conceive of myself as free.[22]

The requirement that I be able to alienate my property leads to the requirement that my existence and rights as a free being be recognized by another being, and that I reciprocally recognize this being as freely existing and bearing whatever rights freedom requires. This is because in order to alienate property, to give up my ownership, I must implicitly recognize that the object is now available to be claimed as property by any other free being who so desires; to alienate my property involves the recognition of the property rights of others, even if there are no others around to claim ownership immediately. Likewise, for another free being to make an ownership claim on an object that I once owned requires her to recognize me as the kind of being who could have both legitimate ownership of the object and the right to renounce that ownership; to claim alienated property involves the recognition of the property rights of others just as much as the alienation of property does.

The result is a further objectification of my freedom. My freedom is no longer objectified solely in the objects that I own, but is now also objectified in another free being: "This relation of will to will is the true distinctive ground in which freedom has its *existence*."[23] In one sense, this is an advance, for shifting the objectification of my freedom from the objects that I own to other free property owners represents a small but important step on the path to finding my freedom in an object or content that is truly mine. This is because other free beings are less alien to me than unfree objects are. At the same time, however, this deepened objectification also amounts to an increased interdependence. For the first time, my freedom is dependent upon the freedom of another, and her freedom is dependent on mine.

This is true not just in the sense in which it is true in the liberal conception of freedom – where the freedom of each depends on others' not interfering with it – but in the more significant sense that without other free beings I cannot be free at all. In the liberal conception I can be a free individual, and in fact it will be easiest for me to be free, if no other people even exist to encroach upon my freedom; choice is something that I can exercise all by myself. Hegel's demonstration of the limitations inherent in understanding freedom as choice, and his further development of the concept of freedom as requiring the ability to alienate property, show that without other free beings who recognize my freedom I myself cannot be free. He thus shows that, paradoxically, increased freedom requires increased interdependence.[24]

Contract, the structure that arises out of this mutual recognition of free property owners, is the second main stage of abstract right. In contractual relationships "the contracting parties *recognize* each other as persons and owners of property," and they undertake to exercise their rights by exchanging property with each other.[25] At this stage, the freedom of a person resides not only in the property she chooses to own, but also in the contracts she enters into, and in her respect for and performance of the obligations contained in those contracts.

Contracts unite the will not only with the objects being exchanged, but also with the will of the other party. Whereas in owning property I raise a particular object to the universal, by externalizing my will in it and making it one means among many of serving my ends, in contractual relationships I also raise my particular will to the universal. This is done by positing a common will that the two contracting, particular wills share. Each will remains distinct, yet also enters into community with the other, by means of this universal will.[26] In this way, contract furthers freedom: it dissolves not only the externality between myself and particular objects, but also the externality between my particular will and other particular wills.[27]

But this reconceptualization of the will that takes place in contract also gives rise to the limiting structure that can ultimately be overcome only by moving into morality. The interdependence involved in freedom as contract effectively doubles the conception of the will. Each individual will is now understood to be composed of two distinct parts: a particular will of its own, and a universal will that it shares with the other wills involved in the contract. As Hegel puts it, "in any relationship of immediate persons to one another, their wills are not only *identical in themselves* and, in a contract, posited by them as *common*, but also *particular.*"[28]

The great significance of this development is that for the first time the particular and universal moments of the individual will are divided. In fact, the universal moment is now understood not to reside within the individual will itself, but to be a creation that it shares with one or more other wills, which exists only in the contracts negotiated between them. Thus the universal moment, upon which the freedom of the individual will depends, is now itself external to the individual will and its particular contents. This means it is now possible for an individual's pursuit of her chosen interests (the particular contents of her will) to diverge from the requirements of her freedom (the particular contents of the universal will); whereas the particular contents of the choosing will are immediately identified with its universality (because its universality is simply *defined* as the sum of its particular contents), their identification is now uncertain or contingent.

This can be seen more clearly with the help of a simple example. I enter into any contractual relationship for two reasons: to satisfy my particular interest in some property or another (I prefer your piece of land in Florida, for instance, to the one I have in Alaska), and to satisfy my universal interest, shared by all free beings, in objectifying my freedom by participating in and respecting contractual arrangements. If all goes well, one and the same relationship will satisfy both of my interests: the contract will enable me to get the particular property I want, and to objectify my freedom with another free being. But all may not go well: "it is purely contingent whether ... *particular* wills are in conformity with the will *which has being in itself,* and which has its existence solely through the former."[29] In some cases, my universal interest will be satisfied (a valid contract is executed and respected), while my particular one is not (I am disappointed with the exchange I have made). In other cases, my particular interest will be satisfied (I get what I want), while my universal one is not (I may violate the mutual respect of rights that contracts require – for example, by defrauding my counterpart). In this latter case I satisfy my chosen interest, yet violate the requirements of my own freedom in the process; in defrauding someone I elevate my particular interest over my universal one, which prevents me from being a free individual:"If the particular will *for itself* is *different* from the universal, its attitude and volition are characterized by arbitrariness and contingency, and it enters into opposition to that which is right *in itself*; this is *wrong*."[30]

If this occurs, if the particular will does not conform to the universal, right is merely a *Schein* (a semblance of what it should be, having an existence inappropriate to its essence), and it, as well as freedom, must be restored by repairing the wrong I have committed.[31] It is important to emphasize that in failing to respect freedom as contract I wrong not only the victim of the fraud or crime, but also myself. I violate the victim's rights as a free property owner and party to a contract, but in doing so I also violate the sphere of contractual rights in general. Since respect for these rights is essential to my own freedom, I wrong myself; as a free will that fails to respect freedom, I fail to respect or to be adequate to my own essence. This is why it is my freedom that must be restored, and not only that of the victim.

There is no guarantee, however, that I will recognize the harm that I have done or, even if I do recognize the harm, that I will take steps to repair it. After all, to commit a crime is to place my particular interests ahead of the universal, and there is no reason to think that I will alter my priorities if left to my own devices. The only solution is that society must punish me if I commit a crime. This punishment is for the sake of both justice and freedom. It serves the former by restoring right, and the latter by restoring my respect for right, which is essential to my freedom. As Hegel puts it, "the injury which is inflicted on the criminal is not only just *in itself*... it is also a *right for the criminal himself*."[32] Punishment, for Hegel, protects us from destroying our own freedom by pursuing our particular interests without respect for right; punishment is a means by which society protects a person from herself for the sake of her own freedom. It does so by turning her will from the particular (her own contingent drives and needs) to the universal (the requirements that stem from her own nature as a free being).

However, punishment can only restore respect for right, and thereby protect freedom, if it is just. Unjust punishment again gives precedence to a particular interest over the universal, and is therefore only another wrong, which restores neither right nor respect for right. But at this stage there is no guarantee that punishment will be just – for the will that exacts punishment has the same basic features as the will that committed the wrong, and is therefore equally capable of placing its particular and subjective interests ahead of the universal. To ensure that justice is done, the punishing will must be "a will which, as a particular and *subjective* will, also wills the universal as such."[33]

But this can only happen if the will is reconceived in such a way that the universal will resides within the individual, if the object in which the freedom of the will resides is again (as it was in the case of freedom as choice) taken to be the individual will itself. Without this reconception, the universal confronts the individual will as something external, to which the conformity of its particular contents is therefore contingent.[34] In this reconception, however, the relationship of particular and universal cannot merely revert to what it was in the choosing will without also reinstating the limitations inherent in choice. This must be avoided, while simultaneously overcoming the limitations produced by the separation of universal and particular in abstract right. The latter requires reuniting the particular and universal moments of the will within the individual, and the former requires that their identification no longer be immediate and abstract; the internalized universal will must not identify with whatever particular contents it happens to find, but instead must determine out of itself the particular contents necessary to the free individual.

We can now recapitulate the development of the will in abstract right. In abstract right, the will tries to give itself internal content and objective existence, which it lacks when conceived as the faculty of choice. It achieves objectivity in property, thus internalizing one of the external factors upon which the choosing will is dependent, but remains formal. The formality of the will, the fact that no particular property is necessary to it, gives rise to its need to be able to alienate its property, which gives rise to the need to engage in contractual relations with other free wills. This deepens the will's objectification, but also separates the particular will and the universal will, and forces the externalization of the latter from the individual. As a result, the will is still formal: the drives of the particular will continue to be given to it externally as natural inclinations, and there is no guarantee that they will coincide with the universal will, which is now a requirement of its freedom. This, finally, is the death of the will of abstract right. As long as the will locates its freedom in an object external to itself, which is what characterizes abstract right, there is always the possibility that the content of the will, its own particular drives, may be at odds with its own freedom, its own universality. Although it is also possible for the will's particular drives to accord with its freedom, if this is in fact the case it is only accidentally or contingently so, not owing to any feature of the will itself.[35] This makes the will of abstract right an inadequate conception of the will and results in the need to reconceive the will in such a way that it determines its own particular contents out of its newly reinternalized universal moment.

3. The Moral Conception of the Will

The needed reconception takes place in the transition from abstract right to morality:

> [The will of abstract right] first posits itself in the opposition between the universal will which has being in itself and the [particular] will which has being for itself; then, by superseding this opposition – the negation of

> the negation – [the moral will] determines itself as will in its existence,
> so that it is not only a free will in itself, but also for itself, as self-related
> negativity... The infinite subjectivity of freedom, which now has being for
> itself, constitutes the principle of the moral point of view.[36]

This says that in abstract right, as we have just seen, the individual will
takes its freedom (the universal will that has being in itself) to exist independent of (that is, in opposition to) itself and its particular contents.
This constitutes a negation, because the individual will is understood
not to be the existence of the universal will. Rather, the universal will is
thought to exist outside any individual will, in the contracts that bind a
number of property-owning wills together, and in the punishments that
enforce breaches of those contracts. The moral will arises when, for the
reasons we saw earlier, this negation has to be negated; the individual
moral will understands that it *is* the existence of the universal will, which
is therefore internal to it.

The moral will's location of its universal moment within itself makes it
not only a free will in-itself (that is, it not only implicitly is the existence
of freedom), but also a free will for-itself (that is, it also takes itself to be
the existence of freedom). This is equivalent to its being self-related, or
an infinite subject, both of which signify that the moral will knows itself
to be determined only by itself, since it knows itself to be the existence of
the concept that determines it.[37]

The moral will is not only self-related, but is a self-related negativity
because it understands itself to be internally divided, to have parts that
"negate" each other in their mutual differentiation, yet are held together
within a single self. Specifically, the individual moral will understands
itself to contain both its particular contents and its universal concept,
and understands that the two are not yet identical but must be made so,
if the moral will is to ensure, as the will of abstract right cannot, that it
wills its own freedom.

We can now recognize that in the transition from abstract right to
morality the will has become particularized, and this recognition allows
us to begin to connect the moral will to the logical concept of judgment:
the moral will is the particular moment of the will, just as judgment is
the particular moment of subjectivity generally. In the moral will, as in
judgment, universality, particularity, and individuality are both divided
and held together, known to be different and assumed to be implicitly
identical.[38]

Its particularization differentiates the moral will from the choosing
will, in the same way that judgment is differentiated from the concept: although the moral will and the choosing will are similar (and differentiated
from the will of abstract right) in locating their universal moment within
themselves, they differ in the sense that the moral will is aware of the

distinction between itself as individual and universal, and is resolved to overcome this difference, to make explicit the implicit identity of these two moments by demonstrating that their particular contents are the same. The choosing will, on the other hand, immediately identifies its universal moment with whatever particular contents it happens to have. As we have seen, this makes it formal, because it is determined by ends and purposes not intrinsic to its universal form, particular ends that are simply given to it as natural instincts. In order to overcome this formality and become free, the individual moral will must determine out of its own universal concept the particular ends and purposes to which it applies itself, transforming its existence from a natural form into a form that it prescribes. Just as the will of abstract right knows that it must own and use property, the moral will knows that it must take genuine ownership of itself or, as Hegel says, have its personhood as its object.[39]

The fact that the individual will's particular contents and universal form are still distinct at the outset of morality (even though the will now understands its universal moment to be internal to itself) means that the contingent identification of the two, which was the undoing of abstract right, has been internalized but not yet overcome.[40] Like judgment, the moral will implicitly assumes the identity of its universal and individual moments, but without initially providing any determinate, particular basis for this implicit assumption.[41] And this leaves open the possibility that the particular contents of universal freedom and the particular contents of the individual moral will may be at odds.

The need to overcome this opposition between the individual will and its universal concept makes morality "the point of view of *relationship, obligation,* or *requirement.*"[42] The course of morality thus presents the attempt to think the moral will in a way that fulfills its obligation by overcoming the internal opposition that keeps its particular contents external to its universal form:

> The process within this sphere is such that the will which at first has being only for itself, and which is immediately identical only *in itself* with the will which has being *in itself* (i.e., with the universal will) is superseded; and leaving behind it this difference in which it has immersed itself in itself, it is posited for itself as *identical* with the will which has being in itself.[43]

Identification of the process of morality as the positing of the determinate identity of its universal and individual moments, which are initially separate and connected only externally, completes the connection between judgment and the moral will, for this is the same process that is required of judgment itself. Judgment, we saw, must unite its individual subject with its universal predicate not through an empty copula, but with a determinate and particular content that belongs to both sides of the judgment. The individual moral will, likewise, must secure its freedom by ensuring the conformity of its particular contents to its universal form, which it can do only if it can determine the particulars that genuinely belong to its universal side.

We can thus conclude that judgment and the moral will are alike in both conceptual structure and process. Initially, they are defined by having a structure that presupposes the mutual externality of their universal, particular, and individual moments, at the same time that it assumes and asserts their identity. Because this structure is self-contradictory, both judgment and the moral will are then defined by the attempt to demonstrate the mutual internality of their moments, by determining the particular contents inherent in the universal that the individual must adopt as its own.

In the case of the moral will, the internalization of its own moments is necessary to its internalization of the external dependencies that plague the choosing will and the will of abstract right: the dependency on external content and an external world. The moral will's internalization of its own moments is thus essential to the spiritual subject's process of self-liberation through coming to know itself as being without insuperable externality.

In the next section we will consider the finitude of judgment, and the requirements that must be met if this finitude is to be overcome. We will then examine in detail how this finitude is connected to the finitude of the moral will, and how the moral will seeks to overcome it. We will identify three distinct stages of the moral will's effort, each of which is connected to its own specific logical structure, and will see that precisely because of their connections to these logical structures all of the moral will's efforts must fail. In the last of these efforts, the moral will seeks to use the power of the highest form of judgment to overcome the finitude built into its structure of judgment. In understanding the failure of this effort, then, we will understand not only the ultimate finitude of the moral will, but also that of judgment itself; in the failure of the moral will we will discover that judgment is unable to internalize the individual and the universal without losing its form of judgment and becoming syllogism. This will show us that a conception of the truly free will must shed the structure of judgment, cease being a moral will, and adopt the structure of syllogism, becoming an ethical will.

4. The Incomplete Freedom of the Moral Will

Recalling our previous discussions of finitude and judgment, it is easy to see that judgment is finite in the sense that it fails to be what it claims to be, and is therefore a limited expression of, or inadequate to, its own concept. Judgment's claim, we have seen, is that its subject and predicate, its individual and universal moments, are implicitly identical even though they appear to be separate and independent. This claim is staked in the copula, which asserts that the individual subject *is* identical to the universal predicate. Judgment fails to make good this claim, we have also seen, because the copula's assertion of identity is merely immediate. The identity claim can be justified only on the basis of a demonstration that the particular contents of the individual subject truly are those of the universal determinacy attributed to it, but the empty copula is devoid of particularity. In failing to make good its own claim, judgment fails to be what it ought to be, and is therefore finite.

The fact that judgment is finite in this sense means that its subject and predicate are finite in the other sense discussed earlier: the individual subject and the universal predicate are mutually external. This is a direct consequence of judgment's failure to demonstrate their identity in virtue of shared particulars. Such particulars, if shown to be contained in both the subject and the predicate they unite, would provide proof of the internal identity of the two, proof that the individual truly is the universal. In the absence of such particulars, however, they are linked only by the empty copula, which is external to the subject and predicate, and which therefore leaves them external to each other.[44] As a result, the individual subject, which is supposed to be infinite in virtue of containing within itself the universal determinacies that define its own nature, experiences those determinacies and that nature as independent of itself, and is therefore finite.[45]

Overcoming the finitude of judgment, and thereby overcoming the finitude of its subject and predicate, requires the development of a logical form in which the connection between the individual subject and the universal moment is not immediate, and therefore external and contingent, but mediated through particulars belonging to both, and therefore internal and necessary. Only in such a form could the individual find its freedom in being bound to a universal that is truly its own.

The development of the various stages of judgment in the *Logic* chronicles the attempts of judgment to become such a form, to become adequate to its own concept. In Hegel's terms, the development of judgment amounts to a process of raising the individual to the universal, or of making the universal not only *an sich* but also *für sich*, by giving the universal existence in an individual subject that knows itself to be the existence of the universal.[46] This is done by gradually forging a determinate identity between the subject and predicate of the judgment. This determination of their identity amounts to what Hegel calls a fulfillment of the copula, a transformation of the implicit and therefore external identity provided by the empty *is* into an explicit and therefore internal identity provided by concrete particularization of the universal.[47] The successive stages of judgment increasingly approximate this final copulation.

However, as the *Logic* ultimately shows, the successful fulfillment of the copula cannot be accomplished by judgment, because that fulfillment amounts to the overcoming of judgment; the fulfilled copula internalizes the universal and individual so thoroughly that it destroys one of judgment's defining features – namely, the essential difference of its moments. The development of judgment thus demonstrates that in all of its stages judgment is a self-contradictory logical concept: what judgment is (the particularization of its universal, particular, and individual moments) is always at odds with what judgment claims to be (the identification of universality and individuality through particularity).[48] Judgment thus remains finite, even in its highest forms. The internalization of individuality and universality necessary for infinitude is found not in judgment, but in syllogism, the concept that follows it in the development of Hegel's *Logic*.[49]

After considering the connection of the finitude of judgment to that of the moral will, and the moral will's failed attempts to overcome its finitude, we will conclude this section by considering the development from judgment to syllogism, and the parallel development from morality to ethical life.

The first sense in which the moral will is finite is a direct result of its having the structure of judgment, and therefore correlates directly to the first sense in which judgment itself is finite: the moral will asserts the identity of its individual and universal moments but, at least initially, provides no proof of its assertion, and thus fails to be what it claims to be. The individual moral will, that is, insists that it can ensure its conformity to its universal concept, but leaves the universal indeterminate and thus leaves its conformity to it contingent.

The consequence of the moral will being finite in this sense is, just as it is in judgment, the finitude of its moments: as long as the particular contents of its universal moment remain undetermined, the individual moral will and its universal concept are mutually external. In other words, the "infinite" moral subject is not truly infinite, because the concept that determines it is not truly internal to it.

The moral will is also finite in the second sense that it experiences the natural world of objects as an external limitation. This limitation – which we have seen to arise because the will is spirit in the form of judgment, taken to be separate from and independent of nature – was transcended by the will in abstract right, but only at the cost of externalizing its universal moment, and with it its own content. The moral will reinternalizes its universal moment in the (as yet unrealized) hope of internalizing its content, but at the cost of again finding itself alienated from the natural world. Whereas the individual will of abstract right located its freedom in objects – such as property and contracts – which therefore came to be internal to it, the individual moral will locates its freedom in itself, and as a result experiences all mere things as external.

These two senses in which the moral will is finite drive the developments that take place in morality; as long as the moral will is finite, it contradicts the concept of the will as that which is free or infinite. Two basic reconceptions are necessary, corresponding to the two types of finitude that must be overcome. First, the individual moral will must determine the particular ends required by the universal concept of freedom and adopt those ends as its own; failing this, it will remain formal or without intrinsic content, dependent upon something external to itself to provide it with ends, and it will fail to be free. Second, the moral will must produce in the objective world the ends it determines to be intrinsic to freedom; failing this, it will remain "the point of view of the difference, *finitude*, and *appearance* of the will."[50] That is, it will be merely subjective (formal in Hegel's second sense), confronted by an alien realm that does not conform to its freedom, and will again fail to be free.[51]

In addition to these basic requirements, there are two additional strictures imposed on the individual moral will, which derive from the developments leading to morality in the *Philosophy of Right.* First, it must recognize the ends that it determines to be required by freedom as also being in accordance with its own subjectivity; if freedom is to be truly internal to the individual will, the requirements of freedom cannot be experienced by that will as alien to itself (as they were in abstract right, leading to the necessary possibility of committing wrong by violating those requirements). Second, these ends must also accord with what Hegel calls universal subjectivity; as we saw for the first time in our consideration of contractual relations, in order to respect its own freedom an individual will must respect the freedom of all other free subjects, who at this stage also insist on determining and actualizing for themselves the contents of freedom.[52]

Hegel sums up these tasks by saying that the moral will must determine and produce content that is simultaneously subjective (recognized as its own) and objective in three distinct senses (existing in the world, in accordance with the concept of freedom, and in accordance with universal subjectivity). He also tells us that the moral will's ultimate failure will lie in its inability to produce content that satisfies all of these criteria.[53]

The requirement that the content of the moral will exist in the world means that its freedom cannot be conceived merely as potentiality, spontaneity, or possibility; rather, the moral will must give its freedom existence in action, since it is action that translates internal ends or purposes into the external world.[54] The moral will must therefore identify itself with its actions, much as in abstract right the will had to identify itself with its property. But an action is the proper expression of freedom only if it meets the criteria described earlier, and so the moral will identifies itself only with actions that meet those criteria.[55]

First, the moral will identifies with an action only if it recognizes it as subjective, or its own. Most basically, the will must recognize the action as something it did on purpose, a quality that Hegel calls being formally its own. He discusses this demand in Purpose and Responsibility, the first main section of morality. In addition, the will must recognize the content of the action as its own, which occurs only if the action is described in accordance with the intention under which the will claims to have performed it. Hegel discusses this in morality's second main section, Intention and Welfare.

But even if the moral will finds satisfaction in an action performed on purpose and under an intentional description that it recognizes as its own, it is still finite, still not completely free. The moral will here is limited in much the same way that the choosing will was: it is able to determine itself to satisfy particular ends with particular means, but the particular ends it happens to have are still given to it: "the as yet abstract and formal freedom of subjectivity has a more determinate content only in its *natural subjective existence* – its needs, inclinations, passions, opinions, fancies, etc. The satisfaction of this content is *welfare* or *happiness*."[56] These ends have now been elevated to the universal, since they are pursued because of their contribution to "welfare," but which particular ends the individual will finds satisfying is still a contingent matter; the individual will remains finite because its particular ends do not stem from its own concept.[57] At this point, the ends it finds satisfying may or may not correspond to the ends of freedom; the individual will may or may not correspond to the universal.[58]

Hegel does not at all mean to downplay the right of subjective satisfaction; in fact, he claims that "the right of the subject's *particularity* to find satisfaction, or – to put it differently – the right of *subjective freedom*, is the pivotal and focal point in the difference between *antiquity* and the *modern age*."[59] His point is rather that subjective freedom is a necessary, but not sufficient, condition of true freedom of the will. Subjective freedom by itself is still formal.

In order to overcome this formality (which is the same formality that plagues the logical concept of judgment) and become truly free, the moral will must take satisfaction in actions that it also knows to fulfill the requirements of its freedom. So far, the content of freedom has been determined only as right – respect for property, contract, and other free beings. At a minimum, then, freedom requires that the moral will's pursuit of welfare not take place at the cost of violating right; *pace* Robin Hood, to break the law in the pursuit of welfare (either one's own or that of some larger community) is to fail to respect the requirements of freedom.[60] At the same time, however, right cannot be upheld at the expense of all welfare whatsoever. Right exists only through the existence of freely willing subjects, so for the moral will to uphold right even if it means the death of those subjects is for right to undermine itself. It is thus consistent with freedom, Hegel argues, for someone facing starvation to ignore right and steal what she needs to survive.[61]

This shows that neither right nor welfare by itself is sufficient to satisfy the demands of freedom; the willing of each is conditional upon the willing of the other. The moral will must manage to will both together if it is to be free. This union of right and welfare, which the moral will must will unconditionally, Hegel calls the good.[62]

Hegel discusses the moral will's attempts to will the good in morality's last main section, The Good and Conscience. At this stage, because the individual will identifies its freedom, its own concept, with the good, these attempts amount to its effort to overcome its finitude by internalizing and actualizing its universal moment. This effort has three distinct stages, each of which corresponds to a particular logical concept; each stage within The Good and Conscience represents the moral will's adoption of a specific logical structure in hopes of overcoming the finitude that plagues the will when it has the structure of judgment.

We will now seek to understand how each of these logical structures in turn fails to enable the moral will to will the good. In the last of these efforts, the moral will attempts to use the power of the highest form of judgment to overcome the finitude built into the structure of judgment. In understanding the failure of this effort, then, we will understand not only the ultimate finitude of the moral will, but also that of judgment itself; in the failure of the moral will we will discover that judgment is unable to internalize the individual and the universal without becoming syllogism. This will show us that in order to be truly free the will must shed the structure of judgment, cease being a moral will, and adopt the structure of syllogism, becoming an ethical will.[63]

Near the beginning of The Good and Conscience, Hegel points out that because the good is initially abstract, the individual will is not posited as being in conformity with it. This is because for the will to be posited as being in conformity is for its conformity to be explicit to it, for it to know that its particular contents do in fact match those of the universal good. But this cannot be the case if the good is abstract: since the content of the abstract good is itself not explicit, there is no way for the particular will to know what contents it is required to have. This means, Hegel also points out, that the good initially confronts the particular will as something that it *ought* to make its end and accomplish, as its unconditional but indeterminate duty.[64]

At this point, then, the moral will's freedom, its attempt to will the good, consists in its being dutiful. What, we might ask, is wrong with this conception of freedom? True, duty is as yet unspecified and indeterminate, but why shouldn't it be? After all, determinate duties might well be willed only conditionally, thereby compromising freedom. Perhaps the freedom of the will is simply its resolve to be unconditionally dutiful, its resolve to act in accordance with the universal, even if it cannot identify any particular duties.

The problem with this conception of freedom is illuminated in the sections on finitude (*die Endlichkeit*) and infinity (*die Unendlichkeit*) in the *Logic*. These sections are relevant because duty, as unconditional or unlimited, is infinite; conversely, the conditional and determinate ends of the individual moral will are finite. The logical relationship of infinity and finitude, therefore, can shed light on the relation of the moral will's duty to its conditional ends.[65]

The *Logic* shows that infinity cannot be thought as the simple opposite of finitude. If infinity is simply opposed to finitude, then the infinite has an other and a limit (namely, the finite), which means that it is not truly infinite, since to be infinite is to be unlimited.[66] The consequence for the moral will is that an unconditioned "ought" that remains apart from all finite determination is not truly unconditioned. This means the moral will cannot become free simply by recognizing the requirement that it do its duty for duty's sake. This would be to understand the ought as simply opposed to all finite or determinate action, which would therefore serve as its limit. To be truly infinite, the *Logic* shows, infinity must be conceived as other than finitude, yet also encompassing it. The same is true for the ought: duty must be thought of as not only unconditional but also determinate – otherwise it is not truly unconditional. This explains the *logical* requirement that the moral will specify its concrete duties as actions to be performed in the world. If it failed to do so, it would be limited and unfree.[67]

Having recognized that the content of the universal will cannot be left indeterminate, the moral will is immediately confronted with the question: what are the particular duties required by freedom? These duties cannot be specified in terms of right or welfare, for the will already knows that these are conditional goods, and duty is unconditional, demanded if the will would simply be what it claims to be – freely self-determining.

As freely self-determining, as infinite subjectivity, the moral will must perform the determination of its duties by itself and out of itself. That the moral will determine its duties by itself Hegel calls the right (as well as the obligation) of the subjective will, the right not to accept anything as good that the will has not itself determined to be such.[68] That the moral will must determine them out of itself means that its duties must be determined strictly from the nature of the moral will itself; duties with any other source would compromise the will's freedom and infinitude, by confronting it as external and alien demands.[69]

This suggests that the moral will must be the "ground" of its own duties, which means that we can learn something about its attempt to determine its duties by looking at the sections of the *Logic* on "ground" (*der Grund*). Two sections are especially relevant: Formal Ground (*formelle Grund*) and Real Ground (*reale Grund*).[70] A formal ground is formal because what it grounds (the grounded) has no content that is not already in the ground itself. The distinction between ground and grounded is therefore merely one of form. In other words, the ground grounds only itself, and the grounding relation is tautological. A famous example is adducing "dormitive powers" as the ground of opium's ability to induce sleep. This ground is formal, since the content of the terms "dormitive" and "sleep-inducing" is identical. By contrast, a real ground is real because its grounded does contain content beyond that contained in the ground. However, precisely because of this, many different things will have equally good claims to be grounded by the same real ground; there is nothing in the real ground itself that can indicate which of several putatively grounded contents is most appropriate to it, since all of those contents differ from its own. The relation of real ground is not tautological, but it is underdetermined.

This discussion of formal and real ground suggests that the moral will's attempt to ground its own determinate duties should fail in two ways: as tautological, the moral will should be able to ground no determinate duty; as underdetermined, the moral will should be able to ground any determinate duty. Let us now return to the *Philosophy of Right* to see why this is in fact the case.

Hegel writes: "all that is left for duty itself, in so far as it is the essential or universal element in the moral self-consciousness as it is related within itself to itself alone, is abstract universality, whose determination is *identity without content* or the abstractly *positive*, i.e., the indeterminate."[71]

This makes sense if we read it slowly. "All that is left for duty . . . is abstract universality." An abstract universal is one whose particulars cannot be specified, that is, one "whose determination is *identity without content*." Hegel's claim is thus that in morality, duty remains an empty word and does not indicate any concrete duties required of the free will. This is because duty "is the essential or universal element in the moral self-consciousness," and this, the moral will, "is related within itself to itself alone."

So the emptiness of duty is supposed to follow from the very concept of the moral will, from the fact that "it is related within itself to itself alone." In order to understand this we need to recall how the moral will emerges from abstract right. Abstract right fails by locating the will's freedom in objects – such as property and contracts – external to it, which makes the will's respect for its own freedom contingent. To solve this problem, the

will is reconceived at the beginning of morality as "infinite subjectivity,"
as a subject that is what it is independent of anything external to itself.
Hegel calls such an infinite subject "reflected into itself" because every
connection or relation it encounters between itself and another thing
points it back (that is, reflects it) into itself: it realizes that such relations
cannot be constitutive of its essence, for they compromise its independence.[72] Every such encounter thus confirms its status as identical with
itself, as being what it is all by itself, not in virtue of anything beyond itself.
The moral will is thus a *negatively* infinite subject: it is *not* this object, *not*
this content, it *is* the thing that is *not* anything else, and *not* essentially
related to anything else.[73] It just is a free moral will, all by itself, conceived
from the beginning as that to which no particular content can belong,
since any particular content would compromise its relation within itself to
itself alone. Thus the moral will by its very concept can have no content,
and "in so far as [duty] is the essential or universal element in the moral
[will] . . . [duty] is *identity without content* or the abstractly *positive*, i.e., the
indeterminate."

This means that every specific candidate for duty is equivalent from
the perspective of the moral will. In one sense, all content fails: any determinate content is alien to the moral will, and therefore cannot be recognized by it as a duty stemming freely from its own nature. The moral will
is thus reduced to the empty tautology "duty for duty's sake." From this
perspective it is a formal ground, unable to ground a duty with content
other than its own, that is, with any content at all.

But in another sense, since all content fails, all is equally successful;
no content is more alien to the moral will than any other. In fact, Hegel
claims, any content can be put in the only form the moral will has been
able to determine duty to have, that of "*absence of contradiction, . . . formal
correspondence with itself*, which is no different from the specification of
abstract indeterminacy."[74] Thus precisely because no content contradicts
itself, and all contents contradict the moral will equally, all contents remain equally plausible as potential duties.[75]

This is to say that because the moral will is a formal ground, it is a
real ground, and its duties are underdetermined. The logic of formal
and real ground, then, which shows how the former turns into the latter,
and how neither is truly a ground, illuminates the failure of the moral
will to determine its duties. Once one sees that the moral will is a formal
ground, and understands this section of the *Logic*, the reasons for the
irredeemable failure of the moral will to overcome its formality through
grounding its own content become clear: the abstract universal that is
the concept of the moral will cannot ground a specific set of particular
contents with which the individual will must identify.

Having failed as a real ground, and faced with a multiplicity of contents
competing to be recognized as duties fulfilling the good, the moral will

can proceed only by comparing the actions it is considering with the concept of "good." To do so is to make a judgment, to subsume a singular (this action) under a universal (the concept of the good), and at this point Hegel describes the moral subject as being "the power of *judgment* which determines solely from within itself what is good in relation to a given content."[76] As this power of judgment, the moral will is known as conscience.

We should note that at this stage the moral will is attempting to use the power of judgment to overcome the finitude of its own structure of judgment. To say that the moral will has the structure of judgment is, we know, to say that it is finite because, as an individual, it is external to its universal nature; the good is indeterminate, and it is therefore contingent whether the particular contents of the individual will are in conformity with it, as they must be if the will is to be free. Overcoming this finitude, we also know, requires that the good, the universal nature of the will, be determined. Here, the moral will is attempting to use the power of judgment to perform this determination of the universal. If the attempt is successful, the power of judgment will provide a determinate identification of the universal will with the individual, fulfilling the copula, and thereby give the will a structure other than that of judgment, a structure liberated from judgment's finitude.

The specific type of judgment that conscience must employ Hegel calls the "judgment of the concept."[77] In a judgment of the concept, the concept of a certain type of object serves as the basis for judging individual instances of that type; the concept, that is, is what the individual objects ought to be, ought to measure up to, and a judgment of the concept judges whether or not they in fact do.[78] In the case of the moral will, the type of object in question is action; the moral will must compare its individual actions with the concept of a good action, so as to judge in each case whether an action is good and required by (or at least in accordance with) its freedom.

The judgment of the concept includes three types of judgment: assertoric, problematic, and apodeictic.[79] The first of these consists of asserting the identity of an individual subject and a universal predicate: "This action is good." It is the kind of claim that conscience makes for the moral will. Such a judgment is called assertoric because it is merely asserted, and its justification is therefore merely subjective. That is, its justification does not rely on an internal determination of the particular contents of the universal concept ("good action"), but on something external to that concept. Therefore, whether or not the particular action in question truly does conform to the universal concept remains contingent.[80]

Because an assertoric judgment is subjective, it is also problematic. A problematic judgment is one whose opposite "confronts it with the same right or rather the same lack of right."[81] In other words, a problematic judgment *might* be true, but then again it might not. Its opposite ("No, this action is *bad, that* action is good") could well prove to be the case. Because both conflicting judgments rely on the same subjective justification, they are equally indefensible, and each is forced to recognize its subjectivity.[82] This is what happens to the moral will, when confronted with the fact that its insistence on the right of conscience gives equal legitimacy to the claims of other wills whose consciences disagree with its own.

The problematic judgment thus points to the need for a type of judgment that can truly distinguish good actions from bad. This leads to the final type of judgment, the apodeictic, which takes the form: "This individual action, being constituted in this particular way, is legitimately classified under the universal 'good'." The distinction between this judgment and an assertoric or problematic judgment is obvious – here there is a specified criterion (having a particular constitution) that justifies the application of the universal predicate. But the difficulty should also be obvious – one cannot know the particular criterion for the application of a universal like "good" unless one *already* knows what the content of that universal predicate is. But if one knew that, one would already be able to make perfectly accurate and well-justified assertoric judgments.

We can now see that the moral will is no more able to determine its duties objectively on the basis of its power of judgment than it is able to ground them in its universal nature as a free being. All that the moral will can use to determine its duties is its subjective certainty that the content of its particular will is attuned to the good. The moral will is reduced to conscience, to "the assertion that what [the particular moral will] knows and wills is *truly* right and duty."[83] The problem, of course, is that "whether what it *considers* or declares *to be good* is also actually good, can be recognized only from the *content* of this supposed good," and the content of the good is precisely what the moral will has proved unable to determine.[84] The moral will is thus dependent, as is judgment, on something other than itself for its conception of the good, and as conscience it is reduced to claiming that what it supposes to be good (subjectively) really is good (objectively). But this is the downfall of the moral will, for it is now clear that it cannot be what it has to be: "[The moral will's] appeal solely *to itself* is directly opposed to what it seeks to be – that is, the rule for a rational and universal mode of action which is valid in and for itself."[85]

We can now recapitulate the development and ultimate failure of the moral will. The moral will arose from abstract right's hope to be able to determine the particular requirements of the universal will out of its individual self, to be able to determine the specific duties that have an unconditional claim on all free beings. But in its attempt to do this, the individual is reduced to the insistence that *it* be the judge of the good. The determinations made by the moral will are thus particular and subjective, and will be acknowledged as binding obligations only by other individual wills that contingently happen to share the same feelings of certainty about what is good. In short, the moral will is not able to produce content that is objective in all three senses that are required of it. The moral will is therefore not the locus of freedom, but rather a perversion of it in which the content of the objective good is subjectively determined via the judgments of an individual will.

This failure of the moral will is analogous to the failure of judgment. We have seen that even the highest form of judgment (the apodeictic) is unable to do its job (to correctly subsume individuals under universals) on its own. Another kind of logical form, that of the syllogism, is required, in which the universal determines its own particular contents, so that judgment may then identify the individuals that have those particulars and can therefore be subsumed under the universal. We have now seen that the moral will is unable to do its job for the same basic reason: it cannot ensure the conformity of the individual will to the universal, because it cannot determine what the universal truly requires. It is thus the logical limitations of judgment that limit the moral will, that make it conceptually incapable of being the actuality of freedom; the power of judgment is unable to overcome the structure of judgment by genuinely uniting the individual with the universal through the particular. The moral will is therefore always in the position of having to specify the content of the good, but being unable to do this in an objective way; ultimately, like judgment itself, the moral will can only determine the particular contents of its universal through a judgment grounded in subjective certainty.

Hegel completes his discussion of morality by arguing that this subjective self-certainty that it knows the good makes the moral will capable of evil: "for both morality and evil have their common root in that self-certainty which has being for itself and knows and resolves for itself."[86] The possibility of evil arises when subjective self-certainty, or conscience, takes itself to be the source of objective good, when subjectivity usurps objectivity. This is because whether conscience is actually attuned to evil or good is both contingent and unknowable (since the will is incapable of determining what the requirements of the objective good are, which it would have to do in order to know whether its conscience were properly attuned). A commitment to conscience and one's certainty of goodness is therefore as likely to produce evil as good, and this risk is unavoidable for the moral will.[87]

A further consequence of the commitment to conscience is the dissolution of any ethical life, any sense that the good might be found in the customs and institutions of a community. For the moral will cannot be satisfied with external arrangements unless they conform to its own particular sense of how things ought to be. A community of moral wills is thus an oxymoron; a community requires its members to understand that the whole is greater than any of its parts, but the moral will always takes itself to be supreme.[88] If a number of moral wills agree about the good, their agreement is only contingent, and their "community" will dissolve as soon as one of them changes its mind.[89]

In the end, then, the moral will produces nearly the opposite of its original intent. Its aim is to overcome its dual finitude by overcoming the dual externality with which it begins; the moral will strives to produce an internal identity of its individual and universal moments, and then purposively transform the objective world to conform to the particular contents of that identity. Its result, however, is a reinforcement of the mutual externality of its individual and universal moments, which in turn reinforces the externality of the objective world and all other individual wills. Thus the moral will, in locating its freedom in itself, prevents itself from being free, for it sets up insuperable boundaries between itself, the contents of its own concept, the objective world, and all other wills.

The moral will is therefore a *Schein*, a semblance of what it is supposed to be, an existence inadequate to its concept. It is perpetually formal and therefore perpetually finite, a hopelessly self-contradictory concept that attempts to conceive freedom in a way that makes freedom impossible.[90] Consequently, at this point there is no choice but to reconceive the will yet again, in a way that overcomes the limitations built into the basic features of both morality and judgment.[91]

We have already seen that the apodeictic judgment in-itself is the transition beyond judgment to syllogism. The apodeictic judgment shows that judgment can never demonstrate the correctness of its own claim to unify the individual and the universal, because all successful judgment presupposes a prior and external unification of particular and universal. Apodeictic judgment exposes, that is, the fact that the contradiction built into judgment – that its moments are truly different yet nonetheless identical – is soluble only through syllogism.[92] Syllogism dissolves the contradiction by reconceiving the moments of universality, particularity, and individuality yet again; in syllogism, the individual is thought not as being connected externally to its universal nature, but rather as being the individual it is in virtue of having the particular constitution appropriate to that nature, which it truly is. Here the moments of universality, particularity, and individuality are reunited – as they could not be in judgment – but without dissolving into each other immediately, as they did in the concept. Here the individual and the universal have the same determinate content – the particular constitution that fulfills the copula – but remain differentiated in terms of form.

We have also already seen that the contradiction of judgment is the contradiction of morality: the individual moral will takes itself to be identical to, yet separate from, its universal nature. It engages in three distinct efforts to overcome this contradiction itself, but we have seen that all of these fail. What remains to be seen is that, just as the self-contradictory finitude of judgment illuminates the self-contradictory finitude of the moral will, the development from judgment to syllogism illuminates the development from morality to ethical life.

As the apodeictic judgment exposes the fact that successful judgment is always already implicitly relying on syllogism, conscience exposes the fact that the moral will's ability to act on the good always already presupposes a prior and external determination of the particular contents of the good, which the moral will must accept as its own. But for the moral will to accept these particular contents as its own is for it to reconceive the relation of the universal, particular, and individual moments of the will in such a way that the will is no longer moral. It is to reconceive the individual will as being what it is not over and against the universal, but in virtue of the particular contents of the universal, which are therefore understood to be truly its own. Such a will overcomes the finitude of morality, because the universal that determines the individual is now internal to it, rather than external. But such a will is an ethical will, not a moral one.[93]

This transition from morality to ethical life takes place when the new relation of universality, particularity, and individuality becomes explicitly posited through the recognition that

> the integration of these two relative totalities [conscience and the good] into absolute identity has already been accomplished *in itself*, since this very subjectivity of *pure self-certainty*, melting away for itself in its emptiness, is *identical* with the *abstract universality* of the good; the identity – which is accordingly concrete – of the good and the subjective will, the truth of them both, is *ethical life*.[94]

That is, the emptiness of the determining conscience (the individual) proves to be indistinguishable from the emptiness of the good-in-need-of-determination (the universal), and neither one can be thought without also thinking the other. At the end of morality, then, the subjective will comes to understand objectivity as identical to itself; it understands the true determinations of conscience and the true determinations of the good to be the same. But this transforms the moral will (which had insisted on the right of subjectivity over and against objectivity) into the ethical will, or the thought that holds subjectivity and objectivity together as inseparable elements of a single unity: "In ethical life as a whole, both objective and subjective moments are present, but these are merely its forms. Its substance is the good, that is, the fulfillment of the objective with subjectivity."[95] In other words, "the *ethical* is a subjective disposition, but of that right which has being in itself."[96]

In order to understand the freedom afforded by ethical life we need to consider the specific forms that it takes: family, civil society, and the state. In all of these forms ethical life surpasses morality by uniting the individual, universal, and particular moments of the will. The three forms of ethical life achieve this unification, however, in their own distinctive ways, each of which is conceptually necessitated by the failure of its predecessor to complete the liberation of the will. Our consideration of the family, civil society, and the state will not be exhaustive; as in our earlier study of choice and abstract right, the essential point to attend to in the development of ethical life is the ongoing transformation of the relationships between the individual, universal, and particular moments of the will. Such attention will reveal how ethical life ultimately liberates the willing subject as fully as possible.[97]

5. The Institutions of Ethical Freedom: Family, Civil Society, State

The family is the first form of ethical life because it provides an immediate unification of the individual with a universal in which her particular interests are satisfied. The unification is immediate because it is based on the feeling of love, which can be satisfied only if the individual is able to unite with the other individual who is the object of her love: "The first moment in love is that I do not wish to be an independent person in my own right and that, if I were, I would feel deficient and incomplete. The second moment is that I find myself in another person."[98] In other words, the person in love simply cannot be the individual she is unless she forms a union with her lover, and thus her particular interest is just the formation and sustenance of this universal relationship.

The family is created when two loving individuals enter into marriage, which originates in "the free consent of the persons concerned, and in particular their consent to *constitute a single person* and to give up their natural and individual personalities within this union. In this respect, their union is a self-limitation, but since they attain their substantial self-consciousness within it, it is in fact their liberation."[99] A true marriage does not compromise the freedom of the individuals who enter into it, but actually makes it possible, because so long as they are bound together by love the individuals' very identity depends on their being members of the union they have formed. Their bond to each other is internal rather than external, which means that they are bound together in freedom rather than in necessity.

Despite its improvement over moral autonomy, however, family life does not completely liberate willing subjects. The reasons for this are twofold. First, because marriage is founded on love, which is a feeling, it is susceptible to dissolution; should one of the partners cease to feel that her identity depends on her bond with the other, then the union would become restrictive rather than liberating, and its essential purpose would be defeated. Because such a development is always possible, there is no guarantee that marriage will secure the freedom of the individuals who choose to enter into it. The persistence of the freedom available through marriage depends on the persistence of love, which is all too obviously contingent.[100]

Second, and more fundamentally, it is certain that even a persistently loving marriage cannot secure the freedom of its offspring, who become family members not through their own consent but rather by the accident of birth. It is, of course, a happy accident to be born into a loving family rather than into one of the many alternatives. Such a family can provide the support every child needs if she is to realize her potential to become an independent adult. But even in such happy cases, when love and support are available and the children flourish, the family ultimately serves to restrict rather than to liberate if it refuses to grant the children the independence for which it has successfully prepared them. The particularity of such independent children must be recognized and respected, which it cannot be if they remain in a union to which their connection is immediate, rather than freely chosen.

The dissolution of the family is, therefore, just as much a requirement of ethical freedom as is its formation. Such dissolution "consists in the fact that the children are brought up to become free personalities and, when they have *come of age*, are recognized as legal persons and as capable both of holding free property of their own and of founding their own families."[101] The result is "a *plurality* of families whose relation to one another is in general that of self-sufficient concrete persons and consequently of an external kind."[102] This plurality of families seeking to provide for their own welfare and to protect their own rights is what Hegel calls civil society.

Civil society is to ethical life what contract is to abstract right: the second moment, in which individuals participate in arrangements with others that make possible the simultaneous satisfaction of the particular interests of each and the universal interest of all in their freedom. In contract, the individual satisfies her interests and objectifies her freedom by entering into contracts with other free beings, and by respecting contractual rights by performing the obligations undertaken in those contracts. In civil society, she satisfies her interests and objectifies her freedom by laboring along with other free laborers in what Hegel calls the system of needs, which is essentially what we think of as a market economy.[103]

In civil society the unification of individuals and the universal is no longer immediate: the bond between fellow laborers is not based on mutual love, and consequently their particular interest does not lie in working together simply for the sake of working together. In civil society the universal is viewed not as an end in itself, but rather as a means to the satisfaction of the particular needs of its members. Everyone, that is, hopes the economy will flourish, but only because it makes it more likely that she will be satisfied and secure, not because she understands that her own good lies in the good of the whole.[104]

By overcoming the immediacy of the connection between individuals and the universal, civil society respects the particularity of everyone as the family ultimately fails to do. At the same time, however, the gap that opens in civil society between each person's particular interests and her universal one creates the possibility that she will violate her freedom in the pursuit of the satisfaction of her needs. This creates the requirement for some means whereby people can be protected from such self-inflicted violations of their freedom. Having already seen how punishment performs this function when contract is violated in abstract right, we must now examine civil society in order to determine the requirements of freedom at this stage, the ways in which individuals' particular interests can diverge from these requirements, and the protections that must be instituted to secure the freedom of all.

As was the case in property and contract, my freedom in civil society is interdependent with that of all free beings, because I can objectify my freedom as a right only if enjoyment of that right is universal. At this stage, since the relevant right is the right to work, I will not be able to objectify my freedom in and through my labor unless everyone who is willing and able to labor can find work in the system. If I am able to find work in a system that fails to provide or respect the right of all free beings to labor, then I enjoy my position not by right but by accident; as long as my ability to labor depends on contingencies such as my natural talents or my level of education, my freedom is not guaranteed as a right. Civil society is therefore

> a system of all-round interdependence, so that the subsistence and welfare of the individual and his *rightful* existence are interwoven with, and grounded on, the subsistence, welfare, and *rights* of all, and have actuality and security only in this context.[105]

Two important things take place in the system of needs, according to Hegel: first, needs proliferate; and second, labor becomes increasingly specialized in order to keep up with the proliferating needs.

The important aspect of the proliferation of needs is that it is endless. Unlike animals, whose needs are limited by their natural instincts, humans are capable of transcending instinct and giving themselves new needs. Hegel mentions a number of factors that drive this process. Among them, and paramount for our purposes, is the fact that in this moment of civil society humans have an insatiable drive to keep up with, and to exceed, their fellow humans:

> On the one hand, the need for . . . equality, together with *imitation* as the process whereby people make themselves like others, and on the other

hand the need of *particularity* (which is likewise present here) to assert itself through some distinctive quality, themselves become an actual source of the multiplication and expansion of needs.[106]

As a result, "need" is always relative; there is no absolute level of wealth at which humans conclude that they have enough. "Enough" is always defined by the society in which one lives, and even when one has enough by that society's standards one will always "need" a bit more to differentiate oneself from everyone else. The manifestations of this phenomenon are familiar: over time, what were once luxuries become necessities (for example, telephones, cars, and computers), and as they become things that everyone has, people differentiate themselves by the *kind* of thing's that they have (for example, the smallest cellphone, the biggest SUV, the fastest microprocessor). This insatiable human drive, and the infinite capacity of the human understanding to multiply our needs by making them more and more specific, guarantee that the production of needs within the system will be endless.[107]

Labor becomes increasingly specialized because specialization allows for increased productivity and efficiency, which are necessary to create enough general wealth to satisfy the endlessly proliferating needs. The important aspect of the specialization of labor is that it further increases our interdependence. At this point, not only am I dependent on the *right* of all to labor for the objectification of my freedom, but I can satisfy my needs only if many people actually *do* labor. As my own labor becomes more specialized and productive, I contribute an increasing amount to the general wealth, and the community becomes increasingly dependent upon me. At the same time, however, as my skills become increasingly specialized they also become increasingly narrow, and I become more and more dependent upon the community. If all I can do is design computer software, then no matter how productive I am, I will depend on others for the means to satisfy almost all of my needs (including my needs for food, clothing, and transportation).[108]

As it did at the level of contract, recognition of this increased interdependence leads to the creation of a new common interest in civil society. In contract, we developed a common interest in the rightful exchange of property; in civil society, we develop a common interest in sustaining an economy that will allow all of us to labor and to satisfy our needs:

> In this dependence and reciprocity of work and the satisfaction of needs, *subjective selfishness* turns into a *contribution towards the satisfaction of the needs of everyone else.* By a dialectical movement, the particular is mediated by the universal so that each individual, in earning, producing, and enjoying on his own account, thereby earns and produces for the enjoyment of others.[109]

But as the creation of a common will at the level of contract led to the divergence of an individual's particular and universal interests, and ultimately to the need for protection from oneself in the name of one's own freedom, so too at the level of civil society. People have two motives for laboring in the system of needs, just as they had two motives for entering into contracts: I labor both in order to satisfy my particular needs (to pay the bills), and in order to satisfy my universal interest in objectifying my freedom. In a perfect system, both my interests would be secured: the economy would function smoothly, all free beings would labor, my freedom would be objectified and my needs sated. But Hegel believes that the system of needs can never be perfected, that it will never be able to satisfy both my particular and my universal interests.

I can satisfy my particular interests in the system of needs if I am able to find work. But it is strictly impossible for me to satisfy my universal interest in freedom in the system of needs, because the very same forces that cause the system to flourish and grow also cause the specialized skills of many laborers to become obsolete, guaranteeing that a segment of society will be unemployed and impoverished.[110] This is the fundamental contradiction of the system: it creates an endless proliferation of needs, which leads to increasingly specialized labor, which creates a situation in which the system is increasingly unable to adapt to the very proliferation of needs that it generates.[111] Thus the system of needs creates structural unemployment and poverty, cannot guarantee labor as a right, and therefore precludes any of its members from satisfying their universal interest in freedom.[112]

This means that even as a successful member of civil society, one who is laboring productively and earning her share of the general wealth, I may not simply regard the structural contradiction in the system of needs as a necessary evil, as "hard luck" for those whose labor has become obsolete. I can do so only at the price of sacrificing my universal interest in my own freedom. As at the level of contract, where crime had to be prevented not only for the sake of the victims, but for the sake of the criminals as well, the structural contradiction in the system of needs must be rectified not only for the sake of the impoverished, but also for the sake of the successful.[113]

The cause of unfreedom in the system of needs is, as it was at the level of contract, a misplaced emphasis on particular interests over universal ones. In contract, this meant that it was possible for individuals to violate right and freedom in order to secure the possessions they wanted. Punishment was required in order to repair freedom by restoring respect for the universal. In civil society, we have seen that the violation of right, welfare, and freedom is no longer merely possible, it is made necessary by the system itself. This means not only that an analogue of punishment is required to repair freedom when it has been transgressed, but also that the system itself must be changed by the addition of new mechanisms to prevent transgressions of freedom before they occur. As with punishment, the efficacy of these mechanisms will derive from their ability to get individuals to focus on the universal as much as on the particular, from their ability to prevent us from pursuing our particular interests without regard for the requirements of freedom. Thus, also as before, these mechanisms will amount to a form of protection from ourselves in the name of our own freedom.

In civil society the function of the administration of justice is precisely the same as that of punishment in contract: to *repair* breaches of the system by restoring the criminal's respect for her own universal freedom: "Through the administration of justice, *infringements* of property or personality are annulled."[114] The additional mechanisms that arise to *prevent* the transgressions of freedom that are built into the system of needs are the public authority and the corporations.[115]

The primary task of the public authority is "that the livelihood and welfare of individuals should be *secured* – that is, that *particular welfare* should be *treated as a right* and duly *actualized.*"[116] Hegel mentions at least four ways in which the public authority tries to discharge this responsibility.

The first is by providing for elements in the system of needs that contemporary economists call externalities – goods or services that are important to all but that no individual would provide if the market were completely unregulated. Examples Hegel gives include street lighting, bridge building, and the maintenance of public health. Because no private party will undertake to pay for these necessary goods, "these *universal functions* and arrangements *of public utility* require oversight and advance provision on the part of the public authority."[117] Second, the public authority must ensure that individuals have the skills necessary to compete in the system of needs, by providing an adequate education for children, if need be even against their parents' wishes.[118] Third, in cases where people prove incapable of securing their own welfare or that of their families, the public authority must be prepared to assume guardianship.[119] Fourth and finally, the public authority also attempts to secure the labor of all, but here Hegel thinks that it is sure to fail. If it creates jobs for those willing to work, it will only exacerbate the root cause of unemployment: overproduction in an economy without sufficient consumption.[120] Ultimately, the economy will be driven to seek foreign markets to boost consumption of its goods. But this too will prove inadequate to solve the problem, as it will result in an international civil society in which unemployment, poverty, and unfreedom remain.[121]

All of these measures amount to society protecting the individual for the sake of her own freedom. However, the inability of the public authority to secure labor for all shows it is incapable of fully actualizing freedom. As long as individuals are driven primarily by the desire to outdo one another, which leads to ever escalating needs and ever more specialized labor in the search for ever increasing productivity and growth, there will be a segment of society unable to labor, and therefore unfree. Since the freedom of each depends for its objectification on a system that ensures the freedom of all, this unfree segment of society renders the freedom of all members of the society incomplete.

The only possible solution is the creation of a system in which people's drive to exceed each other is dampened. Only by reducing this drive can the cycle breeding obsolescent labor be broken, and only by breaking this cycle and securing the right to labor can the freedom of all be ensured.

The corporations succeed where the public authority fails – in diminishing our drive to exceed each other – by transforming not only economic relations but also our very sense of identity. Instead of understanding ourselves as particular beings set off from the universal, we understand that we are both particular *and* universal, that our true interest is bound up equally with each. In the system of needs, we appreciate the good of the universal only because it furthers our particular interests: the growth of the economy enables me to satisfy *my* needs through my labor. In the corporations, we seek the good of the universal, the good of the corporation of which we are a member, for its own sake. We realize that the good of this universal does not just contribute to our particular good, but actually *is* our good in itself, because it is the object in which our freedom resides. The corporations thus restore the unity of subjective particularity and objective universality, which are immediately bound to each other in the family but come apart in the system of needs.[122]

Hegel thinks the realization that the good of the universal is also our own particular good reduces our need to exceed each other. In the system of needs I want to be like others, but I also want to exceed them, partly because that is the only way I can gain their recognition of my worth, and partly because I define myself as over and against them, and thus my own identity requires me to distinguish myself from them. In the corporations, both of these motives for exceeding my peers are diminished. First, I gain the recognition and respect of others simply by being a member of the same corporation: "on condition of [his] *capability* . . . the member of a corporation has no need to demonstrate his competence and his regular income and means of support – that is, the fact that he is *somebody* – by any further *external evidence*."[123] Thus recognition no longer requires excess. Moreover, I do not need to exceed the other members of my corporation in order to establish and solidify my own identity. In fact, since my identity is bound up with theirs rather than defined in contrast to them – I now consider myself one of *us* – I do not even want to exceed them; to seek to exceed or outdo my fellow corporation members would be to seek to outdo myself.[124]

The result of my new self-understanding as a being with a universal aspect and interest is that I can now take satisfaction in the success of my community, and am not continually driven to set myself apart from that community by my particular excess. The person who has been transformed by his corporation now "has *his honour in his estate.*"[125] This transformation eases the pressures on society to create and satisfy endlessly changing needs, which alleviates the structural poverty and unfreedom caused by the extreme vulnerability to obsolescence of highly specialized labor. This limits the growth of the economy, but in a way that enables all to work, which in turn enables all to be free.[126]

Finally, it is important that the corporations that accomplish this dampening of our drives and limitation of the economy are recognized by individuals as their own; any restriction of our particular interests for the sake of our universal freedom must not be effected by the imposition of an external authority. Our freedom requires that our particular interests be limited, but it also requires that we understand that this limitation is in our own interest, and that we therefore understand the limitation to be self-imposed. This is not the case with the public authority. The public authority is experienced as a restriction of freedom, as a hindrance to my ability to pursue my own interests. Its necessity may be acknowledged, but since people do not identify themselves with the public authority, they can never experience the limitations it imposes on their particular interests as an increase in their freedom.[127] It is different with the corporations, which individuals recognize as voluntary associations existing to represent their own universal interest in freedom against their particular interest in excess; people accept the corporations as being consistent with their self-determination, because they understand that the corporations exist to protect them from themselves for the sake of their own freedom.

There might appear to be tension between Hegel's claim that membership in a corporation must be *voluntary*, and his claim that such membership constitutes protection of that person *from* herself. It might seem more natural to understand such a self-imposed measure as protection of an individual *by* herself, rather than *from* herself. But this tension is resolved when we recognize that Hegel is demonstrating precisely that freedom requires that we be protected *both* from ourselves and by ourselves. We need protection from ourselves, as we have seen, because we are both particular and universal, and without such external protection we risk violating our universal aspect in the pursuit of our particular interests. But if such protection is only external, only from ourselves and not by ourselves (as is the case in punishment), its efficacy will be uncertain, for it can accomplish no inner and necessary unification of our particular and universal sides. On the other hand, if such protection is only internal, only by ourselves and not from ourselves (as is the case in morality), it is in fact no protection from particularity at all, but rather the extreme case of particularity determining and dominating the universal. Consequently, we must recognize the protection we receive from

ourselves as being in our true particular interest, while at the same time
recognizing the legitimacy of the universal by not insisting on an absolute
right of particularity. The corporations, unlike punishment and morality,
fulfill both parts of this requirement: membership is voluntary (and so
must appeal to the particular interests of the individuals *by* whom the
decision to join is made), but once entered into confers upon the corporation the right to limit the particularity of its individual members (who
are therefore protected *from* violating their own universal freedom). The
corporations succeed in this, as we have seen, by transforming the self-
understanding of the individuals who join: individuals become members
out of their particular interests, and subsequently membership brings the
individuals to understand that the universal interests of the corporation
that they are obligated to uphold truly are their particular interests. Thus
individuals protect themselves *by* joining the corporations, and corporations protect individuals *from* themselves by preventing them from having a false self-understanding that would allow them to violate their own
freedom.[128]

The corporations represent the conclusion of civil society and the transition to the state. The corporations lead to the state in two senses. First,
by enabling individuals to see themselves as one particular instance of
a universal class (that of "members of this corporation"), the corporations enable individuals to see that their own particular interest *is* that
of a universal, and such seeing of oneself *as* a universal is essential to
making the transition from being an economic actor in civil society to
being a citizen of the state.[129] Second, however, the corporations lead
to the state because the universals with which they unite the particular
interests of their members are still *particular* universals; the corporations
themselves are particular organizations whose interests may conflict, and
so the unification of individual and universal achieved in them is incomplete. Consequently, the state is necessary in order to reconcile these
particular universals with itself as a more comprehensive universal, and
to give individuals an understanding of themselves not only as corporate
members, but as citizens.[130]

The state completes ethical life by overcoming the limitations of both
the family and civil society. We have seen that the family unifies individuals with the universal, but the immediacy with which it does so fails to
respect the particularity of all family members. Civil society, conversely,
grants each person full independence, but as a consequence the relationship of individuals to the universal is always mediated through their
own particular needs. In the state, the relationship of individuals to the
universal is both immediate and mediated, such that individuals view the
good of the state *both* as an end in itself *and* as serving their own particular
good.[131]

Individuals are immediately united with the state through the feeling of patriotism, which functions much like the feeling of love in the family. Hegel describes patriotism as a disposition "of trust (which may pass over into more or less educated insight), or the consciousness that my substantial and particular interest is preserved and contained in the interest and end of an other (i.e., the state), and in the latter's relation to me as an individual. As a result, this other immediately ceases to be an other for me, and in my consciousness of this, I am free."[132] The presence of patriotic feeling thus indicates that individuals identify the good of the state as their own good, which explains their willingness to make extraordinary efforts on the state's behalf, even when such efforts pose great risks to their own particular welfare.

Genuine patriotism is, however, conditional upon, or mediated by, the state's actually securing the freedom and particular welfare of its individual citizens. This distinguishes patriotism from the natural feeling of love that binds the family. In the state, unlike the family, "one is conscious of unity as law; there the content must be rational, and I must know it."[133] The genuinely patriotic disposition is therefore "a consequence of the institutions within the state, in which rationality is *actually* present."[134] If such rational institutions are developed, so that people can "trust that the state will continue to exist and that particular interests can be fulfilled within it alone," then individuals will become patriotic citizens who habitually act in accordance with the universal interest of the state.[135] On the other hand, should a political entity fail to be rational, and fail to secure the freedom and welfare of its citizens, it will risk the loss of their patriotism in both feeling and action.

Hegel's extensive discussion of the state amounts to an attempt to determine the conceptually necessary features of a rational political entity, one that is in fact capable of earning and sustaining the patriotism of its citizens by securing their freedom and welfare. The details of this discussion – which encompass the state's sovereign, executive, and legislative powers, as well as its external relations to other states – are unimportant for our purposes. For we are already in a position to assess how ethical life completes the liberation of the willing subject.[136]

By uniting the disposition of the individual subject with that which is objectively right, ethical life resolves the contradictions of both morality and abstract right. We have seen that neither of those forms of willing is able to unify subject and object as required by freedom. In abstract right, our freedom is objectified in property and contracts, but it is not our own, since those objects remain external to us. In morality, our freedom is our own, developed out of ourselves, but it fails to be objective, as the good is ultimately determined solely by my own conscience. In ethical life, freedom succeeds in being both objective and our own: it is objectified in the institutions that guarantee our freedom, and it is our own because we recognize ourselves in those institutions. The ethical will thus knows that freedom is its own nature, *and* that its freedom exists in the world around it.

Consequently, in ethical life the will is finally thought in a way adequate to its freedom, finally thought as being simultaneously subjective and objective in all of the required senses. The first of these requirements, as we have seen, is that the content of the individual, subjective will be determined by the objective concept of willing itself. Prior to ethical life, in morality, the subjective will is determined as conscience, and the objective will is determined as the good. As we saw, however, conscience can give itself no objective content, and the objective good cannot actualize itself without the efforts of a subjective will. In morality, then, where these two sides of the will are understood to be separate from each other, the subjective will is determined not by the objective concept of willing but rather by its own feeling for what is good, which is why the moral will is not free.

The reconception of the will in the transition to ethical life unifies subject and object, conscience and the good, in this first sense required for the will's freedom. Hegel writes that "whereas morality is the form of the will in general in its subjective aspect, ethical life is not just the subjective form and self-determination of the will: it also has its own concept, namely freedom, as its content."[137] In ethical life, then, the subjective will or conscience is no longer dependent upon the given objects of its natural dispositions for its content. This makes the will truly (as opposed to formally) self-determining, since its content, as well as its determining act, belongs to itself.

The second requirement is that this content of the will that stems from its concept must also have an immediate existence in the world. That is, the ethical will's content cannot remain purely inner or subjective, but must be expressed in an object. In abstract right, this objectification of the subject's content took the form of property and contract. In ethical life, the content is objectified in a system of determinate "*laws and institutions which have being in and for themselves.*"[138] These laws and institutions comprise the family, civil society, and the state, the three main stages of ethical life.

The third and final requirement is that this objective and institutionalized content of the universal will be recognized by the individual and subjective ethical wills as genuinely belonging to them, and therefore as not being an alien force upon which they are dependent. This does not mean that the validity of any particular law or institution is dependent upon the unanimous consent of the polity. Unanimity is not required, because although the legal and institutional objectifications of the good are necessary to freedom, none of the individual wills in the community is; ethical institutions must be actualized by *some* individual subjects, but whether or not any *particular* will is the source of this actualization is purely accidental.[139]

What this requirement does mean is that the subjects who comprise the community must recognize that in themselves, "in these individuals – who are accidental to [the ethical institutions and powers] – these powers have their representation, phenomenal shape, and actuality."[140] This is equivalent to recognizing that the laws and institutions "are not something *alien* to the subject. On the contrary, the subject bears *spiritual witness* to them as to *its own essence*, in which it has its *self-awareness* and lives as in its element which is not distinct from itself."[141] That is, the individual members of the community must recognize that although the ethical content is independent of each of them, it exists only in virtue of all of them, and that they are what they are only in virtue of it; the individuals must recognize that they and the ethical content of the whole reciprocally constitute each other. With this recognition comes the realization that the objective content belongs to each subject, and this allows the individual wills to experience their duty to fulfill the good as liberating:

> A binding duty can appear as a *limitation* only in relation to indeterminate subjectivity or abstract freedom, and to the drives of the natural will or of the moral will which arbitrarily determines its own indeterminate good. The individual, however, find his *liberation* in duty. On the one hand, he is liberated from his dependence on mere natural drives, and from the burden he labors under as a particular subject in his moral reflections on obligation and desire; and on the other hand he is liberated from that indeterminate subjectivity which does not attain existence or the objective determinacy of action, but remains *within itself* and has no actuality. In duty, the individual liberates himself so as to attain substantial freedom.[142]

Individuals experience their liberating unification with ethical universals in two different ways. Their immediate experience of this unity takes the shape of the individual's feeling that she is at home in the universal, which she expresses through the habitual performance of the behaviors – dressing, eating, greeting, celebrating, interacting in particular ways – that are customary in her family and in the larger communities of which she is a member.[143] The immediacy of this experience means that it is unreflective, that the behavior is neither deliberate nor much thought about.[144] Rather, it is simply done, and in doing it individuals feel connected. In custom, Hegel says, ethical content literally becomes a second nature.[145]

But individuals also experience their unity with ethical universals in mediated fashion. This experience has the shape of the individuals' self-consciousness that the ethical institutions are the objective substance of which they are the subjective actuality.[146] While Hegel notes that this reflective awareness is not the same thing as adequate cognition of the unity of individual subjectivity and universal substance, which can only be provided by conceptual thought, it does mean that ethical substance, in the form of the ethical subjects, knows itself as the objectification of the will.[147]

In truly ethical life, then, all three unifications of subject and object are achieved, and the will is finally liberated. The subjective will is informed by the objective content of its own concept; it participates in the purposive actualization of this content in the objective immediacy of the world; and it therefore recognizes this world, including its requirements and duties, as essential to itself, and hence liberating.[148]

The result is that in ethical life the will's self-actualization or objectification (in the laws and institutions of the family, civil society, and the state) is unified with its self-consciousness (that it is essentially one with, and free in, those institutions). This unification of actuality and self-consciousness Hegel calls spirit, and so he concludes that in ethical life the will exists as spirit.[149] As spirit, the ethical will recognizes itself in the objective world; the individual will recognizes itself in the universal, and therefore has a sense of its identity with the totality.[150]

Moreover, in ethical life the spiritual subject understands that it can recognize itself in the world because the strivings of spiritual beings have purposively transformed the initially independent objectivity of nature into something with which such beings are unified, and in which they are therefore free; at the end of objective spirit the subject knows that spiritual beings, by determining their own content and actualizing that content in their families, civil society, and the state, have overcome the independence of nature (that is, internalized the externality) that previously prevented them from being free. As Hegel puts it: "in the *ethical realm* . . . the principle of freedom has penetrated into the worldly realm itself, and . . . the worldly, because it has been thus conformed to the concept, reason, and eternal truth, is freedom that has become concrete and will that is rational."[151] Since this is the case, we must now examine why the willing subject, even in a truly rational state, remains plagued by externality and thus incompletely free.

FREEDOM BEYOND WILLING: FROM THE
PHILOSOPHY OF RIGHT TO ABSOLUTE SPIRIT

Discussions of Hegel's account of freedom often focus exclusively on the *Philosophy of Right*. Although everything Hegel has to say in the *Philosophy of Right* concerns freedom, such an exclusive focus is a serious mistake, for not everything Hegel has to say concerning freedom can be found in the *Philosophy of Right*. The *Philosophy of Right* considers the freedom available to spiritual beings through the activity of willing; it presents a detailed account of what Hegel calls objective spirit. Objective spirit, however, constitutes but one-third of Hegel's philosophy of spirit, and we have seen that the entirety of the philosophy of spirit is an attempt to determine what it means to be free. Understanding Hegel's account of freedom therefore requires not only interpreting the *Philosophy of Right*, but also situating it within its larger systematic context. The goal of this chapter is thus to understand objective spirit in relation to absolute spirit, to understand willing in relation to art, religion, and philosophy.[1]

To accomplish this goal, Chapter 3 employs the same strategy as Chapter 2. Chapter 2 interpreted Hegel's account of the freedom of willing by means of an analysis that emphasized the penultimate conception in the development of the *Philosophy of Right*; attending to the finitude of the moral will illuminated the ultimate liberation of the willing subject in ethical life. Chapter 3 interprets Hegel's larger account of freedom by means of an analysis that emphasizes the penultimate conception in the development of the philosophy of spirit; attending to the finitude of the willing subject in objective spirit illuminates the ultimate liberation of spiritual beings in absolute spirit through the activities of art, religion, and philosophy.[2]

Chapter 3 also employs the same method as Chapter 2. In Chapter 2, the first step in understanding the finitude of the moral will was the identification of its logical structure, and the first step in the identification of its logical structure was an analysis of the development of morality out of abstract right and the Introduction to the *Philosophy of Right*. Having identified the moral will as the will in the form of judgment, we were able to understand the limitations of morality by attending to the limitations of that logical concept. After we had discovered and understood the formality of judgment, its inability to generate its own particular content, we were able to understand Hegel's famous charge that the moral will is formal. Finally, by considering how judgment ultimately transforms itself into syllogism, we were able to see how morality overcomes itself to liberate the willing subject in ethical life.

In Chapter 3, the first step in understanding the finitude of willing is the identification of the logical structure of this activity, and the first step in this identification, provided in section 1, is an analysis of the development of willing out of Hegel's discussion of subjective spirit. This analysis identifies willing as the purposive activity of spiritual beings. Section 2 therefore considers the logical concept of purposiveness. Section 3 attends to the finitude of purposiveness in order to understand the finitude of willing. The insuperable finitude of willing means that even in ethical life spiritual beings are not fully free. Section 4 therefore takes up the transition from objective spirit to absolute spirit, in which spiritual beings are finally conceived in a way that is adequate to their freedom.

1. The Place of Willing in the Philosophy of Spirit

In Chapter 1, we saw that the entirety of the philosophy of spirit is an attempt to conceive spiritual beings in a way adequate to their freedom, and that the freedom of spiritual beings requires that they reconcile themselves with the natural world. The three parts of the philosophy of spirit – subjective, objective, and absolute spirit – thus represent successive efforts to conceive the relation between spiritual beings and the natural world in such a way that the two are genuinely reconciled with each other. These efforts are not only successive but also progressive: each conception is initially assumed to provide an adequate reconciliation; the development of the conception shows that this reconciliation is in fact limited; and the succeeding conception overcomes the identified limitations of its predecessor.

Subjective and objective spirit are both characterized by the assumption that spiritual beings are confronted by a natural world that is independent of them, which serves as their external limit and thereby makes them finite.[3] Because this finitude makes spirit unfree, and "the essential...feature of spirit is freedom," in these shapes spirit is also finite in the sense of being a limited expression of, or inadequate to, its own concept.[4] For these reasons, Hegel calls subjective and objective spirit the two forms of finite spirit.

But subjective and objective spirit are also characterized by the certainty that the separation of spiritual beings from nature is not ultimate. Throughout finite spirit it is thus assumed that spiritual beings can overcome both senses of their finitude, and thereby free themselves, by demonstrating that nature is not truly external to them.[5] Hegel writes that "reason comes to the world with absolute faith in its ability to posit [its] identity [with the objective world] and to elevate its certainty into *truth,* and with the drive to *posit* the antithesis, which is *in-itself* null and void *for it* as null and void."[6]

There are two basic processes or activities through which the identity of spiritual subjects and the objective world can be posited: either spiritual beings can take contents they find in the natural world and give them a spiritual form; or spiritual beings can give their own contents a natural form, by giving them an existence in the objective world. Hegel calls these two activities knowing and willing, and discusses them in subjective and objective spirit, respectively.[7]

In subjective spirit, spiritual beings are conceived as trying to reconcile themselves with the natural world by coming to know it. Through knowing, the spiritual subject is able to "liberate the intrinsically rational object from the form of contingency, singleness, and externality which at first clings to it, and thereby free *itself* from the connection with something which is for it an other."[8] This is accomplished, for example, when it is demonstrated that certain natural phenomena behave in such a way that they can be subsumed under scientific laws. In this accomplishment, rational spiritual subjects recognize that the objects of their cognition – the lawlike natural phenomena – are rational too, and thereby achieve a degree of reconciliation with them.[9]

Hegel calls this conception of spiritual beings "subjective" for two reasons. First, spiritual beings are understood to be the subjects, but not the object, of the activity of knowing. The object of this activity, that with which it is concerned, is the natural world. Second, the contents of the spiritual subject's knowledge are understood to be merely subjective representations of the natural world, which is therefore taken to be real or objective. In the activity of knowing, that is, spiritual beings seek to conform themselves to the natural world with which they are confronted, by developing an adequate conceptual representation of it. In this process the natural world is understood to remain unchanged, and so to be objective, whereas the subjective spiritual beings are altered by internalizing an external content that is given to them.

For example, a rock on the forest floor remains the same before, during, and after it is represented. But the human subject who takes notice of the rock as she walks by is transformed, as the contents of her representations become different than they had been. The subject internalizes the rock by putting its natural contents into a spiritual form, and thus achieves a measure of reconciliation with it.[10]

But the reconciliation with the natural world that the activity of knowing provides is only partial, so in this activity the spiritual subject remains incompletely free. The reconciliation is partial because the spiritual subject still experiences the natural content that it internalizes as externally given. The natural phenomena that the spiritual subject succeeds in representing remain fundamentally independent of the spiritual activity for which they supply the content. Consequently, nature remains alien to the spiritual subject, and the spiritual subject remains bound to it in necessity rather than in freedom.

Since the freedom of spiritual beings is compromised by the dependence of the activity of knowing on an externally given content, spiritual beings must be reconceived as the source of the contents of their own activities. This reconception begins near the end of subjective spirit, in a section entitled Practical Spirit that initiates the transition to objective spirit.

In practical spirit, the spiritual subject is understood to set "only itself for its goal, [it] becomes *will* which . . . does not begin with an isolated object externally given, but with something it knows to be its own."[11] The practical activity of willing thus internalizes the spiritual subject's object in a way that the theoretical activity of knowing does not. The object of knowing is independent of the spiritual subject, but the object of willing, that which is willed, exists only within that subject. The spiritual subject is thus more free in willing than it is in knowing.

But the willing subject, as initially conceived, is still confronted by a double externality. First, although the contents that are willed exist within the subject, the subject still experiences them as given to it: these contents are "the *drives, desires, and inclinations* by which the will finds itself naturally determined."[12] The willing subject is conceived as having the ability to choose from among these natural drives, desires, and inclinations that it finds within itself, but not as having any control over which ones it happens to find.[13] The subject is thus not truly the source of its own contents, even though those contents exist only within it. Second, the willing subject is still confronted by nature as by an independent, external world that may or may not conform to its drives, desires, and inclinations. To become free, the subject must internalize both of these externalities: it must become the source of the contents of its own will, and it must ensure the conformity of the natural world to those contents.[14]

The willing subject seeks to overcome the externality of the natural world not by conforming itself to the contents of the latter, as the knowing subject does, but by realizing its own content in nature. In practical spirit, the subject is conceived as attempting to make the natural world conform to it:

> Unlike theoretical spirit, [practical spirit] does not start from the seemingly alien object, but from its own purposes (*Zwecken*) and interests, that is, from subjective determinations, and *then* proceeds to make these into an

objectivity. In doing this it reacts against the one-sided subjectivity of self-consciousness that is shut up within itself, just as theoretical spirit reacts against the consciousness that is dependent on a given object.[15]

Willing thus amounts to the spiritual subject's effort to "determine the world that it finds already there according to its own purpose."[16]

But no matter how successful the practical spiritual subject is in accomplishing its purposes, it remains unfree as long as its particular contents, the particular things that it aims to accomplish, are still given to it externally by its natural drives, desires, and inclinations. The willing subject can be free only if it makes itself, its own freedom as the overcoming of all externality, into the content, object, or purpose it aims to realize in the natural world.[17]

The transition from subjective to objective spirit occurs when the willing subject is understood to have overcome the first externality by making itself, its own freedom, into the content, object, or purpose that it aims to realize in the natural world. Spiritual beings are considered objective at this stage for two reasons, which correspond to the reasons that they were previously considered subjective. First, spiritual beings are now understood to be not only the subjects but also the objects of their own activity: that which the subject wills to bring about in the world is freedom, its own essential determination. Second, it is now the natural world that is understood to have to conform to the spiritual: in the theoretical activity of knowing, the spiritual subject conforms its contents to those of the natural phenomena it engages; but in the practical activity of willing, the natural world is the malleable field that is made to conform to the contents of the subject's will, which are therefore taken to be what is truly real or objective.

Spiritual beings are more free in objective spirit than in subjective spirit because they are now understood to have overcome their dependence on a naturally given content. The contents of the spiritual subject are no longer those of natural phenomena (as they are in the theoretical activity of knowing) or those of natural drives, desires, and inclinations (as they are in the practical activity of subjective spirit). Rather, the spiritual subject now wills its own freedom, instead of willing something it receives as a command from natural sources over which it has no control.

But despite this increased degree of liberation, at the outset of objective spirit spiritual beings are still understood to be finite, in two senses. First, although the willing subject wills its own freedom, its own reconciliation with the objective world, there are various ways in which it might conceive its freedom, and thus various ways in which it might pursue such a reconciliation. Second, the willing subject remains confronted by and bound to a natural world that has not been determined by its conception of freedom.[18] The subject committed to willing its own freedom "finds itself immediately confronted by differences which arise from the circumstance that freedom is its *inward* function and purpose, and is in relation to an external and already subsisting objectivity."[19] This remains the case as long as "that which is willed . . . is still only a content belonging to the self-consciousness, an unaccomplished purpose."[20]

The willing subject attempts to remedy its finitude by realizing its purpose and thus giving its freedom an external, objective existence: "the purposive action of the will is to realize its concept, freedom, in these externally objective aspects, making the latter a world molded by the former, which in it is thus at home with itself (*bei sich selbst*), locked together with itself (*mit sich selbst zussamengeschlossen*)."[21] Because right (*das Recht*) is the name Hegel gives to the forms of existence that the willing subject is able to give itself in the natural world, the *Philosophy of Right* represents a chronicle of the attempt to develop an adequate conception of the willing subject, one in which that subject truly wills freedom and succeeds in giving that freedom an objective existence.[22]

The *Philosophy of Right* begins, as we saw in Chapter 2, by conceiving the willing subject as a subject with the ability to choose. This is the willing subject considered in practical spirit, which, having yet to grasp its own freedom as its proper object, still belongs to subjective spirit. From this starting point, the *Philosophy of Right* shows how the willing subject must be reconceived if it is to be understood to overcome the dual externality (of given natural content and an indifferent natural world) that prevents it from being free, and therefore prevents it from being a fully adequate spiritual being. This progressive reconception, in which the willing subject becomes increasingly free of these externalities, ends in ethical life, because there the spiritual subject has internalized all of the externality it can through the activity of willing. Hegel writes that ethical life is "the perfection of objective spirit – the truth of subjective and objective spirit itself."[23]

But the perfection of objective spirit is not the perfection or truth of spirit *simpliciter*. Spiritual beings remain burdened, even as they are conceived in ethical life, with externality and finitude, and so never achieve an adequate reconciliation with nature. The perfection of spirit must await absolute spirit, in which spiritual beings are reconceived in such a way that they are truly free.

The finitude of spiritual beings at the end of objective spirit stems from what Hegel calls the contradiction of willing. On the one hand, the willing subject is certain that its content is what is truly real and objective, and that it therefore has the ability to transform the immediate and insignificant shape of the natural world through the realization of its purposes; but on the other hand, the willing subject also presupposes that natural world to be fundamentally independent of itself, and therefore understands its purpose of realizing its own freedom to be only *its* purpose, to be merely subjective.[24] As a result, when it realizes its purposes, the willing subject thinks both that it is determining the natural world to conform to its subjective purposes and, because the natural world is ultimately independent of its will, that the world's conformity to those purposes is only temporary and accidental. The willing subject thinks both that its purpose is essential and that in truth it is inessential; freedom is essential insofar as it is the definitive determination of spiritual beings, but inessential because of the natural world's indifference to it.[25]

This contradiction shows that the willing subject is not just purposive, but externally purposive. It is externally purposive because it understands that its purpose is not the purpose of the found, natural world itself; rather, the willing subject understands its purpose to be external to the world in which it strives to bring that purpose about. The world, according to the willing subject's understanding, does not itself pursue the realization of freedom; rather, spiritual beings must bring about freedom in a world indifferent to it. Willing is the externally purposive striving of spiritual beings to realize their freedom in the natural world.[26]

We can therefore better understand willing, in order ultimately to understand its finitude and the need to reconceive spiritual beings in absolute spirit, if we briefly examine Hegel's discussion of external purposiveness in the section of the *Logic* on teleology.

2. The Logical Concept of Purposiveness[27]

Purpose, according to Hegel, begins with the negative judgment that subject and object are opposed to one another, together with the understanding that the purpose is the subjective side of the judgment, having the power to determine the object, which is therefore a nothing in itself, through its own activity.[28] Because the object is alien to the subject in a judgment, as we saw in Chapter 2, the content of the purpose is external to the object; purpose is thus immediately external purposiveness, and its content is initially limited to the subjective side of the judgment.[29]

As long as it has the form of judgment, external purposiveness is finite in two senses with which we are already familiar. First, it is finite in the sense that its content is given to it. We saw the reason for this in the discussion of judgment in Chapter 2: the content of a judgment is the particular constitution that unites its subject and object, and even the highest form of judgment, the apodeictic judgment, cannot determine these particulars out of itself. In a judgment, the connection of subject and object is immediate, and therefore relies on something external to the judgment for its mediating content; a judgment expresses that "the subject *is* the object," but the *is* remains abstract. In other words, the details of the connection are unexpressed, and therefore cannot be seen to stem from the nature of the subjective purpose itself. As long as this is the case, the content of the purpose is not immanent, but rather given to it, and purpose is finite in the first sense.[30] Second, external purposiveness in the form of judgment is finite because it is limited by and dependent upon an objectivity independent of itself. It might appear that purpose is not limited by objectivity, because it understands objectivity as a nothingness subordinate to its activity of realization. However, because an objective means is necessary if the subject is to objectify itself, and because external purposiveness understands this means to be indifferent to its subjective purpose, the subject's realization is dependent upon conditions external to itself; without external material on which to work, the subject's purpose cannot be realized. This is the second sense in which external purposiveness is finite.[31]

External purposiveness is the attempt to overcome both of these senses of its finitude. External purposiveness is the drive to overcome its second sense of finitude, its dependence on an independent objectivity, by transforming that objectivity in order to demonstrate that its independence is illusory, that its true determinations are those of the subject. This is the drive of subjectivity to objectify itself in an immediate existence, and to join only with itself, rather than with a temporarily mastered other, in that world of immediacy. If accomplished, this amounts to "the *realizing of the purpose*, in which the purpose has sublated the distinction between the two, i.e., subjectivity and objectivity, since it makes itself into the other of its subjectivity and objectifies itself. It has concluded *itself with itself alone* (*sich nur mit sich zusammengeschlossen*) and has *preserved* itself."[32]

But such realization is possible, as we saw in Chapter 2, only if the judgment that separates subject and object is replaced by a syllogism that negates the independent extremes created by that judgment; purpose must be reconceived as a syllogism of realization, as the teleological syllogism, which must reunite the subject and object through a mediating factor, and demonstrate that the subject's translation into objectivity is really a rejoining with itself, rather than a venture into something completely other.[33] Such a syllogism of realization is also necessary to overcome the finitude of purpose's content, by showing that the mediating factor, the concrete connection between subject and object that constitutes the content of the purpose, is identical to the subjective purpose itself, rather than externally connected to it.

Like any syllogism, the teleological syllogism has three terms, which are united in pairs to form a major premise, a minor premise, and a conclusion. In the teleological syllogism the terms are the subjective purpose, the means, and the accomplished purpose. The means itself is twofold, it "is both the purposive *activity* and the objectivity posited *immediately* as subservient to the purpose."[34] The major premise of the teleological syllogism unites the universal subjective purpose with a particular means comprised of both activity and object. The minor premise unites this means with an individual actuality possessing immediate objectivity, the accomplished purpose. The conclusion thus unites the subjective purpose with the accomplished objective purpose, so that this objectivity now appears posited by subjectivity as an external realization of its own determinations.

The stages in the development of the teleological syllogism correspond to its three terms: "*first*, subjective purpose, *secondly*, purpose in the process of accomplishing itself [or means], and *thirdly*, the accomplished purpose."[35]

Subjective purpose initiates the teleological syllogism by making the twofold judgment we have briefly discussed. The subject judges, and in so doing

> it not only particularizes the still indeterminate universal and makes it into a determinate content, but it also posits the antithesis of subjectivity and objectivity... it determines that the subjectivity of the concept, presupposed as confronting the objectivity, is something-deficient, in comparison with the totality that is concluded within itself; and it thereby turns itself outwards once more.[36]

That is, the subject gives itself a content, distinguishes itself from the objectivity confronting it, and resolves to transform this objectivity in such a way that subject and object form a totality in which both sides share the same content in different forms.

This resolve makes the subject into self-completing purpose, into purpose in the process of bringing about its own realization. As subjective purpose, the subject made the negative judgment that objectivity confronts it as independent and indifferent. Now, as self-completing purpose, the subject must negate this negation, positing objectivity as the means subservient to its activity of realization. That is, the subject determines itself as the means-activity with the power to determine the very being of the means-object itself. This makes the being of the means-object merely ideal; it does not have its own character, but is immediately identical with the subject as means-activity: "The relation of the purpose as *power* to this object, and the latter's subservience to it, is *immediate*... inasmuch as the object is posited as *in-itself* null."[37]

The means-object is immediately related not only to the subjective purpose, but also to the end-object in which that purpose is to be realized. It is immediately related to the former, as we have just seen, because the means-object is understood as being nothing in-itself, but rather an extension of the subject's power. It is immediately related to the latter, because both are simply mechanical and chemical things in the objective world. The means-object, once determined by the power of the subject's means-activity, is thus able to communicate the subject's purpose to the objective world.[38] The means-object interacts mechanically and chemically with the objective world in accordance with the physical natures of each, and yet because the means-object is governed by the subject's means-activity, its natural mechanical and chemical interactions bring about the subject's purpose indirectly. This objectification of the subjective purpose is the final stage of the teleological syllogism, that of completed purpose; the fact that this completion is accomplished indirectly, through mechanical and chemical processes completely indifferent to it, amounts to what Hegel calls the cunning of reason.[39]

Hegel's example of the completion of such a cunning teleological syllogism is divine Providence: God's will is the subjective purpose; people are the means-object, used by God's means-activity to carry out his will; and God's will is carried out not through His direct intervention, but indirectly through the natural interactions of people, who do not know that their apparently mundane activities actually serve a divine plan of which they are ignorant. Hegel writes that "God lets men, who have their particular passions and interests, do as they please, and what results is the accomplishment of *his* intentions, which are something other than those whom he employs were directly concerned about."[40]

A more pedestrian example is the use of chlorine to sterilize a swimming pool. Here, the subjective purpose is the prevention of disease. The means-object is a certain quantity of chlorine. As a means-object, the chlorine is immediately subservient to the means-activity of the purposive subject, without which it would not even be in the water; it is also immediately related, as a mechanical and chemical object, to the environment in which it is placed. The chlorine is completely indifferent to the prevention of disease, yet it does prevent disease, simply in virtue of its natural mechanical interactions with the water, which circulate it throughout the pool, and its chemical interactions with the bacteria it thereby encounters and destroys. The cunning of reason thus completes the realization of purpose, for the swimming pool manager no less than for God.

The teleological syllogism unites subject and predicate, universality and individuality, as judgment cannot. It does not, however, completely overcome the finitude of external purposiveness. This is because it is a formal syllogism, and the formal syllogism is irredeemably finite. We will examine the finitude of the formal syllogism, and the finitude of the teleological syllogism and willing that result from it, in the next section of this chapter. We conclude this section with a brief explanation of Hegel's claim that the teleological syllogism is a formal syllogism, and that it therefore "suffers from the defect of the formal syllogism in general."[41]

The formal syllogism shares several basic features with all other types of syllogism.[42] First, every syllogism is composed of a subject and object (the extremes), which are united in a determinate way through a mediating factor (the middle term). Second, this middle term, which posits the determinate unity of subject and object, is the essential feature of every type of syllogism; the middle term distinguishes syllogism from judgment, which has no middle term, and in which subject and object are therefore united only immediately, through the indeterminate *is*. Third, in every type of syllogism each of these three terms – subject, object, and middle term – has the form of either individuality, particularity, or universality.[43]

What distinguishes the formal syllogism from other, more developed types of syllogism is that in a formal syllogism the terms united are understood as having immediate being, and therefore as external to each other and self-subsistent.[44] The subject and the object are both understood to be what they are independent of each other, and the subject is therefore understood to unite not with itself but with an other through the middle term; the being of the individual is thought to be separable from both the universal to which it is attached and the particular through which the attachment is made.

External purposiveness, understood as the teleological syllogism or the syllogism of realization, is therefore a formal syllogism in virtue of the character of its terms and their connections. The connection between the subjective purpose and the accomplished objective purpose is mediated by the means, but, as we have seen, the connections between the subjective purpose and the means and between the means and the objective purpose are immediate. This immediacy of the connections between its terms is what makes the teleological syllogism formal.[45]

3. The Incomplete Freedom of Willing

In the previous sections, we have seen that the willing subject is finite as long as its contents are merely subjective and it is confronted by an independent objectivity. We have also seen that willing is the externally purposive activity of seeking to overcome this finitude by positing the subject's own determinations in the objectivity that confronts it. Externally purposive activity has hopes of overcoming the willing subject's finitude by replacing the judgment that separates it from objectivity with a syllogism in which the subject's will is genuinely realized in the natural world, thus demonstrating that the latter is not truly independent. Finally, we have seen that this syllogism of realization, the teleological syllogism, is a formal syllogism. What is yet to be seen, and what we will examine in this section, is why it is impossible for a formal syllogism to overcome the finitude that plagues judgment, and why it is therefore the case that external purposiveness and willing remain forever finite.

We can represent the formal syllogism by I-P-U, where I, P, and U are understood as immediacies.[46] That the terms are immediacies means that I, P, and U are understood to be independent of and external to each other. This means that although the connection of I to U is mediated by P, the connections I-P and P-U are themselves immediate; there is nothing about the character of I or P that explains why they are connected, nor is there anything about P or U that explains their link.[47] Thus, although the conclusion of the formal syllogism is mediated, which is an advance beyond judgment, no mediating factor is posited to explain the connection of the terms in either premise. Rather, they simply happen to be connected, immediately and therefore externally, not in virtue of any essential feature of the terms themselves.

The consequence of the immediacy and externality of these connections is that the content of the formal syllogism is contingent. This contingency is manifested in two ways. First, the choice of a particular P to mediate I and U is arbitrary.[48] The subject I, as a concrete individual, has many particular qualities, any of which can serve equally well to mediate it with a universal. All of these potential choices for P are equally good, because there is nothing to identify one of them as a quality more essential to I than the others – all of the particular qualities have an immediate connection to the subject, which means that none of them is connected to it in virtue of being part of its essence (or in virtue of anything else, for that matter). This means that the choice to connect I to one P rather than another P must be regarded as contingent. Second, once a particular P has been chosen and connected to I, the choice of a particular U to conclude the syllogism is also arbitrary. Like I, P is concrete, and can therefore be connected to a number of different universals. Again, no reason can be provided for connecting P to one of these rather than to any of the others. As a result, for any given subject I, an indeterminate number of formal syllogisms can be produced. This demonstrates that the logical form of the formal syllogism – namely, the connection of three immediate terms – necessarily makes its content contingent.[49]

As an example, take Sally as our given individual subject. Sally is a woman, a doctor, an African-American, a mother, an aunt, and so on. Any of these particular qualities can serve equally well as the middle term of a formal syllogism. If we choose the first particular quality, Sally's womanhood, as the mediating term of our syllogism, we are then faced with a large number of universals to which it might be connected. As a woman, Sally is a human, an animal, a mammal, a daughter, a biped, and so on. Again, there is nothing to make us prefer using any one of these universals to conclude the syllogism. Sally, like any other concrete individual, can be the subject of a very large number of valid formal syllogisms. But the fact that all of these formal syllogisms are equally valid is precisely the problem. There is nothing about the logical structure of the formal syllogism that can determine which content most truly belongs to its subject, and the content of every formal syllogism is therefore contingent.

Since the contingency of the formal syllogism stems from the immediacy of the connections I-P and P-U, overcoming its contingency requires mediating these connections. This mediation, Hegel points out, requires the construction of two more syllogisms. In the first, a particular aspect of P that explains its connection to I has to be identified in order to mediate the I-P connection. In the second, a particular aspect of U that explains its connection to P has to be found in order to mediate the P-U connection.

But the problem of contingency is only reinstated, rather than overcome, by these two secondary syllogisms. In the first secondary syllogism, P is a universal with respect to I, and their connection is mediated by immediate, and therefore contingent, connections to a particular quality; in the second secondary syllogism, P is an individual with respect to U, and their connection is also mediated by immediate, contingent connections to a particular quality. In other words, each of these secondary syllogisms, designed to mitigate the formality of the original syllogism, is itself a formal syllogism. But this means that the secondary syllogisms cannot mediate the genuine realization of I in U through P in the original syllogism, because their own realization is inadequate in precisely the same way as that of the original syllogism: each secondary syllogism is mediated by immediate connections, so their conclusions are contingent, and I and U remain external to each other in their unification. Consequently, I and U also remain mutually external in the original syllogism. The immediacy and contingency of the original syllogism are not overcome, but only displaced and duplicated in each of the secondary syllogisms.

To complete the mediation of the original syllogism, and to dispel its contingency, each of the two immediate connections in each of the two secondary syllogisms must itself become yet another syllogism: four in all. But these four are also formal syllogisms, and require eight more syllogisms to mediate their immediate connections. The eight require sixteen, the sixteen require thirty-two, and so on. The problem arises again and again, ad infinitum, so the content of the original syllogism remains contingent, and its realization of I in U is never complete.[50]

Formal syllogism, we can conclude, is terminally finite. It does surpass judgment by mediating the connection of its subject and object, of individuality and universality. However, this improvement is largely superficial, because, like judgment, formal syllogism leaves its subject and object external to each other. Formal syllogism is thus a subjective syllogism, in the sense that the connection of its subject and object is not understood to be an objective feature of the subject itself, but rather to be externally attributed to that subject by the subject performing the syllogism.[51] It therefore has a contingent content, as we have seen. Overcoming this contingency, by demonstrating an internal and objective connection of subject and object, thus requires not an infinite multiplication of formal syllogisms, but rather overcoming the logical structure of formal syllogism altogether. Since the formal syllogism is therefore dependent on a logical form other than itself for its realization, it is finite.[52]

External purposiveness, we have noted, seeks to overcome its finitude by replacing its initial judgment that subject and object are mutually external with a syllogism that unites the two in a way that demonstrates their internal connection. We have also noted, however, that this syllogism of realization, the teleological syllogism, is a formal one. Having now seen the failure of formal syllogism to overcome its finitude, we should therefore expect external purposiveness to fail in a similar fashion. This is, in fact, what eventually happens, but the insuperable finitude of external purposiveness is not immediately obvious.

For example, in the following summary of the result of the teleological syllogism, Hegel makes it sound as though finitude has indeed been overcome:

> [T]he realized purpose is the *posited unity* of the subjective and the objective ... the objective is subordinated to and brought into conformity with the purpose, which is the free concept and hence the might over it. The purpose *preserves* itself against and within the objective, since it is not only the *one-sided* subjective [moment], the particular, but also the concrete universal, the identity (of both the subjective and the objective) that is in-itself. As simply reflected inwardly this universal is the *content*, which remains *the same* through all three terms of the syllogism, and throughout their movement.[53]

Here it appears that the purposive subject, by positing its unity with the object, has demonstrated that its connection to that object is an internal one. After all, the subject is responsible for the determination of the object, and in the determined object the subject finds its own content. By finding its own content in the object, the subject transforms its initial understanding of that object as something other than and external to itself. The finitude of the subject is thus apparently overcome in the realization of purpose.

But the teleological syllogism's overcoming of finitude proves to be merely illusory. Because the teleological syllogism is a formal syllogism, the realization of the subject in the object proves to be incomplete, and the two remain external to each other. This means that a genuinely objective realization of the subjective purpose depends on a logical structure other than that of external purposiveness, which is therefore finite. We will now examine the teleological syllogism, in order to understand how its formality consigns external purposiveness to finitude.

Recall that the teleological syllogism is formal because of the immediacy of the connections between its terms. The consequence of immediacy for the teleological syllogism, as for the formal syllogism itself, is contingency. Because the means is only immediately connected to the subjective purpose, it is not the only possible means. On the contrary, a number of different means-objects can be linked with the subjective purpose, and the selection of a particular means-object is therefore arbitrary and contingent.[54] Likewise, given a particular means-object, the immediacy of its connection with the objectified purpose makes this connection equally contingent; a given means-object can be linked with a number of different objectifications. The result, as in formal syllogism, is the contingency of the teleological syllogism's conclusion; the subjective purpose happens, contingently, to be connected with this particular objectification, but many other conclusions are equally possible.

We can illustrate this contingency by returning to our previous example of external purposiveness: the prevention of disease in a swimming pool. In that example, the chosen means-object was chlorine, and the associated means-activity was the distribution of the chlorine throughout the pool. But the subjective purpose of disease prevention might well be connected with a variety of different means-activities and means-objects. These could include: closing the pool (means-activity) by putting a lock (means-object) on the gate; draining the pool with a pump; preventing anyone from entering the pool with a crew of strong lifeguards; inoculating each prospective swimmer with certain drugs. Furthermore, each of these potential means could objectify itself through mechanical and chemical interaction in numerous ways. If we choose the traditional means of adding chlorine to the pool, disease might well be, and often is, prevented. But other objectifications include red and painful eyes, damaged hair, itchy skin, and a peculiar smell. Still others, in certain conditions, include the failure to prevent disease, and the causation of illness and even death. The upshot is that an indeterminate number of formal syllogisms connect the goal of aquatic disease prevention with an objectification, and the logical structure of formal syllogism cannot tell us which of these syllogisms realizes the subjective purpose more truly than the others.

The apparent solution to the problem of contingency, again as with formal syllogism, is to mediate the immediate connections. The subjective purpose and the objectified purpose must be connected to the means-object not immediately, but through mediating particulars. However, as we saw earlier, this "solution" only duplicates the problem, replacing the original formal syllogism (subjective purpose, means, objectified purpose) with two secondary formal syllogisms (subjective purpose, particular quality, means; means, particular quality, objectified purpose). These secondary formal syllogisms cannot solve the problem, cannot produce a noncontingent unification of subject and object in the original syllogism, unless they can unify subject and object in themselves in a noncontingent way. But since the connections between their terms are also immediate, they cannot do this. Their immediate connections must be mediated by four further syllogisms, which require eight mediating syllogisms, which require sixteen, and so on. Again, the quest to provide a noncontingent conclusion to the original syllogism leads to an infinite regress of mediation, which never overcomes the contingency.[55]

A contingent connection between two terms is an external connection. To say that a connection is contingent means that whether or not it is made has no bearing on the terms it connects, and that the nature of those terms does not determine whether or how they are connected. In other words, the connection is external to what the terms are in-themselves; being connected in this way is not an internal aspect of their nature. An immediate consequence of two terms being externally connected is their being external to each other. Since both terms are what they are regardless of whether they are connected, each must be what it is independent of what the other is. In other words, each externally connected term is external to what the other term is in-itself; neither term's nature is an internal aspect of the nature of the other.

Here, in the teleological syllogism, we have seen that the subjective purpose and the objectification are contingently connected. We can thus conclude that they are externally connected: what they are is independent of their being connected, and what they are does not determine the nature of their connection, or whether they are connected at all. Further, we can conclude that they are external to each other: because the character of the subjective purpose and the character of the objectification are independent of their being linked, they are independent of each other; each is what it is, regardless of what or whether the other is. In the teleological syllogism, the subjective purpose and the objectification are mutually external.

The mutual externality of the subjective purpose and the objectification means that the objectification is not truly the objectification of the subjective purpose itself. Rather, the fact that the two are external to each other means that the objectification does not contain the complete determinacy of the subjective purpose, and what determinacy it does receive from the subject is external to its own character. In other words, the object in a teleological syllogism does not objectify the subjective purpose, and thus does not serve as that subject's genuine end. On the contrary, Hegel writes, "the conclusion or the *product* of the purposive act is nothing but an object determined by a purpose external to it; *consequently it is the same thing as the means... only a means*, not *a realized purpose*, has resulted, or the purpose has not truly attained an objectivity in it."[56]

This demonstrates that the apparent overcoming of finitude is illusory. In the accomplishment of purpose, "only a form that is *externally* posited in the pre-given material is established thereby."[57] In other words, the form that the externally purposive subject succeeds in communicating to the object is not that of the object itself, but rather something imposed upon it from without. That the object now has this particular form, rather than the one it used to have or some other form entirely, is therefore contingent; there is nothing about this form that is intrinsic to the object.[58]

The immediate solution to this problem would seem to be a further purposive transformation of the object, one that invests the object with a form truly internal to itself, and that thereby truly unifies the subject with the object. But this fails to solve the problem, for every further purposive transformation of the object also has the form of a teleological syllogism. Thus every further purposive transformation has a result as contingent as the first, and posits a form in the object that is external to the nature of the object itself. Even if the object were to undergo an infinite sequence of purposive transformations, therefore, it would remain merely a means, external to the subject with whose purpose it has been informed.

This shows that no matter how many times the purposive subject performs its activity of positing a new form in the objective world, it always remains limited by the independence of the objectivity from which it distinguishes itself. Although the subject has the ability to transform the objective world an infinite number of times, to make it accord again and again with whatever finite purpose it happens to have, it remains forever conditioned "by an objectivity that it has not itself determined but which still confronts it in the form of indifference and externality."[59] In short, the externally purposive subject remains forever finite, unable to claim a genuine identity with objectivity.[60]

The final conclusion to draw from the finitude of the externally purposive subject is the finitude of teleological syllogism and external purposiveness themselves. The teleological syllogism strives to overcome the finitude of external purposiveness by accomplishing a genuine realization of the subject in the object, by demonstrating that the determinations of the subject are genuinely internal to the object itself. However, as we have seen, it is unable to do this. Not only is the subject external to the object at the beginning of the teleological syllogism, but it remains that way throughout this logical form; as Hegel points out, not only is purposiveness immediately external purposiveness, it is never able to get beyond external purposiveness.[61] In the teleological syllogism, we have seen, the externally purposive subject is able to posit its unity with the object, but this unity is *only* posited, it is not genuine or in-itself.[62] The genuine realization of the teleological syllogism, therefore, depends on a logical structure other than that of teleological syllogism. Teleological syllogism and external purposiveness, like formal syllogism before them, are finite.

It was demonstrated earlier that willing is the externally purposive activity of the spiritual subject and that, like external purposiveness, willing is doubly finite, finite in both form and content. Willing and external purposiveness are finite in form because both initially involve judgments, in which their subjects are determined as confronting an objectivity external to themselves, in which they have yet to achieve immediate existence. They are finite in content for slightly different reasons. External purposiveness is finite in content because its content is contingent, not a product of its form, which means that its content is given to it externally. Willing is finite in content not because its content is accepted as given (on the contrary, the willing subject develops its content out of its own form), but because its content is particular and limited. That is, the content of the self-determining will is underdetermined by its form: there are many forms of life compatible with the basic conceptual necessities of ethical freedom, so the particular one willed in any given instance is only one possibility among others, and is therefore finite.[63] We might say that the will's content remains contingent, although it has internalized that contingency.[64]

We also noted earlier that external purposiveness and the willing subject both try to overcome their twofold finitude by taking on the form of syllogism instead of judgment. External purposiveness becomes the teleological syllogism, in which it hopes to achieve a genuine and noncontingent unification of subject and object. Willing becomes the syllogism of realization, in which the activity of the spiritual subject takes on the form of the teleological syllogism.

We have now seen, however, that the teleological syllogism is unable to overcome the finitude that plagues external purposiveness. In the teleological syllogism, the externally purposive subject initially appears to overcome its finitude, as it posits its unity with objectivity. However, this posited unity proves to be merely posited, not true in-itself, and the externally purposive subject therefore remains externally purposive and finite.

Willing, as the activity of the spiritual subject in the form of the teleological syllogism, suffers the same fate. Like the externally purposive subject, the will in the form of syllogism, the ethical will, initially appears infinite, but ultimately proves not to be. The ethical will transforms the objective world of nature with which it is confronted, giving it the determinations of the rational state, in which it finds itself and therefore feels at home and free; in other words, the ethical will posits its unity with the natural world by informing that world with its own subjective determinations. However, as in the case of the teleological syllogism, this posited unity proves not to be true in-itself, the ethical will remains external to natural objectivity, and the spiritual subject remains finite as long as it is engaged in the activity of willing. Hegel makes this limitation of willing clear in the following passage:

[T]he consummation of the realization of the concept of objective spirit is achieved only in the state, in which spirit develops its freedom into a world posited by spirit itself, into the ethical world. Yet spirit must pass beyond this level too. The defect of this objectivity of spirit consists in its being only posited. Spirit must again freely let go the world, what spirit has posited must at the same time be grasped as having an immediate being. This happens on the third level of spirit, the standpoint of absolute spirit, i.e., of art, religion, and philosophy.[65]

The ethical will is finite because in it the spiritual subject's objectivity is merely posited, not grasped as having immediate being. The spiritual subject's objectivity, the unity of the subject and the natural world, is not understood by the ethical will to be truly the case. The willing subject, that is, even in its highest form, continues to understand natural objectivity as external to and other than itself. Although it understands itself to be capable of transforming the natural world to accord with its subjective determinations, it understands those determinations to be not those of objectivity itself but a form externally posited in the object. Thus, in willing, as in the teleological syllogism, the object is never truly the objectification of the subject, but is always informed by that subject as by an external purpose; the object remains merely a means, something worked upon by a subject external to it.[66]

Consequently, even at the culmination of objective spirit the spiritual subject understands the actualization of its own determinations in the rational state to be merely its subjective achievement, only true for it, rather than the way things genuinely are in themselves; it understands that the natural world does not have as its purpose the construction of a rational state, but has this form imposed on it from without by willing subjects. The willing subject, therefore, is only externally connected to the natural world, and so it is finite.[67]

The solution to this finitude might appear, as it did briefly in our consideration of external purposiveness, to be a further transformation of the objective world by the willing subject. But all further transformative acts of willing must also have the form of the teleological syllogism and, as we have seen, this means that their realizations are equally external to the subject. At the end of each realization, the willing subject remains confronted by an objectivity other than itself, and therefore experiences the need to transform it yet again. Even after an infinite number of realizations, the externality of subject and object remains, and requires overcoming.

We have already seen that this infinite striving that fails truly to unify subject and object is as far as external purposiveness can go; no matter how many times the purposive subject transforms the object, "external purposiveness... really only comes to be a means, not an objective end."[68]

We can now see that this is also as far as the willing subject can go. For the willing subject,

> this contradiction presents itself as the *infinite progress* in the actualization of the good, which is fixed in this progress as a mere *ought*... the will... is concerned to make the world finally into what it *ought* to be. The will holds that what is immediate, what is given, is not a fixed being, but only a semblance, something that is *in-itself* null and void... the good ought to be realized; we have to work at this, to bring it forth, and the will is simply the good that is self-activating.[69]

For the willing subject, then, the perspective of the "ought" is insuperable; the willing subject repeats endlessly the presupposition that the objective natural world is truly its other. Even when it has posited its unity with the objective world in the rational state, "there are still two worlds in opposition, one a realm of subjectivity in the pure regions of transparent thought, the other a realm of objectivity in the element of an externally manifold actuality that is an undisclosed realm of darkness."[70]

This shows, as we saw in our discussion of external purposiveness, that the act of positing a new form in the objective world cannot make the subject truly infinite, no matter how many times it is performed; in objective spirit the spiritual subject always remains subjective. Even at the pinnacle of objective spirit, the ethical will characterizes itself as the subjective other yet to be realized in objective nature. The willing subject is therefore perpetually committed to an infinite struggle to realize itself in this objective other. But it is precisely this commitment, born of its understanding of itself and nature, that dooms the willing subject to subjectivity and finitude:

> This repetition of the presupposition of the unrealized purpose after the actual realization of the purpose consequently assumes this character, that the *subjective bearing* of the objective concept is reproduced and made perpetual, with the result that the *finitude* of the good in respect of its content as well as its form appears as the abiding truth, and its actualization appears always as a merely *individual* act, and not as a universal one.[71]

Thus, because willing has the form of external purposiveness, which has the form of formal syllogism, spiritual beings are irredeemably subjective as they are conceived in objective spirit, and are therefore finite with respect to both form and content.

It may sound strange to conclude that the defect of spiritual beings in objective spirit is their subjectivity. But Hegel confirms in several places that subjectivity is the willing subject's ultimate fate and flaw. In the Introduction to the *Philosophy of Right*, he writes that "the will, as freedom *with inward being (in sich seiende)*, is subjectivity itself; subjectivity is accordingly the will's concept and hence its objectivity; but its subjectivity, as opposed to objectivity, is finitude."[72] In the section of the *Lectures on Aesthetics* entitled The Position of Art in Relation to the Finite World and to Religion and Philosophy, he expounds on this point at length:

> Nature stands over against spirit, not as spirit's opposite, set down by spirit itself (*durch ihn gesetzte*), in which spirit reverts into itself, but as a restricting otherness, not overcome. Spirit as subjective, existent in knowing and willing, remains related to this otherness as to an object just found, and it can form only the opposite of nature. In this sphere [of spirit's mere subjectivity] there falls the finitude of both theoretical and practical spirit, restriction in knowing, and the mere "ought" in the pursuit of realizing the good. Here too, as in nature, spirit's appearance is inadequate to its true essence; and we still get the confusing spectacle of skills, passions, purposes, views, and talents, running after and flying away from one another, working for and against one another, crossing up one another, while their willing and striving, their opining and thinking, are advanced or deranged by an intermixture of the greatest diversity of sorts of chance. This is the standpoint of spirit which is purely finite, temporal, contradictory, and therefore transient, unsatisfied, and unblessed. For the satisfactions afforded in this sphere are themselves in their finite shape always still restricted and curtailed, relative and isolated.[73]

Here, Hegel makes it quite clear that not only in subjective spirit, but also in objective spirit, spiritual beings remain subjective. Finally, he also makes this point throughout the sections of the *Logic* on the idea. There, he continually emphasizes that willing, as the idea of the good, is a moment of the subjective idea, which is subjective and finite, and so in need of reconceptualization in the absolute idea.[74]

We can make sense of the claim that spiritual beings are subjective as they are conceived in objective spirit, if we distinguish the different senses in which Hegel uses the terms objective and subjective.[75] The willing subject is objective in the sense that it has itself for its content, and in the sense that it actualizes that content, its conception of freedom, in the external or objective world; willing is the spiritual subject's attempt to produce arrangements in the objective world that correspond to its understanding of itself as a free being. Yet spiritual beings remain subjective in objective spirit in two distinct senses.

First, as we have noted, the willing subject confronts the objective world of immediate being as an independent other. This means that even when it succeeds in actualizing its content in that world, it has to understand what it has produced as merely its production, as a subjective content that happens to have been successfully externalized and objectified. That is, although the willing subject recognizes the achievement of a unification of the subjective and the objective, of spiritual beings and the natural world, it considers this achievement to be merely its own doing. The willing subject does not know that the unity of spiritual beings and nature must always already be the case in order for willing to take place. Rather, it understands itself to have forged a unification with nature, *despite* the fact that nature is fundamentally other than itself. Thus the willing subject always understands the objective natural world as other than itself, and in this sense remains subjective.

Second, the willing subject is also subjective in the sense that the details of its content, of its conception of freedom, may not accord with the objective requirements of freedom itself. The content of the willing subject, as we have also noted, is only one particular conception of freedom among many. Willing therefore can and does manifest itself in a wide variety of political arrangements.[76] As long as these external arrangements fairly reflect the willing subject's internal understanding of freedom, it will feel at home and free in them; as noted at the end of Chapter 2, the features of ethical life literally become a second nature for the willing subject. But a particular shape of ethical life can become natural to citizens without being in accordance with all of the conceptual requirements of freedom. This is possible because citizens experience freedom as a feeling, rather than as a thought. And this means that the feeling of a people that they are free cannot in fact guarantee that they are; such a feeling, experienced as patriotic obedience to the state, does not prevent the content of the willing subject from being subjective in this second sense.[77]

The fact that the willing subject is merely subjective leads Hegel to claim that its freedom has the form of necessity.[78] We saw earlier that necessity involves two or more things being both bound together and understood as alien or external to one another, which is precisely the case with the freedom of the willing subject. The freedom of the willing subject is bound to or dependent upon the conditions it finds in the external, objective world, upon the objective requirements of the concept of freedom, and, most importantly, upon that which enables it to know those requirements and genuinely realize itself in that objective world. Yet the willing subject experiences all of these as irreducibly other than itself; its freedom, therefore, has the form of necessity.

We can now conclude that willing, like external purposiveness, depends for its genuine realization on a logical form other than its own, other than teleological syllogism, and is therefore finite. Willing cannot forge the spiritual subject's unification with an objectivity that is truly other; rather, it is only if the unification of the spiritual subject and the objective natural world is always already the case prior to their being judged to be independent that the activity of willing can then reposit their unity after this differentiation. Such a genuine unification of subject and object, which makes the realization of willing possible, is itself not achieved through willing, not merely forged by the subject, but true in-itself. It therefore requires the spiritual subject to engage in activities other than willing, activities in which its unity with nature is recognized as always already the case.

The spiritual subject is driven to engage in these activities other than willing because, as we saw earlier in the passage from the *Lectures on Aesthetics*, the satisfactions of willing are ultimately unsatisfying. Therefore, that passage continues,

> discernment, consciousness, willing, and thinking lift themselves above [the finite satisfactions of willing], and seek and find their true universality, unity, and satisfaction elsewhere – in the infinite and the true. This unity and satisfaction to which the driving rationality of spirit raises the material of its finitude is then and only then the true unveiling of what the world of appearance is in its essential nature. Spirit apprehends finitude itself as its own negative and thereby wins its infinity. This truth of finite spirit is absolute spirit.[79]

The claim, then, is that willing itself, doomed to finitude by its logical structure, somehow lifts itself above that structure to produce a truly infinite form of spiritual activity, which Hegel considers in absolute spirit. In the next and final section of this chapter, we will investigate this claim, seeking to understand how willing produces its own self-overcoming and thus leads to the most comprehensive liberation of the spiritual subject.

4. From Willing to Art, Religion, and Philosophy

We have seen that the willing subject – the spiritual being as it is conceived in objective spirit – is finite because its activity is externally purposive, and that externally purposive activity is finite because it has the logical structure of formal syllogism. So in order to understand the transition from objective spirit to absolute spirit – the transition from conceiving of spiritual beings as willing subjects to conceiving of them as subjects engaged in the most fully liberating activities – we need to understand at least something of the transitions in Hegel's *Logic* from external purposiveness and formal syllogism to the succeeding conceptual determinations that overcome their finitude.

In Hegel's *Logic*, the formal syllogism develops into the reflective syllogism, which develops into the syllogism of necessity, which finally develops beyond syllogism altogether. Likewise, external purposiveness develops into the idea. We do not need to work through the details of all of these developments, but do need to note the features of the syllogism of necessity and its development beyond syllogism, since it is these features and this development that external purposiveness and the willing subject must replicate in order to shed their externality and finitude in the idea and in absolute spirit, respectively.

The terms of the syllogism of necessity, unlike those of the formal syllogism, are not immediacies; they are not externally connected, but rather contain each other.[80] This means that the middle term of the syllogism of necessity is not a contingent content alien to the extremes, but is the reflection of those extremes into themselves in the form of a universal; the middle term is the substantial nature of the extremes, and its content is not different from those extremes, but is only the necessity of differentiating itself into the individuals and particulars that are its forms of existence.[81] This mediating term is therefore the identity of the entire syllogism, which differentiates itself into the extremes and gathers itself out of that difference.[82] In other words, the syllogism of necessity mediates itself, as universal, with itself, as individual and particular.[83]

Such a mediating term, however, supersedes the logical form of syllogism altogether. For syllogism is defined by its threefold structure: a mediating term posits the unity of distinct subject and object terms. But the mediation of the syllogism of necessity dissolves this structure; the middle term of the syllogism of necessity contains the extremes of the syllogism completely, and is no longer distinct from them.[84] In other words, the syllogism of necessity overcomes the distinctions between mediator and mediated, and between subject and object, by showing that each is identical to the other. It thus overcomes the last remnants of their externality, and in so doing overcomes syllogism itself.[85]

With the supersession of the syllogism also comes the supersession of its formality and subjectivity. The formality of syllogism derives from the fact that its content, represented by its middle term, is external to the determinations of form connected with that content in the extremes. But this is no longer the case. In the syllogism of necessity, the content of the middle term is posited *as* its manifestation in the extremes, and is therefore no longer external to the formal distinctions of those extremes. The subjectivity of syllogism also derives from the externality of the middle term and the extremes; as long as any externality remains in these connections, the subject and the object also remain external to each other, and whatever determinations the object receives through the syllogism are merely posited in it by the subject, and do not belong to it in itself. But this too is no longer the case. Because the subject of the syllogism of necessity is mediated not with an other but with itself in the object, its determinacies truly are those of the object, and are no longer merely subjective.[86]

Another way to express this result is to say that in the overcoming of syllogism the subject is finally genuinely realized in the object. In judgment (and therefore in external purposiveness and finite spirit), subject and object are separated and considered to be independent extremes. In syllogism (and therefore in the activity of willing), the subject claims to be realized in the object through the mediation of a third term. But, as we have seen, the unity achieved in syllogism (and by the willing subject) is only a posited and subjective unity; there remains a distinction between the determinacy of the subject and what the object is in itself. The object is not taken to be immediately identical to the subject, but rather to be something that ought to be made that way contingently and temporarily through the subject's activity, to which the object is indifferent. In the overcoming of syllogism, however, a genuine unity of subject and object is achieved. The subject is now seen really to be the inwardness of the object; and the object is now seen really to be the expression of the subject. The object, which had appeared to be other than the subject, is now seen to be identical to it. Their unity is therefore no longer something that *ought* to be produced by the subject, but something that has always already been brought forth prior to, and as a precondition of, the subject's engagement with objectivity.[87]

The finitude of external purposiveness, we saw, is due to the immediacy of the connections between the means and both the subjective purpose and the objectification. This immediacy means that the subjective purpose and objectivity are never genuinely united, but rather remain external to each other. As a consequence, the object never takes on the character of a genuine objectification of the subject; the subject posits its determinations in the object, but continues to understand that those determinations do not belong to the object itself, but have instead imposed on it a form external to itself. The object, then, is not truly the end of the subjective purpose, but only its means. Consequently, the purposive subject remains forever subjective, forever finite, because no matter how many transformations of the object it may make, it can never genuinely find itself in objectivity, which remains alien.

The transformation required to overcome this finitude of external purposiveness should now be apparent. Since the problem is an objectivity that is never more than a means, the solution is an objectivity that is truly the end of the subject, that truly has in itself the determinations that the subject posits in it. The solution is for the subject and the object, which are divided in external purposiveness, to become reunited. Since this is prevented in external purposiveness by the immediacy of the connections in the premises of the teleological syllogism, the solution requires transforming this syllogism into one in which the immediacy is overcome, but without producing the infinite regress that we encountered before. This requires replacing the formal syllogism with the syllogism of necessity.

Although external purposiveness appears to reconstitute continually the presupposed division of the subject and the object with which it begins, Hegel contends that if we attend to external purposiveness carefully we see that in truth it overcomes itself and this presupposition. He writes that "in the realizing of the purpose what happens *in-itself* is *that the one-sided subjectivity* is sublated, along with the semblance of an objective independence standing over against it."[88] Or, in other words, the result is not only an externally purposive relation (*äussere Zweck-beziehung*), but the truth of it, an internally purposive relation (*innere Zweck-beziehung*) and an objective purpose (*objektiver Zweck*). The externality of the object, self-subsistent as against the concept, which the purpose pre-supposes for itself is *posited* in this presupposition as an illusory show and is also already sublated in and for itself; the activity of the purpose is there-fore, strictly speaking, only the representation of this illusory show and the sublating of it.[89]

This self-sublation of external purposiveness occurs through the sub-ject's immediate grasping of the means-object, through which it accom-plishes its purpose.[90] In this immediate grasping, the subject posits itself as the essence of the means-object. It must, because in order to dominate the mechanical and chemical processes into which the means-object en-ters, which is required if the means-object is to be its means, the deter-minations of the means-object must truly be those attributed to it by the subject. If the determinations of the means-object were impenetrable by the subject, if immediate objectivity were truly other than the subject, then the subject could never successfully employ an object as a means at all. Rather, to employ a means successfully, the determinations of the subject's purpose must be the determinations of both the subject's means-activity and the means-object, which together must be the two forms in which those determinations exist. In the realization of purpose, there-fore, these determinations are not mediated by the subject with an ex-ternal object, but rather mediate themselves as content with themselves as these existent forms. Consequently, the fact that the purposive subject can make a means out of immediate objectivity shows that the means-object is not merely a means, but truly the objectified end of the subject, which is therefore no longer externally purposive.

The activity of purposiveness, then, does not amount to transforming objectivity by giving it a foreign content that originates in an external subject; rather, it amounts to giving a different form (that of objective immediacy) to the content that subjectivity and objectivity already share. This makes the content of this activity, what it has for its purpose, nothing other than its own activity itself, its own alteration of form. The opposi-tions of form and content, of mediator and mediated, are thus overcome, and it is revealed that the purpose of purpose is to show that the presup-position of purpose is false, to show that subject and object are already identically determined though existing in different forms.[91]

This recognition that the subject and the object have the same con-tent, albeit in different forms, means that external purposiveness has overcome its externality and mere subjectivity. The independence and externality of the object, which is presupposed by external purposive-ness, is now revealed to be an illusion; the unity of subject and object is no longer merely posited, but is now understood to be objective in-itself.

The externally posited subject *is* its manifestation in its object, to which it is immediately and internally identical.[92]

The ultimate result of the self-overcoming of external purposiveness, then, is the overcoming of its finitude; external purposiveness ultimately demonstrates that what it initially is, the merely implicit and therefore external unity of subject and object, is in fact the transition to the explicit and therefore internal unity of subject and object, which Hegel calls the idea. The self-overcoming of external purposiveness accomplishes this by overcoming the illusion of finitude, the illusion that purpose is always yet to be attained, that objectivity is always in need of transformation by an externally purposive subject:

> The finitude of purpose consists in the fact that, in its realization, the material used as means is only externally subsumed under it and adapted to it. But in fact the object is *implicitly* (*an sich*) the concept, and when the concept, as purpose, is realized in the object, this purpose is only the manifestation of the object's own inwardness. So objectivity is, as it were, only a wrapping under which the concept lies hidden. In the sphere of the finite we can neither experience nor see that the purpose is genuinely attained.[93]

The overcoming of this illusion of finitude is the realization of the infinite purpose, whose only purpose is to overcome the illusion that it has not yet been realized. The infinite purpose is realized when it becomes apparent, as it now has, that subject and object are not truly other, constantly in need of external reconciliation, but that "the concept is . . . essentially this: to be distinct as an explicit identity from its *implicit* objectivity, and thereby to possess externality, yet in this external totality to be the totality's self-determining identity. As such, the concept is now the idea."[94]

We have already seen that the willing subject, the spiritual being as it is conceived in objective spirit, is finite because it understands itself to be merely subjective in two senses. First, the willing subject presupposes an insurmountable distinction between its own subjective self and the objective world of nature. Second, the willing subject does not comprehend the form of ethical life required by the concept of freedom. In ethical life, the particular willing subject experiences the customs of the community – the content of the universal will – as necessary to itself, and therefore feels at home and free in them, but it cannot know whether those customs are necessary to freedom itself. These two senses in which it is subjective mean that the willing subject is only externally connected to the two things upon which its freedom depends, and that its freedom therefore has the form of necessity. The willing subject thus contradicts the concept of the spiritual being, that which is fully free, and must therefore give rise to a new conception of the spiritual subject, one in which that subject has an adequate self-understanding.[95]

By now the solution to the problem of finitude born of subjectivity and externality should be familiar: the spiritual subject must take on the form of the syllogism of necessity, rather than that of the formal syllogism. The method by which this transpires should also be familiar: as the self-overcoming of external purposiveness is analogous to that of the formal syllogism, the self-overcoming of the willing subject is analogous to that of external purposiveness.

We saw earlier that external purposiveness overcomes itself when the subject reflects on its own activity as a syllogism that unites a subjective purpose with external actuality through a means-object. In this syllogism, the ability of the purposive subject to use objectivity as a means demonstrates the falsity of the subject's presupposition that subject and object are alien. The willing subject overcomes itself analogously by reflecting on its own activity as a syllogism of realization.[96] In the first premise of this syllogism, the willing subject relates its subjective purpose to a means-object. But for this to happen, the subjective purpose and the objective means must be immediately identical, which directly controverts the pre-supposition of willing that it is alien to objectivity.[97] This is confirmed in the second premise, in which the means-object, now known to be identical to the subjective purpose, is related to a further objectivity. But for this to happen, the means-object and the further objectivity must be identical, which transitively demonstrates the identity of the subject and its final objectification.[98] As with external purposiveness, then, the very act of successful willing demonstrates that in objective spirit the spiritual subject's understanding of itself and of its relation to its other must be mistaken, and therefore must be revised.[99]

A central feature of the spiritual subject's revised self-understanding is its understanding of the status of its content. Whereas in objective spirit the subject understands the determinations of its content to be merely subjective and external to the object in which it posits them, it now understands that its content, its own determinations, also belong to the object; the spiritual subject now understands itself and the objective natural world to be different forms in which one and the same content is actualized or manifested.

This means that the spiritual subject no longer understands immediate objectivity to be a nothingness. Recall that in subjective spirit the spiritual subject understands itself as a nothingness, an empty form that seeks to fill itself with the substantial content of objectivity through the activity of knowing; in subjective spirit, objectivity is considered to be actual, but alien to the spiritual subject. In objective spirit, on the other hand, the spiritual subject understands objectivity as a nothingness, which it seeks to fill with its own substantial content through the activity of willing; in objective spirit, the spiritual subject is considered to be actual, but alien to the indifferent world of objectivity. The self-overcoming of objective spirit has now restored immediate objectivity to the status of true actuality. The spiritual being no longer understands the object as a nothingness to be determined by a willing subject external to it, but rather understands that the object has its own inner determinations, which the subject is able to grasp and therefore employ and transform in the realization of the purposes that it wills.

The spiritual subject's awareness that objectivity is not a nothingness but is substantial and true constitutes the recovery of what Hegel calls the theoretical attitude, the attitude that the spiritual subject had in subjective spirit. This recovery is crucial to the overcoming of the practical attitude that the spiritual subject has in objective spirit, according to which objectivity is assumed to be external to the subject, because the subject's determinations are assumed not to be those of objectivity itself. Hegel writes that

> what is still lacking in the practical idea is the moment of conscious-ness proper itself; namely, that the moment of actuality in the concept should have attained on its own account the determination of *external being*. Another way of regarding this defect is that the *practical* idea still lacks the moment of the *theoretical* idea. That is to say, in the latter . . . what *truly is* is the actuality there before it independently of subjective positing. For the prac-tical idea, on the contrary, this actuality, which at the same time confronts it as an insuperable limitation, ranks as something intrinsically worthless that must first receive its true determination and sole worth through the purposes of the good. Hence it is only the will itself that stands in the way of the attainment of its goal, for it separates itself from cognition, and exter-nal reality for the will does not receive the form of a true being; the idea of the good can therefore find its integration only in the idea of the true.[100]

But the spiritual subject's recovery of the theoretical attitude cannot amount to a mere reversion to the theoretical attitude. For we have seen that in subjective spirit the spiritual subject is as external to objectivity as it is in objective spirit. What is required, and what takes place in the self-overcoming of the willing subject, is the development of a conception of the spiritual subject in which the theoretical and practical attitudes are integrated. The spiritual subject must understand that objectivity has the determinations posited in it by the subject (it has the practical attitude) *and* that the object is true in itself because those determinations are its own (it has the theoretical attitude). The spiritual subject must under-stand that *both* itself and immediate objectivity are actual, and that they are therefore identical, rather than external to each other.[101]

The spiritual subject's recognition that it is identical to immediate objectivity amounts to the awareness of the inseparability of thought and being, an awareness that is produced by the self-overcoming of the form of syllogism, which the subject undergoes in reflecting upon the self-overcoming of willing. The spiritual subject now understands that although it is initially determined (in both forms of finite spirit) as merely subjective, as mere thought, one of the determinations of subjective thought is to appear in a form other than its own, that of immediate objectivity or being, which it is therefore both identical to and different from. In Hegel's words:

> [T]he concept... in its determinacy as determinacy of the *concept* alone... passes over into a form that is diverse from determinacy as it belongs to the concept and appears *in it*... the result may be *correctly* expressed by saying that the concept (or even, if one prefers, subjectivity) and the object are *in-themselves the same*. But it is equally correct to say that they are diverse. Precisely because each statement is as correct as the other, each of them is as incorrect as the other; expressions of this kind are incapable of presenting the genuine relationship.[102]

The genuine relationship, it would seem, is that the determinacies of thought include determining themselves to take the shape of both spiritual subjectivity and natural objectivity. Because the spiritual subject and nature have different forms, they are diverse; because they have the same content, the determinacies of thought, they are in-themselves identical. In subjective and objective spirit, spiritual subjects can understand only their diversity from nature, but the self-overcoming of willing enables them to understand themselves as also being identical to nature, and as being that which comprehends the determinacies in virtue of which both the identity and the diversity of thought and being are the case.

As a result of this transformed self-understanding, spiritual beings are no longer subjective in the first sense that we have discussed. The spiritual subject has overcome its presupposition that it is confronted by an independent and indifferent objective world, in which it must continually strive to realize its purposes, despite that indifference.[103] The willing subject's self-overcoming activity has demonstrated that in the object the subject unites only with itself in the form of externality.[104] Although the willing subject continues to encounter objective immediacy as a limitation, resistant to its purposes, in moving beyond willing the spiritual subject has come to know that this limitation is a necessary manifestation of the determinacies of thought, and is thus a limitation internal to the spiritual subject itself.

The knowledge that the objective world of nature is not irreducibly external to the spiritual subject makes the latter no less bound to or dependent upon the natural world, but it does show the spiritual subject that in this bond it is bound to itself, and is therefore free. As Hegel puts it, "We make ourselves finite by receiving an other into our consciousness; but in the very fact of our knowing this other we have transcended this limitation ... therefore to know one's limitation means to know of one's unlimitedness."[105] Thus by overcoming the externality of the objective world, by recognizing the determinacies of that world as also being its own, the spiritual subject overcomes the finitude that characterizes it in subjective and objective spirit. The spiritual subject that understands nature as not only different from but also identical to itself is infinite, and is considered in Hegel's account of absolute spirit.[106]

The self-understanding of the spiritual subject in absolute spirit finally overcomes the infinite repetition of the "ought" that plagues it in objective spirit, and in absolute spirit the spiritual subject is thus absolved from the infinite struggle to transform objectivity that torments the willing subject. The "ought" persists in objective spirit because in it the unity of subject and object is posited, or *für sich*, but is not recognized as being actually true, or *an sich*. In objective spirit, the spiritual subject thus always experiences the unification of subject and object as something in need of doing. In absolute spirit, however, the unity of subject and object is posited as being actually true, and is therefore *an und für sich*. In absolute spirit, the spiritual subject thus experiences the unification of subject and object as always already accomplished and self-accomplishing.[107]

Consequently, the spiritual subject is now *für sich* what the willing subject is *an sich*; in absolute spirit, the spiritual subject is explicitly aware of itself as that which it has been implicitly all along: infinite and free.[108] Implicitly contained in the concept of the willing subject and its successful activity is the presupposition that spiritual beings and nature have always already been unified, but the willing subject remains finite in both form and content. The freedom of spiritual beings, which depends on their being truly unified with natural objectivity, therefore always remains merely implicit, or *an sich*, in the activity of willing. In absolute spirit, on the other hand, the spiritual subject not only is the self-producing unity of subject and object, but grasps itself as such. In absolute spirit, the spiritual subject is thus the *self-aware*, self-producing unity of subject and object, of thought and immediate actuality. The spiritual subject's freedom is therefore *an und für sich*, actually the case and explicitly so, in absolute spirit.

Making its own freedom explicit to itself is not incidental to the spiritual subject's actually being free. For, as we noted in Chapter 1, spiritual beings are only what they know themselves to be, what they have internalized.[109] To be free, therefore, the spiritual subject must know that it is free. As a willing subject, the spiritual subject is implicitly free, implicitly already unified with nature in a way that makes willing possible, but the fact that this freedom appears external to the spiritual subject is one of the reasons that it remains finite in objective spirit. The self-overcoming of willing, however, makes the spiritual subject's freedom explicit to itself.[110] In absolute spirit, the spiritual subject finally internalizes itself as that for which there is truly no externality, thus *making* itself that which is without externality, and making itself free.[111]

We have now seen that the spiritual subject's freedom lies in both its production and its awareness of its freedom, that the achievement of this awareness is the final step in this production, and that it achieves this awareness by grasping the truth of itself as that for which there is no externality. The spiritual subject is thus most free in the activities in which this truth is produced and grasped. We have also seen that the activity of willing does not produce or grasp this truth, for the willing subject in fact always presupposes an externality upon which to work, and in its work produces only a posited unity. The most complete freedom of the spiritual subject thus resides not in willing, but in the activities that result from the willing subject's self-overcoming. These are the activities presented in absolute spirit, the activities in which Hegel contends that spiritual subjects produce and grasp their own truth: art, religion, and philosophy.[112] Chapter 4 will conclude Part I by considering the liberation afforded by these activities, which will enable us finally to understand why Hegel considers philosophy to be "the highest, the *freest*, and the wisest configuration of spirit."[113]

FREEDOM THROUGH HEGEL'S PHILOSOPHY

1. Art, Religion, and Philosophy: Overcoming the Subjectivity of Willing

Hegel thinks that all three activities considered in absolute spirit – art, religion, and philosophy – overcome the subjectivity of willing, the first sense in which it is finite; all of them, that is, overcome the presupposition (common to both subjective and objective spirit) that spiritual beings and the natural world, subject and object, are fundamentally alien to each other. In the theoretical activity of knowing, recall, the contents of the natural world are understood to be imposed on a receptive spiritual subject. And in the practical activity of willing, spiritual contents are understood to be imposed on an indifferent natural world. The activities of absolute spirit, however, are precisely those in which spiritual subjects come to understand that the theoretical and practical presumption of the mutual alienation of the spiritual and the natural must be false, for only if the spiritual subject and the natural world are always already reconciled is it possible for successful knowing and willing to take place. Art, religion, and philosophy, that is, show spiritual beings that the very condition of the possibility of the theoretical and practical activities through which they strive to unify the determinations of thought and being is that thought and being must have always already been unified. In the activities of absolute spirit, then, spiritual beings recognize that the unity of the spiritual and the natural is not merely made but also found.

This recognition by spiritual beings of the unification of subjective thought and objective immediacy is not incidental, but actually completes the unification itself, because it is only through this recognition that spiritual beings fully reconcile themselves with the natural world. In art, religion, and philosophy, that is, spiritual beings make themselves explicitly infinite and free through their discovery that they always have been implicitly infinite and free:

> Nature and [finite] spirit are in general different modes of [the absolute
> idea] presenting its existence (*ihr Dasein darzustellen*), art and religion its
> different modes of apprehending itself (*sich zu erfassen*) and giving itself an
> adequate existence (*ein sich angemessenes Dasein zu geben*). Philosophy has
> the same content and the same purpose as art and religion.[1]

That is, although willing gives immediate existence to the unification of
spiritual beings and nature through its construction of a rational state
(i.e., finite spirit presents the existence of the absolute idea), it is only
in art, religion, and philosophy that spiritual beings recognize that this
unity is not merely posited but true in itself. Through this recognition,
spiritual beings complete their unification with nature and thus their
liberation (i.e., absolute spirit apprehends itself as the absolute idea, and
in so doing gives itself an adequate existence).

In art, religion, and philosophy, then, spiritual beings finally understand themselves as those beings that grasp and demonstrate that the
apparent opposition and self-sufficiency of the spiritual and the natural
are an illusion. In all three activities, spiritual beings know themselves to
be truly self-determining, infinite, and free, for they know that they have
no absolute other. The activities of absolute spirit thus finally overcome
the distinction between determining spiritual subject and determined
natural objectivity, and the contingency and externality of the unification of the two, that plague the willing subject.[2]

Although all three activities of absolute spirit overcome the subjectivity
of willing, the presupposition of the willing subject that it is insuperably
alienated from the natural world, Hegel thinks that only philosophy overcomes its formality, the inability of the willing subject to determine its own
content entirely out of itself. Thus only philosophy overcomes the second
sense in which spiritual beings, as conceived in objective spirit, are finite
and unfree. To understand how philosophy, unlike art and religion, accomplishes this final and ultimate liberation of spiritual beings, we must
briefly consider Hegel's conception of what philosophy is.[3]

2. Philosophy as Conceptual Systematization

Hegel lectured numerous times on the history of philosophy, and at the
beginning of these lectures he always emphasized that in order to determine what is to qualify as an important moment in philosophy's history
one must possess a conception of philosophy itself. A summary of his
own conception of philosophy can be found in the Introduction to the
lectures he gave in Berlin between 1823 and 1827:

> Thought, being what is essential, fundamental, and actual in man, is con-
> cerned with an infinite multiplicity and variety of objects. Yet it will be at its
> best when it is occupied solely with man's best possession, i.e., with thought

itself, where it wants only itself and is concerned only with itself. Its occupa-
tion with itself means to appear to itself, to find itself, and this happens only
by its producing itself. Thought is only actual by producing itself, and it
produces itself by its very own activity. It is not just *there*; it only exists by
its own self-production. What it produces in this way is philosophy. What
we have to explore [in the history of philosophy] is the series of these pro-
ductions, this more than millennial labor of thought to produce itself, this
voyage of discovery on which thought embarks, the voyage of self-discovery.[4]

By philosophy, then, Hegel means the self-discovery and self-
production of thought. Philosophy is thought's self-discovery because
it is thought's attempt to know the truth about itself. In other scientific
disciplines, thought relates itself to or thinks objects other than itself: for
example, the zoologist uses thought to comprehend animals. Animals are
the object or content of the zoologist's work, that about which she would
like to discover the truth, and she uses thought to put that content into
conceptual form, to comprehend her discoveries. In philosophy, however, thought relates itself to or thinks only itself; thought is not only the
form in which the philosopher comprehends and expresses her discoveries, but also the content about which she would like to discover the
truth.

Philosophy is thought's self-production, as well as thought's self-
discovery, because thought is not an object in the same way that, for
example, a snail is. Snails, and other objects of zoological study, are natural products. Although the zoologist who wishes to discover the truth
about them must find appropriate samples, she is not responsible for the
production of those samples. So in zoology, as well as in the other scientific disciplines outside of philosophy, producing the objects of study
is an activity distinct from that of discovering the truth about them. The
philosopher, however, is charged not only with discovering but also with
producing the object that she studies. For without a thinker, there are
no thoughts, and thus no truths about thinking to discover. The philosopher's production and discovery of the object of her study are therefore
two sides of the single activity that is philosophy; the philosopher discovers the truth about thought just to the extent that she contributes to
thought's production.

To engage in philosophy, however, is not simply to produce and discover any thoughts whatsoever. We have just seen that the philosopher
does not think about objects or contents other than thought itself. Moreover, Hegel is especially insistent that philosophy is not equivalent to the
production and elaboration of the personal opinions or convictions of
any particular thinker. Of course, philosophy is practiced by particular
thinking subjects, but Hegel's point is that these thinkers are philosophers only insofar as they are able to shed their particular subjectivity –
their own interests in objects other than thought, and their own opinions

about the objects they think – and let an objective determination of the nature of thought itself emerge.[5]

Hegel thus understands philosophy to be thought's *self*-determination, a determination necessarily free from the influence of objects external to thought, and from the influence of subjective thinkers. As such, philosophy must be the self-development of a self-contained totality of thoughts, for if it failed to be self-developing and self-contained, philosophy would be externally influenced and so would fail to be self-determining. A self-developing and self-contained totality is what Hegel calls a system, and thus he concludes that philosophy, by its very nature, is necessarily systematic:

> Philosophy is thought which brings itself into its consciousness, is preoccupied with itself, makes itself its object, thinks itself, and, at that, in its different specific steps and stages. Thus philosophy (as science) is a development of untrammeled thinking, or rather it is the entirety of this development, a circle turning back into itself, remaining wholly at home with itself, being entirely itself, and wanting only to revert to itself . . . Consequently, philosophy is a system . . . The real meaning of "system" is totality, and only as such is a system true, a totality beginning from what is simplest and becoming ever more concrete as it develops.[6]

For Hegel, then, philosophy is systematic philosophy, and systematic philosophy is the immanent development of thought. It begins with the most simple thought of all – a completely indeterminate thought, or the thought of sheer indeterminacy, which Hegel calls "being" (*Sein*) – and then follows the development of this thought into other, more determinate thoughts: "This process involves making distinctions, and by looking more closely at the character of the distinctions which arise – and in a process something different necessarily arises – we can visualize the movement as development."[7] The result of this developmental process is the production and discovery of thought as a concrete totality, as a unified but internally differentiated system of discrete thoughts.

Following Aristotle and Kant, Hegel calls the discrete thoughts that systematic philosophy produces and discovers *categories*; as the form of thought itself, they are the pure concepts that make possible all conceptual activity whatsoever. The categories are assumed and used in everything we think and do, but typically without our being aware of them. Hegel describes the concrete totality of categories as

> the net which holds together all the concrete material which occupies us in our action and endeavor. But this net and its knots are sunk in our ordinary consciousness beneath numerous layers of stuff. This stuff comprises our known interests and the objects that are before our minds, while the universal threads of the net remain out of sight and are not explicitly made the subject of our reflection.[8]

He also gives several examples of the categories and their everyday, implicit use: "Everyone possesses and uses the wholly abstract category of *being.* The sun *is* in the sky; these grapes *are* ripe, and so on *ad infinitum.* Or, in a higher sphere of education, we proceed to the relation of cause and effect, force and its manifestation, etc. All our knowledge and ideas are entwined with metaphysics like this."[9] Hegel concludes that "the task and business of philosophy [is]... to display... the thought-out and known necessity of the specific categories."[10]

Hegel's own philosophical system is the result of his efforts to complete this task that he understands to define philosophy. The *Logic* begins with the simplest pure thought, that of indeterminacy or pure being, and develops from it a concrete totality of other pure thoughts. The course of this development increasingly refines our understanding of what it is to be. The *Philosophy of Nature* begins with the simplest thought of that which exists in a form other than thought, the thought of nature, and develops from it a concrete totality of thoughts that increasingly refine our understanding of what it is to be natural. And the *Philosophy of Spirit* begins with the simplest thought of that which exists in a form other than thought but which itself is able to think, the thought of spirit, and develops from it a concrete totality of thoughts that increasingly refine our understanding of what it is to be spiritual.

Ultimately, then, in the course of producing and discovering the *Philosophy of Spirit,* the philosopher develops conceptual knowledge of herself. She first comes to know that she is not merely natural in virtue of her ability to think.[11] She then learns, in working through the development of subjective spirit, that to be a thinking being is to be a knowing being. In working through objective spirit, as we did in Chapter 2, she learns that to be a thinking being is to be a willing being, which is to be a legal, moral, familial, economic, and political being. And finally, in working her way from objective spirit to absolute spirit, as we did in Chapter 3, and then working through absolute spirit, she learns that to be a thinking being is to be an aesthetic, religious, and philosophical being.

Thus philosophy concludes when the philosopher comes to comprehend her own philosophical activity, the activity in which she has been engaged since commencing the *Logic.* She comes to know that to be a thinking being is to be a being that thinks the categories of thought that determine what it is to be, what it is to be natural, and what it is to be spiritual, which she herself is. That is, she comes to know that to be a thinking being is to be a self-knowing being.

In coming to *know* that she is a self-knowing being, the philosopher finally *becomes* a self-knowing being. Prior to attaining the knowledge that she is self-knowing, the philosopher, as a thinking being, has the potential for self-knowledge. But this potential for self-knowledge is actualized only when she in fact knows herself, which she does fully only when she knows herself to be self-knowing. This she does through philosophy, and it is thus through philosophy that the thinking or spiritual being most fully succeeds, to use Nietzschean language, in becoming what she is. As Hegel puts it in the concluding lecture of his course on the history of philosophy:

> Spirit is actual as spirit . . . only in virtue of knowing itself as absolute spirit, and this it knows in philosophical science (*Wissenschaft*) . . . In the deeds and life of history, and also in art, spirit brings itself forth to consciousness, and knows various modes of its actuality, but these are only modes. Only in philosophical science does it know itself as absolute spirit, and this knowledge alone, or spirit, is its true existence.[12]

3. Freedom through Systematic Philosophy

The spiritual being and the free being, we already know, are one and the same. So in becoming what she is by developing self-knowledge through the activity of systematic philosophy, the spiritual being comes to know herself as, and so becomes, free. Hegel thus writes that "a man is free only when he knows himself . . . it is this knowing alone which makes one free."[13]

Freedom, recall, requires that spiritual beings overcome both of the senses in which they remain finite as willing subjects, both their subjectivity, or alienation from nature, and their formality, or inability to determine their own content, the determinations of freedom, out of themselves. We saw earlier that Hegel understands all three activities considered in absolute spirit – art, religion, and philosophy – to overcome the subjectivity of spiritual beings. Each of the three activities overcomes the subjectivity of spiritual beings by enabling them to discover that the assumption that they are alienated from nature is false, and through this discovery to reconcile themselves with nature and thus to produce the assumption's falsehood.

The principal difference between the three activities presented in absolute spirit lies in the form in which each grasps and manifests the unity of spiritual subjectivity and natural objectivity: art presents it in sensuous intuitions and images, religion instills spiritual beings with a feeling of it, and philosophy generates conceptual knowledge of it.[14] Although all three activities present as their content the unity of thought and being, it is only in philosophy that this unification becomes known or conceptually comprehended, rather than intuited or felt.

The difference between the forms or media in which art, religion, and philosophy present spiritual beings with an awareness that they are reconciled with nature, and are thus infinite and free, is important for several reasons. First, thought is the medium or form most appropriate to deliver the content or message that thinking beings are infinite and free. In religion and art, the awareness of infinitude is made through, and therefore depends upon, particular finite objects: particular religious mythologies and rituals enable adherents to experience the feeling of infinitude, and particular artworks and performances enable audiences to experience the intuition of infinitude. But in philosophical thought there is no difference between the content delivered and the form of delivery. For philosophical thought is itself infinite and free, fully self-determining. This means that in the practice of philosophy, but not in religious or aesthetic experience, the spiritual subject finds herself at home in, and is thus reconciled with, the very medium through which she discovers and produces the reconciliation with nature that makes her infinite, free, and self-determining.[15] Hegel writes:

> Intelligence as such in its manifestation, its utterance, only goes as far as the *word*, this fleeting, vanishing, completely *ideal* realization which proceeds in an unresisting element, so that in its utterance intelligence remains at home with itself, satisfies itself internally, demonstrates that it is its own purpose (*Selbstzweck*), is divine and, in the form of comprehensive cognition, brings into being the unlimited freedom and reconciliation of spirit with itself.[16]

Second, self-determining thought is not only the medium most appropriate for overcoming the subjectivity of willing subjects, but also the only medium capable of overcoming the formality of willing subjects. Only philosophy, that is, is able to determine its content – the knowledge of both the general truth that thought and being are unified (developed at the end of the *Phenomenology*) and the specific determinations of that unity (developed throughout the system) – out of itself. Art and religion present this same content but cannot generate it for themselves, because the content of intuitions and feelings is external to their form.[17] That is, although art and religion present spiritual beings with their freedom, only philosophy can ultimately justify the claim that spiritual beings are free by making explicit exactly that in which their freedom consists.[18] Art and religion, like willing, are therefore dependent for their content, their conception of freedom, on something external to themselves. Philosophy, on the contrary, depends for its content only on its own form, that of conceptual thought, has no external other, and is therefore not finite in either of the senses in which willing is.[19]

We can now understand why Hegel calls philosophy "the highest, the freest, and the wisest configuration of spirit."[20] Philosophy is the only activity in which spiritual beings are dependent upon nothing other than themselves, have overcome all externality, and are no longer subjective or formal, no longer finite in either sense. In art and religion, as in philosophy, spiritual beings achieve an adequate self-understanding as those beings in which the unity of thinking and being is realized. Only in philosophy, however, is this self-understanding raised to self-knowledge, through being demonstrated by thinking beings to themselves in the form of thought. Only in philosophy, then, do spiritual beings conceptually comprehend themselves as fully free, and thus become fully free.[21] As Hegel writes:

> The need for philosophy can be determined more precisely in the following manner. As feeling and intuition spirit has what is sensible for its object; as fantasy, it has images; and as will, purposes, etc. But spirit needs also, in *antithesis to*, or merely in *distinction from these forms* of its thereness and its objects, to give satisfaction to its highest inwardness, *to thinking*, and to make thinking into its object. In this way, spirit comes *to itself*, in the deepest sense of the word; for its principle, its unadulterated selfhood, is thinking.[22]

To recapitulate: spiritual beings are free as they are conceived in absolute spirit because it is understood, in art, in religion, and most clearly in philosophy that they are not confronted with an alien material in which they must struggle to manifest themselves. Philosophy knows spiritual beings as thinking beings, and it knows thought as that which determines both the natural and the spiritual, determines them to appear self-sufficient and opposed to each other, and then demonstrates the illusion of the apparent opposition. Philosophy is thus absolute absolute spirit. Absolute spirit is absolute because in it spiritual beings are absolved from the externality of nature that they experience in the activities of subjective and objective spirit. Philosophy is absolute absolute spirit because in it spiritual beings are absolved from the externality that persists in art and religion between their content and the media of its recognition and expression. Through philosophy, spiritual beings thus free themselves by coming to know

> that [spirit] is itself the creator of its other, of nature and finite spirit, so that this other loses all semblance of independence in the face of spirit, ceases altogether to be a limitation for spirit and appears only as a means whereby spirit attains to absolute being-for-self, to the absolute unity of what it is in itself and what it is for itself, of its concept and its actuality.[23]

With this philosophical comprehension of philosophy, Hegel's system comes to an end. The speculative philosopher finally comprehends her philosophical practice as the activity of coming to comprehend herself as a free spiritual being, and she comprehends that it is through this philosophical self-comprehension that she becomes a free spiritual being by completing her reconciliation with the natural world. She thus realizes in retrospect that ever since she adopted the standpoint of speculative philosophy at the beginning of the *Logic*, she not only has been thinking about the meaning of freedom, but also has been participating in her own liberation. She can finally justify the assertions of the *Phenomenology*:

> Pure self-recognition in absolute otherness, this ether as such, is the ground and soil of science or knowledge in general . . . [In philosophical science] the moments of spirit . . . no longer fall apart into the antithesis of being and knowing, but remain in the simplicity of knowing . . . In thinking I am free, because I am not in an other, but rather remain completely with myself (*bei mir selbst*) . . . My movement in conceptual thinking is a movement within myself (*in mir selbst*).[24]

4. Epilogue: Reconciliation, Resignation, Theory and Practice

I want to conclude Part I by considering and responding to three objections that are commonly raised against Hegel's conception of freedom. First, it is often objected that although becoming reconciled with, or "at home" in, that which is other than ourselves might indeed be a desirable achievement, it is not the achievement of freedom. Freedom might be the ability to choose without constraint, or freedom might be autonomy, the objection runs, but freedom and reconciliation are simply different things.

To understand Hegel's answer to this objection we must begin with the reiteration that Hegel understands freedom initially, and most generally, as self-determination (i.e., as not being subject to external necessitation), and with the observation that this understanding is shared by those who charge him with ultimately talking about something other than freedom. For example, those who understand freedom as choice do so precisely because being able to choose means being able to determine one's own actions. And those who understand freedom as autonomy do so because being autonomous means being able to determine one's own will. So those who object to Hegel at least agree with him that freedom involves self-determination.

The real question at issue is thus: what exactly is involved in self-determination? As I have argued, Hegel's entire philosophy of spirit represents an attempt to answer this question. In the course of this attempt, Hegel comes to the conclusion that choice and moral autonomy are indeed indispensable elements of freedom. But he also concludes that they are *only* elements of freedom, and that they are elements of freedom only *because* they contribute to our reconciliation with the world. Defending these claims requires the kind of engagement with and explication of Hegel's *Logic* and philosophy of spirit that I have provided in Part I. But so does criticizing them. That is, if one agrees with Hegel that freedom is self-determination, but disagrees with his account of what this involves, then simply asserting that Hegel has ceased to talk about freedom begs the question. Instead, one must point out exactly where his argument goes awry. If and when that is done, it is incumbent upon the Hegelian to explain and defend the portion of the argument that has been called into question. But until that is done, the Hegelian can have little more to say by way of response to the general and dogmatic charge that in talking of reconciliation "Hegel is no longer talking about freedom."[25]

Second, if it is granted that in talking about reconciliation with that which is other than oneself Hegel is indeed talking about freedom, it is sometimes objected that Hegelian reconciliation amounts to resignation, that what he calls freedom is not the overcoming of but rather the recognition and acceptance of necessity. His ultimate shifting of the discussion of freedom from politics to art, religion, and philosophy, so it is thought, represents a renunciation of the practical concern with changing the world in favor of the theoretical project of comprehending its current condition. In other words, the activities considered in absolute spirit represent precisely the kind of escapist flight from reality that Hegel himself has found to fall short of real freedom.[26]

But this objection falsely assumes that in the transition to absolute spirit the lessons of objective spirit are forgotten. To say that art, religion, and philosophy are necessary conditions of freedom does not imply that they are sufficient. In Hegel's view, freedom is a concrete concept that unites a number of essential determinations, including those developed in subjective, objective, and absolute spirit: to be a free being is to be an aesthetic, religious, and philosophical being, but it is also to be a legal, moral, familial, economic, and political being.

Moreover, the liberating role that Hegel assigns to art, religion, and philosophy is not that of resigning us to stoic acceptance of the situation in which we currently find ourselves. Hegel would not claim, for example, that the bachelor we considered in Chapter 1 becomes free by resigning himself to the long-term continuation of whatever relationship he happens to be in at the moment. Freedom is not to be found in a bad relationship or a bad marriage. Hegel's point, however, is that freedom is also not to be found in the absence of personal relations. Freedom involves neither an escape from relationships, nor a resignation to the relationships one currently has, but rather the development of relationships in which one is genuinely reconciled with that which is other than oneself.[27]

Hegel applies this general conclusion not only to personal relationships, but also to legal, moral, economic, and political ones. In the *Philosophy of Right*, we have seen, Hegel discusses property and contract rights, moral autonomy, economic markets, and the state, all of which he considers to be essential to freedom because he considers them to be relationships or structures that we must develop in order to reconcile ourselves with, and thus find ourselves at home in, the world. But again, his point is not that one becomes free by coming to accept the social and political institutions with which one is immediately confronted. Rather, one becomes increasingly free by helping to transform the social and political institutions with which one is confronted in such a way that they become more freely acceptable.

The degree to which one is free is thus determined by the degree to which one successfully accomplishes these various types of reconciliation. A person at home in her social and political situation (i.e., one who enjoys *Sittlichkeit*) is more free than one who is not. Given two people who enjoy *Sittlichkeit*, one is more free than the other if her social and political situation more closely accords with the concept of objective freedom. Given two people with roughly equal degrees of objective freedom, one is more free than the other if she also has the kind of awareness of herself as a free being that Hegel thinks is developed in art, religion, and philosophy. And, finally, given two people who have such an awareness, one is more free than the other to the extent that her self-understanding is more explicit and complete, which is why Hegel concludes that philosophy ultimately offers a degree of freedom not available through other activities.

So the most comprehensive freedom requires both *Sittlichkeit* and the activities of absolute spirit, including philosophy. The citizen at home in her state is free, but not as free as if she also enjoyed philosophical self-knowledge. Conversely, the person with philosophical self-knowledge is free, but not as free as if she were also the citizen of a rational state (i.e., her freedom, like that of the slave, is significantly diminished if she is in chains). In other words, there is a theoretical or cognitive component to freedom, but it is only a component, and the most comprehensive freedom simply cannot be had in the absence of certain social and political conditions. Freedom, that is, requires both the theoretical comprehension of the world, and its practical transformation.

Third and finally, however, even if it is granted that for Hegel freedom is never equivalent to resignation, and that freedom has practical as well as theoretical components, it is sometimes still objected that these diverse components have nothing to do with each other. In other words, the objection runs, the freedom available through art, religion, and philosophy is simply different in kind from that available through social and political institutions, and the two kinds of freedom are mutually irrelevant. Art, religion, and philosophy, it is contended, contribute nothing to practical freedom, and thus enjoyment of the kind of freedom peculiar to aesthetic, religious, and philosophical experience can only function as a diversion of time and energy from our efforts to bring about a distinctly social and political liberation.

It is true that art, religion, and philosophy serve to provide a break from the unending labor of social and political struggle, since they are activities that are not subject to the same kinds of frustration that plague us in our practical endeavors. But this stepping back from the world cannot be their only function, lest they do amount to a retreat into stoic contemplation, which would threaten our freedom by allowing our homes to deteriorate around us. That is, art, religion, and philosophy cannot be the activities in which spiritual beings are most free if they replace social and political struggle, but rather only if they help us to sustain and guide it.

The most important way in which art, religion, and philosophy sustain our attempts to achieve reconciliation within the social and political world is, paradoxically, by educating us to understand the impossibility of ever perfecting such a reconciliation. We have seen that Hegel thinks our legal, moral, social, and political freedom will always be limited, always be frustrated by the necessary contingency that characterizes the natural world. If freedom is becoming at home in the world, our homes will always need maintenance and repair. And this implies that we can reconcile ourselves with the world only by recognizing and accepting that any such reconciliation will always be imperfect and fragile, only by recognizing the insuperable finitude of willing. Because this recognition and acceptance are achieved in art, religion, and philosophy, participation in these activities constitutes an important step toward achieving freedom *in* the world. They allow us to feel at home in a home that necessarily remains less than perfect, no matter how incessantly we work to improve it.

But the necessity of learning to feel at home in an imperfect house does not imply the necessity of accepting the current state of affairs. On the contrary, what is called for (in politics and marriage, no less than in home ownership) is a continual effort to improve the present, in the full knowledge that there will be no future in which such an effort will have completely succeeded. In Hegel's view, art, religion, and philosophy sustain our efforts to improve existing social and political conditions, by allowing us to realize that the importance of this work is not diminished by the fact that it will always need to be done.

Moreover, in Hegel's view, art, religion, and philosophy not only sustain but also direct our striving for social and political freedom, by providing the self-understanding, the conception of ourselves as free beings, that guides our efforts to transform the world. He insists that "the way in which the subject determines its goals in worldly life depends on the consciousness of its own essential truth . . . Morality and the political constitution (*Moralität und Staatsverfassung*) are governed wholly by whether a people grasps only a limited representation of the freedom of spirit, or has the true consciousness of freedom."[28]

Hegel's point is that the social and political conditions that we strive to bring about, and in which we are able to feel at home, depend upon the details of our self-understanding: we strive to realize the social and political conditions that we take to be most appropriate for beings like us, and thus our theoretical understanding of the sort of beings we are plays a crucial role in determining the direction of our practical undertakings.

Of course, what we are, most basically, is free. But to say that is not to say very much, and thus, as Hegel emphasizes in the passage just cited, everything depends on exactly how we understand our freedom: people with different understandings of freedom develop very different social and political arrangements.

This insight regarding the relationship between theoretical comprehension of ourselves and practical transformation of the world is, Hegel believes, nothing less than the key to understanding human history, in which he finds a development toward an increasingly adequate understanding and realization of freedom.[29] He summarizes the entirety of this development, as he sees it, in a single extended passage from the Introduction to his lectures on the philosophy of history:

> In the world of the ancient Orient, people do not yet know that spirit, or the human as such, is free. Because they do not know this, they are not free. They know only that *one* person is free, but for this very reason the freedom of this one is either a mere arbitrariness, ferocity, and stupidity of passion, or else a mildness and tameness of the same, and which of the two is itself a mere accident of nature and therefore quite arbitrary. This *one* person is therefore only a despot, not a free man. It was among the Greeks that the consciousness of freedom first arose, and thanks to that consciousness they were free. But they, and the Romans as well, knew only that *some* persons are free, not the human as such. Even Plato and Aristotle did not know this. Not only did the Greeks have slaves, therefore – and Greek life and their splendid freedom were bound up with this – but their freedom itself was partly a merely arbitrary, transient, and limited flowering, and partly a hard servitude of the human and the humane. It was first the Germanic peoples, through Christianity, who came to the consciousness that *every* human, as human, is free, and that it is the *freedom* of spirit that constitutes its ownmost nature (*eigenste Natur*).[30]

Whether or not this story in fact reveals the truth of history, it clearly reveals that for Hegel the practical realization of freedom is dependent upon its theoretical comprehension. In order to make ourselves free, we must first know that we are free, and what freedom is. If we do not know that we are free, we may willingly submit ourselves to unjust authorities (Hegel's diagnosis of the ancient Orient); and if we know ourselves to be free but misunderstand freedom, we may submit others to our own unjust authority (Hegel's diagnosis of the Greeks). In either case, it is not only the freedom of those subject to authority that is compromised, but also the freedom of the authorities themselves, for as we saw in Chapter 2, Hegel's analysis shows that no one is free unless all are free. The realization of universal freedom thus depends upon its becoming widely known that freedom is, and can only be, universal.

Hegel's discussion of history also makes clear, however, that he does not claim that the practical realization of freedom depends upon distinctly *philosophical* self-knowledge spreading far and wide. All must know that all are free, but certainly not all, nor even very many, need be philosophers. As the end of the passage just cited shows, Hegel considers religion, rather than philosophy, to be the primary means by which the self-consciousness of human freedom is disseminated broadly enough that it can, eventually, become an effective practical force. The passage continues:

> This consciousness [that every human is free] arose first in religion, in the innermost region of spirit. But to introduce this principle [of freedom] into worldly reality as well was a further task, which to solve and carry out required a long and difficult labor of development. For example, slavery did not end immediately with the acceptance of the Christian religion, still less did freedom suddenly predominate in Christian states, nor were governments and constitutions organized in a rational way, or even based on the principle of freedom. This application of the principle to worldly reality, the thorough permeation and formation of the worldly situation by it, is a long process that makes up history itself.[31]

Hegel thus attributes to Christianity the origin of the awareness that all are free, from which grew the essentially modern refusal to accept either the word or the power of unjustified authorities, the demand that both theoretical claims and practical arrangements be justifiable to *all* thinking beings. This demand, when made by a sufficient number of people, proved to be truly radical, issuing in the "long and difficult labor of development" that uprooted traditional social and political institutions incompatible with the principle of freedom.[32]

Philosophy is, thus far, conspicuously absent from Hegel's account of the historical realization of freedom. It is neither the primary source of people's increasingly adequate self-understanding, nor a direct contributor to the ensuing practical struggle to transform the world. But philosophy does have an indispensable role to play, because religion is incapable of discharging the very demand to which it gives rise, the demand that all knowledge claims, as well as all social and political institutions, dispense with reliance on authority and be justified to free thinking.

The inability of religion to satisfy its own demand results from the fundamental contradiction at its core: on the one hand, the truth that religion presents (its content), according to Hegel, is the fact of human freedom, the fact that we are self-determining and therefore should reject all unjustified authority; but on the other hand, religion asks us to accept this truth on faith (its form), and so it asks us to accept an unjustified authority as the basis for our belief that no unjustified authority should be accepted.

Hegel's criticisms of Catholicism and Judaism as religions that subject people to unjustified authorities are well known. In the Catholic priesthood and the Judaic law he sees sources of purported truth and undeniable power that people are asked to accept without justification.

He considers Lutheran Christianity to be the ultimate religion, the one most in harmony with the teaching that each and every human is free and subject only to the authority of her own reason. But Hegel points out that even Lutheran Christianity, *qua* religion, necessarily presents its teaching regarding the self-determination of rational beings in the form of mythological representations that appeal to human feelings, rather than in the form of thoughts that appeal to our reason. This appeal to feeling is precisely what makes religion a more powerful means for the broad dissemination of truth than philosophy, for everyone is susceptible to the pull of feelings, whereas relatively few have the appetite and aptitude for conceptual thinking. But the appeal to feeling that makes religion so popular and powerful is also what makes philosophy indispensable.

Because religion relies on the arbitrary "authority of inner feeling," it can justify neither its theoretical claims about the truth of human freedom nor their practical implications. The modern response to this situation must be an attempt to produce a nonarbitrary justification of the truth, one that appeals to reason alone and is therefore justifiable to all rational beings. Failing this, there will be no choice but to acknowledge that theoretical and practical commitments are relative to whatever presuppositions or authorities one happens to take as a starting point. As Hegel puts it in the Preface to the *Philosophy of Right*:

> The *truth* concerning *right, ethics, and the state* is at any rate *as old* as its *exposition and promulgation* in *public laws and in public morality and religion* . . . [But] it needs to be *comprehended* as well, so that the content which is already rational in itself may also gain a rational form and thereby appear justified to free thinking. For such thinking does not stop at what is *given*, whether the latter is supported by the external positive authority of the state or of mutual agreement among human beings, or by the authority of inner feeling and the heart and by the testimony of the spirit which immediately concurs with this, but starts out from itself and thereby demands to know itself as united in its innermost being with the truth.[33]

In other words, although many religious people do in fact have an awareness of, and try to live in accordance with, the truth that humans are free, it is only in virtue of philosophy that we can know this truth to be the case. For only philosophy, understood as the presuppositionless and systematic self-determination of thought, can provide a nonarbitrary justification of the truth that the religious person so deeply feels.

We might further explicate Hegel's view of the relationship that philosophy bears to religion, and of the relationship that both of these activities of absolute spirit bear to practical freedom, by means of an analogy. Hegel is to Luther as Andrew Wiles is to Fermat, the great French mathematician who scribbled his incredible last theorem in the margin of a book, together with the unsubstantiated claim that he had discovered a beautiful proof of it that the margin was unfortunately too narrow to contain. Fermat's purported proof was never found, and more than 300 years passed before Wiles, a contemporary British mathematician, was able to produce the demonstration that justified the conjecture. Likewise, 300 years separated Luther's nailing of his theses to the church door in Wittenberg from Hegel's development of the philosophical system that, in his own view, as expressed in the *Philosophy of Right*, serves to demonstrate the truth that Luther grasped but could not justify: "What Luther inaugurated as faith in feeling and in the testimony of spirit is the same thing that spirit, at a more mature stage of its development, endeavors to grasp in the *concept* so as to free itself in the present and thus find itself therein."[34]

This analogy illuminates the role that philosophy plays in the realization of freedom, for in both cases the production of the proof does more than just verify what we already knew to be true. In the course of the attempt to prove Fermat's last theorem, Wiles and his predecessors had to develop an enormous amount of previously unknown mathematics, so that in the end we know not only that the original conjecture is true, but also many other things besides. Likewise, Hegel's systematic philosophy not only justifies the simple claim that humans are free, but in the course of this justification discovers a great deal about that in which our freedom consists. Philosophy does more, that is, than ratify the religious feeling that we are free: it also discovers that freedom necessarily involves all of the legal, moral, familial, economic, and political structures Hegel identifies in his discussion of objective spirit. And it is thus philosophy, rather than religion, that is best able to serve us as a guide in our struggle to realize practical freedom.

Hegel made these points most explicitly in 1831, just before his death, when he added a new section to his lectures, entitled The Relationship of Religion to the State.[35] In this section, he first reemphasizes that the concept of freedom that comes to popular consciousness in religion is the basis of social and political development:

> Universally speaking, religion and the foundation of the state are one and the same . . . The laws are the development of the concept of freedom, and this concept, reflecting itself in this way in existence, has as its foundation and truth the concept of freedom as it is grasped in religion. What this expresses is that these laws of ethical life and legal right are eternal and unchangeable regulations for human conduct, that they are not arbitrary but endure as long as religion itself. It can even be expressed in the form that one is hearkening to God in obeying the laws and the governmental authority.[36]

Hegel then immediately warns, however, that in this religious formulation the principle of freedom definitive of modern life remains dangerously abstract, precisely because it lacks the kind of rational justification that could give it a determinate content:

> This tenet is in one way correct, but is also exposed to the danger that it can be taken wholly abstractly, since it is not determined how the laws are explicated and which laws are appropriate for the basic constitution. Expressed formally, the tenet thus reads: One ought to heed the laws whatever they may be. Ruling and legislation are in this way relegated to the arbitrariness of the government.[37]

In other words, as we have seen, the authoritarian form of religion contradicts the religious truth that humans are free, even in Protestant states in which "religion does not have its own principles that conflict with those that are valid in the state."[38] The problem in such states is that "through adherence to the formal principle [of obedience to the laws, whatever they may be] a wide scope is granted to arbitrariness, tyranny, and oppression."[39] Consequently, Hegel reasons, the religious truth that humans are free must be coupled with determinate knowledge of what freedom is:

> Thus, along with the truth that the laws are the divine will, it is particularly important that it be determined what these laws are. Principles as such are only abstract thoughts that have their truth only in their development; held fast in their abstract form, they are what is wholly untrue.[40]

This determination of the laws of freedom, however, in the absence of which political freedom is always at risk of devolving into an arbitrariness that is potentially oppressive or even tyrannical, is a task charged to philosophy:

> To posit these principles of freedom is to assert that they are true because they cohere with the innermost self-consciousness of human beings. But if in fact it is reason that discovers these principles, then, to the extent that they are genuine and do not remain formal, it has their verification only in virtue of the fact that it traces them back to the cognition of absolute truth – and this cognition is only the object of philosophy.[41]

Hegel's conclusion is clearly that philosophy, as the only science capable of providing a determinate and rationally justified conception of freedom, has an indispensable role to play in guiding the realization of freedom in the social and political world.[42]

It is important not to misinterpret Hegel's claim that philosophy can guide us toward political freedom. He is not advocating a reincarnation of the Platonic philosopher-king. Nor is he suggesting that legislators, judges, and civil servants need professional training in philosophy. To be of use in such capacities, and so to help a given nation move from its current condition toward a fuller realization of freedom, philosophers would have to comprehend not only the conceptual conditions of freedom but

also the existing state of affairs, and then would have to determine the
appropriate policies to implement in order to bring about the required
changes. But in Hegel's view philosophy is capable of only one of these
three tasks: philosophers can grasp the conceptual conditions of freedom, but they can comprehend their own time and place only after the
fact (the import of Hegel's famous admonition that "the owl of Minerva
begins its flight only with the onset of twilight")[43] and have no special
talent for prescribing empirical remedies. Consequently, Hegel does not
believe that political freedom depends upon philosophy to provide the
state with rulers, representatives, or bureaucrats of any kind.

The role that philosophers *can* play in guiding us toward freedom
is perhaps best conceived as analogous to the role that scientists can
play in guiding us toward public health. The scientist can use her expertise to determine, for example, that smoking causes cancer. But she
cannot dictate that people stop smoking (as a scientist-king would), nor
does she have any special ability to figure out which policies are most
likely to lead to a cessation of smoking (as a skilled scientist-legislator or
civil servant would), nor will the elaborate experiments supporting her
conclusions inspire smokers to quit (as the exhortations of a successful
scientist-preacher would). This does not make the scientist's knowledge
useless, however, for she can strive to educate people about the implications of her discovery. If she can teach people that smoking is not, as was
once believed, beneficial, then all people (including rulers, representatives, bureaucrats, and religious leaders) can put this knowledge to work
in improving public health.

Likewise, the philosopher who comprehends freedom can strive to educate people about the conditions of their liberation. She cannot force
people to be free, nor does she have any expertise in designing or imple-
menting plans for social and political change, nor will the intricate details
of her arguments motivate people to pursue freedom. But for those who
already desire to be free, the dissemination of philosophical knowledge
of the conditions of freedom can help to ensure that they are in fact
aiming at the right target. If philosophers can teach people, for example, that freedom demands finding a solution to poverty, then all people
can make use of this knowledge in their pursuit of social and political
liberation. Consequently, philosophical knowledge, when coupled with
education, harbors transformative and even revolutionary potential:

> Philosophy in general has, as philosophy, other categories than those of
> ordinary consciousness: all education (*Bildung*) reduces to the distinction
> of categories. All revolutions, in the scientific disciplines no less than in
> world history, arise only on account of the fact that spirit, to understand
> and comprehend itself, in order to possess itself, has changed its categories,
> and so has grasped itself more truly, more deeply, more intimately, and more
> in unity with itself.[44]

Hegel thus identifies philosophy as the capstone of the most comprehensive freedom. Freedom certainly requires the practical transformation of the world, such that we come to be increasingly at home in our social and political situation. But freedom also requires the theoretical consciousness that we are free, and once people develop this consciousness they cannot be fully at home in their social and political situation unless they know that it is in accordance with the concept of freedom. Although people attain self-consciousness of their freedom through art, religion, and philosophy, we have seen that only philosophy can determine the content of the conception of freedom that all three of these activities present. Modern practical freedom therefore depends on philosophy to comprehend the conditions of freedom, against which the existing social and political situation must be measured, and toward the realization of which all people must work if they are to enjoy the fullest liberation. In the absence of such a worldly realization people's freedom will be incomplete, but in the absence of philosophy such a worldly realization will be not only less likely to occur, but also impossible to recognize if it does, and therefore harder to sustain in the face of destructive demands for abstract freedom. Thus although Marx was right that the world needs changing, he failed to understand, as Hegel did, that political change and theoretical comprehension are thoroughly interdependent, and that both are essential to the most comprehensive freedom.[45]

FREEDOM IN AND THROUGH NIETZSCHE'S PHILOSOPHY

THE PLACE OF FREEDOM IN NIETZSCHE'S PHILOSOPHY

1. Nietzsche's Lack of System

Whereas Hegel's readers are immediately confronted with the systematic character of his works, Nietzsche's readers encounter a corpus that is decidedly unsystematic. And as is the case with Hegel, the character of the whole of Nietzsche's corpus is not without consequences for those who would attempt to extract from it an account of any particular topic.

On the one hand, Nietzsche's lack of systematicity makes it difficult to locate the appropriate texts and passages that treat the topic in which one is interested. Although Nietzsche clearly has much to say about art, for example, unlike Hegel he does not provide us with a set of lectures on aesthetics. Locating Nietzsche's remarks on a particular topic therefore requires trolling through his many texts, and reading much material that seems irrelevant to one's concerns. On the other hand, the lack of systematic ordering makes it tempting to think that once Nietzsche's remarks on a topic have been located they can be neatly extracted from his larger body of work. Since that body does not form a system, so the tempting thought goes, it must instead be a collection of insights, loosely connected if at all, that suffer no loss of meaning when removed from the context in which they happen to have been placed.

If this were in fact the case, then we would be compensated for the difficulty of finding Nietzsche's thoughts on a particular topic by the ease with which those thoughts could be disentangled from his thoughts on other matters. His remarks on art, for example, would be fundamentally independent of his remarks on history, politics, and religion. Although we would still have to sift through the latter in search of the former, after we had found the relevant nuggets the rest could be discarded and forgotten as dross.

Things are not so simple, however. Nietzsche is not a systematic philosopher, but neither is he merely an aphorist. The topics he treats are not arranged in a determinate order, as they are in Hegel, but they are

interrelated nonetheless. This means that not only is there no compensa-
tion for the difficulty of finding Nietzsche's remarks on particular topics,
but in fact this difficulty is compounded by that of having to build an
interpretive context for the remarks once they have been found. Because
his corpus does not specify the interrelations of the texts it contains, and
those texts do not specify the interrelations of the passages they contain,
Nietzsche's readers must determine these relations, and their bearing on
particular topics, for themselves.[1]

Nietzsche's unsystematic corpus therefore presents a challenge that
Hegel's system does not. Hegel, in effect, hands each of his readers a map
of his philosophy (the skeletal outline of his *Encyclopedia*) and challenges
them to learn to read it. Nietzsche, however, distributes no maps of his
works, and thus challenges each of his readers to produce her own; he
invites, but also requires, every reader to chart his writings in her own
way.

This challenge functions as both an opportunity and a burden.
Nietzsche's readers, unlike Hegel's, do not have to offer justifications
for beginning somewhere other than the beginning, or for proceeding
without taking into account something that has come before. For there is
no given beginning, and no given order that could determine what must
function as a "before" with respect to anything else. But this means that
the expositor of Nietzsche is, perhaps even more than the expositor of
Hegel, obligated to justify her interpretive choices. One's point of entry
and one's mode of proceeding must be justified by demonstrating that
they lead one somewhere worth going, and that they get there in a way
that responds responsibly to Nietzsche's texts.

One standard way to approach and organize Nietzsche's texts is
chronologically. If this were our method, we would begin by reading *The
Birth of Tragedy* (or perhaps even earlier unpublished essays and notes)
and work our way straight through to the end of Nietzsche's productive
life. When we were finished, we would attempt to classify the insights
we had found according to when they were produced: perhaps we would
be able to identify an "early," a "middle," and a "late" Nietzsche, all of
whose accounts of freedom might differ slightly or substantially from
each other.

But such an approach is most valuable if one's primary interest lies,
as mine does not, in the development of Nietzsche's thought. Since I am
not interested in whether Nietzsche understood freedom in different
ways at different times, but rather in what Nietzsche can teach us about
the way in which freedom is best understood, classifying his thought into
different periods is not important to my project.

Another common approach to Nietzsche is to focus on a carefully
circumscribed subset of his texts. This approach makes the most sense if
one's primary interest is in interpreting a particular book or essay – such

as *Zarathustra*, or the *Genealogy* – rather than in learning about a topic that Nietzsche addresses throughout his corpus. It might also make sense if one were interested in learning about a topic and knew, having read all of Nietzsche's corpus, that Nietzsche's treatment of that topic is limited to certain works.

But neither of these situations in which it makes sense to focus on a subset of Nietzsche's texts applies to my project. For I am interested in the topic of freedom rather than in a particular text, and, having read all of Nietzsche's corpus, I am convinced that freedom is at issue throughout. Consequently, my approach to Nietzsche is neither strictly chronological nor oriented toward a few texts to the exclusion of the rest. Instead, I consider all of Nietzsche's texts, while focusing on those that are most helpful for understanding freedom.

Of course, as I noted at the beginning of this introduction, finding those of Nietzsche's texts, and the passages within them, that are most helpful for understanding freedom is no trivial task. Like Hegel, Nietzsche provides no "lectures on freedom." But, unlike Hegel, Nietzsche also provides no "philosophy of spirit" that we can determine to be equivalent to a sustained account of freedom. Strictly speaking, then, there is no fixed "place" that freedom occupies within the corpus of Nietzsche's philosophy. We therefore have no choice but to organize Nietzsche's texts around the theme of freedom for ourselves, and in so doing to demonstrate that freedom is in fact a topic about which those texts themselves have something to say.

In what follows, then, I draw on all of Nietzsche's published works, and many of his unpublished notes and essays, in my attempt to determine the conditions of freedom. I deliberately ignore, however, the aspects of Nietzsche's thinking and writing that have nothing to teach us about those conditions. So, for example, I have little to say about Nietzsche's deep-seated political elitism, because such elitism cannot illuminate freedom. But we should not make the mistake of thinking that because Nietzsche was deeply elitist we cannot learn anything about freedom from him: the fact that Nietzsche believed most humans to be incapable of attaining the fullest liberation does not mean that he did not develop a profound understanding of what such liberation involves. It is this understanding of the conditions of freedom that I have tried to reconstruct from Nietzsche's works, in part so that those of us who do not share his elitism can better grasp the task that confronts us if we are to work toward the liberation of all human beings.[2]

2. Nietzsche's Unsystematic Account of Freedom

Nietzsche's account of freedom, as I suggested in the introduction, is implicit in his discussions of decadence, nobility, and tragedy. Part II of this book constitutes an extended demonstration that the decadent, the noble, and the tragic represent three stages of increasing freedom. Nietzsche's well-known preference for nobility over decadence can thus be understood as a preference for the greater degree of liberation achieved by the former. Moreover, Nietzsche's less well known, but equally demonstrable, preference for the tragic over the noble can be understood in the same way; the noble figure is more free than the decadent, but less free than the tragic, who represents the most liberated figure of all.

Nietzsche's account of freedom, like those of Kant and Hegel before him, begins with the recognition that the subject's ability to choose, which liberalism equates with freedom, does not guarantee that its willing is autonomous. The willing of a choosing subject may remain determined by forces external to itself, in which case the subject fails to be free.

In Chapter 2, we saw that Hegel makes this critique of liberalism in the Introduction to his *Philosophy of Right*, and we analyzed the development of his attempt to offer a more adequate conception of willing in his discussions of abstract right, morality, and ethical life. Only in ethical life, Hegel argues, is the subject conceived in such a way that its willing is truly free. In Chapter 6, we will see that Nietzsche's version of this critique of liberalism is implicit in his discussions of decadence. For the decadent subject, it turns out, is precisely one whose will fails to be self-determining. Free willing is reserved for, and is the determining characteristic of, the noble subject, with whom Nietzsche contrasts the decadent. Nietzsche's discussions of decadence and nobility can thus fruitfully be understood as addressing the question of the necessary requirements of a free will.[3]

Nietzsche also recognizes, like Hegel but unlike Kant, that even the most freely willing subject remains incompletely free, and that an adequate account of freedom must therefore discuss the activities that provide a liberation that willing cannot. In Chapter 3, we saw that Hegel considers these to be the activities that he discusses in absolute spirit. Art, religion, and philosophy, according to Hegel, all overcome the subjectivity endemic to willing, while philosophy alone overcomes the formality that persists not only in willing but also in art and religion. In Chapter 7, we will see that Nietzsche's account of the limitations of willing is implicit in his critique of nobility. The noble subject manages to will freely, but nonetheless remains externally determined and so incompletely free. This incomplete freedom of nobility is overcome only by those individuals and communities able to develop the stance that Nietzsche characterizes as tragic.

As we will see in Chapter 8, with which Part II concludes, Nietzsche understands the development of the tragic stance required by freedom to depend upon philosophy. He thus agrees with Hegel that freedom is not only treated in philosophical works, but also produced through philosophical practice.

Nietzsche's philosophical practice, however, is quite obviously not the same as Hegel's. We saw in Chapter 4 that for Hegel philosophy is always systematic philosophy. Nietzschean philosophy, as we noted at the beginning of this chapter, is resolutely unsystematic. And thus, although Hegel and Nietzsche agree that philosophy has a role to play in our liberation, the liberating roles that they envision for philosophy, and consequently their conceptions of freedom itself, are significantly different. The conclusion of this book will therefore consider the relationships between the conceptions of freedom developed by Hegel and Nietzsche, and between the corresponding philosophical practices that Hegel and Nietzsche identify and recommend as liberating. We will see that these conceptions and practices, while undeniably different, are complementary. The most comprehensive sort of freedom, that is, will turn out to require us to engage in philosophical practices that are both Hegelian and Nietzschean, both systematic and genealogical.

Before we can consider these relationships between Hegel and Nietzsche, however, we need to understand Nietzsche's conception of freedom, his manner of philosophical practice, and how this sort of practice is supposed to contribute to and complete our liberation. The rest of Part II, to which we now turn, thus examines the treatment of freedom in, and the attainment of freedom through, Nietzsche's philosophy.

THE FREEDOM OF WILLING: DECADENCE AND NOBILITY

1. The Decadent Failures to Will Freely: Two Types of Sickness

In *Ecce Homo*, Nietzsche associates freedom with those who are capable of initiative and thinking for themselves, in contrast to those who are mere reagents, capable of acting and thinking only as a reaction to external stimuli.[1] To understand the former, it will be easiest to begin with the latter; Nietzsche's understanding of freedom is best illuminated by his critique of those he considers most unfree.

The paradigm of reactive unfreedom for Nietzsche is what he calls the decadent. The decadent is one who experiences her own instincts as an independent and external force against which she must struggle.[2] Such decadents are unfree because they are not capable of the self-mastery required for genuine action. Instead, they are ruled tyrannically by instincts they can neither harness nor enjoy, but to which they can only react.[3]

DISGREGATION: THE UNFREEDOM OF NOT WILLING

In Nietzsche's terms, the decadent suffers from a disgregated will. Instead of having a will that integrates her disparate instincts into a larger whole, apart from which those instincts have no function and are not exercised, the decadent is merely a composite, an aggregate of instincts and drives whose expression is not organized by any larger purpose. As such a disgregated aggregate, the decadent is not even fully a self, and properly speaking has no will at all. For to be a self and to have a will requires being a genuine whole, which gives purpose to its component parts. But the decadent is not a genuine whole. Rather, she is only an artificial whole, lacking organizing force, one in which the parts, the anarchic instincts and drives, are sovereign.[4]

Since the decadent is defined by her struggle with and suffering from her own instincts, her opposite is the person for whom happiness and instinct are one.[5] Nietzsche calls such people noble, and whereas he considers decadence a sign of degeneration, he considers nobility an indication of what he calls the ascending movement of life; for Nietzsche, the decadent is an ill-constituted or sick human being (because she is constituted in such a way that she is at odds with herself), and the noble is a well-constituted or healthy one.[6]

Nietzsche also characterizes the difference between decadents and nobles as that between weakness and strength. Decadents are weak in two important senses. First, as we have seen, they are too weak to organize and direct their own instincts. As Nietzsche puts it, they are weak-willed, too weak to impose a measure on themselves.[7] This, as we have also seen, means that decadents inevitably suffer, both from their own instincts, which they do not enjoy and cannot control, and from the nobles, whose instinctive happiness and indifference to the decadents' plight they resent. The decadents' second form of weakness is their incapacity to endure the suffering caused by their first form of weakness. Corresponding to the two senses in which the decadents are weak are the two senses in which the nobles are strong: able to direct and enjoy their instincts, nobles suffer less than decadents do; but in addition, when they do suffer, nobles are more able to endure it, for they can understand their suffering as a necessary condition of living a life that, on balance, they consider enjoyable and worthwhile.[8]

Too weak either to overcome or to endure their suffering, the decadents are left, Nietzsche thinks, with no choice but to attempt to flee it and its sources. Such flight cannot be actual, for the problem necessitating the flight is precisely that the decadents are unable to avoid their instincts, the nobles, or the suffering caused by both. It must therefore be imaginary, a fictitious flight in which the decadents invent an alternative actuality in which they do not suffer:

> Who alone has grounds to lie himself out of actuality? He who suffers from it. But to suffer from actuality is to be a misfortunate (*verunglückte*) actuality... The preponderance of unpleasurable feelings over pleasurable feelings is the cause of fictitious morality and religion: such a preponderance, however, provides the formula for decadence.[9]

The decadents believe that in the resulting imaginary world they will enjoy both the rest from their own tormenting instincts that they so desperately want, and superiority over the nobles, whose evil self-indulgence will finally be recognized as such.

In order to hide their weakness from themselves and the nobles, however, the decadents must disguise the character of their imaginary flight and the fictitious world that it produces. Specifically, they must deny (to both themselves and the nobles) that the flight is a flight, and that the fictitious world is a fiction. Rather, the weak and cowardly invention of a fictitious world in which decadents do not suffer and the evil character of the nobles is exposed must be redescribed as the *discovery* of the *true* world. In comparison to this "true" world, the actual world – and with it the suffering of the decadents and the instinctive virtue of the nobles – becomes merely apparent or false.

From this decadent perspective, the actual world is false in two senses. First, it appears to be the ultimate reality but is not; somewhere behind or beyond the actual world in which we live is the "true" world, in which the decadents hope to live in some indeterminate future. Second, the actual world inverts, and thus falsifies, the values that the decadent considers "true." In the actual world the instinctive nobles are esteemed and rewarded, judged to be "good" and given power, when the fact of the matter is that they are "evil." Only in the "true" world will this finally be acknowledged, allowing both nobles and decadents to get their just deserts.[10]

The "true" world is one of the important elements of what Nietzsche calls the metaphysics of weakness, developed by the decadents to alleviate their suffering from actuality. The true world, as we have seen, accomplishes this by holding out the hope of a time and place in which the decadents will not suffer and the nobles will, since the former will be at peace, and the latter will be punished for their wickedness. But in order to support the claim that the nobles are truly evil and the decadents truly good, and thus the claim that the former are deserving of punishment and the latter of reward, the metaphysics of weakness needs a few more elements. The most important of these are the soul and free will.

The first function of the soul in its role as a decadent metaphysical prop is to make possible the proffered hope of a future life in the true world. Without a soul, each human life would end with the death of the body, and since the body can be observed to decay upon death, it cannot reasonably be supposed that it has a future post mortem. The chief characteristic and virtue of the soul, however, is precisely its immortality. Thus if a person is primarily identified with her soul, which can be detached from her body, then she can expect to continue living after the death of the latter, and can hope that such a life will take place in the true world, rather than in the apparent one.

The second function of the soul is to justify the decadents' condemnation of the nobles for their failure to treat all people equally. The nobles, recall, find joy in the activities that come to them instinctively, which means that they naturally value others who share their enjoyment of and success in these activities more highly than they value those who do not. Supposing that there were no souls, this would be perfectly reasonable, for then people could be evaluated only according to their earthly actions and accomplishments. But the introduction of the soul, and the primary identification of people with it rather than with their bodies, makes such noble valuations appear to be unjust. For all souls are understood to be of equal value, regardless of the achievements or failures of the body to which they happen to be temporarily attached in this life. On this reasoning, then, justice requires that all be treated equally, in virtue of having an immortal soul.[11]

Whereas the soul makes it possible to hope for eternal life in the true world, and to condemn the nobles as unjust, the postulation of free will makes it possible to blame the nobles for their injustice, and to consider the decadents virtuous and therefore deserving of the hoped-for eternal blessedness. Without free will, it would be no less true that the nobles indulge their own instincts, treat people unequally, and are indifferent to the decadents' suffering, but they could hardly be blamed for this; as Nietzsche writes, "that lambs dislike great birds of prey is not strange: only it gives no ground to blame the birds of prey for carrying off little lambs."[12] Likewise, it would remain true that the decadents do not enjoy their instincts, treat all alike, and attempt to alleviate suffering at all costs, but they could not be praised for this, or be said to deserve eternal life as a reward for so living. Without free will, decadents too would be like any other animal, not deserving either praise or blame, but simply acting on their instincts. Only if people are understood to have free will can the decadents blame the nobles and judge them to be "sinful" and "evil," while praising their own weakness and self-denial as virtuous and "good." Nietzsche concludes:

> Revenge and hatred . . . maintain no belief more ardently than the belief that *the strong are free* to be weak . . . for they thus gain the right to hold the bird of prey *accountable* for being a bird of prey . . . [and to act] as if the weakness of the weak – that is, their *essence*, their effects, their sole ineluctable, irremovable reality – were a voluntary achievement, something willed, chosen, a *deed*, something *meritorious*. This type of man *needs* to believe in an indifferent, free-choosing subject . . . because it makes possible the sublime self-deception that interprets weakness itself as freedom, and his being so-and-so as something *meritorious*.[13]

Finally, the metaphysics of weakness is completed with the supposition of an omniscient, omnipotent, benevolent God. Such a God ensures not only that the nobles *can* be blamed and the decadents be praised, but also that they actually *will* be so judged, and by a Being with the power to attach appropriate sanctions to His judgments. God ensures that the decadents will spend eternity in a Heaven where no one suffers, and that the nobles will suffer eternally in Hell.[14]

Nietzsche grants that the metaphysics of weakness is beneficial for those who need it in order to endure their worldly suffering. In fact, he considers it an expression of the instinct of the weak for their own self-preservation.[15] But it also has other consequences that inspire his notorious critique of decadent morality. The most significant of these, which we will treat in turn, include the exacerbation of bad conscience and the spreading of nihilism. The former intensifies suffering and decadence, and together with the latter entrenches reactive unfreedom, both of which the metaphysics of weakness was intended to overcome.

Nietzsche understands bad conscience to be a sickness, peculiar to humanity, in which people suffer from themselves, from their own instincts. Nietzsche thinks that this sickness, almost synonymous with decadence, develops when people find themselves living in stable, peaceful societies. In such situations, acting on certain instincts, which Nietzsche takes to be basic, becomes unacceptable; for example, one can no longer take pleasure in cruelty, hostility, persecution, destruction, or change, because these are damaging to the social whole of which one is a part, and to which one owes one's own security and prosperity.

Consequently, people suffer in three distinct ways. Most obviously, if they continue to act on these unacceptable instincts, people suffer by being punished. But they also endure twofold suffering even if they avoid punishment by successfully restraining themselves. First, such people suffer from having to fight and suppress their natural inclinations, from having to live in the world in an unfamiliar and uncomfortable way. Second, they suffer because these instincts do not simply disappear and, since they cannot be exercised externally, tend to seek their satisfaction by turning inward, by acting upon the very self to which they belong. Thus, Nietzsche thinks, a person who cannot take her natural pleasure in shaping the external world through creative destruction will find her pleasure in shaping the only thing she still can, namely, herself. Though pleasurable, this is also painful, and really the essence of what Nietzsche means by bad conscience: the person suffers from, and so comes to consider "bad," her most natural and pleasurable instincts. Her own instincts plague her; she is sick from herself.[16]

So far, this analysis of bad conscience does not involve any of the elements of the metaphysics of weakness. It might seem that it should, for bad conscience is obviously related to feeling guilty for having and exercising certain instincts, and guilt is quite naturally associated with free will. But Nietzsche makes it clear that he believes bad conscience can and did arise independent of and prior to the notion of free will.

Bad conscience is logically independent of free will because the sense of guilt required for bad conscience is different from the sense of guilt that only free will makes possible. Bad conscience, Nietzsche thinks, requires only that a person be aware that every injurious act incurs a debt, so that in committing such an act a person feels "guilty" in the sense that she knows she is obligated to repay the injured party. But this sense of guilt as indebtedness does not require that either the person committing the injury (the debtor) or the person injured (the creditor) hold the violator responsible for her act. It does not matter whether the person "could have done otherwise," which would indeed depend on having free will. Punishment can be and, according to Nietzsche, for a long time prior to the invention of free will actually was, justified simply on the grounds that an inflicted harm demands an equal response. Bad conscience arises as soon as one internalizes this understanding of punishment and couples it with the recognition that one harms others by acting on one's instincts; this combination drives one to suppress instinctive behavior, which leads to the suffering from oneself described earlier.[17]

Although free will is not necessary to bad conscience, it does exacerbate it, adding yet another dimension to the suffering bad conscience produces. As we have already seen, the postulation of free will enables the decadents to blame the nobles, to hold them responsible for the expression of their instincts and the harm it produces. It also allows the decadents to praise themselves, to give themselves credit for their own meekness and self-restraint. But free will is a double-edged sword. It not only allows the decadents to blame the nobles, but at the same time demands that the decadents blame themselves. Having endowed themselves with free will, the decadents have no choice but to take responsibility both for the occasions on which they do indulge their "evil" instincts, and for simply having such instincts in the first place, for failing to purge themselves of their "evil" drives. Consequently, the decadents suffer not only from punishment, self-suppression, and internal violence, but also from guilt, from the belief that all of this suffering is their own fault, deserved in virtue of their sinfulness, and could be avoided if only they were better people who exercised their free will purely for the "good."

Ultimately, then, a vicious circle is produced. Decadence and suffering lead to a metaphysical belief in free will, but the guilt produced by such a belief creates both greater suffering and greater pressure to suppress and struggle with one's instincts; the intensification of this suffering and struggle is the intensification of bad conscience and decadence, which in turn intensifies the need for the belief in free will, yet again increasing suffering and struggle, and so on. By exacerbating bad conscience through the doctrine of free will, then, the metaphysics of weakness actually intensifies the decadence that it is supposed to alleviate.

Moreover, the metaphysics of weakness not only exacerbates bad conscience, but also leads to nihilism, in three senses.[18] In the first sense, nihilism means that this world, the actual world, is literally "nothing." This belief is a direct consequence of the supposition, central to the metaphysics of weakness, that there is a "true" world behind, beyond, or above this one. As we have seen, this supposition demotes the actual world to being but a false appearance of the true one. According to the metaphysics of weakness, then, the true world is what *is*, and the actual world is a mere apparition.

Nietzsche calls this belief that actuality is only an appearance "world-slandering" (*weltverleumderisch*).[19] It is slander because it is not only mendacious (recall that Nietzsche considers the invention of the true world to be an attempt by the decadents to lie their way out of the reality from which they suffer), but also malicious and defamatory; the claim that actuality *is* nothing also implies that actuality is *worth* nothing. This is the second sense of nihilism to which the metaphysics of weakness leads. It convinces its adherents that this world is valueless and meaningless, or at least that if anything in this world has value or meaning it is only in virtue of the contribution it makes toward attaining the true world, the achievement by which all value is measured.[20]

Convinced that nothing in this world has value in itself, adherents of the metaphysics of weakness become nihilistic in yet a third sense: they are unable to *will* anything, unable to set themselves any positive goal, since no such earthly goal could have any ultimate value or meaning.

Nihilism in this sense, then, is the entrenchment of the condition of reactive unfreedom that defines decadence in the first place; it is a condition that prevents disgregated decadents from forging a will out of which they could act. Nihilism in this sense thus represents the failure of the metaphysics of weakness to overcome decadence and liberate the weak.[21]

THE MORALITY OF SELFLESSNESS: THE INCOMPLETE FREEDOM OF WILLING NOTHING

The consequences of the metaphysics of weakness – the exacerbation of bad conscience and nihilism – combine to encourage the development of a particular kind of morality. This is the morality of selflessness, which has three main purposes, the first two of which correspond to the consequences of the metaphysics of weakness just discussed.[22]

The first purpose of the morality of selflessness is to alleviate suffering. In part, this is a response to the exacerbation of bad conscience by the metaphysics of weakness, since such exacerbation is tantamount to an increase in suffering.

The most effective way to alleviate the suffering produced by bad conscience would be to effect a reconciliation between the decadent and her instincts; if a person could learn to control the expression of her instincts, to direct them so that they served a goal whose accomplishment she valued highly, then she would not consider her instincts bad and would enjoy rather than suffer from their expression. But because the adherents of the morality of selflessness are by definition those too weak to organize their instincts to serve such a positive goal, their morality cannot alleviate their suffering by effecting such a reconciliation.

Instead, the morality of selflessness can alleviate the suffering of its adherents only by encouraging and enabling the extirpation of those instincts that are the source of the pain.[23] It thus advocates absolute resistance to the natural instincts one cannot control. One means of bringing about this resistance is the subjection of oneself to logic and reason, and the equation of such subjection with happiness; too weak to be one's own master, and suffering under the tyranny of instinct, one opts for subjection to a master still more powerful, but believed to be more benevolent.[24] Famously, Nietzsche takes Socrates to embody such developments in ancient Greece:

> If one needs to make a tyrant of *reason*, as Socrates did, then there must exist no little danger of something else playing the tyrant . . . The fanaticism with which the whole of Greek thought throws itself at rationality betrays a state of emergency: one was in peril, one had only *one* choice: either to perish or – be *absurdly rational* . . . The moralism of the Greek philosophers from Plato downwards is pathologically conditioned: likewise their estimation of dialectics. Reason = virtue = happiness means merely: one must imitate Socrates and counter the dark desires by producing a permanent *daylight* – the daylight of reason.[25]

Such subjection to reason is thus inevitable for the weak, necessary for their self-preservation, but the metaphysics of free will enables them to regard it as the voluntary self-denial of evil instincts, and therefore virtuous. Their decadence thus gets cloaked in positive language: weakness and subjection to reason become admirable self-sacrifice, self-abnegation, lack of egoism – in a word, "selflessness" (*Selbstlosigkeit*)[26].

Having made a virtue of selflessness in the sense of denying and extirpating one's own instincts and drives, decadent morality also makes a virtue of selflessness in the sense of caring for others more than one cares for oneself. This is quite natural, since caring for oneself by definition involves the attempt to satisfy at least some of one's own desires and instincts, which is a vice from the perspective of decadent morality. Caring for others can thus serve the negative function of distracting one from the instincts that always threaten to retake control of one's life. But caring for others also serves the positive function of reducing *their* suffering, which the decadent assumes that they must experience simply in virtue of dwelling in this world, and which she also assumes that they would be better off without.

The morality of selflessness thus values not only the extirpation of one's own positive instincts, but the inculcation of instincts directed toward the helping of others. In the Christian tradition, these highly praised instincts are known as the virtues of pity and love of one's neighbor, which Nietzsche categorizes as the "selfless" (*selbstlos*) virtues.[27]

The first purpose of the morality of selflessness, then, is to reduce suffering, whether that of oneself or of another; the highest value of decadent morality is not a positive achievement but rather the *lack* of suffering. If such a morality can be said to have an earthly aim, it aims at no longer having earthly aims, for that is the surest way to avoid suffering from their inevitable frustration.[28] In Nietzsche's terms, the highest goal of the morality of selflessness is the taming of humanity, the turning of humanity toward the ascetic ideal, with the hope that this will make life on Earth as comfortable as possible while also making eternal life in the true world as likely as possible.[29]

Since some degree of earthly suffering is inevitable, however, the second purpose of the morality of selflessness is to give meaning to the suffering it cannot eradicate. This goal corresponds to the problem of nihilism, which we saw results from the metaphysical postulation of a true world, of which the actual world is merely an appearance. Given this postulation, nothing that takes place in the actual world, whether pleasurable or painful, truly *is*, and therefore nothing that takes place in the actual world truly *matters*. This is maddening, and prevents the decadent from mustering the strength to forge a will, for it means that all of the suffering that she endures is for no good reason, indeed, for no reason at all.[30]

The morality of selflessness responds to this problem by linking one's suffering to one's degree of virtuousness in the actual world, and one's degree of virtuousness in the actual world to one's chances of attaining the true world. The latter link is direct and straightforward: the more virtuous one is, the more one denies one's instincts and conforms to the ascetic ideal, the more likely one will be to enjoy life in the true world, where, of course, there is no suffering. The former link, between suffering and virtuousness, is twofold.

Some suffering, according to the morality of selflessness, is incurred *because* one is virtuous; being a virtuous ascetic means denying oneself earthly pleasures and earthly power, and consequently having to endure certain deprivations and having to suffer at the hands of the powerful, rich, and worldly. Other suffering, however, indicates that one is not *sufficiently* virtuous; the morality of selflessness interprets this kind of suffering as punishment inflicted for sin.[31]

These two interpretations enable decadent morality to give meaning to all possible suffering, and thus enable its adherents to avoid the madness of the third type of nihilism, that of being unable to will because one suffers without reason. When the decadent suffers, her morality counsels her, she must first examine her life for signs of sin. Surely she will find some, for to live in the actual world is by definition to be impure, and she must try to improve herself before she can legitimately expect the associated suffering to diminish. It is also likely, however, that she will honestly be able to conclude that she is afflicted with more suffering than her sins alone would justify. This being the case, she must learn to accept the incremental suffering as the unfortunate price of ascetic virtue, and thus the price of future admission to the true world. As Jesus advised, she must turn the other cheek, and have faith that the meek shall inherit the Earth.[32]

These first two purposes of the morality of selflessness – reducing suffering and giving meaning to suffering that cannot be eradicated – are interrelated. Specifically, the success of the first purpose depends on the success of the second: reducing suffering through denial of one's instincts and concern for others requires that one have sufficient motivation to adopt such ascetic measures, and such motivation depends on the belief that asceticism will be rewarded, and that the suffering it inflicts is therefore meaningful.

The success of each of these two purposes therefore ultimately depends upon the adherents' of the morality of selflessness retaining their faith in the metaphysics of weakness. For the belief that ascetic suffering is meaningful and will be rewarded cannot be maintained apart from belief in all four major components of this metaphysics: to expect reward in the true world for living virtuously in this one, one must believe that there is a true world, that one has an immortal soul that can survive earthly death, that one has a free will in virtue of which one can be judged to be deserving of a place in the true world, and that an omniscient, omnipotent, benevolent God will observe one's life and reward one accordingly.[33]

The third purpose of the morality of selflessness, designed to make possible the accomplishment of its first two purposes, is thus the reinforcement of faith in the metaphysics of weakness, out of which the morality itself grows. The morality of selflessness accomplishes this by making it a sin even to doubt the faith, or to ask that it be grounded in reason; the morality of selflessness, based on a lie and therefore threatened by knowledge, makes knowledge itself the forbidden fruit.[34] This rejection of reason and knowledge tries to ensure that both the morality of selflessness and the metaphysics upon which it rests are impervious to intellectual attack.[35]

Initially, when metaphysical faith and moral asceticism are new to a people, such an explicit prohibition on dangerous knowledge is extremely important. For such people are both the most vulnerable to losing the faith or lapsing morally, and the most likely to be in the habit of the kinds of investigations that could trigger such losses or lapses. But as time goes on, Nietzsche points out, such a prohibition becomes self-sustaining, and hardly needs to remain explicit. Successive generations, living under such a prohibition, gradually lose their *capacity* for knowledge, since this capacity, as Nietzsche understands it, depends essentially on being in the habit of seeking out sound causal explanations for phenomena, rather than being content to rest with (i.e., to take on faith) "explanations" that are at least as mysterious as the things they purport to explain (e.g., accepting "sin" as an "explanation" of suffering). As Nietzsche puts the point:

> The concept of guilt and punishment, including the doctrine of "grace," of "redemption," of "forgiveness" – *lies* through and through and without any psychological reality – were invented to destroy the *causal sense* of man: they are an outrage on the concept of cause and effect! ... When the natural consequences of an act are no longer "natural" but thought of as effected by the conceptual ghosts of superstition, by "God," by "spirits," by "souls," as merely 'moral' consequences, as reward, punishment, sign, chastisement, then the precondition for knowledge has been destroyed.[36]

Faith thus becomes increasingly difficult to displace, as the ban on causal investigation produces more and more people who not only have no idea how to perform one, but do not even perceive the absence of one as a lack.[37]

The third purpose of the morality of selflessness is thus achieved by an explicit ban on knowledge, the success of which ultimately overcomes the very need for itself. Faith in the metaphysics of weakness is secured by destroying people's capacity to think, destroying not only their ability to challenge their faith, but more fundamentally their very ability to recognize the difference between relying on faith and seeking an explanation.

The destruction of the preconditions for knowledge is the final key to the success of the morality of selflessness and the metaphysics of weakness. Such destruction makes the displacement of the metaphysics all but impossible,[38] which both secures the need for the morality (to ward off the exacerbation of bad conscience and the third type of nihilism),[39] and makes the adoption of the morality likely by providing an incontrovertible hope that it will reduce earthly suffering and lead to eternal life in the true world, with no suffering at all.[40]

Nietzsche concludes *On the Genealogy of Morals* with the following positive evaluation of the adoption of the morality of selflessness by decadent humanity:

> [T] *he ascetic ideal offered man meaning!* It was the only meaning offered so far; any meaning is better than none at all ... In it, suffering was *interpreted* ... the door was closed to any kind of suicidal nihilism ... man was *saved* thereby, he possessed a meaning, he was henceforth no longer like a leaf in the wind, a plaything of nonsense – the "sense-less" – he could now *will* something; no matter at first to what end, why, with what he willed: *the will itself was saved.*[41]

Thus, although Nietzsche is famously hostile to the morality of selflessness, he also recognizes it and its metaphysics as a genuine improvement, if only for those people who without it would remain merely decadent and ill-constituted. Such people, with disgregated wills that are no wills at all, unable even to form a self, are as sick as the human animal can be.

The metaphysics of weakness and the morality of selflessness improve on such wanton disgregation by enabling the weak to will. As we have seen, faith in the metaphysics of weakness, which gives meaning to earthly suffering, allows the weak to avoid the third type of nihilism. They remain decadent and ill-constituted, suffering from themselves, but in virtue of their metaphysical faith they are nonetheless capable of willing.

On the one hand, the only thing that morality makes the weak capable of willing is nothing – they desire rest, an end to and transcendence of the suffering and struggles of this world.[42] Putting words in the mouths of such people, Nietzsche writes, in a section headed *At the freezing point of the will*, that they all feel that

> "It will come, one day, that hour that will envelope you in a golden cloud where there is no pain: where the soul has the enjoyment of its own weariness and, happy in a patient game with its own patience, is like the waves of a lake which, reflecting the colors of an evening sky on a quiet summer's day, lap and lap against the bank and then are still again – without end, without aim (*Zweck*), without satiation, without desire . . . "[43]

But on the other hand, willing nothing is still an improvement over not willing, over a nihilism so deep that it can find nothing worth willing, not even nothingness itself. So the metaphysics of weakness and the morality of selflessness allow the weak to affirm themselves and their lives, in a sense:

> [T]he "tame man," the hopelessly mediocre and insipid man, has already learned to feel himself as the goal and zenith, as the meaning of history, as "higher man" . . . he has indeed a certain right to feel thus, insofar as he feels himself elevated above the surfeit of ill-constituted, sickly, weary, exhausted people of which Europe is beginning to stink today, as something at least relatively well-constituted, at least still capable of living, at least affirming life.[44]

Unlike those who are merely decadent and ill-constituted, those who forge a moral will to nothingness are capable of thinking and acting in accordance with their own adopted moral valuation, no longer merely reacting to external stimuli, and are thus more free than those who do not.

Although Nietzsche praises the moral will as an improvement compared to the disgregated will, compared to no will at all, he also makes it clear that the moral will is neither a cure for the decadence and weakness out of which it grows, nor completely free. Indeed, the moral will is both a symptom of weakness, and a means of reinforcing it, of further weakening the weak, so that they become increasingly dependent on morality and its metaphysics as their only hope of avoiding disgregation and nihilism.

Morality is a symptom of decadence rather than its cure because it does not represent the genuine ability to organize oneself and one's instincts in a way that one can affirm, but is rather only the imitation of this achievement.[45] Recall that on Nietzsche's account the moral will, the will to the nothingness of ascetic self-denial, is created when those too weak to create a will on their own, faced with nihilistic disgregation and suffering at the hands of their own tyrannical instincts, subject themselves to reason as the more benevolent master. Nietzsche grants that reason is a better master than anarchic instincts, but emphasizes that it is still a master, and that those with a moral will are therefore still subjects, still ruled by something other than themselves. They are not self-organized, and not reconciled with their instincts. Rather, the fact that one has a moral will indicates precisely that one still struggles with one's instincts, and that one is capable of managing this struggle only by subjecting oneself and one's instincts to the greater force of morality:

> It is self-deception on the part of philosophers and moralists to imagine that by making war on *decadence* they therewith elude *decadence* themselves...what they select as an expedient, as a deliverance, is itself only another expression of *decadence* – they *alter* its expression, they do not abolish the thing itself...the harshest daylight, rationality at any cost, life bright, cold, circumspect, conscious, without instinct, in opposition to the instincts, has itself been no more than a form of sickness, another form of sickness – and by no means a way back to "virtue," to "health," to happiness...to *have* to combat one's instincts – that is the formula for *decadence*: as long as life is *ascending*, happiness and instinct are one.[46]

Thus rather than overcoming the decadent inability to resist one's instincts, the moral will simply pretends to have overcome it. Moreover, Nietzsche thinks, there are two distinct ways in which morality exacerbates the decadence and weakness of its adherents.

First, morality's central values of asceticism and pity not only fail to overcome the decadent incapacity to resist external stimuli, but actually make such lack of resistance into a virtue. Asceticism does demand resistance to one's own instincts, but it also demands that one not resist those who inflict earthly suffering on oneself, that one instead await revenge in the true world.[47] And to feel pity instinctively, which the morality of selflessness requires of its adherents, is to be unable *not* to react to the suffering of another, to be unable to be indifferent to another.[48] Asceticism and pity, then, combine to make into a virtue the incapacity to resist either the suffering inflicted upon oneself, or the moral instinct to alleviate the suffering one observes in others. Because such lack of resistance is a chief characteristic of decadence, these moral virtues give decadence itself the status of a virtue.

Establishing the incapacity to resist as a virtue, and thus entrenching this incapacity more firmly in its adherents, is the first way in which the morality of selflessness actually reinforces the decadence out of which it arises. But it also reinforces this decadence through its destruction of the preconditions of knowledge.

Whereas asceticism and pity reinforce the decadent's inability to resist external stimuli, the destruction of the preconditions of knowledge reinforces the decadent's dependence on external sources for her own thoughts and actions. It does this by making it impossible for the adherents of morality to think, and therefore to act, for themselves.

The ban on knowledge and doubt makes faith the only possible ground of judgment and purposive action. But submitting to faith as the ground of judgment, Nietzsche thinks, is equivalent to submitting to common judgments, the judgments conventionally agreed upon by the mass of moral adherents, as to law.[49] For to act on faith is to act on one's conscience, and conscience has no content other than obedience to authority; to act on faith is to be directed by the authorities one fears, who in this case are the moral authorities and by extension the whole moral community.[50] The morality of selflessness is thus what Nietzsche calls herd morality, because its adherents cannot be said to have individual wills but rather make judgments and initiate actions based on the beliefs of the group of which they are a part.[51]

As we saw earlier, the ban on knowledge quickly turns into an incapacity for knowledge in those who have accepted the ban and in their descendants. The consequence is that herd morality, dependence upon external authority initiated by the ban on knowledge, is also self-perpetuating and self-enhancing. As people lose their ability to make judgments about the appropriateness of the moral judgments of the community, they become increasingly dependent on those herd pronouncements. This increases the force of the herd's judgments, as more and more people subscribe to them blindly, and with increasing fervor and righteousness born of the certainty that comes from the inability to see any alternative.[52] Resistance and independence thus become increasingly difficult, requiring ever more strength, while at the same time the chances that any individual will have a certain amount of strength decrease due to the undermining of the preconditions of knowledge and independent thought. The combination makes the reach and power of herd morality nearly absolute; no one can escape the influence of its judgments entirely, and even if one could, the backlash of the community would be so great as to make dissent extremely unwise. Herd morality is threatened by independent individuals, and thus one of its main tenets, taken on faith by its adherents, is that such independence is evil and conformity is morally good.

As a corollary, herd morality considers itself the only morality, to which all should subscribe.[53]

Again Nietzsche grants that there is some benefit to these develop-ments, from a particular perspective. The development of herd morality is clearly beneficial to the community, and therefore indirectly to the weak, who need the community to protect them. It is beneficial to the former because by making conformity a virtue and individual dissent a vice, herd morality tends to foster the community's preservation.[54] It is thus beneficial to the latter, because Nietzsche understands this kind of community as an organization designed to protect the weak, to provide security and equality for all through the rule of law.[55]

But at the same time that it is beneficial to the community, whose preservation is one of its central virtues, herd morality is detrimental to the virtuous, to those who adopt its judgments and practice asceticism, pity, and faithful conformity. Although herd morality benefits these weak people by protecting them, it is precisely in so doing that it also harms them, for it protects and preserves them *as* weak and dependent, and thus prevents them from becoming strong, independent, and free.

In Nietzsche's words, the virtues of the morality of selflessness "take from a human being his noblest selfishness (*edelste Selbstsucht*) and the strength for the highest care for himself (*höchsten Obhut über sich selber*)."[56] They do this by teaching him to value himself only insofar as he serves some function of the community or herd, teaching him to subordinate himself as an individual to the needs and judgments of the majority.[57] Although Nietzsche acknowledges that such identification of oneself with the laws and values of one's community can provide the feeling of a cer-tain kind of freedom, on balance he considers it bad for the individual.[58] Because the community by definition values stability, to serve the com-munity the individual must give up change, learning, and the possibility of self-transformation.[59] Worse, the individual must give up himself, in the sense that the ends to which he dedicates himself are those of the community, and the means he uses to pursue those ends are prescribed for him by the herd.

In other words, although morality enables the weak to will, the will it gives them is not their own. The moral adherent overcomes the third type of nihilism and subjection to the tyranny of his instincts, but only by subjecting himself to the "rational" instincts of the herd, which provide the content of "his" will. The ultimate content, purpose, or goal of this will is nothingness; the moral will wills only escape from this world to the true world, has no earthly goals that are ends in themselves, and thus remains nihilistic in the senses that for it this world is nothing and is worth nothing. Its earthly purposes are merely intermediate means, those things the moral authorities (the priests, the churches, the herd) designate as necessary to achieve the ultimate goal of an eternal, pain-free life.[60]

For this reason, Nietzsche also calls the morality of selflessness, or decadent morality, "unselfing" (*Entselbstung*) morality.[61] Dependence on faith literally prevents one from being or becoming a genuine self with a will of one's own, out of which one could think and act:

> The man of faith, the "believer" of every sort is necessarily a dependent man – such as cannot out of himself posit (*ansetzen*) goals (*Zwecke*) at all. The "believer" does not belong to *himself*, he can be only a means, he has to be *used*, he needs someone who will use him. His instinct accords the highest honor to unselfing morality... Belief of any kind is itself an expression of unselfing, of self-alienation (*Selbst-Entfremdung*) ... If one considers what need people have of an external regulation to constrain and steady them, how compulsion, *slavery* in a higher sense is the sole and final condition under which the person of weaker will... can prosper: then one also understands the nature of conviction, "faith".[62]

This passage makes it clear that Nietzsche does not think that the development of morality can solve the problem of freedom. As we saw at the very beginning of this chapter, Nietzsche associates freedom with thinking and acting for oneself. But instead of enabling people to develop these capacities, to develop a self and a will, morality simply disguises the fact that people lack them. In so doing, it "unselfs" and enslaves them even more profoundly than before: although it is true that prior to morality the decadent have no self, no will, but merely react to external stimuli, at least such disgregated souls are capable of feeling the lack of a self as a lack, and struggling to overcome it (if too weakly to succeed); morality, however, overcomes not the lack but the *sense* of lack, providing not a self or a will, but the mere feeling that one is a self with a will. As a result, one no longer struggles to forge a will for oneself, but rather relies on faith for direction, allows oneself to be "steadied" by the "external regulation" and "compulsion" of morality. Morality offers the false feeling of freedom one gets from conforming to a herd, and the alleviation of suffering one gets from ascetic denial of one's instincts, but it is precisely in virtue of enjoying these moral pleasures that one allows oneself to be "enslaved," that one sacrifices the possibility of the genuine freedom of thinking and acting out of one's own will.[63]

THE CONTAGIOUS CIRCLE OF DECADENCE

We can now understand Nietzsche's concern that the reactive unfreedom of decadence will not overcome itself, but instead will intensify in a self-reinforcing cycle. We have already seen that disgregation and weakness, the lack of a will, leads to metaphysical flight, which leads to the morality of selflessness, a will to nothingness. Now we can see that this morality ultimately generates a circling back to and deepening of the very decadence and unfreedom that it pretends to overcome.[64]

We have seen that morality originates in ill-constitutedness and weakness, in people both unable to enjoy their instincts and incapable of resisting them. Unable to enjoy their instincts, decadents must struggle with them; incapable of resisting them, the weak must enlist allies in the struggle, which they do by inventing the metaphysics of the true world and the morality of selfless asceticism and pity. Although this avoids the third type of nihilism, making it possible for the decadent to will and to affirm her life, it not only fails to overcome decadence and weakness, the need to struggle with one's instincts and the inability to do so successfully on one's own, but actually reinforces them; the morality of selflessness both increases the decadent's need to struggle with her instincts, as it codifies her own feeling that her instincts are bad, and decreases her ability to resist them or to form a will out of them on her own, as it makes her increasingly dependent on the judgments of the herd. The content of these judgments, finally, further reinforces decadence and completes the cycle, since in deeming the decadent adherents of morality to be good and virtuous, the herd deems decadence and weakness to be good and virtuous and brands as evil any attempts to overcome these conditions of impotence and dependence.[65]

As already noted, Nietzsche grants that for those too weak to have any hope of forging their own will, for whom the only alternative to moral enslavement is complete nihilism, morality is an improvement. Given this, Nietzsche's extreme hostility to morality might seem perplexing. For it would be highly unreasonable to castigate morality for inhibiting the freedom of those constitutionally incapable of being free. On Nietzsche's understanding, the weak must necessarily be enslaved, either to instincts they cannot control, or to a moral authority outside themselves. That being so, and moral enslavement being the better of the two, one would almost expect Nietzsche to be an advocate of morality.

Nietzsche, however, understands morality to have not only the positive effect of preserving the weak, but also deleterious consequences for the entire future of humanity. Specifically, morality endangers those strong enough to aspire to overcome enslavement altogether, to aspire to forge an independent earthly will for themselves, in two specific ways.

First, Nietzsche is concerned that the pity of the weak for all who suffer can interfere with the efforts of the strong to develop themselves. Nietzsche suggests that suffering and solitude may be requirements of greatness, and that sickness may be a requirement of knowledge and self-knowledge.[66] If this is so, then the strong and noble, who by definition are those capable of enduring suffering, need protection not from suffering, but from those who would offer them such protection; the strong need protection from pity.[67]

Second, Nietzsche worries that the values of the morality of selfless-ness will spread even to the strong, to those capable of living healthily and happily without them. This is possible because, as we have seen, deca-dent morality institutes a ban on knowledge. Over time this ban destroys the preconditions of knowledge, thus making an increasing number of people reliant upon faith. Once this has transpired, even the strong may succumb to pity, which will entice them away from their healthy concern with self-development in favor of concerning themselves with mitigating the suffering of others.[68] Consequently, even the strong will begin to suf-fer from life, contracting suffering from the sympathy they have for those they pity.[69]

These two specific concerns about the ways that the morality of self-lessness might negatively affect those strong enough to flourish without it both represent Nietzsche's single larger concern about such morality: namely, that it will make humanity extremely short-sighted, willing to sacrifice the possibility of its future development and elevation for the certainty of its present comfort.[70] To Nietzsche the latter goal – pleasure without suffering – is contemptible, and fails to see that

> the discipline of suffering, of *great* suffering ... it is *this* discipline alone that has created every elevation of mankind hitherto ... In man, *creature* and *creator* are united: in man there is matter, fragment, excess, clay, mud, madness, chaos; but in man there is also creator, sculptor, the hardness of the hammer ... do you understand this antithesis? And that *your* pity is for the "creature in man," for that which has to be formed, broken, forged, torn, burned, annealed, refined – that which has to *suffer* and *should* suffer?[71]

Because this contemptible future would result from the contagion of the morality of selflessness, which itself would ultimately result from the de-struction of the presuppositions of knowledge, Nietzsche concludes that such destruction, at which Christianity and other religious movements aim, is the greatest crime against humanity.[72]

We can now conclude that although the morality of selflessness is in some ways, for some people, an improvement on mere decadence, it not only fails to liberate its adherents, but also threatens the possibility of liberation for those strong enough not to need it. It saves the weak from the third type of nihilism, makes it possible for them to will, but at the cost of destroying the preconditions of knowledge and thus both intensifying the decadence of the already decadent and increasing the ranks of the decadent to include those formerly at home with their instincts and strong enough to forge their own wills; that is, it spreads and deepens the first two types of nihilism. The decadent destruction of the preconditions of knowledge thus threatens to destroy the possibility of a future in which humanity, or at least some part of it, is genuinely free, genuinely able to think and act for itself, out of a will that is truly its own.[73]

2. From Decadence to Nobility: Convalescence

DESTRUCTION OF THE MORAL WILL

We have seen that the chief failure of the morality of selflessness is that it enslaves humanity by unselfing it. Morality makes freedom impossible by creating an empty will to nothing whose contents are provided by the herd, which prevents the creation of an independent will out of which one could set goals, think, and act. We have also seen that the key to this moral unselfing is the destruction of the preconditions of knowledge, the displacement of the sense that one needs to investigate and discover causes and grounds by the complacency of faith, conviction, and conscience. Overcoming the enslavement of morality and preparing the way for the creation of independent selves and wills, then, requires first that the hammerlock of faith be broken. In turn, this requires that the lack of knowledge again be felt as a lack, and that this sense of lack spur people to restore the preconditions of knowledge.

Nietzsche sums this up by describing the recovery from moral unselfing as a matter of education. But by education Nietzsche emphatically does not mean schooling, at least not of any conventional kind. For education in the sense of conventional schooling is one of the primary means by which herd morality is inculcated and disseminated, by which morality constructs the will to nothing of its adherents and maintains them as a herd.[74] Since the goal of the kind of education that Nietzsche has in mind is precisely the restoration and expansion of noble individuals and cultures, this education must not be a process of learning how to see and think in conventional ways, but of learning how to see and think beyond convention.[75]

Although learning how to see and think beyond convention involves shedding the moral perspective of the herd, the point is not to replace it immediately with another perspective. On the contrary, the primary problem with herd morality is not so much the particular contents of its conventions (although they are far from unproblematic), but the simple fact that its contents are conventional, that they comprise an established perspective. As an established perspective, herd morality interprets every experience through the same fixed set of categories, even when those categories are not the most appropriate ones for the phenomenon at hand. Indeed, the ultimate problem is that an established perspective is incapable even of entertaining the possibility that there are phenomena for which its categories are inappropriate, much less of recognizing the specific situations in which that is the case. Consequently, established perspectives in general, and herd morality in particular, interpret the world too *quickly*; the moral self reacts immediately and decisively to the external stimuli it receives (which, recall, is the hallmark of a lack of freedom for Nietzsche), forcing them into its own preestablished framework of categories and values, imposing its own will upon them.[76] As a result, the herd experiences not the phenomenon at hand, but merely its reflection in the lights of morality. Education, for Nietzsche, is thus a process of developing the ability to experience phenomena, a process of acquiring the habit of *deferring* judgment and decision, of *not* imposing one's will, of letting phenomena come to oneself and investigating them carefully before stamping them with an interpretation. Learning to see and think is a process of becoming *slow*, of not presuming familiarity with everything one encounters.[77]

Developing these habits of slowness and deferral is, for Nietzsche, a matter of intellectual integrity. For assimilating all experience into the categories of an established perspective, whose adequacy one accepts as a matter of faith, is dishonest and indecent.[78] Intellectual integrity demands that one make one's assent to or dissent from any particular belief or doctrine a matter of conscience – not in the sense that one avers the truth of whatever accords with the contents of one's conscience (for that is precisely the moral approach being criticized), but in the sense that one is committed to deferring all assent or dissent until one has thoroughly investigated the matter in question, has sought grounds for one's judgment in the hope of replacing blind conviction with reasonable certainty.[79]

To fail to display such intellectual integrity and conscience is both to be overly tolerant of and dishonest with oneself and to be unjust to the phenomena one encounters. It is overly tolerant and dishonest because it allows one to have any number of conflicting convictions without shame or discomfort. In other words, the convictions of the moral self have no consequences; since all of its convictions are accepted on faith and without grounds, there is no reason, fact, or competing belief that could compel the rejection of any of them.[80] It is unjust because, as we noted above, it amounts to encountering new phenomena only as they appear in the light of one's old prejudices, and thus to failing truly to encounter anything new at all.[81]

Nietzsche points out that what is needed to replace morality's intellectual deceit with intellectual integrity, ironically, is to become *increasingly* moral – again, not in the sense that one should cling more tenaciously to the convictions of the herd, but in the sense that one should take seriously the moral injunction to seek and tell the truth.[82] Taken seriously, Nietzsche thinks, this moral commitment to truth undermines trust in morality and its "truths," undermines both its specific lies and its insistence that whatever lies it tells be accepted on faith; through its commitment to truth, then, morality can overcome itself.[83]

This overcoming of morality in which people become more "moral," in the sense of truthful, amounts to the rejection both of the herd's established interpretive framework and of faith as an adequate basis for establishing a framework of interpretation. Consequently, it restores people's ability to be interested in and retain what is new in an encounter; in virtue of their commitment to truth, people no longer simply re-create the familiar but rather become, in Nietzsche's words, more "subtle, faithful, cautious organs of knowledge (*Erkenntniss*)," more faithful to the phenomena than to their faith.[84]

This increased interest in and capacity for the new requires two "losses" that are crucial gains from the perspective of knowledge and freedom. One of these is the loss of self, specifically, the loss of the moral self, the faithful self, the self whose contents are those of the herd. This self must perish if knowledge is to be possible because, as we have seen, for it "knowledge" means making the strange familiar, interpreting the strange through the categories of its convictions, and this precludes genuine knowledge of the strange and new, knowledge of that which by definition is not best captured by those categories.[85] Through the moral command that one always have control of oneself, that one always maintain the proper and established perspective, the moral adherent "has been cut off . . . from all further *instruction*! For one must be able to lose oneself at times, if one wants to learn something from things which we ourselves are not."[86] Nietzsche concludes that the virtue of the subtler soul, the soul capable of knowledge, consists not in tenacious self-control, in rigid conformity of one's will to the dictates of morality, but on the contrary in "deep mistrust of oneself and all virtue."[87] Knowledge, and thus freedom, require losing oneself, losing one's will, losing one's perspective.

Gaining this ability to lose one's perspective is a prerequisite for achieving the second "loss" demanded by knowledge and freedom. This is the loss of the belief that one's perspective, or any other perspective, is eternally adequate. Herd morality, recall, demands above all that one believe precisely this, that one believe its tenets to be not only true but altogether and forever beyond doubt.[88] It is when people adopt this belief that they begin to lose the *capacity* to doubt and question, the capacity to know, and so it is in discarding this belief that they regain those capacities. Thus losing oneself, losing the faith that one's perspective is eternally adequate, and losing the general belief that it is possible in principle for a perspective to be adequate once and for all are the prerequisites for restoring the preconditions of knowledge. They represent the first step in the overcoming of morality at the hands of its own truthfulness, and thus the first step in the overcoming of the enslavement of humanity by unselfing moral conviction.

We have seen that the key to the beginning of the overcoming of morality lies in gaining the ability to encounter phenomena as new. Initially, the most important phenomenon that can be encountered as new is morality itself. As long as morality reigns, everything must be interpreted through its perspective, including morality. From this perspective, morality is simply true, not open to doubt, and not in need of any justification beyond that conferred in virtue of its presumed truth. In particular, morality does not require of itself a utilitarian justification. Although it may have originated in utilitarian concerns about the alleviation of suffering, and although such concerns may continue to attract its adherents to it, once in power morality disowns such concerns as unnecessary and irrelevant to justifying its existence and hegemony.[89] Morality justifies itself simply by claiming that its metaphysics is true and that the practices stemming from that metaphysics are therefore necessary, not in virtue of any claims about the good that it does for individual adherents or for humanity in general. Certainly it also makes these claims about its power to reward its adherents, but strictly speaking they are not part of its self-justification; even if its adherents suffer terribly, or if humanity seems to be on the brink of precipitous decline, these are not grounds for questioning morality.[90]

But the power to see morality anew, from outside morality's perspective, is precisely the power to question morality, to ask about its utility. This point in the development of humanity, the point at which humanity can call its own values into question, is of tremendous importance in Nietzsche's view. He calls it the highest self-reflection of humanity (*Selbstbesinnung der Menschheit*), the revaluation of all values (*Umwerthung aller Werthe*), and the great midday; it is the point, he tells us, at which humanity achieves a perspective beyond good and evil and ushers in the twilight of the idols.

This moment of questioning is one of self-reflection because it involves humanity's achieving sufficient distance from its own perspective, from its own values, to reflect upon those values from a new perspective for the first time.[91] This makes it a revaluation of values, because it is the moment at which humanity no longer accepts the values on faith, but demands that the *value* of the values be explained, the moment at which humanity resolves to value the values only if they can be shown to have value.[92] Nietzsche considers this moment to be the great midday of humanity both because it is the moment of greatest brightness, in which things that have lain in the shadows come to be seen clearly, and because it is a moment of transition from one phase to the next, from the rise of the moral sun to its descent.[93]

Under all of these descriptions, the moment at which humanity repudiates its habitual moral mendacity amounts to its "placing itself beyond good and evil" (*sich jenseits von Gut und Böse zu stellen*). By this Nietzsche means arriving at the insight that "there are no moral facts," getting the illusion of the eternal truth of the moral perspective beneath oneself, getting the self-deception of moral concepts (i.e., the belief that they are always applicable, or ever applicable) behind oneself.[94] As a result, one is able to question the idols of morality – God, the "true" world, the soul, free will; humanity's great midday thus ushers in the twilight of these idols, the moment at which their unquestioned power and authority begins to wane.[95]

Four related questions are most important to the revaluation of values: Where did morality come from? Of what does it consist? For whom and in what sense is it beneficial? And, where is morality taking us? In other words, how did the morality of selflessness come to dominate? How does it draw the distinction between "good" and "evil"? Whose "good" is served by that way of drawing the distinction? And what sort of future will humanity have if it retains these values, and this metaphysics?[96]

Asking these questions for the first time exposes morality's lies as lies.[97] Whereas before this decisive moment the mendacity of morality was impossible to discover because of the insistence that even to challenge faith was a sin, now the metaphysics of weakness and the values and practices it supports are in full view.

Exposing the metaphysics of weakness means showing that its main elements – the "true" world, the soul, free will, and God – are more likely to be inventions than discoveries, more likely to be useful fictions than ultimate truths. Nietzsche does not aim to show, nor does he think that he needs to show, that these metaphysical elements definitively do not exist. Instead, his more modest goal is to show how strong and widespread belief in them could well have come about even if they do not exist, and how, once established, such belief could become nearly impossible to dislodge. In the absence of strong evidence and good arguments supporting the claim that these metaphysical elements do exist, Nietzsche thinks that such demonstrations will suffice to make it unconscionable for people to persist in their old moral beliefs.[98]

We have already encountered Nietzsche's explanation of how belief in the elements of the metaphysics of weakness could have arisen and become entrenched: the metaphysics was invented by people who could endure actuality only through an imaginary flight from it; it spawned a set of values and practices designed to ease and make meaningful their suffering; one of those values was that of unconditional faith, which ultimately eroded the capacity for knowledge and ensured enduring belief in the metaphysics.

But we have not yet encountered what is arguably the most important element of this explanation – namely, Nietzsche's account of how the very functioning of "reason" and language help to establish and shore up metaphysical belief. The central contention in this account is that "reason" and language are structured in such a way that they introduce unity, thinginess (*Dinglichkeit*), substance, duration, identity, and being where there is only becoming, passing away, and change.[99] Language initiates this process, Nietzsche believes, because it is made up of discrete words and concepts, which divide its material into discrete subjects, objects, and properties. "Reason" completes the process by reifying the discrete words and concepts with which language provides it; reason infers from the fact that linguistic subjects, objects, and properties are independent of each other that the world itself must be made up of the kind of independent entities to which the words purportedly refer:

> The word and the concept are the most manifest ground for our belief in this isolation of groups of actions: we do not only *designate* things with them, we think originally that through them we grasp the *true* in things. Through words and concepts we are still continually misled into imagining things being simpler than they are, separate from one another, indivisible, each existing in and for itself. A philosophical *mythology* lies concealed in *language* which breaks out again every moment, however careful one may be otherwise.[100]

The most important entities in which belief is sustained through this collaboration of language and reason are, of course, those central to the metaphysics of weakness: the soul, free will, and God. Each of these, Nietzsche thinks, is a word without a referent. More precisely, each is a word that refers not to a thing, as most people assume, but rather to a multiplicity whose thingliness is merely linguistic. Nietzsche discusses both the will and the soul at length in *Beyond Good and Evil*. Of the will, he writes:

> Willing seems to me to be above all something *complicated*, something that is a unity only as a word... in all willing there is, first of all, a plurality of sensations... in the second place... thinking: in every act of will there is a commanding thought – and do not imagine that this thought can be separated from the "willing"... thirdly, will is not only a complex of feeling and thinking, but above all an *affect*... what is called "freedom of the will" is essentially the affect of superiority... a man who *wills* – commands something in himself which obeys or which he believes obeys.[101]

And of the soul:

> One must also... finish off... that belief which regards the soul as being something indestructible, eternal, indivisible, as a monad, as an *atomon*: *this* belief ought to be ejected from science... But the road to new forms and refinements of the soul-hypothesis stands open: and such conceptions as "mortal soul" and "soul as multiplicity of the subject" and "soul as social structure of the drives and emotions" want henceforth to possess civic rights in science.[102]

Although the "true" world is not a single entity, in the way that the soul, free will, and God are thought to be, Nietzsche thinks that belief in it is also fostered by the tendency of language and reason to introduce stability into the world.[103] This tendency leads not only to belief in the existence of particular stable substances, but also to the more general belief that what is most real must be that which is most stable and unchanging. Given this assumption, and the observation that the actual world is clearly unstable, continually changing and subject to becoming, the conclusion that the actual world is not the real world cannot be avoided. On this account, then, the "true" world must be devoid not only of suffering, but also of any change or decay whatsoever.[104]

With these complementary suggestions about the provenance of the metaphysics of weakness – that it has resulted from the combination of the need of weak sufferers to invent an alternate reality and the tendency of language and "reason" to produce one – Nietzsche believes that he has exposed the falsity of the "truth" claims of morality. By trusting the evidence of the senses – the evidence, that is, that reality is manifold and changing – Nietzsche has undermined the basis for belief in the "true" world, and in the God, souls, and wills that inhabit it. The only world is the actual world in which we live, the "apparent" world, which can no longer be considered "apparent" because there is no "true" world of which it could be the appearance. Nietzsche exults: *"With the true world we have also abolished the apparent world!* (Midday; moment of the short-est shadow; end of the longest error; high-point of humanity; INCIPIT ZARATHUSTRA.)"[105]

Exposing the falsity of the metaphysics of weakness also exposes the fact that the values and practices of the morality of selflessness, which appeared to be "necessary" as long as the metaphysics held sway, are in-deed optional. And this makes it possible to examine those values and practices from the perspectives of history and utility, to ask the ques-tions mentioned earlier: How did the morality of selflessness arise and become dominant? How does it draw the distinction between "good" and "evil"? And for whom are that distinction and the morality of selflessness beneficial?

We have already discussed Nietzsche's answer to the first question. The morality of selflessness arose as a natural consequence of, and comple-ment to, the metaphysics of weakness; once established, the metaphysics and the morality were mutually reinforcing and combined to destroy the preconditions of knowledge, which in turn served to make them virtually impossible to displace.

But just as Nietzsche's explanation of the establishment and domi-nance of the metaphysics of weakness has two strands, so does his expla-nation of the parallel rise, expansion, and entrenchment of the morality of selflessness, and again the second strand emphasizes the role of lan-guage in these developments. Whereas we have just seen Nietzsche argue that the structure of language reinforces belief in the kinds of elements central to the metaphysics of weakness, he now argues that language naturally helps to create, support, and spread herd morality.

This argument consists of two claims. First, Nietzsche contends that "moralities are... only the sign-language of the emotions (*Affekte*)."[106] That is, moral valuations express in words the feelings of their adherents. The question then arises: what feelings are most likely to be expressed in words? Nietzsche's answer is the second contention of the argument: the feelings that come to words are those of which we are most conscious, and those of which we are most conscious are those that we share with the most people. In other words, the feelings most likely to come to words are those of the herd, and the moral valuations represented by those words are therefore most likely to express the herd's perspective. Nietzsche expounds this view of language in *The Joyful Science*[107] and then again in the following passage from *Beyond Good and Evil*:

> Words are sounds designating concepts; concepts, however, are more or less determinate images of frequently recurring and associated sensations, of groups of sensations. To understand one another it is not sufficient to employ the same words; we have also to employ the same words to designate the same species of inner experiences, we must ultimately have our experience *in common*... which groups of sensations are awakened most quickly within a soul, grasp the word (*das Wort ergreifen*), give the command, decides the whole rank-ordering of its values... Now supposing that need has at all times brought together only such human beings as could indicate similar requirements, similar experience by means of similar signs, it follows that... the more similar, more ordinary human beings have had and still have the advantage... Tremendous counter-forces have to be called upon to cross this natural, all too natural *progressus in simile*, the continuing development of mankind into the similar, the ordinary, average, herdlike – into the *common!*[108]

According to Nietzsche, then, the morality of selflessness arises out of the common need of weak and decadent people to alleviate and give meaning to their suffering. Because this need is so common, it is easily communicable, and the values to which it gives rise readily "grasp the word"; what the weak and decadent deem good for themselves comes to be referred to by the word "good," and thus appears to *be* the good, in itself and for everyone.[109]

Having exposed the fact that what the morality of selflessness calls "good" may not in fact be the good in itself allows Nietzsche to turn to the second and third questions posed above: How does decadent morality define "good"? And for whom and in what way is this "good" truly beneficial?

Nietzsche's discussion of the difference between decadent morality, whose primary distinction is that between "good and evil," and noble moralities, whose primary distinction is that between "good and bad," is among the best known in his entire corpus.[110] Briefly, he defines a noble morality as one whose value judgments are essentially affirmations of

the instincts of its adherents; noble people act on their instincts sponta-
neously, find their happiness in doing so, and the moralities they produce
are codifications of their judgment that their instincts and actions are
good. Noble moralities are thus yes-saying moralities, in which people
joyously say yes to themselves, call themselves "good," and only as an af-
terthought, if at all, apply the judgment "bad" to those unlike themselves.

Decadent morality, by contrast, is the result not of action but of reaction. Unlike nobles, decadents do not find their happiness in their
instincts, and so cannot affirm those instincts or the actions expressing
them. Rather, as we have seen, their happiness lies in passivity, in narcosis
or rest from the instincts that tyrannize them. Decadent morality is thus
neither joyous nor yes-saying, but rather the codification of negative judgments; the adherents of decadent morality say no to their own instincts
(and thereby to themselves), and to the noble people who indulge their
instincts without shame and without concern for whether such indul-
gence causes the decadents further suffering. The primary judgment of
decadents is thus that those unlike themselves are "evil." Only secondarily
do they determine themselves to be "good," and then not in virtue of any
positive characteristics but only because they are *not* like the instinctively
happy nobles. The creative work of decadent morality is thus a negative
reaction to that which is external to it, rather than an active affirmation
of itself, and is therefore the supreme expression of the decadents' lack
of freedom.[111]

By drawing the distinction between the pair of distinctions "good and
evil" and "good and bad," Nietzsche is able to show that what the morality
of selflessness deems "good" is good only for a subset of humanity, not for
humanity itself, and even for that subset only in a circumscribed way.[112]
Herd morality is good only for those too weak to endure without it, and
even for them only in the sense that it alleviates their suffering. But, as
we have already noted, the price of this present comfort is the sacrifice of
the future of humanity: the morality of selflessness unnecessarily enslaves
both the weak and the potentially strong to a false metaphysics and an
unselfing set of values and practices.[113] In so doing, it forecloses the
possibility of freedom.

The highest self-reflection of humanity reveals

> that humanity is *not* at all by itself on the right way, that it is by no means
> governed divinely, that, on the contrary, it has been precisely among its holi-
> est value concepts that the instinct of denial, corruption, and decadence
> has ruled seductively. The question concerning the origin of moral values
> is for me a question of the very first rank because it conditions the future
> of humanity... Humanity has so far been in the *worst* of hands... has been
> governed by those who have come on the bad path (*Schlechtweggekommenen*),
> the craftily vengeful, the so-called "saints," these slanderers of the world and
> violators of man.[114]

The recognition that humanity is not on the right way, which results from self-reflection on the values through which that way is determined, allows humanity to "step out of the mastery of accident (*Zufall*) and priests."[115] This is the first step toward achieving the genuine self-mastery that freedom requires, for priests and accident represent the two forces by which Nietzsche thinks humanity has been ruled for thousands of years.[116] Of the two, mastery by the priest – the condition of being directed by the external commands of unselfing morality – has been the more prevalent and oppressive. But Nietzsche grants that such priestly mastery has not been universal; there have been times and places in which particular cultures and individuals have managed to avoid the dominance of the morality of selflessness. He contends, however, that even where humanity has escaped such enslaving decadence, the escape has been accidental, rather than deliberately willed as a means to a better future:

> [T]here is a continual success of individual cases in the most various parts of the earth and out of the most various cultures, with which a *higher type* indeed presents itself: something that in relation to the whole of humanity (*Gesammt-Menschheit*) is a kind of *Übermensch*. Such lucky accidents (Glücksfälle) of great success were always possible and perhaps will always be possible. And even entire races, tribes, peoples can under certain circumstances represent such a lucky hit (*Treffer*).[117]

Historically, then, even in the rare cases in which humanity has escaped moral enslavement it has still not achieved the independence and freedom of self-mastery and self-direction. On the contrary, it has remained subject to the mastery of accident, to having its present and thus the course of its future determined by forces outside itself. If humanity is to be free, therefore, it must not only overcome the false and empty will of unselfing morality, the mastery of the priest, but it must *will* this overcoming, and so also overcome the mastery of accident:

> The problem that I pose here . . . what type of human one ought to *breed* (*züchten*), ought to *will*, as more valuable, more worthy of life, more certain of the future. This more valuable type has already existed often enough: but as a lucky accident, as an exception, never as *willed*. Rather has he been the most feared . . . and out of fear was the opposite type willed, bred, *achieved*: the domestic animal, the herd animal, the sick animal man – the Christian.[118]

The value of the revaluation of values, the value of exposing the metaphysics of weakness as a lie and the values of selflessness as detrimental and enslaving, is precisely that it makes possible this double overcoming of both priests and accident. It obviously overcomes the former, by making explicit their mendacity and perniciousness. But in so doing it also opens the possibility of overcoming the latter, which is a condition of the possibility of freedom: if humans are to be free, they must will their own wills and deliberately make themselves into a higher type; they must no longer be enslaved by disgregation (lack of a will), unselfing (possession by a false moral will), or accident (possession through chance of an externally given noble will).[119]

THE DANGERS OF DESTRUCTION

Overcoming decadent morality and destroying the moral self does open the possibility of overcoming accident and willing a more genuine, more liberated self, but it opens two other possibilities at the same time. Each of these possibilities represents a way in which the attempt to forge a self without morality can fail, in which the promise of a liberated will can be dashed in a regression to dependence.

In the very last section of *Dawn*, headed *We aeronauts (Luft-Schifffahrer) of spirit!*, Nietzsche portrays these two possibilities facing those escaping morality and trying to make their own way into the unknown as those facing birds flying over a sea that has never been crossed:

> All those brave birds which fly out into the distance, into the farthest distance – it is certain! Somewhere or other they will be unable to go on and will perch on a mast or a bare cliff-face – and they will even be thankful for this miserable accommodation! But who could venture to infer from that, that there was *not* an immense open space before them, that they had flown as far as one *could* fly! . . . *Other birds will fly farther!* . . . And whither then would we go? Would we *cross* the sea? . . . Will it perhaps be said of us one day that . . . it was our fate to be wrecked against infinity? Or, my brothers. Or? –[120]

The two ways in which the birds could fail to be up to the challenge of the open sea correspond to the ways in which humans newly liberated from morality could "wreck against infinity" and fail to achieve genuine liberation. Either we might never dare to cross the sea, falsely believing that the birds before us have flown as far as possible, and that we too must therefore seek rest on a familiar fixed point; or we might risk the crossing, flying farther than any previous bird and refusing to rest, yet fail to be up to the challenge and perish along the way.

Nietzsche is particularly concerned about the first possibility. Since humanity has lived within the moral perspective for so long, and since for many it is only that perspective that has enabled them to overcome nihilism by serving as the ground upon which they could forge a will, it is reasonably likely that the prospect of living without morality will be disorienting and frightening. Those for whom this is the case will shrink before the task of willing their own future, of leaving the ground and flying out over the infinite sea to give themselves a will. Instead they will seek the comfort of an alternative ground, "a mast or a bare cliff-face" on which to rest in the middle of the ocean, yet another externally given will.

In a section of *The Joyful Science* headed *In the horizon of the infinite,* Nietzsche warns against this nostalgic urge for a set of metaphysical truths and moral facts by which to live, when we have only so recently become aware of the impossibility of any eternally adequate perspective. Again he uses the imagery of the infinitely open sea:

> We have abandoned the land and embarked by ship! We have destroyed the bridges behind us – still more, we have destroyed the land behind us! Now, little ship, look out! Beside you lies the ocean – true, it does not always roar ... But hours will come when you will realize that it is infinite and that there is nothing more terrible than infinity. Oh, the poor bird that felt free and now strikes the walls of this cage! Woe, when homesickness for the land befalls you, as if there had been more *freedom* there – and there is no longer any "land."[121]

For those who experience the infinite horizon beyond good and evil, created by toppling the view-constricting idols of morality, as a terrible cage, it will be tempting to return to the old moral ground, on which they felt at home and so more free. These people will abandon ship and swim for land, only to discover that there is no way back; the truthfulness that exposed morality prevents our readopting its perspective with the requisite blind faith in its adequacy. Consequently, those who find the ocean's infinite horizon unbearable will have to reclaim other lands from the waters to serve as solid ground upon which they can will.

Nietzsche suggests several ways in which this has been done. One is by replacing the abandoned belief in a God who providentially organizes and directs the universe for the best with a belief in personal providence, a belief that everything happens for the best *for us.* Nietzsche considers the abandonment of the former belief a high point of freedom, in which "we have denied all providential reason and goodness to the beautiful chaos of existence." But he recognizes that for those who experience this "beautiful chaos" as a terrible infinity, "the thought of a personal providence presents itself ... with the most penetrating force," and "we are ... once more in the greatest danger of spiritual unfreedom and have to pass our most difficult test."[122] This most difficult test is that of forging a will without a ground, whether that of God or of personal providence, of forging a will while remaining at sea.

Nietzsche thinks that modern humanity has cheated on this test in another way as well; in its indomitable pursuit of science it has surreptitiously crept back onto the land of faith while loudly proclaiming its independence from it. The scientific age is able to tout its independence from the land of faith because science is simply the natural outgrowth of the same moral and religious commitment to truth that has killed morality and

God. By refusing to allow any unexamined conviction to stand as true, this commitment ultimately issues in science, as the institutionalization of this refusal. The scientific method of demoting every conviction to the rank of an unproven hypothesis would thus appear to place modernity far from faith's shores.

Nietzsche insists, however, that science's self-proclaimed independence from the land of faith is illusory. In a section of *The Joyful Science* headed *How we, too, are still pious*, he asks:

> *To make it possible for this discipline to begin*, must there not already be a conviction? . . . science also rests on a faith . . . The question, whether *truth* is needed, must not only have been affirmed beforehand, but affirmed to the degree that the principle, the faith, the conviction finds expression: "*nothing* is needed *more* than truth, and in relation to it everything else has only second-rank value."[123]

Nietzsche calls this conviction underlying science an "unconditional will to truth," and proceeds in the same section to ask exactly what this will might amount to.

The first possibility is that the scientific will to truth is the will not to allow oneself to be deceived (as one had been deceived by religion and morality). But Nietzsche quickly rejects this interpretation. Such a will, he argues, would have to stem from the belief that to be deceived is harmful and dangerous, which would make the pursuit of science, as the discipline preventing us from being deceived, a matter of prudence and utility. But Nietzsche considers this belief to be patently false, as it can easily be demonstrated that the truth is dangerous in many cases, whereas being mistaken and deceived are often among the very conditions of life.[124] This means that the will to truth, the conviction that truth is the most valuable of all things, can actually be harmful, and must have developed for a reason other than its utility, other than the desire not to be deceived.

Nietzsche concludes that the "'will to truth' does *not* mean 'I will not allow myself to be deceived', but rather – there remains no choice – 'I will not deceive, not even myself'; *and with that we stand on moral ground*."[125] We stand on moral ground with this interpretation of the will to truth because, Nietzsche thinks, there is no utilitarian reason that one would want to avoid deceiving oneself and others; we have already noted that to be deceived is sometimes beneficial, and so surely are deceiving oneself and deceiving others. The will to avoid deceiving can thus be grounded only in the same way that the moral will was: namely, in a metaphysical conviction that the world has a certain character that demands a certain set of values and practices.

In the case of science and the will to truth, this metaphysical conviction is the "faith in a world that is supposed to have its equivalent and measure in human thought and human value concepts, in a 'world of truth' that one can master once and for all (*leztzgültig beikommen*) with the help of our four-square little human reason."[126] But this belief, like that of the metaphysics of morality, is contrary to the evidence of the senses, and so "the truthful, in that audacious (*verwegenen*) and ultimate sense presupposed by the faith in science, *thus affirm another world* than the world of life, nature, and history."[127] The scientific will to truth thus merely disguises the very hostility to and negation of the actual world that it condemns in morality. With this recognition, the same questions that were put to morality in the revaluation of values begin to be directed to science: Why be scientific when the world is not? Whom does the will to truth benefit, and in what sense? What effect will the spreading of the will to truth have on the future of humanity and the chances of its flourishing?

For Nietzsche, then, the erection of the modern idols of personal providence and scientific rationality represents not an improvement in the wake of the destruction of the moral will, but a failure to capitalize on the opportunity that this destruction represents. Both of these responses to the revaluation of values allow people to will, as did morality. But they prevent us from developing a will out of our instincts and our experience of the actual world; instead, like morality, they enable willing only on the basis of a false metaphysical faith, only on the ground of a finite and limiting perspective. Both responses indicate a fear of the infinite, idol-free horizon, and both preclude the formation of an ungrounded and independent will.[128]

If one response to the experience of infinity and chaos is to flee it for the more familiar and secure "freedom" of an externally grounded will, another response that Nietzsche judges to fall short of freedom is that of wallowing in the chaos without forming a will at all. In the parable of the birds, this is the fate of those who fly out over the sea, forsaking rest on land or any other perch, but who lack the instincts or stamina to make the journey successfully; in the terminology of our main theme, it is the fate of those no longer able to believe in morality or any of its surrogates, but too weak to form a will without them. For these people, the twilight of the idols signals a reversion to the initial state of decadence, in which they are subject to the immediate demands of their own instincts as to an external force, unable to form those instincts into a genuine whole, self, or will.

Nietzsche is aware that from the modern perspective these individuals do appear to be free; no longer constrained by belief in God, moral valuations, or appeals to tradition, they are free to act on their instincts, free to do as they please. But he is contemptuous of this understanding of freedom, this "freedom of the individual."[129] In a section of *Twilight of the Idols* headed *Critique of modernity*, Nietzsche writes that the "modern spirit... lives for today, lives very fast – lives very irresponsibly: it is precisely this which one calls 'freedom'."[130] Two sections later he makes clear that this is not what *he* calls freedom, in a paragraph headed *Freedom as I* do not *mean it...*:

> In times like these, to be turned over to (*überlassen sein*) one's instincts is one fatality more. These instincts contradict, disturb and destroy one another... Today the only way to make the individual possible would be by *pruning* him: possible, that is, *whole*... The opposite happens: the claim to independence, to free development, to *laisser aller* is made most heatedly by precisely those for whom no reining in (*Zügel*) *could be too strong* – this applies *in politicis*, it applies in art. But it is a symptom of *decadence*: our modern concept "freedom" is one more proof of the degeneration of instinct.[131]

Thus the celebrated modern "freedom" is really a sign that "individuals" are again at the mercy of, rather than masters over, their own instincts and drives, that they are not really individuals. They may now enjoy this condition of disgregation and dissolution, because they experience it as a liberation from morality, but their enjoyment makes it no less dissolute, and no more fully liberating.

NOBLE HEALTH: THE ESTABLISHMENT OF A FREE WILL

We have now examined both the requirements and the dangers of what Nietzsche calls the no-saying part of convalescence. The chief requirement is saying no to decadent morality, destroying the moral will through a process of education that enables the self-reflective revaluation of values. The chief dangers are the two ways in which one can destroy the moral will yet lapse back into decadence: one can replace the moral will with another external authority to which one is subject, which also gives one a will by extirpating the instincts that one is too weak to organize; or one can eschew such authority and, still too weak to organize one's instincts into a will, be subject to those instincts themselves, reacting immediately to their demands and calling this "freedom."[132]

If convalescence is to succeed, liberating the will, the requirement must be met and both dangers avoided. To do this, the unselfing of morality must be not just undone but repaired; the moral will must be not just destroyed but supplanted with a will that is truly independent. In other words, the process of convalescence must involve not only saying no but also saying yes. In the wake of saying no to morality the convalescent must say yes to herself, forge her own will with its own convictions and values, if she is to avoid the two modes of lapsing back into decadence that threaten those newly emergent from the morality of selflessness.[133]

In *Ecce Homo*, Nietzsche describes his personal experience with embarking on this process:

> My instinct decided inexorably against any longer giving in (*Nachgeben*), going along (*Mitgehn*), mistaking-myself-for-another (*Mich-selbst-verwechseln*) ... Everything seemed to me preferable to that shameful "selflessness,"

into which I was thrown (*geraten*) originally out of ignorance, out of youth, and in which I remained suspended later out of inertia, out of so-called "sense of duty"... That deepest (*unterste*) self, as it were buried and silenced under a continual having-to-listen to other selves... awoke slowly, shyly, doubtfully – but finally it spoke again... To comprehend what this "return to myself" was: a highest kind of convalescence (*Genesung*)![134]

In this final section of Chapter 6 we will examine the yes-saying part of the process of convalescence, by which the self recovers from its unselfing and gives itself a free will.

We have seen that recovering oneself requires both liberating one's instincts from the false will of morality (and its substitutes) and not taking this negative liberation for liberation itself, not turning oneself over to the chaos of unbridled and disorganized instincts. This second requirement means that after having liberated one's instincts one must somehow give them form, organize them as parts of a genuine whole. We have also seen that Nietzsche associates the failure to do this with modernity, with understanding freedom as *laisser aller*, which is necessarily opposed to any form or organization.

Nietzsche provides these interpretations of modernity and selfhood as early as the *Untimely Meditations*. There, in "Richard Wagner in Bayreuth", he writes of the "impotent many-sidedness (*unkräftige Vielseitigkeit*)" of modern life, which inhibits one from being one's "own proper self (*eigentlichen Selbst*)." This quality of "simply being one's own proper self" (*schlichten Eigen- und Selbstheit*) he calls "naïveté." Although naïveté is usually associated with the innocence of the ancient Greeks, Nietzsche makes it clear that in the modern age it is an achievement, something one must work for, something one attains only after one has "simplified" (*vereinfacht*) the many-sidedness of one's nature (*Natur*). The modern, then, has to struggle to be naïve, to be her own proper self, and exhibiting these childlike qualities is actually a sign of "spiritual and ethical manliness (*geistige und sittliche Mannbarkeit*)."[135]

Nietzsche takes up related concepts in the even earlier *Meditation*, "On the Uses and Disadvantages of History for Life", where he associates having become "whole and mature" (*fertig und reif*) with having a "harmonious" personality.[136] This suggests that being one's own proper self, which requires the maturity characteristic of manliness, requires being whole and harmonious. Nietzsche makes this suggestion explicit in "Richard Wagner in Bayreuth," in the context of a discussion of Wagner's concept of loyalty (*Treue*). Wagner's great achievement, according to Nietzsche, lay in remaining loyal to himself, loyal to the idea of being a whole, in the face of the modern pressures to disintegrate. This loyalty was "the great necessity through which alone he could remain whole and himself," but it was threatened by the fact that "each of his drives strove without measure (*in's Ungemessene*), all his talents, joyful in their existence, wanted to tear themselves free individually and satisfy themselves; the greater their abundance, the greater was the tumult and the more hostile was their crossing."[137] Nietzsche goes on to ask, rhetorically, "How is it possible under such conditions to stay loyal, to remain whole?" and to marvel at the fact that Wagner did somehow remain "loyal to his higher self, which demanded of him total-acts (*Gesamttaten*) from his many-voiced being (*vielstimmigen Wesens*), and called him to suffer and learn in order to be capable of these deeds."[138]

Nietzsche thus finds Wagner's genius in his ability to organize and master his many drives, which always threatened to degenerate into chaos, but in such a way that his drives were not extirpated or disarmed: "the bigger and heavier the structure became, the more tightly stretched the arch of ordering and mastering thought . . . And yet neither did this whole (*Summe*) stifle (*erdrücken*) his will to act nor did the individual and most attractive aspects of it lead him astray."[139] In a word, Wagner was a *simplifier* of himself, which for Nietzsche

> consists in . . . having become master over the monstrous abundance and wilderness of an apparent chaos, and in condensing (*zusammendrängen*) into one what was previously incompatible with each other[140] . . . [while also being] the opposite of a polyhistor, a spirit that only carries together (*zusammentragen*) and orders; for [the simplifier] is a unifier (*Zusammenbildner*) and ensouler (*Beseeler*) of what is brought together (*Zusammengebrachten*).[141]

This conception of genius as the ability to simplify, in the sense of being able to master and unify chaos into a mature, harmonious, living whole, is not confined to Nietzsche's early writings. A very similar conception is offered in *Beyond Good and Evil*, in which Nietzsche claims that there are two kinds of genius, whose respective roles are akin to those of male and female in sexual reproduction. One type of genius, to which we will return, impregnates, introducing new material to an existing structure; the other type, with which we are concerned here, enables the material within to develop until it is ready to enter the world and then gives birth to it. This feminine genius has the "task of shaping (*Gestalten*), ripening (*Ausreifens*), completing (*Vollendens*)."[142]

To achieve the proper selfhood that is so elusive for moderns, such a feminine genius must bring her powers of shaping, ripening, and completing to bear on herself. If such a genius were to give birth to herself, as an ensouled unity of formerly disparate drives, she would have forged her own will and thereby have avoided the polar dangers of chaos and external subjection.[143]

But in order to do this she must resist not only the inclination of her individual drives to disgregate, but also the tendency of the values of selflessness to entice her away from herself. Recall that one of Nietzsche's primary criticisms of the dominant modern morality is that it replaces

people's healthy interest in their own long-term development and elevation with a misguided and short-sighted interest in mitigating the current
suffering of others. Should this happen to one with the potential for independence, one with the feminine genius for giving birth to herself, she
will be distracted from the effort required to forge her own will, and will
thus remain unfree.

To give birth to one's own proper self, then, requires that one not
be swayed from the task; it requires that one be selfish, as Nietzsche
acknowledges in *Ecce Homo*: "At this point giving the proper answer to the
question, *how one becomes what one is*, can no longer be avoided. And thus
I touch on the masterpiece of the art of self-preservation – of *selfishness*
(*Selbstsucht*)."[144] So, Nietzsche concludes: liberation requires becoming
your own proper self, becoming your own proper self requires being
selfish, and therefore "the free, the fearless, grow and blossom out of
themselves in innocent selfishness (*unschuldiger Selbstigkeit*)."[145]

Before we examine in more detail what this "innocent selfishness"
involves, we should note two things that it does not involve. First, such
selfishness does not amount to seeking to satisfy one's current needs, or
to pursuing the current purposes of one's will. On the contrary, such
selfishness actually requires sacrificing the needs and purposes of one's
current self for the sake of the development of the self to which one
hopes to give birth. In a section of *Dawn* headed *Ideal selfishness*, Nietzsche
writes:

> Is there a more holy condition than that of pregnancy? To do all that one
> does in the unspoken belief that it must somehow accrue to the good of
> that becoming in us! . . . We have to every essential bringing to completion
> no other relation than that of pregnancy and ought to blow to the wind the
> presumptuous talk of "willing" and "creating." This is *ideal selfishness*: always
> to care and to keep watch and to hold the soul still, so that our fruitfulness
> shall *come to a beautiful end* (*schön zu Ende gehe*).[146]

Second, being innocently selfish does not mean that one is concerned
with ends valuable only to oneself, even when one's "self" is understood
in the larger sense just discussed. On the contrary, Nietzsche's point is
precisely that the revaluation of values should show us that we can be
most valuable to humanity not by making it comfortable in the present,
but by paving the way for its liberation in the future.[147] And since the
future liberation of humanity depends on the liberation of those few
individuals in the present who are capable of it, which in turn requires
that those individuals selfishly devote themselves to becoming what they
are, their "selfishness" is actually the greatest gift they can offer to others.
Nietzsche is trying to demonstrate the truth of a claim that he makes
in *Ecce Homo*: namely, that it is a "naïve conceptual error (*Naivetät des
Fehlgriffs*)" to believe that "'unegoistic' and 'egoistic' are opposites."[148]

Since being enticed away from oneself, either by short-term concern for others or by one's own chaotic drives, is the greatest threat to carrying one's pregnancy to full term, this healthy, nonvulgar variety of selfishness involves having what Nietzsche calls an instinct of self-defense:

> Much not to see, not to hear, not to let approach oneself (*an sich herankommen lassen*) – first cleverness (*Klugheit*), first proof that one is no accident but a necessity. The appropriate (*gangbare*) word for this instinct of self-defense is taste ... to *react as rarely as possible*, and to avoid situations and conditions where one would be condemned to suspend, as it were his "freedom," his initiative, and to become a mere reagent.[149]

Earlier in *Ecce Homo*, Nietzsche describes this instinct as a kind of "self-walling (*Selbst-Vermauerung*)," and argues that it is necessary to a successful "spiritual pregnancy," because "in the deep tension to which pregnancy condemns the spirit and, at bottom (*im Grunde*), the whole organism, the accident (*Zufall*), every kind of external stimulus has too vehement an effect, 'strikes' ('*einschlägt*') too deep."[150]

Moreover, the closer one is to having become one's own proper self, the more difficult such defense of this self becomes. Recall that one of Nietzsche's models for a highly developed self is that of a carefully constructed "ordering and mastering arch," which gives shape to what was previously a mere heap of independent stones. The larger and more complicated this arch is, and the closer it is to completion, the less the chance that any stone still external to it can be successfully incorporated, and the more likely it is that such stones will imprecisely fill the remaining gaps in the arch, weakening the existing structure and ultimately destroying the whole.

Returning to the organic model of spiritual pregnancy, Nietzsche describes this problem of incorporating the right stimuli in order to complete one's development, while at the same time rejecting those that would cause one to miscarry, as a "question of nutrition (*Ernährung*)." Specifically, the question is: "How must *you* nourish yourself, to attain your maximum of force, of *virtu* – of moraline-free (*moralinfrei*) virtue in the Renaissance style?"[151] Again, he thinks this problem becomes more acute as one gets closer to term: "according to the degree to which a spirit is *sui generis*, the limits of what is permitted to him, that is, beneficial (*nützlich*) to him, are narrow and narrower."[152]

We can also see from these remarks that Nietzsche thinks the problem has no generic solution, the question no generic answer. Just as the stone that completes one arch might cause the collapse of another, the food best for one person might make another seriously ill. There is a generic solution only in the sense that each person who would give birth to herself must know what nourishment *she* requires to make a successful delivery.[153]

The precondition of knowing what to allow into one's system, according to Nietzsche, is that one be healthy and well-constituted. This might appear backward, for we usually think of health as the *result* of a good diet, rather than its cause. But as we saw earlier, Nietzsche thinks that this usual understanding confuses cause and effect. In his view, only if one is already healthy will one have the instinct to do what is healthful and productive of virtue:

> How does one recognize the well-constituted?...He has a taste only for what is salubrious (*zuträglich*) for him; his pleasure and delight cease where the measure of salubriousness is transgressed (*überschritten*)...He instinctively collects *his* sum from all he sees, hears, lives through: he is a principle of selection, he lets much fall through. He is always in his own company...He honors by *choosing*, by *admitting*, by *trusting*...He tests the stimulus that approaches...He knows how to forget – he is strong enough that everything *must* turn out best for him...[he] is the opposite of a decadent.[154]

By contrast, if one is unhealthy and decadent, if one's instincts are not good, one may be able to imitate healthy and virtuous behavior, but such imitation cannot make one truly healthy or virtuous. An unhealthy person might be able to go on a diet, but the very fact that "going on a diet" is a deliberate and unusual step indicates that such a person is only imitating virtue and health, and suggests that the diet will not last very long. A healthy person does not need to go on a diet, because her regular diet is naturally what is good for her – the foods she enjoys and the foods she needs to flourish are identical.

We should note that in the preceding passage Nietzsche includes knowing how to forget among the attributes of the well-constituted. This might seem odd, but forgetting is important, because no matter how carefully one tests the stimuli one encounters to see if they are salubrious, and no matter how instinctively one takes in only those that are, in the process one is certain to encounter those that are not. The ability to forget such encounters with stimuli that are at best unhelpful and at worst actively detrimental is crucial, lest one become distracted and burdened to the point that one's carefully constructed will disintegrates. When building an arch, one must be able to drop heavy stones that one has picked up but that prove not to be useful; when nourishing oneself, one must be able to discard those things on one's fork or in one's mouth or stomach that cannot be productively incorporated. Without forgetfulness, which he describes as "an active...positive capacity of inhibition (*Hemmungsvermögen*)...a doorkeeper, a maintainer of soulful (*seelischen*) order," Nietzsche writes, there is "no happiness, no cheerfulness, no hope, no pride, no present,"[155] no action and no belief in oneself.[156]

On the other hand, being one's very own self, being the master of one-self, being able to take responsibility for oneself, also requires memory; forging a will requires not only that one forget what cannot be incorpo-rated, what would destroy the will, but also that one remember what has already been internalized, that one not allow the will to be broken by dis-tracting impulses and encounters. In her eagerness to find the keystone that would complete the arch, the builder must not allow the stones pre-viously placed to shift or fall; in her quest for the ultimate nourishment that would best allow her to complete her pregnancy, the mother cannot neglect to feed the partially developed fetus. Nietzsche describes mem-ory, the capacity with which the genius of giving birth to herself must be endowed, as that

> with the help of which forgetfulness is suspended in certain cases – namely, in the cases where promising ought to be... [memory is] an active *willing* not to let go again (*Nicht-wieder-los-werden-wollen*), a continued and continual willing (*Fort- und Fortwollen*) of the once willed, a proper *memory of the will*: so that between the original "I will," "I will act" and the proper discharge of the will, its *act*, a world of strange new things, conditions, even acts of will may be interposed harmlessly, without breaking this long chain of will.[157]

We can finally conclude that such a genius is one who can strike an appropriate balance between memory and forgetting.[158] She must forget all that she cannot incorporate, while remembering everything that she has already incorporated. This appropriate balance will therefore vary from person to person, as each will have a different measure or limit to what she is able to internalize.[159] In Nietzsche's terms, this ability to internalize is proportional to the strength of the person: the stronger one is, the more one will find nourishing, the more one will be able to master and order in the arch that is one's will. The weakest person, then, who is least able to incorporate external stimuli successfully, has the greatest need of forgetting, and the strongest, who can incorporate the most, has the greatest need of memory.[160]

Since memory is necessary to forging a long will and becoming what one is, whatever is necessary to the creation of memory is indispensable to the prospect of independence. Surprisingly, Nietzsche considers one of the most important preconditions of memory to be the development and dominance of the very herd morality from which independence is sought.

Herd morality is necessary because it makes humanity calculable and regular, which it must be if memory is to be possible. Continuing the passage just cited, Nietzsche writes: "But how many things [memory] presupposes!... Man himself must first have become *calculable* (*berechen-bar*), *regular* (*regelmässig*), *necessary*, even in his own representation of him-self, in order finally to be able to vouch for (*gut sagen zu können*) his

own future, in the way that one who promises does!" He then describes
the role of herd morality in this process of making humanity regular, as
he recounts what he calls the "long history of the origin of responsibility": "The monstrous work of what I have called the 'ethics of custom'
(*'Sittlichkeit der Sitte'*) ... has here its meaning, its great justification, however much severity, tyranny, stupidity and idiocy also dwells within it: with
the help of the ethics of custom and the social straightjacket, man was
actually *made* calculable."[161]

The means by which herd morality has made humanity calculable
should be familiar, for they are precisely the same means by which we saw
it unself humanity earlier. The most important of these for the creation
of memory, according to Nietzsche, were ascetic codes of behavior and
strict punishment for violating those codes. First, he addresses asceticism:

> "How does one create a memory for the human-animal?" ... Pain is the
> most powerful means of aiding mnemonics. In a certain sense the whole
> of asceticism belongs here: a few ideas ought to be made ineliminable
> (*unauslöschlich*), omnipresent, unforgettable, "fixed" ... and ascetic proce-
> dures and forms of life are means of detaching (*lösen*) these ideas from
> concurrence with all other ideas, in order to make them "unforgettable."[162]

Then he turns to punishment:

> Without question we must seek the proper (*eigentliche*) *effect* of punish-
> ment above all in a sharpening of prudence (*Klugheit*), in a lengthening of
> memory, in a will henceforth to go to work more cautiously, mistrustfully,
> secretly, in the insight that one is once-and-for-all too weak for many things,
> in a kind of improvement in self-judgment. That which can in general be
> achieved through punishment, in men and animals, is the increase of fear,
> the sharpening of prudence, the mastery of desires.[163]

Prior to the institution of such social codes, Nietzsche imagines, people lived instinctively, without the regularity necessary for memory, and
therefore without the self-mastery and responsibility necessary to independent willing. But with the appearance and dominance of classes who
organized and gave form to the social world according to their own instincts, imposing their own codes on others, people who were not in those
classes were no longer able to express their own form-giving instinct. Consequently this instinct, which Nietzsche also calls the instinct of freedom
or the will to power, became latent and turned inward; the weak became
capable of discharging their will to power only on themselves.[164]

As we saw earlier, this development is the beginning of bad conscience.
But whereas before we examined the role of bad conscience in furthering
the unselfing process of morality, we can now see that it also has a role
in overcoming the morality of selflessness and enabling the creation of
genuine and liberated selves. This is because bad conscience completes

the forging of memory and will begun by asceticism and punishment. Bad conscience is

> the *instinct of freedom* (spoken in my language: the will to power): only here the matter (*Stoff*) on which the form-developing (*formbildende*) and ravishing (*vergewaltigende*) nature of this force vents itself (*sich auslässt*) is the man himself, his whole ancient animal self – and *not*, as in that larger and more conspicuous phenomenon, the *other* man, the *other* men. This secret self-ravishment, this artist's cruelty, this delight in giving himself – as a hard, recalcitrant, suffering material – a form, in burning in a will, a critique, a contradiction, a contempt, a No... eventually this whole active "bad conscience"... as the proper womb of ideal and imaginative events (*Ereignisse*) also brought to light an abundance of strange new beauty and affirmation (*Bejahung*).[165]

So bad conscience, together with the asceticism and punishment from which it is inseparable, and the ethics of custom from which they all spring, serves to prune and form desires and instincts that have grown unruly. The "ripest fruit" of this pruning Nietzsche calls

> the *sovereign individual*, equal only to himself, liberated (*losgekommene*) again from the ethics of custom, the autonomous, supra-ethical (*übersittliche*) individual (for "autonomous" and "ethical" are mutually exclusive), in short the man who *may promise* out of his own long, independent will – and in him a proud... consciousness of a proper power and freedom, a feeling of perfecting humanity. This free-become individual, who actually *may promise*, this master of *free* will, this sovereign... the "free" man, the possessor of a long, unbreakable will, has in this possession also his *measure of value*: looking out upon others from himself, he honors or he despises... The proud knowledge of the extraordinary privilege of responsibility, the consciousness of this rare freedom, this power over himself and fate has penetrated into his deepest depths and has become instinct, the dominating instinct... The sovereign man calls this [instinct] his conscience...[166]

Bad conscience is thus a self-negation or no-saying that ultimately enables a wholly new kind of yes-saying, a self-affirmation indispensable to freedom. It says no to the instincts that society deems unacceptable, forces those creative (and therefore necessarily destructive) instincts to turn inward, and thus forces the individual to create herself and her will, to achieve mastery over the instincts that once dominated her by giving them form. The pride that results from this achievement, from being able to vouch for her own future, is what then allows the sovereign individual to affirm herself.[167] She no longer has to take pride in being an adherent of morality, because she is now capable of willing without it.

In Nietzsche's view, then, the arrival of bad conscience through the imposition of herd morality is a development of genuinely historical significance, one that changes the entire future of humanity. Indeed, it

even changes the ontological status of humanity, making what would otherwise be just another animal beholden to its instincts *into* humanity. By
giving itself the ability to promise, humanity gives itself promise, makes
itself the promise of and the bridge to something other than what it has
been.[168] In the vocabulary of giving birth to oneself, bad conscience is "a
sickness ... but a sickness like pregnancy is a sickness."[169] In other words,
it makes humanity ill, but this illness is indispensable if humanity is to give
birth to itself as something new, as the species of animal whose members
are capable of giving birth to themselves as self-responsible, sovereign,
free individuals.

The temporary dominance of decadence, then, is necessary if humanity is to achieve a future in which it is no longer decadent. Certainly, this
future cannot arrive if, as Nietzsche fears it may, decadence becomes permanent through the destruction of the preconditions of knowledge. But
risking this danger has proved to be unavoidable if such a future is to
arrive, for humanity can only forge an independent will out of strength,
instead of accepting one given to it in weakness, by suffering through the
transformative, decadent sickness of bad conscience.[170]

We have already noted that Nietzsche understands nobility to be the
opposite condition of decadence, so we should expect that in overcoming
decadence by giving birth to themselves as sovereign individuals people
should also become noble. If we compare Nietzsche's descriptions of
nobility to his descriptions of the process of forging a will and of the
resulting sovereign individual, we see that this is indeed the case.

In the first place, recall that becoming a sovereign individual requires
an instinct for self-walling, for incorporating only what is nourishing for
oneself, and that this instinct is especially important, and especially rare,
in a modern age that offers many unhealthy choices and is unaccus-
tomed to self-restraint. The same instinct is required for nobility, and
again modernity presents the same obstacles:

> Whoever has the drives of a high, selective soul, and only rarely finds his
> table laid, his nourishment prepared, will be in great danger at all times:
> but today the danger is extraordinary. Thrown into a noisy and rabble-filled
> (*pöbelhaftes*) age, with which he does not want to eat out of the same dish,
> he can easily perish of hunger and thirst, or, in case he finally "sets to"
> (*zugreift*) – of sudden nausea.[171]

Being noble, then, like becoming sovereign, requires not letting everything come to oneself, not tasting everything. In Nietzsche's phrase, both
require giving oneself a measure and living within its limits, even when
confronted by the unlimited, infinite possibilities and temptations arising
from the death of morality.[172]

Second, in both cases the aim of such measured self-walling is becoming who one is, instead of being enticed away from oneself, unselfed, by

the herd; rather than thinking and acting out of a common and empty moral will that one has been given, those who would be noble, sovereign individuals seek to give themselves a will that is neither common nor empty, not shared by many ("equal only to itself") and defined by its positive virtues. In seeking to think and act out of this self-developed will, they seek independence and responsibility, both of which are foreign to the moral adherent.[173]

We can conclude, then, that the noble and the sovereign individual are one and the same. The noble individual results from the development of an independent will, and subsequently takes responsibility for the actions she performs out of it, evaluating herself not according to an externally given code but out of her own will. Such individuals, who take pride in their "free will" – in being responsible for what they will and do, but *only* for what they will and do – evaluate themselves according to their own measure."[174]

It goes without saying that the noble individual's self-evaluation is not at all equivalent to self-indulgence or *laisser aller*; the noble individual is not distinguished from the moral adherent by a lack of obedience. Rather, the difference is that the noble, sovereign individual obeys commands that she gives herself, instead of commands imposed by an external authority.[175] The will of the noble individual, as evinced again by Wagner, is "a single inner lawfulness," "a mastering passion become conscious of itself and grasping-together (*zusammenfasst*) [the individual's] whole nature."[176]

From the perspective of the herd and the community the development of such individuals, who have the strength to develop evaluations out of themselves and live according to those evaluations, is a threat. For the displacement of faith and herd judgment by individual evaluation can only signal social corruption, the decay of the belief that one way of thinking and acting is best for all, and thus the decay of such uniform behavior.[177]

Replacing the single social code of decadent morality is a plurality of noble codes.[178] A noble code is not primarily distinguished from the decadent one by its content, but rather by the mode of its production (although this will also lead to differences in content). As we have seen, noble moralities affirm the virtues of their adherents as "good," whereas decadent morality brands the traits of those who do *not* adhere to it as "evil" and only secondarily defines as good the general trait of *not* being like those who are evil. Now we can see that this is because noble moralities are produced by those who evaluate out of themselves, who forge their own wills, which are in effect tables of their own virtues. The development of noble individuals is thus at the same time the development of noble moralities, the creation and naming of noble values.

There is necessarily a plurality of noble moralities because there are many ways in which an individual can organize her instincts under a ruling passion in order to form a will. By contrast, there is only one decadent morality because its will is empty, its only content being the denial of instinct and self, the negation of whatever positive noble contents its adherents should encounter.[179] Decadent morality thus insists, as we saw earlier, that it *alone* is morality, that it is the best way of life for everyone. Noble moralities do not make this claim and, moreover, do not *want* their way of life to appeal to everyone; noble individuals struggle to develop their *own* virtues, the virtues that set them apart and make life worth living *for them*, and would find these virtues cheapened if they were adopted by all.[180]

For Nietzsche, this makes noble moralities significantly more "moral" than decadent morality. Recall that decadent morality begins the overcoming of itself by pursuing its own central value of truthfulness to the point that it undermines its own metaphysical foundation. We can now see that this ultimately brings to light another truth denied by the morality of selflessness: not only is decadent morality not best for everyone, but *no* single moral code is best.

Nietzsche makes this point repeatedly in *Beyond Good and Evil*, where he writes that "it is immoral to say: 'what is right for one is appropriate (*billig*) for another'," that "what is appropriate for one can be inappropriate for another," and that moralities addressing themselves to all people "generalize where generalization is impermissible."[181] In *The Joyful Science* he expresses it in the language of spiritual health and nourishment with which we have been concerned:

> The beloved medical moral formula... "Virtue is the health of the soul" – must... be changed: "*Your* virtue is the health of *your* soul." For there is no health in-itself... and the more one abjures (*verlernt*) the dogma of the "equality of men," the more must the concept of a *normal* health, along with a normal diet, and a normal course of illness be abandoned by our physicians... Only then would it be time... to locate (*setzen*) the peculiar (*eigentumlich*) virtue of each in the health of his soul: which certainly could appear in one person like the opposite of health in another.[182]

Decadent morality's claim to be morality for all is immoral, and not merely mistaken, both because morality's lies harm those who cannot flourish under them and thereby threaten the future of humanity as a whole, and because those making the claim *know* that it is a harmful lie.[183] As we have already noted, the morality of selflessness is detrimental to those who are strong enough to flourish without it but who are liable to catch the decadent contagion if forced to live with it. It is detrimental to the future of humanity because its insistence that it is the one eternal norm, horizon, or perspective threatens humanity with stagnation, with permanent confinement to decadent dependence.[184] Contrary to decadent morality, there is no single path to the future. What is needed is not morality but a plurality of amoral moralities, a varied nobility, gods but no God.[185]

Noble moralities will thus necessarily be both similar to and different from each other. They will necessarily share a commitment to the moral perspectivism just described, a commitment to fighting the decadent, antiperspectival belief in the good-in-itself. They will therefore also share a process of formation; without belief in a single good, noble moralities will have to arise through experimentation intended to determine the particular good for those conducting the experiment. Each noble table of virtues will represent the summation of such an experiment. The difference between noble moralities will lie in the contents of these tables, which will differ because each is a recipe for the healthy spiritual nourishment of a particular person or group of people with particular needs and goals.[186]

Nietzsche emphasizes that each of these noble moralities will, like decadent morality, be a tyranny, in the sense that they will compel their adherents to think and act in certain ways. But unlike decadent tyranny, noble tyranny is compatible with freedom, and even makes it possible. This is because, to reiterate a point already made, for Nietzsche freedom is opposed not to compulsion – freedom is not the chaos of *laisser aller* – but rather to *external* compulsion, to the tyranny of a will forged not by oneself but by an alien authority. Freedom actually requires tyranny, in the sense that compulsion is required to organize disgregated instincts into a unified will out of which one can take responsibility for one's actions and vouch for one's future, but the tyranny must be internal and noble, rather than external and decadent.[187] If successful, such internal tyranny is ultimately not experienced as tyrannical – as behavior that originally had to be compelled comes to be automatic, so that one feels at home and free in performing it – but it remains tyrannical nonetheless.[188]

The internal tyrannies of noble moralities are liberating because the virtues they codify and instill in people are invented out of personal needs, out of the conditions of the lives of their adherents, rather than (as in the case of decadent morality) out of respect for the abstract concept of virtue itself.[189] The virtues of these moralities, then, are natural and native to their adherents, rather than foreign to them.[190]

In such naturalistic, noble moralities the "shalls" determine the "shall nots," and both fulfill the instincts of the people obeying them. In other words, these moralities command people to "do this again and again," so that what is done determines what is foregone, and over time what does not belong to a person or a people drops away, and no longer needs to be resisted or warned against.[191] Nietzsche calls this a "return to nature," but one that is not a regression to unorganized instinct, but rather an elevation in which we recover those instincts as component virtues of an organized will.[192] Whereas decadent morality linked our natural instincts to bad conscience, made us feel guilty for having and expressing them, and strove to extirpate them altogether, this return to nature links the *un*natural instincts of that morality – to slander this life and aspire to transcend it in a beyond – to bad conscience, and links the instinct to follow our own instincts, even where they contradict the customs of the herd, to good conscience.[193]

With this achievement – the development of a noble table of virtues, the goals of which are exclusively oriented to this actual world – convalescence is complete, and the will is liberated. The nobles have transformed the conditions of their life into spiritual form, and in the process have transformed themselves into different people and attained self-mastery.[194] They are now able to dispose of themselves (*über sich selber verfügen*), which Nietzsche calls the opposite of slavishness, through having given style to their character. This "great and rare art"

> is practiced by he who surveys all the strengths and weaknesses offered by his nature, and then fits them into (*einfügt*) an artistic plan, until each appears as art and reason and even the weaknesses delight the eye . . . Finally, when the work is completed (*vollendet*), it becomes evident how it was the compulsion of a single taste, which mastered and formed (*bildete*) both large and small . . . It will be the strong and domineering natures that find their finest joy in such a compulsion, in such a restriction (*Gebundenheit*) and perfection (*Vollendung*) under their own law . . . Conversely, it is the weak characters without power over themselves that hate the restriction of style: they feel that if this bitter and evil compulsion were imposed on them they would be demeaned – they become slaves as soon as they serve; they hate to serve. Such spirits . . . are always out to shape or interpret themselves and their environment as free nature – wild, arbitrary, fantastic, disorderly, surprising.[195]

The nobles have created their own justification for their way of living and thinking; in Nietzsche's terms they have created their own sun.[196] And in so doing they have liberated their wills. In *The Joyful Science*, at the end of a long passage primarily devoted to criticizing Wagner for his Schopenhauerian errors, Nietzsche nonetheless insists that only if we remain faithful to Wagner's characteristic of remaining faithful to himself, which the nobles just described have done, will we make ourselves free:

> Enough, that his life had justification (*Recht*) before itself, and remains justified – this life, which calls to each of us: "Be a man and do not follow me – but yourself! But yourself!" *Our* life also ought to remain justified

before ourselves! We also ought to grow and blossom out of ourselves, free and fearless in innocent selfishness! And in the contemplation of such a man, these sentences still sound to me today as before: "that passion is better than stoicism and hypocrisy; that to be honest, even in evil, is better than losing oneself to the ethics of tradition; that the free man can be good as well as evil, but that the unfree man is a disgrace to nature, and has a share in no heavenly or earthly comfort; finally, that each who wants to become free must become so through himself, and that freedom falls into the lap of no one as a miraculous gift."[197]

FREEDOM BEYOND WILLING: FROM NOBILITY TO TRAGEDY

1. The Incomplete Freedom of Nobility

In the previous chapter, we examined why Nietzsche understands freedom to require that one forge one's own will. Failing to do so amounts to being condemned to one of two styles of decadent dependence: either one is determined by a will forged and imposed externally, or one is determined by instincts and drives that, subject to no will, serve as master and tyrant.

We also examined what forging one's own will involves. Primarily, it involves giving birth to oneself as a living whole, by simplifying and integrating the chaos that results from the destruction of the moral will. For this process to succeed, we saw that one must be selfish. One must build a wall that excludes what one cannot integrate, and one must forget that which one encounters but cannot use in the building of the wall. Furthermore, once built, the wall must also serve to retain what has been integrated; one must remember what one places in one's will. If one employs the combination of forgetfulness and memory appropriate to one's strength, to one's ability to incorporate the external without destroying the whole that one is developing, one will succeed in giving oneself a measure. This measure, the limit that determines what one can incorporate and what one must exclude, is one's own will, from which one evaluates, and the evaluations of which one obeys.

Finally, we also examined the consequences of forging one's own will. Such a process necessarily results in a separation of the individual from the herd, as the individual no longer accepts the judgments and customs of the herd unreflectively, but rather makes her own judgments and gives herself new customs more appropriate to her own needs. These new customs that distinguish noble individuals and groups from the herd and from each other are no less tyrannical than the customs they replace, but their tyranny is internal rather than external, and thus liberating.

Such noble liberation is an improvement on the liberation made possible by the moral will, just as moral liberation is an improvement on the complete lack of freedom suffered by the merely disgregated. But nonetheless, Nietzsche thinks that noble liberation remains incomplete and, if freedom is to be realized, must be overcome.[1]

The primary problem with the sovereign, noble will is that, like the moral will before it, it is fixed and stagnant. It improves on the moral will, as we saw, by not insisting that its particular measure is the appropriate measure for all, that its particular nourishment is conducive to the health of everyone. This improvement reduces the stagnation of humanity to a degree, as it enables various groups and individuals to transform themselves in ways that were previously impossible. The result is a proliferation of genuinely different wills, customs, and nobilities. However, each of these noble wills is still constituted by a fixed measure that determines both what it must exclude and how it must evaluate or interpret what it allows itself to engage. In other words, once forged, each noble will represents an established perspective that is limiting in exactly the same way that the established moral perspective was. Such a perspective, as we saw, prevents one from truly experiencing what is external to oneself. Thus the noble will, like the moral will, is fixed and stagnant, unable to experience the new as new, and therefore unable to grow or transform itself.[2]

The noble will is more free than the moral will because it has developed its own customs out of itself, has given itself its own measure. However, the fixing or forging of this measure, and the consequent exclusion of what is external, other, and new, makes its freedom incomplete. For the noble will is determined not only by what it has experienced and integrated into its measure, but also by what it has excluded from its measure and not experienced.[3] To be determined by such an external other is to be dependent upon something other than oneself, which is to fail to be independent and completely free.

The lesson to be learned is a Hegelian one: independence cannot be won outside an other, but must be won in the other; by fleeing or refusing to engage an other, one allows it to determine oneself externally. One can therefore liberate oneself only by engaging the other and making its determination of oneself one's own.[4]

But this is precisely what the noble, sovereign individual refuses to do. Having built her wall, set herself apart, and justified her own way of living to herself, the noble individual has no need or use for the new or the strange, for that which exceeds her measure. In the previous chapter we saw that this noble characteristic is necessary to overcome the typically modern susceptibility to distracting stimuli that can prevent one from ever forging a will out of chaos. But now we can see that by itself this same characteristic can frustrate liberation by allowing one's will to stagnate and to be determined by an externality to which it stands in fixed opposition.[5]

What freedom calls for is clearly a complementary combination of nobility and modernity, of setting oneself apart from and holding oneself open to the chaotic stimuli beyond one's measure. Nietzsche highlights these differences between modern and noble individuals, and makes it clear that he finds advantages in the strengths unique to both, in the following lengthy passage from *Beyond Good and Evil*. First, he emphasizes the distinctively modern virtue and its advantages:

> The historical sense ... to which we Europeans lay claim as our specialty, has come to us in the wake of the mad and fascinating semi-barbarism into which Europe has been plunged through the democratic mingling of classes and races ... The past of every form and mode of life, of cultures that formerly lay close beside or on top of one another, streams into us "modern souls" thanks to this mingling, our instincts now run back in all directions, we ourselves are a kind of chaos – : in the end, as I said before, "the spirit" perceives its advantage in all this. Through our semi-barbarism in body and desires we have secret access everywhere such as a noble age never had ... "historical sense" means virtually the sense and instinct for everything, the taste and tongue for everything: which at once proves it to be an ignoble taste ... but we – accept precisely this confusion of colors, this medley of the most delicate, the coarsest and the most artificial, with a secret confidence and cordiality.

Then, he explains why the nobles cannot share it:

> The very definite Yes and No of their palate, their easily aroused disgust, their hesitant reserve with regard to everything strange, their horror of the tastelessness even of a lively curiosity, and in general that bad will of a noble and self-sufficient (*selbstgenügsamen*) culture to admit to a new desire, a dissatisfaction with what is one's own, an admiration for what is foreign: all this disposes them unfavorably towards even the best things in the world which are not their property or *could* not become their prey – and no sense is so unintelligible to such men as the historical sense and its obsequious plebian curiosity.[6]

Finally, he turns to the noble virtue unavailable to the moderns:

> That which we men of the "historical sense" find hardest to grasp, to feel, taste, love, that which at bottom finds us prejudiced and almost hostile, is just what is complete and wholly mature in every art and culture, the proper nobility in works and in men, their moment of smooth sea and halcyon self-sufficiency, the goldness and coldness displayed by all things which have become perfect. Perhaps our great virtue of the historical sense stands in a necessary opposition to good taste, or to the very best taste at any rate ... We are able ... only with difficulty, hesitation, and compulsion to reproduce in ourselves moments and miracles when a great power voluntarily

halted before the measureless (*Maasslosen*) and unlimited (*Unbegrenzten*) – when a superfluity of subtle delight in sudden restraint and petrifaction, in standing firm and fixing oneself (*Feststehen und Sich-Fest-Stellen*), was enjoyed on a ground still trembling. Measure is alien to us ... what we itch for is the infinite, the unmeasured ... we let fall the reins before the infinite, we modern men, we semi-barbarians – and there first attain our state of bliss, where we are also most – in danger.[7]

This passage nicely summarizes the complementary features of modernity and nobility, and enables us to see why freedom requires both: in isolation, both the modern and the noble "virtues" are vices that prevent the achievement of genuine independence; but together, these "vices" become truly virtuous, and make freedom possible. Modernity, as we saw in the preceding chapter, is unable to give itself a measure, to develop self-sufficiency, to forge its own will while at sea. Instead, it mingles instincts of all kinds without being able to combine them into a mature whole, and succumbs to the chaos of infinity. Nobility, on the other hand, as we have just discussed, voluntarily gives itself a measure and a self-sufficient will, but only by permanently excluding the strange, the foreign, and the new. On its own, the modern "virtue" of continual and indiscriminate openness precludes freedom by preventing the formation of a will. And on its own, the noble "virtue" of self-sufficient closure precludes freedom by allowing its forged will to be dependent on the other that it excludes as external. In the preceding chapter we saw how the process of noble will formation is able to overcome the sickness of modern decadence. In this chapter, we must now examine Nietzsche's explanation of how nobility can be reinfected with modern openness in order to overcome the limitations of its own healthy closure.[8]

DESTRUCTION OF THE NOBLE WILL: HEALTHY REINFECTION

We have already seen that for Nietzsche the path to freedom involves a series of stages in which a variety of selves and wills is found and forged, lost and destroyed. The moral will is created in order to liberate humanity from disgregated decadence. But morality enslaves humanity by unselfing it, by giving each person the same empty will to nothing, and so the moral will must be destroyed. The destruction of the moral will through the revaluation of values offers the possibility of liberation, but also the possibility of regression, either to the state of disgregation, or to a condition of dependence on another externally given will (such as the will to truth). Consequently, a new will, a sovereign and noble will, must be created. Such a will, not given to the individual but forged by her, increases liberation by internalizing the instincts and customs that the individual obeys. However, as we have just seen, even this will that is one's own becomes a hindrance to freedom, by making one dependent on a fixed and external other for one's determination. Thus the noble self, like the moral self before it, must be lost; freedom requires that the noble will, no less than the moral will, be destroyed.

The noble self must be lost, the noble will destroyed, in two senses. First, the memory that allows the will to retain its constructed measure must fail; the measure that defines the limits of the self must be forgotten. This will prepare the self to be lost in the second sense. For limits that have been forgotten can be transgressed, and in this case such transgressions amount to an active destruction of the will, a loss of the self in which its measure is not only forgotten but redefined.[9]

The first self-losing amounts to a kind of amnesia, in which the tremendous efforts that went into developing a memory strong enough to construct and stabilize a noble will are undone. The struggle to develop a memory, we recall, was the struggle to develop the ability to remain committed to a goal or purpose that could serve to organize a variety of drives into a single will, even in the face of competing goals that might intervene before the achievement of the original goal. The problem introduced by success in this struggle, we have now seen, is that such a commitment forces one to exclude everything external to it, everything new and strange. Consequently, the commitment and the memory must be weakened, the all-consuming goal and purpose forgotten, in order to reopen oneself to the new.

Nietzsche makes this point in *Ecce Homo*, where he emphasizes that such self-forgetting is central to becoming what one is:

> That one becomes what one is, presupposes that one does not suspect in the least (*nicht im Entferntesten ahnt*) what one is... Where *nosce te ipsum* would be the recipe for perishing, forgetting oneself, misunderstanding oneself, making oneself smaller, narrower, mediocre, become reason itself... The whole surface of consciousness... must be kept pure of all great imperatives. Beware even of every great word, every great attitude! Nothing but dangers, should the instinct "understand itself" too soon.[10]

He then concludes the passage by describing his own experience with such self-forgetting as precisely that of lacking the kind of will fundamental to nobility: "In no case did I suspect what was growing in me... I cannot remember that I troubled myself (*mich bemüht*) – no trace of struggle is evident in my life, I am the opposite of a heroic nature. 'Willing' something, 'striving' for something, 'envisioning' a 'purpose' (*Zweck*), a 'wish' – I know none of that from experience."[11]

In other words, although forging a memory and a will is indispensable to becoming what one is, having too good a memory, too strong a will, can actually prevent one from becoming what one is by locking one into an inappropriate goal and by refusing to allow that goal to be transformed over time. To "know" what one is too soon, to decide upon a purpose before one is mature and to strive single-mindedly to achieve that purpose, is thus a great danger. If one has forged such a will and such a purpose, freedom demands that one renounce them, forget them, in order to allow oneself to continue to develop in unforeseeable directions through new experiences that they exclude.[12]

Having forgotten itself, the self still must be lost in the second sense; the measure that constitutes the will must be changed by the introduction of new material. If the first loss of self occurs through amnesia, this second loss is the child of self-impregnation.

The ability to impregnate is the second of the two types of genius to which we alluded above. The first was the ability to give birth to a complete and perfected whole out of an originally chaotic material. This second genius is the ability to disrupt an existing whole with the introduction of new material. Returning to a passage from *Beyond Good and Evil* considered in the previous chapter, we see Nietzsche describe individuals and peoples possessed by this genius as those who "must fertilize (*befruchten*) and become the cause of new orders of life," as those "irresistibly driven outside of themselves, enamored of and lusting after foreign races (after those which 'let themselves be fertilized') and at the same time seeking mastery (*herrschsüchtig*), like everything that knows itself full of begetting force (*Zeugekrüfte*)."[13]

Recall that the sovereign, noble will is the offspring of the genius of giving birth applied by the individual to herself. Now the transformative destruction of this will results from such a reflexive application of the genius of impregnation; the individual transgresses her own measure, going outside herself in search of new material with which she can be impregnated.

The contrast to the noble individual, or to the individual in the process of becoming noble, is straightforward. Whereas the noble individual excludes the strange and foreign, the genius of self-impregnation not only welcomes it but also actively seeks it out. Whereas the noble individual has "a very definite Yes and No," the self-impregnating genius deliberately seeks to undermine her own established perspective.

In both *Human, All Too Human* and *Ecce Homo*, Nietzsche reports on his own experience with such self-transgression. In the former, he again uses the language of health, describing the effort to go outside of himself in order to incorporate what is *not* nourishing for his current established self, as a *remedy* for the sickness of the "healthy" stasis that results from ingesting only what one knows, from always excluding the strange:

> I . . . took sides *against* myself and *for* everything painful and difficult precisely for *me* . . . I, as physician and patient in one person, compelled myself to an opposite, unexplored *climate of the soul*, and especially to a curative journey into strange parts, into *strangeness*, to a curiosity for every kind of strange thing . . . A long wandering around, seeking, changing followed, an

aversion (*Widerwille*) to all remaining-fast (*Festblieben*), to every blunt affirmation and denial; likewise a dietetic and discipline that wanted to make it
as easy as possible for the spirit to run far, to fly high, above all to fly forth
again and again.[14]

Later, in *Ecce Homo*, he describes this process as that of philosophy:
"Philosophy, as I have understood and lived it, is the voluntary living
in ice and high mountains, the seeking out of everything strange and
questionable in existence."[15]

The result of this process is a further overcoming. The destruction of
the moral will was the overcoming of herd morality. The creation of the
noble will constructed a new, noble morality, which stood in opposition to
other noble moralities and, especially, to herd morality, to the dominant
customs of the individual's time. Now the movement out of and away from
the noble will is the overcoming of what Nietzsche calls the individual's
opposition to her time. Only with this last overcoming is the individual
truly free within her time for, as we have seen, to remain opposed to
something is to continue to be determined by it.[16]

As she overcomes her opposition to her time, the individual also overcomes herself, in the sense that she is no longer defined by the measure
that constituted her noble will and held what was strange to her at bay.
By forgetting this limiting measure and wandering out in an attempt to
know what lies beyond it, the individual transforms and enlarges herself.
Paradoxically, by forgetting who she is, she is able to become what she is,
as her fixed self-conception no longer limits her.[17]

We have seen previously that freedom requires the creation of a noble
will, which in turn requires that one have or develop certain characteristics. One must be selfish, have an instinct for self-walling, be healthy
enough to allow in only what will be nourishing, be able to forget what
one cannot use, and be able to remember what one has incorporated.

Now we have seen that freedom also requires the destruction of one's
noble will. Nietzsche emphasizes that the capacity to destroy a noble will
that has been forged, no less than the capacity for such forging, demands
certain traits. Three can be distinguished: one must be brave; one must
be hard; and one must have what Nietzsche calls excess force.

First, one must be brave even to attempt to destroy one's will and lose
one's self. The reason is fairly obvious: having carefully constructed a self
in the wake of the destruction of the moral will, reopening the measure
of this self in an attempt to enlarge it puts one at risk of remaining unmeasured, of not being able to put the disassembled arch back together.
One's degree of bravery, courage, or daring can thus be measured by
one's willingness to open oneself to the strange. One is courageous to
the extent that one is unwilling to stand pat with a healthy but closed and
limited self.[18]

But daring to reopen oneself is not enough. In order to make such reopening worthwhile and productive, one must also be hard, or resolute. When confronted with the strange and the new, the temptation will be to return to the familiar, to seek comfort too quickly, to close oneself prematurely. To alter one's measure, to overcome the instincts that have been so tightly woven into oneself, one must resist such temptation. One must be a kind of ascetic, who can resist the instincts and passions that come to her easily, for the sake of a larger goal (which, in this case, is the goal of divesting oneself of one's current goals). Only if one has the strength characteristic of such an ascetic will one enjoy holding one's measure open, continually turning over the ground on which the arch of one's will is constructed. And only if one enjoys such difficult tasks will one be able to persist in them; if one takes no pleasure in the work of losing oneself, one will eventually refuse to do it. In virtue of such a refusal, paradoxically, one will truly lose oneself; by refusing to let go of one's measure, one imposes a limit on oneself and cannot become what one is.[19]

Such resolution and strength manifests itself as skepticism. The measure of one's will is determined by one's convictions and one's virtues, both of which serve to limit growth and transformation when they become fully internalized and accepted unreflectively. The strength to hold this measure open, therefore, amounts to having the fortitude to maintain a persistent skepticism toward all such fixed beliefs and proficiencies. One must have the strength to question continually and honestly both the constituents of one's own measure and that which is excluded from and forbidden by that measure.[20]

In *Beyond Good and Evil*, Nietzsche expresses this need for skepticism as a need for individuals to avoid clinging to what they know and love:

> One must test oneself to see whether one is destined (*bestimmt*) for independence and command. One should not avoid one's tests, although they are perhaps the most dangerous game one could play and are in the end tests which are taken before ourselves as witness and before no other judge. Not to cling to (*hängenbleiben*) another person, though he be the one you love most – every person is a prison, also a nook and a corner. Not to cling to a fatherland, though it be the most suffering and in need of help . . . Not to cling to a feeling of pity, though it be for higher men into whose rare torment and helplessness chance allowed us to look. Not to cling to a science, though it lures us with the most precious discoveries seemingly reserved precisely for *us*. Not to cling to one's own detachment . . . Not to cling to our own virtues and become as a whole the victim of some part (*Einzelheit*) of us . . . One must know how to preserve (*bewahren*) oneself: the sternest test of independence.[21]

And in "Opinions and Maxims," in a section headed, *To be a good German means to degermanize* (entdeutschen) *oneself*, he makes the same point at a cultural and political level:

All argumentation on the basis of national character is so little incumbent upon him who labors at the *transformation (Umschaffung)* of convictions, that is to say at culture . . . If we consider, for example, all that *has been* German, we shall at once improve the theoretical question "what *is* German?" into the counter-question "what is *now* German?" – and every *good* German will give it a practical answer precisely by overcoming his German qualities. For whenever a people goes forward and grows it bursts the girdle that has hitherto given it its *national* appearance; if it remains stationary, it wastes away (*verkümmert*), a new girdle closes itself around its soul; the crust, becoming ever harder, constructs around it as it were a prison whose walls continually grow. If, therefore, a people has a great deal that is firm, this is a proof that it wants to petrify and would like to become wholly and really a *monument* . . . Thus he who wishes the Germans well should for his part see how he can grow more and more beyond what is German. The *change into the ungermanic* has therefore always been the indication of the most able of our people.[22]

Finally, having found the courage to open oneself, and the skeptical resolution to hold oneself open, one must also have the force to incorporate what one encounters. The force one has is measured by the amount that one is able to incorporate, by the amount that one has overcome. One has force to the extent that one is able to bear new truth and expand one's measure and one's proficiencies.[23]

Since one is what one has overcome, what was formerly external that one has incorporated into one's measure, one's measure increases in proportion to the success one has in overcoming.[24] One's freedom also increases with this success, for by increasing one's measure one reduces the extent to which one is externally dependent. Freedom is thus reserved for those who are courageous, hard, and forceful enough to attempt and carry out repeated self-overcomings.

Those capable of the repeated self-overcoming necessary to freedom go by many names and descriptions in Nietzsche's texts. One thing they certainly are is *unsittlich*, unethical in the sense of not being firmly attached to any given set of customs. This is in contrast not only to the *Sittlichkeit* of herd morality, but also to that of nobility. The important distinction between noble and decadent *Sittlichkeit* is whether the customs by which one lives are self-imposed or imposed externally and accepted as given. But the important distinction between those who are *unsittlich* and both of these forms of *Sittlichkeit* is whether one lives by any fixed set of customs, any closed measure; here, whether this measure has been internally or externally forged is irrelevant. The *Unsittliche* release themselves (*sich auslösen*) from any such measure, from any fixed customs that define a stable community.[25]

In doing so, these free spirits honor their capacity to change their opinions, to replace one set of convictions and virtues with another, which

Nietzsche calls a "rare and high distinction."[26] In fact, it is a capacity and distinction so rare and high that Nietzsche suggests that free spirits might be willing to die for it: "Dying for 'truth'. – We would not let ourselves be burned to death for our opinions: we are not so certain of them. But perhaps so that we may have and alter our opinions."[27]

To become the free spirits that they are, these *unsittlich* beings must have overcome not only their certainty of their opinions and convictions, but more fundamentally the very desire to be certain of such beliefs. For without overcoming that desire, one may overcome the particular opinions of which one is initially certain, but will inevitably replace them with others of which one is no less certain. Thus one fixed measure will be exchanged for another, but the basic problem of being limited by a fixed measure and dependent upon an external other will remain. Instead of this, we need to imagine, Nietzsche writes,

> a pleasure and power of self-determination, a freedom of the will, by which a spirit would bid farewell to every faith, to every wish for certainty (*Gewissheit*), being accustomed, as he is, to being able to maintain himself on flimsy ropes and possibilities, and even to dancing near abysses (*an Abgründen*). Such a spirit would be the *free spirit* par excellence.[28]

This passage makes explicit that the free spirit not only gives up her convictions, but also her very desire to be convinced, her very wish for certainty. It also makes clear that giving up this wish for certainty is possible because she does not need such a fixed ground upon which to erect her will. On the contrary, she is accustomed to maintaining herself, to being able to will, on flimsy ropes stretched out *above* the ground, on possibilities rather than certainties. She is even at home where there is no ground at all, near the abyss. The free spirit is not only sanguine about approaching the abyss, but actually appears both to celebrate it and to risk falling into it, by dancing at its edge. In the terms we used earlier, the free spirit is brave enough to jeopardize her will by abandoning the ground of its construction, and strong enough not only to continue willing in the ground's absence, but also to enjoy the fact that her will is no longer tied to the ground, that there are no more grounds for established perspectives. It is in this bravery and strength that she finds the power of self-determination in which she takes such pleasure, her freedom of will, for it is her bravery and strength that allow her will to avoid being determined and measured by fixed convictions, and so by a fixed externality.

Nietzsche contends that the strongest drive of these spirits capable of freedom is the drive for freedom itself – presumably because they enjoy exercising the bravery and strength that they possess and that the quest for freedom demands – and further, that the freedom toward which they are driven is that of bursting the limits of fixed convictions,

conventions, and wills. In a passage from "Opinions and Maxims" entitled "Free-moving (*freizügige*) spirits," Nietzsche writes: "We may well be
called 'free-moving spirits' in all seriousness... because we feel the pull
(*Zug*) of freedom as the strongest drive of our spirit and, in opposition
to the bound and fast-rooted intellects, see our ideal almost in a spiritual
nomadism."[29]

As spiritual nomads, these free spirits find no cultural climate permanently to their liking, permanently nourishing and healthy. Instead, they
are driven to drive themselves through a series of climates, a series of
convictions and virtues, pausing to rest in a temporarily adopted home
when that is conducive to their health, moving on again when it threatens
them with stagnation and limitation.

Nietzsche emphasizes, however, that the free spirit's nomadic adoption and abandonment of a series of convictions and values is to be distinguished from the practice of the person who, too weak to construct
her own will, hides herself in the currently prevailing opinions of her
culture. The latter, whom we have already encountered in our discussion of the moral will, cannot create a genuine self, and so presents as
her "self" the mask that the herd of her culture wants to see. Behind
that mask, however, is an emptiness no more suited to one mask than
to another, and therefore equally well suited to any mask.[30] By contrast,
the free spirit adopts and discards convictions from strength rather than
weakness, from overfullness rather than emptiness. The free spirit adopts
a particular set of convictions and virtues because they are well-suited to
the self she has created, and she eventually abandons them because no
set of convictions and virtues can permanently contain or measure that
self. She presents to the world, therefore, not a mask for an emptiness
she must hide, but an expression of the health that the current state of
her genuine self enjoys:

> *Opinions.* – Most people are nothing and are regarded as nothing, until
> they have clothed themselves in universal convictions and public opinions,
> in accordance with the tailor-philosophy: clothes (*Kleider*) make the man
> (*Leute*). Of exceptional people, however, it must be said: *only the wearer*
> (*Träger*) *makes the clothes* (*Tracht*); here opinions cease to be public, and
> become something other than masks (*Masken*), finery (*Putz*), and disguise
> (*Verkleidung*).[31]

The weak individual is thus an *imitation* of the herd culture around her,
whereas the strong, spiritually nomadic free spirits practice *experimentation*
on themselves and their culture.[32]

Nietzsche recognizes, however, that although imitation out of weakness and experimentation out of strength are vastly different, they are
also closely related, and in fact may be inseparable. Both are, after all,
different responses to being made sick by the present. The imitator is

always sick, in every present, because she has no self for which any set of convictions or virtues could be healthy. Her "health," as we have seen, thus consists in adopting the convictions and virtues of the prevailing culture, which allows her to will but only masks her sickness without curing it. The experimenter is always sick, in every present, because her self consists in continually transgressing the measure that defines the health of her "self" at any given time. Her health thus consists in overthrowing her own convictions and virtues, transforming her own will, deliberately making her present self sick in order to avoid being restricted by the limits within which it can flourish. Both the imitator and the experimenter, then, are uncertain and malleable, the one from weakness, the other from strength:

> Man is more sick, uncertain, changeable, indeterminate than any other animal, there is no doubt of that – he is *the* sick animal: how has that come about? Certainly he has also dared more, done more new things, braved more and challenged fate more than all the other animals put together: he, the great experimenter with himself, discontented and insatiable, wrestling with animals, nature, and gods for ultimate dominion – he, still unvanquished, eternally directed toward the future, whose own restless energies never leave him in peace, so that his future digs like a spur into the flesh of every present – how should such a courageous and richly endowed animal not also be the most imperiled, the most chronically and profoundly sick of all sick animals?[33]

This passage suggests that the experimentation of courageous free spirits produces both of the types of sickness just discussed. In the first place, it produces the dire sickness of those who cannot will on the shifting grounds that experimentation continually plows under. This is the sickness of the truly decadent, who need a firm ground, any ground, in order that they may will nothing, rather than not will at all. But it also produces the sickness of the experimenters themselves, the sickness of never being fully at home in the present, of being eternally prodded by the future, of always needing to become what one is by destroying who one currently is.

The sickness that the experimenters produce in themselves is necessary to their freedom, and thus to the possibility of a future in which the freedom of humanity is more fully realized. Their sickness in the present causes them to "run through the range of human values,"[34] which prevents these free spirits from becoming limited by a particular established valuation. Instead of willing the goals of a single value system, the free spirits will the experimental "running through" of all value systems, in a quest for knowledge and freedom. Nietzsche calls this goal of experimenting with all goals the "most universal" goal,[35] and claims that in this quest for knowledge "no sacrifice is too great."[36] Indeed, nothing less than humanity itself must be sacrificed – in the sense that the non-experimental, stagnant herd must give way to a culture of experiment and self-transformation.

In the end, however, this sacrifice of humanity will produce a culture that sacrifices fewer humans than does the "moral" culture of the herd:

> At the present time it seems that . . . those who do not regard themselves as being bound by standing customs and laws are making the first attempts to organize themselves and therewith to create for themselves a *right*. . . One ought to find this on the whole *fair (billig) and good*, even though it may make the coming century a dangerous one . . . It constitutes a counter-power which is a constant reminder that there is no such thing as a morality with an exclusive monopoly of the moral, and that every morality that affirms itself exclusively destroys too much good force and is too expensive for humanity. The deviants, who are so often the inventive and fruitful, shall no longer be sacrificed; it shall not even be considered shameful to deviate from morality, in deed and thought; numerous novel experiments of life and community shall be made; a tremendous burden of bad conscience shall be expelled from the world.[37]

In other words, the experiments of these initial free spirits, through which they make themselves into "monstrous multiplicities,"[38] will lead to a culture that is itself such a multiplicity, and which will therefore encourage the multiplication of free spirits. This self-reinforcing cycle of individual and cultural self-transgression, self-transformation, and self-multiplication must replace the self-reinforcing cycle of individual and cultural decadence, if freedom is to be possible.[39]

THE DANGERS OF DESTRUCTION REDUX

The aim of the noble's self-infection is to inoculate herself against the sickness of being healthy, and thus against the failure to be free. The noble has to guard against finding herself permanently at home in, and therefore limited by, an established perspective and orientation. She guards herself, as we have just seen, by dropping her guard, by allowing herself to become sick; she endeavors to develop a thoroughgoing skepticism that enables her to lose her perspective and become disoriented.

Put in the terms of self-losing and self-preservation used earlier, the paradox comes sharply into focus. The noble will lose herself precisely if she tries to preserve herself, precisely if she tries *not* to lose herself by protecting her perspective against incursion by all others. By refusing to lose her perspective, she will become limited by what is external to that perspective, and will thus lose herself by failing to become the free being that she is.[40] Conversely, it is only if she allows herself to be lost, if she infects and impregnates herself with material external to her measure, that she will be preserved. Only by transgressing the boundary between herself and her external other, only by losing her hard-won nobility, will the noble preserve herself as the possibility of freedom.

Like all experimental inoculations, however, this one can go awry; when one attempts to prevent disease by deliberately introducing an infection, one runs the risk that the vaccine will make the patient sick. In this case, the disease the noble wishes to avoid is that of being overly measured, and the vaccination is a heavy dose of measure-transgressing skepticism. The concomitant risk should be apparent: the noble may become so infected with skepticism that she is incapable of reconstructing her measure in the wake of its transgression.

Should this occur, the noble will not progressively transcend her nobility but instead lose it in a regress to one of the stages of disease, one of the two forms or styles of decadence previously considered. She may return to a state of disgregation, dissolution, and convulsion, a state of dependence on her unmeasured instincts. Or, fearing that state, which Nietzsche considers to be the worst human sickness, she may opt for the familiar "cure" of surrendering herself to an external authority that can provide her with a measure and a will. In either case, she will fail to become free.[41]

Freedom thus requires not only that the noble inoculate herself with skepticism against her own measured health, but that she also emerge from that skepticism able to reconstruct her measure, give herself new values, rebuild her will. Nietzsche emphasizes this tension, between being a skeptic and being *merely* a skeptic, at length in Part 6 of *Beyond Good and Evil*, entitled "We Scholars." There, he distinguishes between scientists and scholars, who are merely skeptics, and genuine philosophers, who are skeptical in the service of constructing a larger whole with new values:

> It may be necessary to the education of a philosopher, that he himself has also once stood on all those steps on which his servants, the scientific laborers of philosophy, remain standing – *must* remain standing; he himself must perhaps have been critic and skeptic and dogmatist and historian and, in addition, poet and collector and traveler and guesser of riddles and moralist and seer and "free spirit" and practically everything, in order to run through the range of human values and value feelings, and to be *able* to gaze from the heights into every distance, from the depths into every height, from the corner into every expanse, with manifold eyes and conscience. But all these are only preconditions of his task: this task itself wants something else – it demands that he *create values*.[42]

In other words, freedom requires that the noble lose her nobility and keep it too. Nietzsche writes that although the philosophers he has in mind will have to be skeptics and experimenters, they will at the same time have to manifest qualities recognizably noble: "certainty of value-measures, conscious employment of a unity of method, clever courage, and the ability to stand alone and be self-responsible."[43] He insists that their task is not just to be an enemy of ideals, armed with "dangerous question-marks," but to undertake this questioning "in order to know a new greatness (*Grösse*) of man, a new untrodden path to his enlargement (*Vergrösserung*)."[44] The passage continues:

> A philosopher, assuming there could be philosophers today, would be compelled to place (*setzen*) the greatness of man, the concept "greatness," precisely in his spaciousness (*Umfänglichkeit*) and multiplicity, in his being-whole-in-many (*Ganzheit im Vielen*). He would even determine value and rank according to how much and how many things one could bear and take upon oneself, how *wide* one could stretch one's responsibility... In the philosopher's ideal, precisely strength of will, hardness and the capacity for long decisions must belong within the concept of "greatness"... Today, being noble, wanting to be for-oneself (*Für-sich-sein*), the ability to be different (*Anders-sein-können*), standing alone and having to live by one's own means (*auf-eigne-Faust-leben-mssen*) belong to the concept "greatness"; and the philosopher will betray something of his own ideal, when he offers: 'he shall be the greatest, who can be the most solitary, the most concealed, the most deviant (*Abweichendste*), the man beyond good and evil, the master of his virtues, the overrich of will; this shall be called greatness: to be able to be as multiple as whole, as wide as full.'[45]

BEYOND NOBILITY AND DECADENCE: THE ENDLESS CYCLE OF SICKNESS AND CONVALESCENCE

We have now distinguished three basic ways in which we can fail to be free for Nietzsche. First, there are the two styles of decadence: the peculiarly modern sickness of having no will, of enjoying the "freedom" of being turned over to one's instincts after shedding the constraints of traditional custom; and the premodern moral sickness (and its modern substitutes, such as the scientific will to truth) of having an externally imposed will, within which one "feels" free. And then there is nobility, in which one has convalesced from both forms of decadence and has imposed one's own will on oneself, but in a way that permanently excludes everything strange and external to one's measure, by which one is therefore limited.

We have also seen how these inadequate forms of will must complement each other if freedom is to be possible. Noble wills and measures, which ultimately limit those who have created them, must from time to time be transgressed through self-infection and self-impregnation. Yet this introduction of modern multiplicity and disgregation into the noble must be followed by the convalescing re-formation of a will, by a new giving birth to oneself.

We can conclude that freedom exists neither in sickness nor in health. Instead, it demands that one become, and feel at home in being, a perpetual cycle of self-infection and self-recuperation, of self-destruction and self-creation. As Nietzsche writes, in reference to thinkers: "Once one has found oneself, one must understand how to *lose* oneself from time to time – and then how to find oneself again."[46] To cling to either pole between which this cycle moves is to be limited and dependent: to cling to sickness, to live "without limitation" in pursuit of "freedom of the individual," is to be dependent upon one's unlimited instincts; to cling to health, to live within established limits, is to be limited by one's own establishment.[47]

To be such a perpetual cycle is, in the terms Nietzsche uses in *Human, All Too Human*, to be an "infinite melody." This phrase appears in two paragraphs in the book, numbers 113 and 134 of "Opinions and Maxims," which discuss the writing and music of Laurence Sterne and Richard Wagner, respectively.[48] Before letting the passages speak for themselves, we should note several important points. First, Nietzsche is praising the *work* of Sterne and Wagner, and not the men themselves (in fact, in the case of Sterne, Nietzsche explicitly expresses disappointment with the man's life in comparison to his writing). Second, what Nietzsche finds praiseworthy is that the work refuses to rest content within established forms and measures, continually disrupts the bounds of form, but at the same time avoids degenerating into a superficial formlessness. Third, the risk of this kind of degeneration, which cannot be avoided by those who transgress form, makes Sterne and Wagner bad examples for lesser artists; only the exceptional can repeatedly burst their measure and always manage to regain wholeness.

In the paragraph on Sterne, headed *The most free writer*, Nietzsche writes:

> What may be praised in him is not the closed (*geschlossene*), the transparent, but the "infinite melody": if with these words a style of art is named, in which the determinate form is continually broken, displaced (*verschoben*), translated back into the indeterminate, so that it signifies the one and at the same time the other. Sterne is the great master of ambiguity... Ought it be necessary to add that Sterne, among all the great writers, is the worst model and the truly unexemplary author?... He elevates himself, as the masterly exception, above that which all literary artists demand of themselves: discipline, closure (*Geschlossenheit*), character, constancy of intention, comprehensibility (*Überschaulichkeit*), simplicity, composure in movement and expression (*Haltung in Gang und Miene*).[49]

And in describing the music created and inspired by Wagner, he contends:

> The artistic intention that recent music pursues, which is now designated, very strongly but unclearly, as "infinite melody," one can make clear to

oneself: one goes into the sea, gradually loses the certain step on the ground, and finally gives oneself over to the waving elements, come what may: one ought to *swim*. In previous, older music, one had . . . to *dance*: whereby the measure necessary for this, the maintenance (*Einhalten*) of determinate units of time and force of equal weight, compelled the soul of the listener to a continual *possession of its senses* (*Besonnenheit*) . . . Richard Wagner wanted another kind of movement of the soul . . . related to swimming and floating . . . His notorious artistic means, sprung from and appropriate to this will – "infinite melody" – strives to break all even-measuredness (*Ebenmässigkeit*) of time and force . . . He is abundant in the invention of effects which sound to the older ear like rhythmic paradoxes and blasphemy. He fears petrifaction, crystallization, the transition of music into architectonic . . . A great danger for music can arise out of a complacent imitation of such art: alongside this overripeness of rhythmic feeling has always lurked in hiding the return to the wild, the ruin of rhythm . . . [for] such music . . . has no measure in itself.[50]

The latter passage returns us to the language of the sea, which we encountered earlier when considering the overcoming of morality and its substitutes.[51] Here again, Nietzsche praises, in those capable of it, leaving behind the ground for the water, giving up the established perspective of walking in favor of allowing oneself to be carried by the waves, the oscillation of which produces a perpetual shift of horizons; he prefers taking leave of one's senses to the continual possession of them. But again he also emphasizes the dangers involved in entering the depths where one can no longer stand. Most obviously, one can drown. Avoiding this fate requires either finding land upon which to stand (allowing one to live, but only by failing to liberate oneself), or learning to float or swim. Floating is perhaps preferable to standing up, but it too falls short of freedom; floating is only an imitation of swimming, in which one's horizon and perspective are determined entirely by the current upon which one is carried. Only swimming in the sea is adequate to freedom. Even one strong enough to swim in the ocean is carried by the tides, currents, waves, and winds, which continually disrupt perspective, disorient, and take one to places beyond one's horizon; but at the same time, a true swimmer is able to direct and reorient herself within these currents, able to reestablish a horizon and a perspective in the new waters to which she has been carried, knowing full well that before long the tides will change yet again. The swimmer is thus free, for she avoids both the petrifaction of standing on the shore and the dissolution of floating, managing to keep her senses *while* taking leave of them, managing to maintain a course *while* her head is swimming; the swimmer retains the ability to reconstruct her will, but without clinging to any particular construction itself.

Sterne and Wagner thus teach writing and music to swim, and in so doing bring a new kind of freedom to those art forms. Sterne's writing is determinate and indeterminate at the same time, not a closed unity, but a unity without closure. Wagner's music is rhythmic at the same time that it shuns the determinate and even measures of traditional rhythm.

This freedom is not just unavailable, but actually imperceptible, to lesser writers and readers, composers and listeners. This is owing not only to a lack of talent or training, but also to conceptual failure. For them, unity is impossible without being fully determinate and closed, and rhythm is impossible without being determinate and even. These are the lesser artists and critics who demand of themselves and of those whom they judge constancy, comprehensibility, and simplicity, and the older ears who hear in Wagner paradox and blasphemy rather than freedom.[52]

Finally, however, freedom demands that not only works of art but also people and cultures learn to swim.[53] In the previous sections on nobility and its deliberate destruction, we considered two types of genius, and saw that the production of freedom requires such geniuses to apply their talents to themselves: becoming noble requires giving birth to oneself; overcoming nobility requires deliberately allowing oneself to be impregnated with external material. We can now see that freedom requires that individuals and cultures combine both types of genius and apply them both continually and simultaneously to themselves. Such an individual will be a swimmer, with a self that is "structured" like Sterne's writing or Wagner's music: she will at the same time be both the will to the unification of her will and the will to overcome that unified will through self-multiplication. She will neither lack a will nor possess one, will thus have no established perspective or limit, and will thus be free.[54]

In the language of experimentation, the free swimmer will be a perpetually repeated two-stage cycle. In the first stage, she will destroy her will through experiments that draw her beyond its measure and enable the current to carry her away. In the second, she will return from these experiments with her instincts for reunifying her will intact, using her strength to emerge from the current and reestablish a perspective in her new location. Then the cycle will begin again: she will surrender to the current once more, performing further experimentation on herself, exposing herself yet again to the hard struggle to find the horizon in an unfamiliar place at sea, but seeing that struggle as a stimulus to self-mastery and unification.[55]

At stake in the effort to develop people who can swim is the hope of developing swimming cultures. As noted earlier, herd cultures (which here include noble cultures) are self-reinforcing: composed of individuals who are confined by definite measures of conviction and value, such cultures are prone to sacrifice potentially productive deviants, precisely the individuals who might transgress the culture's limits.[56] Only if such deviants are able to teach themselves to swim, and are then permitted to stay in the water, will a culture itself become a cycle of experimentation and reunification in which freedom can emerge.[57]

Nietzsche makes this point about the interconnectedness of the flourishing and liberation of individuals and of culture explicitly in a section of "The Wanderer and His Shadow" headed *The tree of humanity and reason.* He begins by describing "the great task of the hopeful":

> Humanity ought one day to become a tree, which overshadows the whole earth with many billions of blossoms, which all alongside one another ought to become fruit, and the earth itself ought to be prepared for the nourishment of this tree. That the *presently still small* roots (*Ansatz*) of this should increase in sap and force, that the sap should flow throughout countless canals for the nourishment of the whole and the individuals – from these and similar tasks is the standard to be derived, as to whether a person of the present is useful or useless.[58]

So present individuals must be engaged in preparing the conditions under which humanity can grow both strong and diverse, nourishing an immense variety of fruitful people and cultures. Because, Nietzsche continues, humans have no instinct for developing into such a tree, this preparatory work can consist only of tremendous experimentation, which is not without its costs:

> Whole peoples, whole centuries, struggle to discover and *test-out* new means, with which one could benefit a great human whole and finally the great total-fruit-tree (*Gesammt-Fruchtbaume*) of humanity; and whatever injuries individuals, peoples, and ages may always suffer in the course of this testing, through these injuries individuals have always become intelligent (*klug*), and from them intelligence slowly streams out over the measure-constituting-rules (*Massregeln*) of whole peoples, whole ages.[59]

Finally, then, we have a description of the liberation of humanity and of human individuals from their limiting measures. In delicate symbiosis, individuals and cultures must experiment with themselves, with their convictions and values, undertaking a wide survey in a quest for knowledge that will transform and enlarge them. Such experimentation will involve turning over the ground on which they stand, but it cannot be merely disruptive. Rather, it must amount to a tilling and fertilization of the soil out of which the whole of humanity can grow increasingly strong, capable of producing and sustaining ever more numerous and diverse blossoms of people and cultures. As the fruits of these blossoms ripen, drop to the ground, and decay, they will contribute to the continual repetition of this liberating cycle.

But if this vision sounds horribly fruitopian, Nietzsche is not unaware of the difficulties that its actualization faces. In fact, he acknowledges that the activity that is its precondition – the repeated transgression of measure in order to encounter the external and new *as* new – is contrary to what he calls the "basic will of spirit" (*Grundwillen des Geistes*).[60] This basic will is the will to simplify, to assimilate the new to an old measure and to exclude what cannot be assimilated by that measure, to preserve unity by extinguishing multiplicity:

> The commanding something, called "spirit" by the people, wants to be master in itself and around itself, and to feel itself as master: it has the will to simplicity (*Einfachheit*) out of multiplicity (*Vielheit*), a lacing-together, binding, mastery-seeking and actually mastering will... The force of the spirit to appropriate (*sich aneignen*) the strange to itself manifests itself in a strong tendency to assimilate (*anähnlichen*)[61] the new to the old, to simplify the manifold, to overlook or push away the wholly contradictory: just as it arbitrarily (*willkürlich*) underscores, plucks out, and falsifies to suit itself determinate traits and lines in the strange, in every piece of "external world." Its intention thereby is the incorporation of new "experiences," the classification (*Einreihung*) of new things under old classes (*Reihen*) – that is, growth; more precisely, the *feeling* of growth, the feeling of increased force. An apparently opposed drive of spirit serves this same will, a suddenly breaking-out decision (*Entschluss*) for ignorance, for willful exclusion (*Abschliessung*), a closing of its windows, an inner no-saying to this or that thing, a not-letting-it-approach, a kind of defensive-condition against much that is knowable, a satisfaction with the dark, with the closed (*abschliessenden*) horizon, a yes-saying and approval of ignorance: all of this is necessary according to the degree of its appropriating force.[62]

It is against this will, in herself and others, that the free spirit struggles in her drive for knowledge and freedom. This will

> to semblance (*Schein*), to simplification, to the mask, to the cloak, in short to the surface – for every surface is a cloak – is *counteracted* by that sublime tendency of the knower, which takes things deeply, multiply, and thoroughly (*gründlich*) and *will* take them thusly: as a kind of cruelty of intellectual conscience and taste, which every brave thinker will recognize in himself, assuming that he, as befits him, has hardened and sharpened for long enough his eyes for himself, and is habituated (*gewöhnt*) to severe discipline and also severe words.[63]

The free spirit thus has a will to overcome the will to power, which is one of Nietzsche's names for the appropriating, assimilating will just described; the will to power wills the overcoming of what is other, wills its annihilation through an incorporation that assimilates, and simply refuses to engage what it cannot so incorporate.[64] The will to power thus leaves intact the limiting measures that define the one who exercises it and her other. In contrast, the free spirit wills the overcoming of these limiting measures through an overcoming of the will to power's violent sort of overcoming. The free spirit pursues the overcoming of the fixed boundary between herself and her other through an open engagement that allows the other to remain other, that neither annihilates it by making it the same nor rejects it because it is too different.[65]

a. Tragic Great Health

We can now see that the healthy, noble spirit, in the senses in which we have so far understood health and nobility, is precisely the spirit that must be overcome – spirit at home in its measure, with a strong will to power, a strong will to assimilate and exclude. Freedom demands that this health and nobility indicative of self-satisfaction, self-justification, and a pathos of distance be replaced with a new kind of healthiness and nobility.[66] This new health will indicate one who can flourish in a continual cycle of the old kinds of health and sickness, one who is at home in a home whose walls are continually being torn down and rebuilt from new materials, one who can remain whole while experimenting with the limits of her convictions and values.[67]

Nietzsche discusses this new health at length in the penultimate paragraph of the fifth book of *The Joyful Science* (added to the first four books in 1886), headed *The great health*. The importance of such great health to Nietzsche, and his satisfaction with his expression of it here, are both suggested by the fact that he repeats this paragraph in its entirety, with very few changes, as the second paragraph of his discussion of *Thus Spoke Zarathustra* in *Ecce Homo*. There he introduces the paragraph by saying that great health is the "physiological presupposition" of the type represented by Zarathustra, and that he does not know how he could explain the concept any better than he has already done in *The Joyful Science*:

> *The great health* ... For a new goal we also need a new means, namely, a new health ... Whoever's soul thirsts to have lived through the whole range of previous values and desiderata, and to have sailed around all the coasts of this ideal "Mediterranean"[68] ... has need of one thing above all, the *great health* – a health such that one not only has, but also continually still acquires and must acquire, because one relinquishes it ever again, must relinquish it! And now, after we have long been underway in this manner, we argonauts of the ideal ... dangerously-healthy, ever again healthy – it will appear to us as if, as a reward, we have before us an as yet undiscovered land, whose limits (*Grenzen*) no one has yet surveyed, a beyond of all previous lands and nooks of the ideal, a world so overrich in the beautiful, strange, questionable, terrible, and divine, that our curiosity as well as our thirst to possess it have gotten beside themselves (*ausser sich*) ... Another ideal runs before us, a wondrous, tempting ideal, rich in danger ... the ideal of a spirit which plays naïvely, that is, without willing (*ungewollt*) and out of an overflowing abundance and power, with everything previously called holy, good, untouchable, divine; for which the highest thing, in which the people rightfully (*billigerweise*) had its measure of value, would signify

precisely as much as danger, decay, debasement or, at least, as recreation, blindness, temporary self-forgetting; the ideal of a human-*übermenschlich* well-being and well-willing, that often enough will appear *unhuman*, for example, when it comports itself (*sich hinstellt*) in the presence of all previous earthly-seriousness, every kind of solemnity in gesture, word, tone, glance, morality, and task, as their most incarnate, involuntary parody – and despite all this, perhaps with it the *great seriousness* first arises, the proper question-mark is first posed, the fate of the soul turns itself, the clock-hand moves, the tragedy *begins*.[69]

If such great health is the precondition of Zarathustra's type, if it brings into view the ideal of *übermenschlich* well-being, alters the fate of the soul, and marks the beginning of tragedy, we now need to consider these phenomena and their interrelations, since they are tantamount to the achievement of freedom for Nietzsche.

The most obvious connection is that between Zarathustra's type and the ideal of the *Übermensch*, which are linked in several passages, including the one just considered and its reiteration in *Ecce Homo*. As noted, in *Ecce Homo* the passage is introduced by saying that the great health it describes is the presupposition of the type Zarathustra represents. Within the passage itself, we learn that the great health leads to the ideal of an *übermenschlich* well-being. That Zarathustra's type is the herald of this latter ideal is further suggested earlier in *Ecce Homo*. In the first paragraph of the section entitled "Why I Write Such Good Books," Nietzsche says that "the word '*Übermensch*' [is the] designation of a type of higher well-constitutedness (*Wohlgeratenheit*)," which "in the figure of Zarathustra has been brought to appearance."[70]

The next link is between the *übermenschlich* type and the beginning of tragedy, which Nietzsche claims marks a turning point in the fate of the soul. We must now investigate what it means to say that the *Übermensch* is tragic, and why the arrival of tragedy is a fateful turning point.

Nietzsche indicates the importance of tragedy in the same way that he indicates the importance of great health – by devoting one of the last sections of one of his late works to its discussion, and then incorporating that discussion into *Ecce Homo*'s reflections on his earlier books. The following passage is from the final paragraph of *Twilight of the Idols*:

> The psychology of the orgiastic-orgasm (*Orgiasmus*),[71] as an overflowing feeling of life and force, within which even pain works as a stimulus, gave me the key to the concept of *tragic* feeling . . . Tragedy is . . . the affirmation (*Jasagen*) of life even in its strangest and hardest problems; the will to life rejoicing in its own inexhaustibility through the *sacrifice* of its highest types – I called *that* Dionysian, I correctly guessed *that* was the bridge to the psychology of the *tragic* poet . . . *to be oneself* the eternal joy of becoming – that joy which also encompasses the *joy in destruction* . . . And with that I again touch down at the place from which I first set out – the "Birth of

Tragedy" was my first revaluation of all values...I, the last disciple of the philosopher Dionysus – I, the teacher of the eternal return.[72]

Here we find tragedy, which has already been linked to Zarathustra and the *Übermensch*, linked to most of the other concepts central to Nietzsche's late work: affirmation, Dionysus, and the eternal return.[73] The links are strengthened when Nietzsche expands on the passage in *Ecce Homo*:

> I have the right to understand myself as the first tragic philosopher ... The affirmation of passing away *and destruction*, the decisive thing in a Dionysian philosophy, the affirmation of opposition and war, *becoming*, with the radical repudiation of the very concept of "*being*" – therein must I under all conditions recognize what is more closely related to me than what has previously been thought. The teaching of the "eternal return," that is, of the unconditional and infinitely repeated circular course of all things – this doctrine of Zarathustra.[74]

And finally, all of these concepts and figures – Dionysus, Zarathustra, affirmation, *Übermensch*, eternal return – are brought together and strongly connected to each other in *Ecce Homo*'s reflection on *Thus Spoke Zarathustra*, in a passage that begins with Nietzsche declaring that perhaps no other work ("leaving aside the poets") has been done from such an excess of strength as produced *Zarathustra*.[75]

To understand freedom, we must make something of this welter of associations that spill out of the tragic disposition characteristic of great health. For great health is necessary to freedom, the tragic disposition is necessary to great health, and understanding the tragic disposition requires understanding Dionysus, Zarathustra, affirmation, the *Übermensch*, and the eternal return.

AFFIRMATION OUT OF OVERFULLNESS

We do well to begin with affirmation. Returning to the passages just cited, we find that the tragic soul affirms the following things: pain, the strangest and hardest problems, passing away and destruction, opposition and war, becoming. In order to understand why she affirms these things, we must know what affirmation itself involves.

In English, something can be affirmed in two senses. In one sense, to affirm something is merely to acknowledge its existence. In this sense, if I say that I "affirm" pain, I mean only that the existence of pain is undeniable. But this sense of affirmation leaves open the question of whether I *approve* of the existence of the thing affirmed. I can acknowledge the existence of pain, while also fervently wishing that I lived in a pain-free world. The second sense of affirmation registers this approval. In this sense, to affirm or say-yes to something is positively to want it to be part of my world. But this second sense of affirmation leaves open the question of whether the thing of which I approve does in fact exist. I can, for example, "affirm" certain political principles or programs that have never been realized.[76]

The tragic soul's affirmation of pain, destruction, opposition, and becoming encompasses both of these everyday uses of the term; the tragic soul is one who has first acknowledged, and then come to approve of or celebrate, the things just mentioned.

This double affirmation by the tragic soul separates her doubly from the nontragic. The nontragic certainly acknowledge that pain and destruction exist, but they do not acknowledge the *necessity* of their existence. Moreover, the nontragic would prefer a world without pain and destruction, a world in which there were only pleasing things that never had to be destroyed. The tragic soul differs on both counts, both acknowledging the necessary existence of pain and destruction, and approving of their existence.

To understand the tragic soul's approval of pain and destruction, we must first understand her acknowledgment of their necessity. This acknowledgment is the result of her scientific voyage through the worlds of nature and culture, a voyage of experimentation made possible by her great health. On this voyage, the most important lessons learned are that nothing is possible without the necessary conditions of its existence, and that those conditions often, paradoxically, include what would appear to be the very opposite of the thing conditioned.

Light, for example, can only be experienced in virtue of the shadows and darkness in distinction from which it appears. Pleasure can only be experienced as pleasure against the background of a normal state that is less dramatically pleasant, and of an opposing state that is positively painful. Creation can only take place in virtue of destruction, for to create is to give new forms to the materials at hand, but this can only be done by destroying the forms that they currently have.

Consequently, to wish for a world without darkness is to wish for a world without light. To wish for a world without pain is to wish for a world without pleasure. And to wish for a world in which nothing is destroyed is to wish for a world in which nothing is created.

The tragic soul acknowledges this fact. But more importantly, having acknowledged the necessary existence of pain and destruction, the tragic soul also comes to approve of their existence, to affirm them in the stronger sense. This second affirmation obviously does not necessarily follow from the first. One possible response to the necessity of destruction and pain in this world is the decadent desire to live in another world altogether, a world in which nothing ever changes and no one ever suffers. Avoiding this decadent response in favor of the tragic one thus depends on preferring a world in which there is both creation and destruction to a world in which there is neither.[77]

The tragic soul has this preference, on Nietzsche's account, because of her overfullness, or superabundance. In the passages cited earlier, we saw Nietzsche claim that the tragic ideal to which great health leads is that of a spirit who "plays naïvely" out of an "overflowing abundance and power." This tragic soul rejoices "in its own inexhaustibility through the *sacrifice* of its highest types."[78]

I take this to mean that the tragic soul is one who is aware of both her own inexhaustible capacity to create, and the fact that such creation inevitably involves destruction and sacrifice. But because she values and enjoys her *capacity* to create more than any of her creations themselves, the tragic soul celebrates this world as a place in which she can exercise this capacity, in preference to any other world in which nothing she loved would ever be destroyed but at the price of the inability to discharge her creative superabundance. Thus the tragic soul "plays naïvely" with the existing creations of herself and others, unconcerned that her play may be destructive, for only by risking such destruction is there any possibility of new creation. And only in such new creation is there any possibility of the ongoing transfiguration of herself and her world that is the necessary condition of her liberation, of her continual overcoming of the fixed measures defining herself and her other.[79]

By contrast, the decadent, who is exhausted rather than inexhaustible, empty rather than overfull, who has nothing to contribute and nothing to create, has no reason to approve of destruction and pain. She therefore clings to her idols and her measure tenaciously, somberly, and without a trace of playfulness, dreaming of a world devoid of becoming, which is therefore devoid of freedom as well.[80]

The tragic soul thus recognizes, as the decadent does not, that the world must either be affirmed or denied, approved or rejected, *in toto*. The decadent would have an impossible world of pleasure, light, and being without pain, darkness, and becoming. The tragic soul relishes her capacity to generate pleasure and light so enthusiastically that she actually relishes pain and darkness as the necessary conditions of that generation.[81]

Nietzsche makes this point repeatedly, throughout his works, in various ways. In a short paragraph from "Opinions and Maxims," headed *The fruitful field*, he writes: "All rejection and negation demonstrates a lack of fruitfulness: at bottom, if we were only good, arable land, we would be able to let nothing perish unused and would see in every thing, event, and person welcome manure, rain, or sunshine."[82] In "The Wanderer and His Shadow," he has the former say to the latter: "I love shadow as I love light. For there to be beauty of face, clarity of speech, goodness and firmness of character, shadow is as necessary as light. They are not opponents: they hold each other (*halten sich*), rather, lovingly hand in hand, and when light disappears, shadow slips away after it."[83] In *Twilight of the Idols*, he adds that we immoralists have [as distinguished from the degenerate] opened our hearts wide to every kind of understanding, comprehension, *approval* (*Gutheissen*). We do not easily deny, we seek our honor in being *affirmative*. Ever more have our eyes been opened to that economy which needs and knows how to use all that the holy lunacy (*Aberwitz*) of the priest, the *sick* reason of the priest throws away... To what advantage? We ourselves, we immoralists, are the answer.[84]

And in *The Antichristian*, he concludes: "'The world is perfect', so speaks the instinct of the most spiritual, the affirmative instinct."[85]

The overfullness and consequent affirmation of the tragic soul are what makes her Dionysian:

Dionysus... is only explicable as an *excess* (*Zuviel*) of force... What did the Hellenic Greek guarantee himself with these [Dionysian] mysteries? *Eternal* life, the eternal return of life; the future augured and sanctified in the past; the triumphant Yes to life over death and change; the *true* life as the total-continued-life through procreation, through the mysteries of sexuality... In the doctrine of the mysteries *pain* is pronounced holy: the "pains of childbirth" make pain in general holy – all becoming and growing, everything vouching for the future is *conditioned* by pain... For there to be the eternal pleasure of creation, for the will to life to affirm itself eternally, there *must* also eternally be the "torment of childbirth"... The word Dionysus signifies all of this.[86]

They also place the tragic soul "beyond good and evil," beyond the perspective that divides the world into positive and negative aspects and dreams of a time and place in which the latter have been eliminated. And this makes her *übermenschlich*. In the section of *Ecce Homo* entitled "Why I Am a Destiny," Nietzsche writes:

Zarathustra, the first psychologist of the good, is – consequently – a friend of evil... He does not conceal the fact that *his* type of man, a relatively *übermenschlicher* type, is *übermenschlich* precisely in relation to the good, that the good and the just would call his *übermensch devil*... This type of man, which he conceives, conceives reality *as it is*: it is strong enough for that; this type is not estranged or removed from reality but is reality itself, it has everything terrible and questionable in itself, *and only thus can man have greatness*.[87]

We have now connected the tragic soul of great health with affirmation, Dionysus, Zarathustra, and the *Übermensch*. Of the original welter of associations, only the eternal return remains to be discussed. That Nietzsche connects the eternal return with these other associated concepts is clear from the fact that it has surfaced in several of the passages we have just examined. How it is connected will be clarified later.

First, we must note that the concept of the tragic soul, having traveled through all of its various associations, has deposited itself in the concept of greatness. The tragic soul is great both in the sense that she is an enlarged spirit – containing and affirming good *and* evil – and in the sense that she is an extraordinary spirit – a rare creature who herself promises rare creations. It is the tragic soul's greatness that connects her to the eternal return, indirectly, through *amor fati*: "My formula for human greatness is *amor fati*: that one wants to have nothing different, not forward, not backward, not in all eternity. Not merely to bear the necessary, still less to conceal it – all idealism is mendaciousness before the necessary – but to *love* it."[88]

Amor fati, the love of fate, is thus the state of the great, tragic soul who has come to affirm the character of this world in both senses. Having acknowledged the necessity of destruction as a condition of creation, the tragic soul does not need to conceal this necessity from herself, does not need to be mendacious before it. And having come to approve of such destruction, out of an overfullness that cannot bear not to create, the tragic soul actively loves this necessity, loves everything about the world that makes it the kind of place in which she can unleash and give form to her superabundance.[89]

Amor fati is linked to the eternal return in the fourth book of *The Joyful Science*, whose first paragraph introduces the former concept to Nietzsche's corpus, and whose penultimate paragraph marks the debut of the latter. Nietzsche describes *amor fati* as

> the thought that ought to be for me the ground, guarantor, and sweetness of all further life! I want ever more to learn to see the necessary in things as the beautiful – thus will I be one of those who makes things beautiful. *Amor fati*: let that be my love from now on! I want to lead no war against the ugly. I do not want to accuse, I do not want to accuse the accusers even once. Let *looking away* be my only denial! And, all in all and on the whole: I want someday to be only a Yes-sayer![90]

And then he presents the eternal return, in a section headed *The greatest heavy-weight*:

> What if one day or night a demon were to steal after you in your loneliest loneliness and say: "This life, as you live it now and have lived it, will you have to live once more and countless times more ... The eternal hourglass of existence is turned over ever again – and you with it, speck of dust!" Would you not throw yourself down and gnash your teeth and curse the demon who spoke thus? Or have you once lived through a monstrous moment, when you would have answered him: "You are a god and never have I heard anything more divine!" If this thought gained control (*Gewalt*) over you,

it would change you as you are and perhaps crush you; the question of each and every thing, "do you want this once more and countless times more?" would lie upon your actions as the greatest heavy-weight! Or, how well-disposed would you have to become (*gut werden*) to yourself and to life, in order *to long for nothing more fervently* than this ultimate, eternal confirmation and seal?[91]

How the relation between *amor fati* and the eternal return is understood depends on how the eternal return is interpreted. For what it is to love one's fate depends on what one understands one's fate to be, what one understands to return eternally and the sense in which one understands it to return.

The eternal return has been interpreted quite variously, but we can organize this variety in two ways. First, we can distinguish interpretations according to the *kind* of thing that they take Nietzsche's presentation of the eternal return to be: some consider it a metaphysical hypothesis or assertion, Nietzsche's own view about how the world really is constituted; whereas others understand it as a kind of psychological challenge or test, in which individuals are encouraged to *imagine* a particular metaphysical scenario and to gauge what their reaction would be to living in the world *if* it were so constituted.[92] Second, we can identify subcategories within these two classes of interpretation based on the *content* of the metaphysical scenario that readers take Nietzsche either to be asserting or to be encouraging us to imagine: perhaps what is eternal is only the general condition of becoming, the perpetual process of destruction and creation that guarantees that the existence of any particular being will be temporary; or, perhaps what returns is not merely becoming in general, but every single particular being that has ever been created or destroyed.

The schema we have just constructed leaves us with four possible types of interpretation. But, given my reading of the other concepts central to the tragic spirit, we can make the most sense of the eternal return with an interpretation that is none of these four. I want to consider a hybrid interpretation, which will both make sense of what we already know about the eternal return and enable us to see a dimension of it that has so far remained concealed.

In my view, the eternal return has both a metaphysical and a psychological component. It is undeniable that Nietzsche thinks that the general process of becoming returns eternally in a metaphysical sense. We have seen that on the tragic soul's journey of knowledge she learns that nothing is created without destroying something else, and that no matter how permanent a particular construction may appear, whether human or natural, a more careful and honest assessment will show that it too eventually must pass. This metaphysical view is well presented in the second paragraph of the third book of *The Joyful Science*, one book before the eternal return makes its first official appearance:

> The astral order in which we live is an exception; this order and the relative duration which is conditioned by it have again made possible the exception of exceptions: the development of the organic. The total-character of the world is, on the contrary, in all eternity chaos, not in the sense of a lack of necessity, but a lack of order, structure, form, beauty, wisdom, and all our aesthetic anthropomorphisms (*Menschlichkeiten*) ... The exceptions are not the secret aim, and the whole music box eternally repeats its tune, which may never be called a melody.[93]

But this does not commit Nietzsche to the view, much more difficult if not impossible to defend, that the whole series of particular beings created by the play of becoming returns eternally in exactly the same sequence. In fact, one could argue that this view and the view that unordered chaos is eternal are mutually exclusive. For if the world were the infinite repetition of the creation and destruction of a fixed sequence of particular beings, it would have, at the most general level, the kind of order, structure, and form that Nietzsche denies to it in the passage just cited. Thus the only metaphysical fate that the tragic soul must love, the only metaphysical fate that she can love, is the eternal return of chaos, the eternal destruction of what has been created, and the eternal creation of new forms out of what has been destroyed.[94]

Nietzsche does, however, ask us in several places to imagine that every detail of our lives will be repeated eternally, without variation. In the passage headed *The greatest heavy-weight*, partially cited earlier, the dwarf suggests not only that the hour-glass of existence will be eternally turned over – which would imply a repetition of general chaos but not of determinate forms – but also that "there will be nothing new [in your life], but every pain and every pleasure and every thought and sigh and everything unspeakably small and great in your life must come again to you, and all in the same succession and sequence – even this spider and this moonlight between the trees, and even this moment and I myself."[95]

We have just seen that we need not interpret this as Nietzsche's own metaphysical view.[96] Instead, we can read it as a psychological test of one's capacity for affirmation. This is explicitly suggested in the first paragraph of the section in *Ecce Homo* on *Zarathustra*, in which Nietzsche calls "the thought of the eternal return" not only the "fundamental conception (*Grundconception*) of the work [*Zarathustra*]" but the "highest formula of affirmation."[97] Combining this with the suggestions of the dwarf, the psychological test asks us whether we love ourselves enough that we could hypothetically will the eternal return of both the specific constructions we presently are and the entire sequence of constructions and destructions that has preceded us. In order to will the eternal return of ourselves, we would also have to will the eternal return of this entire sequence, because we are incapable of disentangling our fate from its fate, incapable of attaining a perspective outside the world from which we could understand how we could have come to be exactly what we are without all the events leading up to us being exactly what they were.[98]

What I have distinguished as the metaphysical and psychological components of the eternal return might appear to be incompatible. For the former asks us to love the fact that everything that exists, including ourselves and our most valued creations, will be destroyed. And the latter asks us to love ourselves and our world, as both are specifically constructed at this very moment, so much that we would love being fated to repeat eternally everything painful and awful in history if only we could enjoy such repetition too.

But this incompatibility is only necessary for those without the great health of the tragic soul, for those clinging to either noble health or skeptical sickness. Those with noble health, self-satisfied in their will and at home in their world, will have no trouble passing the psychological test, affirming the entirety of history out of love for themselves. And those sick with skepticism, incapable of forming and maintaining a determinate will, will easily affirm the metaphysical fate that condemns all determinate forms to destruction. But the latter will fail the psychological test, and the former may acknowledge, but will surely never love, their metaphysical fate. Only the tragic soul will love both fates at once. In virtue of her great health, her capacity to infect her will and nurse it back to health repeatedly, she will affirm both her self as currently constructed and the fact that this construction must and will be destroyed, both the world as it is and the fact that the world is nothing but the chaotic process of destroying what it is and becoming something else. She can do this because although she is at home in her current self and her current world, loving who she is and where she is, she loves equally if not more her capacity to become someone else who is at home somewhere else.[99]

We might ask what sort of effect, if any, this tragic affirmation of both the metaphysical and psychological senses of the eternal return, this dual *amor fati*, could have. For on the surface, by asking one to accept a number of different necessities, it appears to be profoundly conservative, perhaps even nihilistic. The tragic soul must accept and even love the fact that nothing she cares about – indeed, nothing at all – will last forever. And she must accept the fact that, if she loves herself or anything else, she must also love the entire history that made these objects of love possible. The latter necessity would seem to rob the past of any transformative potential it might impart to the future; for if we must love what has been, exactly as it was, how could we be critical of it in a way that would give us specific direction toward a different construction of what will be? And the former necessity would seem to rob the present of any motivation to alter the future; for if all of our efforts will one day be undone, why should we bother to make such efforts in the first place? Is not the effect of tragic affirmation then an indifferent Stoicism, a passive acceptance of and acclimation to whatever fate throws at one, whatever constructions arise and whatever destructions transpire?[100]

Nietzsche's response is clearly no.[101] Without question, one must acknowledge the universality of impermanence, the fact that all form is temporary and destined to be destroyed and re-formed. But this acknowledgment leads to nihilistic ennui only in those who think that the permanent alone can have value. For them, there is no reason to act in the present, for the results of their actions cannot enjoy an eternal future and therefore have no value (except insofar as they supposedly enable the agents to transcend this world of impermanence upon their death).

The tragic spirit of great health, as we have seen, does not subscribe to this equation of value and permanence. She is able to love the impermanent, not only *despite* its impermanence, but in *virtue* of it. For her, impermanence actually increases a thing's value, because it means that the thing has value not only in its current form, but also through the contribution its destruction will make to the creation of valuable things beyond itself.[102] This means that the tragic spirit is not indifferent to the impermanent present and the uncertain future; unlike the decadent, she is not indifferent to what gets created and what gets destroyed in this world. Instead, for her the eternal return as psychological test functions as a challenge: can she *make* herself and the present, again and again, so lovable that she is able to love the entire past?[103]

Meeting this challenge charges the tragic spirit with three tasks. First, she must determine the extent of the unalterable, so that she may expend her energy improving what can be altered. Second, she must improve the alterable to such an extent that she can indeed affirm the entire past as the precondition of the present that she has made lovable. Third, she must not act in ways that make the present less lovable, because this not only makes it impossible to affirm the past now but makes it less likely that the past will be affirmable in the future. For every present action becomes a part of the past, and thus becomes something that eventually has to be made affirmable through one's love of some future present. By performing unlovable acts in the present one thus ultimately adds to the burden that the past imposes on the future, making it increasingly difficult to meet the challenge and pass the test.

As early as the *Meditation* on Wagner, Nietzsche identifies the first two of these tasks with philosophy, which he specifically contrasts with the decadent quest for rest and passive accommodation to the world that most people associate with it:

> Philosophy: most people want to learn nothing other from it than an approximate – very approximate! – understanding of things, in order then to resign themselves to them (*sich in sie zu schicken*). And its soothing and consoling power is so strongly emphasized even by its noblest representatives, that those seeking rest and the indolent must believe that they seek the same thing philosophy seeks. The most important question of all philosophy appears to me on the contrary to be to what extent things have an unalterable nature (*Artung*) and shape (*Gestalt*): in order then, when this question has been answered, to set about *improving the part of the world recognized as alterable* with the most reckless courage.[104]

And in *Dawn*, he provides further evidence that he is far from advocating Stoic acceptance of the prevailing mode of life. There, in a section headed *Ethical life* (Sittlichkeit) *and making stupid* (Verdummung), he writes:

> Ethical custom (*Sitte*) represents the experiences of earlier people with the supposedly useful and harmful – but the *feeling for ethical custom* (ethical life) is related not to these experiences as such, but to the age, the holiness, the indiscussability of ethical custom. And thereby this feeling works against the having of new experiences and the correcting of ethical customs: that is, ethicality works against the arising of new and better ethical customs: it makes stupid.[105]

The first two tasks of the tragic soul thus amount to distinguishing what is truly necessary and unchangeable from what only appears to be so in the light of the currently established perspective, and improving upon the "necessities" that prove to be both alterable and less than perfect.[106] It is these tasks that are the point of the tragic soul's voyage of experimentation. Such experimentation is the attempt to give new and better goals and customs in the wake of destroying the old.[107] If it is successful,

> a time will come when, in order to further ethical rationality (*sittlichvernünftig*), one will prefer to take up the memorabilia of Socrates rather than the Bible... The pathways of the most various philosophical ways of life lead back to him; they are at bottom the ways of life of different temperaments, established through reason and habit, and all are directed toward joy in life and in one's own self.[108]

But the third task of the tragic soul threatens to impose a restrictive burden on her experimentation. For this task – that of *not* doing anything that would make oneself and one's world harder to love – stems from the realization that every action taken in every moment will return eternally as a part of the past that the tragic soul and all of her human descendants must come to affirm. This realization that no act, no matter how small, can ever be escaped is what threatens to crush the person who thinks the eternal return, threatens to paralyze her, in fear of the eternal guilt that would follow from acting in a way that can never be affirmed. It is this realization, then, that makes the eternal return the most terrible thought that lays upon the tragic soul and her actions like the heaviest weight.[109]

THE GLAD TIDINGS OF WORLDLY SELF-REDEMPTION

But one who can think this heaviest thought without collapsing, who can continue to act in full knowledge of both the eternal weight of her actions and the necessary impermanence of the results of those acts, has the opportunity to improve the present in such a way that she can affirm both it and the past. Such a tragic soul has the opportunity to meet the challenge of the eternal return and to present humanity with its greatest gift, the gift of its redemption. Specifically, the tragic soul can redeem humanity from the need to have itself, its present, and its past redeemed, and it is this capability that makes her a fateful "turning point" as the harbinger of freedom.

The world stands in need of redemption for those incapable of the tragic affirmation of the present and the past, incapable of affirming either what is valuable but impermanent in the present or what is horrible and eternal in the past. Since such people cannot redeem the world for themselves through such affirmation, they stand in need of an external redeemer. For Christians, of course, it is Jesus who is supposed to provide this service in his Second Coming. Jesus is to redeem humanity (in the sense of setting it free) from the world by redeeming (in the sense of paying for) the sinful acts that we have committed in the world.[110]

But the tragic soul can dispense with the need for such an external redeemer. In the first place, she does not need to be set free from the world, for she is able to affirm it as it is. Moreover, she does not need someone else to pick up the tab for the past, for her affirmation of the world's present state "pays for" all previously committed "sins." Speaking more strictly, her affirmation changes the status of these past acts so that they are no longer something for which payment is required; because the tragic spirit's affirmation of the present cannot be distinguished from a wholesale affirmation of the past, acts committed in that past cannot be regarded as sins. In other words, because the tragic soul can think of nothing more divine than an eternal recurrence of her present world, she must regard the past, as the price of bringing about this present, as more than worth its cost.

The ultimate task of the tragic soul is thus to redeem the world eternally, in each and every moment, through her own acts of making it affirmable and actually affirming it. She does not wait for redemption, neither requiring nor desiring a Second Coming of someone else, but instead seeks to make redemption something that comes eternally through herself.[111]

Not surprisingly, then, given the connections we have already seen him draw between the tragic soul, Zarathustra, and himself, Nietzsche writes in *Ecce Homo*:

> Zarathustra once determines, strictly, his task – it is also mine – and there is no mistaking his meaning: he is affirmative to the point of the justification (*Rechtfertigung*), also of the redemption (*Erlösung*) of all of the past. "I walk among people as among fragments of the future: the future which I envisage. And this is all my creating (*Dichten*) and striving, that I create (*dichte*) and carry together into one what is fragment and riddle and dreadful accident. And how could I bear to be a man if man were not also creator and guesser of riddles and the redeemer of accidents? *To redeem the past* and to re-create (*umschaffen*) all 'it was' as a 'thus I willed it!' – that alone I call redemption."[112]

That the tragic human task is to redeem the world from within is, I think, the ultimate meaning of the eternal return, the final payoff of the various components of this teaching that we have considered. The point of the *ewige Wiederkunft* (eternal return) is to demonstrate the inadequacy and superfluity of the *Wiederkunft Christi* (Second Coming of Christ). The tragic soul who can bear the heaviest weight of the thought of the eternal return gains the opportunity to redeem the world from its need for a future, external, one-time redemption by redeeming it internally in each and every present moment.

This opportunity for self-redemption is liberating in two senses: it frees us *from* our dependence on a Christlike savior, and it enables us to be free *in* our world, since we no longer need to escape that world in order to be redeemed. The tragic soul who redeems the world thus liberates herself at the same time.[113]

In *Twilight of the Idols*, Nietzsche characterizes Goethe as such a soul, as one who succeeded in liberating himself by redeeming the world from within:

> He did not sever himself (*sich ablösen*) from life, he placed himself within it; he was not despairing and took as much as possible on himself, over himself, in himself. What he wanted was *totality*; he struggled against the separation (*Auseinander*) of reason, sensibility, feeling, will (– preached in the most horrible scholasticism by Kant, the antipode of Goethe), he disciplined himself to wholeness, he *created* himself ... Such a *free-become* (*freigewordner*) spirit stands with a joyful and trusting fatalism in the midst of the universe, in the *faith* that only the individual is condemnable (*verwerflich*), that in the whole everything is redeemed and affirmed – *he denies no more* ... But such a faith is the highest of all possible faiths: I have baptized it with the name *Dionysus*.[114]

The tragic soul can rightfully take pride in her ability to redeem her world and to liberate herself through her own activity. But she recognizes that this pride is justifiable only as long as her ability is useful – that is, as long as she lives in a world that needs redemption, and for which no external redeemer is available. The tragic soul would therefore have the world no other way. Unlike the decadent, she would not prefer to live in a heavenly, atemporal world of permanence that needs no redemption; the tragic soul needs a world of destruction and pain in order to take pride in her ability to create things that give pleasure.[115] And, again unlike the decadent, given that she lives in an earthly world of impermanence and temporality that must be redeemed, the tragic soul does not wish for someone else to shoulder the burden of the redeeming; she needs to perform the redemption herself, if she is to take pride in making herself free.[116] In Nietzsche's terms, the tragic soul sees the abyss (*Abgrund*) with pride,[117] and experiences the death of God as a dawn.[118]

To see the abyss, to think the most abyssal thought,[119] to see that all seeing is seeing abysses,[120] is to know that there is no firm ground on which the world has been or could be permanently constructed and secured, or from which a permanent perspective for judging the world could take its bearings. It is to know, that is, that the world is eternally in need of redemption, because the past must always be justified in terms of the present, and because every such justification, no matter how successful, is necessarily impermanent, given that the world is temporal and subject to becoming.

To see this abyss with pride, then, is to see it not as a reason to condemn the world and seek to flee it, as the decadent does, but as a reason to celebrate, for it gives one the opportunity to redeem the world, which one would not have if the world had the kind of ground that absolved it from the need for redemption. It is to be like Zarathustra, "he who has the hardest, most terrible insight into reality, who has thought the 'most abyssal thought', but nevertheless finds therein no objection to existence, not even to its eternal return – but rather one more reason (*Grund*) to be himself the eternal Yes to all things, 'the monstrous unlimited Yes and Amen saying'."[121]

The death of God signifies, among other things, both the death of Christ – as God's incarnation – and the death of Heaven, the otherworldly paradise purportedly created by God in preparation for our arrival. It signifies, that is, both the fact that redemption of this world cannot take place through a severance from it that removes us to an other-world, and the fact that our redemption cannot be performed by someone else. Redemption of this world must take place in this world, through the efforts of those who live here.[122]

If to see the abyss with pride is to celebrate the fact that our world is in need of redemption, to experience the death of God as a dawn is to celebrate the fact that it is we who must redeem the world from within. It is to exclaim, as Zarathustra's good taste does to the old Pope, "Away with *such* a God! Rather no god, rather make destiny on one's own, rather be a fool, rather be a god oneself!"[123]

For the tragic soul, then, the abyssal character of the world and the fact that there is no possible escape from this world and its abysses to a grounded other-world are causes for celebration, reasons for joy. However, this joy that she finds in the opportunity to redeem the world will be short-lived if she does not seize the opportunity and actualize such redemption, if she does not act to improve the present so that she can affirm the entire past. But the improvement required to achieve redemption is nothing less than the transformation of humanity; our redemption requires the displacement of the prevailing decadent morality – with its hostility to knowledge and experimentation, its cowardly flight from reality, and its hope for an external redemption – by the tragic soul's tragic spirit, with its honesty and justice toward all things, its brave persistence in the face of the abyss, and its pride in its ability to redeem itself. The tragic soul, therefore, must somehow communicate her ability to affirm the world to others, must somehow share the joy she has found.

The tragic soul attempts to share her joy by bringing her discoveries to the world as "glad tidings."[124] The tidings are the discoveries themselves: existence and becoming cannot be redeemed in a flight to an other-world of permanent being; and no external redeemer can provide our redemption. The gladness with which the tidings are to be received stems from the implications that the tragic soul has drawn from those discoveries: right and innocence have been restored to existence and becoming, in which we eternally dwell;[125] and we need not pray for an external redeemer to accept the punishment that will pay for our sins, because we can bring about our own absolution from the *guilt* of those sins by redeeming them in the present, so that no punishment is required.[126]

Amazingly, Nietzsche considers these thoroughly anti-Christian glad tidings, the announcement that we are redeemed from the need for a redeemer, to be precisely those brought by Jesus himself:

> In the whole psychology of the "Gospel" the concept guilt and punishment is lacking; likewise the concept reward. "Sin," every kind of distance-relationship between God and human is abolished – *just that is the "glad tidings."* Blessedness is not promised, it is not tied to conditions: it is the *only* reality – the rest is signs, in order to speak of it... The *consequence* of such a condition projects itself in a new *practice*, the proper evangelic practice. Not a "faith" distinguishes the Christian: the Christian acts, he distinguishes himself through a *different* acting. Neither in word nor in his heart does he contradict he who does him evil. He makes no distinction between foreigner (*Fremden*) and native (*Einheimischen*), between Jew and

non-Jew... The life of the redeemer was nothing other than *this* practice – his death was also nothing other... He no longer had need of any formulas, any rites for trafficking with God – not even prayer... He knows that it is only through the *practice* of life that one feels himself "divine," "blessed," "evangelic," at all times "a child of God." It is *not* "penance," *not* "prayer for forgiveness" that are ways to God: *only evangelic practice* leads to God, it *is* even "God"... The profound instinct for how one would have to *live* in order to feel himself "in heaven," in order to feel himself "eternal," while in every other relation one does *not* "feel in heaven": this alone is the psychological reality of "redemption" – A new way of life (*Wandel*), *not* a new faith.[127]

This is in stark contrast to Christianity's own interpretation of its founder:

> Nothing is more unchristian than the *churchly crudities* of God as a *person*, of a "kingdom of God" which *comes*, of a "kingdom of heaven" *beyond*, of a "son of God," the *second person* of the trinity... It is obvious what is touched on with the signs "father" and "son"... with the word "son" is expressed the *entry* into the feeling of the total-transfiguration (*Gesammt-Verklärungs-Gefühl*) of all things (blessedness), with the word "father" *this feeling itself*, the feeling of eternality, of perfection. – I am ashamed to recall what the church has made out of this symbolism... The "kingdom of heaven" is a condition of the heart – not something that comes "upon the earth" or "after death"... The "kingdom of God" is not something that one awaits; it has no yesterday and no tomorrow, it does not come in "a thousand years" – it is an experience in a heart; it is everywhere, it is nowhere.[128]

Nietzsche concludes that Christ neither lived nor died to redeem humanity, as his followers think, but to show us how to live in freedom from the need for redemption, in freedom from resentment toward this world and that within it which opposes us. Christ lived and died for, and brought as his glad tidings, a new kind of practice that would produce happiness within the world, and divinity and freedom within humanity.[129] These are the very same glad tidings brought by the tragic soul. Christ and the tragic soul, Zarathustra and Nietzsche – all bear as their gift to humanity the glad tidings of its liberation.

Humanity, however, has not only produced too few tragic souls bearing this ultimate gift, but has also failed to receive them properly when they have arrived. The misinterpretation of Christ exemplifies this phenomenon. Presented with the gift of Christ's glad tidings, humanity not only failed to grasp and share his tragic spirit, with which they could have redeemed and liberated themselves, but actually inverted it, inaugurating two millennia of decadence and nihilism.

Nietzsche's highest hope, which we have seen him express in several contexts and in various vocabularies, is that humanity will again give rise to tragic souls, and that this time it will also be prepared to receive them. His hope is that humanity can prepare itself to receive and nourish the tragic spirit of these tragic souls, so that this spirit can spread and become self-reinforcing. Ultimately, if tragic great health can replace decadence as the dominant human condition, humanity will be enabled to take up the ongoing work of its own worldly redemption and liberation.

But this hoped-for future can only be realized if, somehow, the decadent age within which we live can be transformed sufficiently to allow the first few tragic souls to emerge and begin to communicate their spirit. At the end of the second essay of the *Genealogy of Morals*, Nietzsche pleads for such an emergence:

> Some day, in a stronger age than this rotten, self-doubting present, he must come to us, the *redeeming* (*erlösende*) man of great love and contempt, the creative spirit whose compelling force always drives him again out of every remoteness (*Abseits*) and beyond, whose isolation is misunderstood by the people, as if it were a flight *from* actuality – while it is only his immersion, entombing (*Vergrabung*), penetration (*Vertiefung*) *into* actuality, so that when he again comes out of it into the light, he brings home the *redemption* of this actuality ... from the previous ideal [and] from that which had to grow out of it, from the great nausea, from the will to nothing, from nihilism; this bell-stroke of midday and the great decision, who makes the will free again, who gives back the earth its goal and man his hope, this anti-Christian and anti-nihilist, this victor over God and nothing – *he must come one day*.[130]

FREEDOM THROUGH NIETZSCHE'S PHILOSOPHY

We have seen that the tragic soul is necessary to freedom, and we have considered many of the prerequisites for this soul's emergence. Such a soul must combine modernity and nobility, amnesia and memory, the abilities to impregnate and to give birth to herself. Such a soul must be courageous, skeptical, and forceful. Such a soul must be *unsittlich* and experimental, yet whole, a monstrous multiplicity. Such a soul must be an infinite melody and a swimmer. Above all, such a soul must have great health: she must be able to affirm the world out of overfullness, loving the fated eternal return of chaos at the same time that she loves the current construction of the world and herself enough to wish that it were their fate to return eternally.

But all of these prerequisites are themselves conditioned by a further prerequisite, which is therefore itself a condition upon which the tragic spirit, redemption, and liberation depend: the tragic soul must have available to her a kind of language through which she can experience the world tragically, and in which she can communicate her tragic spirit and great health to others.

For Nietzsche, then, freedom depends on the emergence of a kind of language capable of facilitating the transition from the noble to the tragic. The ultimate condition of freedom is therefore the practice of those activities that enable tragic language to emerge. Nietzsche identifies philosophy as one of these activities, and thus concludes that our liberation is made possible by and completed through philosophical practice.

Section 1 of this chapter examines what Nietzsche means by the language of tragedy, and how he understands the emergence of such language to be necessary to freedom. Section 2 concludes Part II with a discussion of how philosophy, as Nietzsche understands and practices it, can serve as a liberating source of tragic language.

1. The Language of Tragedy as a Condition of Freedom

Nietzsche's contention that the fate of the tragic spirit turns on find-ing or developing an appropriate kind of language should not be overly surprising. For we have already seen him argue that certain features of ordinary language are central to the hegemony of decadent metaphysics and morality.[1]

Specifically, recall, Nietzsche argues that decadent metaphysics is sup-ported by our tendency to reify linguistic subjects and objects; we are prone to assume that the discrete and stable units of language – words – must refer to units of reality that are equally discrete and stable. We assume, for example, that the words "soul" and "will" must refer to dis-crete things or substances, which have as their properties or accidents the attributes contained in the definitions of those words. Additionally, Nietzsche contends that decadent morality is supported by the tendency of language to bring to words only the most common feelings, the feel-ings of the herd. So, for example, although the word "good" has come to signify what the herd considers good, it is used and understood as if it connoted the good-in-itself. In this way, the most common feelings become even more widespread and more deeply entrenched.

To recapitulate the relationships Nietzsche takes to obtain between most Indo-European languages and the hegemony of decadence: the very structure of such languages, their neat division of the universe into discrete subjects and objects identifiable by individual words, lends cre-dence to a decadent metaphysics of being; this metaphysics, in which souls, free wills, God, and the true world thrive, encourages a decadent morality of selflessness, the goal of which is to escape this apparent world of becoming for the postulated real world of being; as this morality comes to predominate, its valuations "grasp the word" ever more strongly, the specific words we use to indicate what is valued become imbued with deca-dent content; this result then reinforces the entire process by spreading and strengthening decadent feeling, which both increases belief in the metaphysics of being and further tightens the decadent grasp on the words in circulation.[2]

The triumph of this process is indicated by its complete invisibility. The metaphysics of being and the morality of selflessness ultimately acquire such a chokehold on language that it becomes impossible to imagine that language once might have been, or could someday be, possessed by a different spirit. More strictly speaking, it becomes impossible to imagine or notice that language is possessed at all; decadent language is simply taken for language-in-itself.[3]

It is at this point that the prospects for the tragic spirit, and so for freedom, are most bleak. For this point is analogous to that at which the preconditions of knowledge are destroyed, so that the decadent is no longer aware of the difference between knowledge and faith, and therefore no longer struggles against the conditions of her enslavement. Now language, the very medium of thought for Nietzsche, has itself become decadent, so the decadent literally has no means for thinking, articulating, or expressing the difference between her decadent thought and any possible alternative. At this point, it is impossible to think outside of the metaphysics of being and the morality of selflessness within which one is trapped by decadent language. The would-be tragic soul, therefore, has no access to the tragic spirit.[4]

Before turning to Nietzsche's discussion of how the tragic spirit can wrest language from decadence, we should briefly consider the relationship of language to nobility. Just as the noble represents a midpoint between the decadent and the tragic in terms of liberation, so she is also a midpoint with respect to her relationship to language. The noble, in escaping the morality of selflessness through her reconstruction of the preconditions for knowledge and subsequent revaluation of values, regains possession of words like "good" and "bad," replacing their decadent content with content from her own experience. But although these noble values are self-generated, rather than externally imposed, the noble continues to share with the decadent a firm commitment to her established perspective, to her fixed set of convictions and values. This means that noble values and feelings grasp the word as forcefully as do their decadent counterparts, and noble language is therefore equally likely to foster a metaphysics of stability and being (albeit with different specific contents). Consequently, noble language is hardly more helpful to the would-be tragic soul than decadent language is; just as the healthy noble will must be overcome through an infection with multiplicity, so must noble language be overcome to make possible the thinking characteristic of the tragic soul.

But if neither decadent nor noble language is adequate to tragic thinking, the question, asked by Nietzsche near the end of his discussion of *Zarathustra* in *Ecce Homo*, obviously becomes, "What language will such a spirit speak, when he speaks to himself?"[5] In what kind of language, that is, could the tragic experience of the world possibly be thought?

We can approach this question by recollecting the central features of tragic experience, which tragic language must be capable of thinking and communicating. First and foremost, the tragic soul must be able doubly to affirm her double fate; she must be able to acknowledge and celebrate both the fact that everything in existence must someday be destroyed, and the fact that she and her world are currently constructed as they are. That is, she must have a sense for what is necessary (the eternal return of chaotic becoming) and for what is not (any given construction or valuation). With this sense she will be able to value what is impermanent, both for what it temporarily is and for the fact that its impermanence makes possible the creation of things beyond it, and she will therefore regain the motivation to alter and improve the present in a way that leads to a future in which the past is redeemed. That is, she will be able to work at becoming free through her own activity, rather than working at not being, as the decadent does.[6]

It is also central to tragic experience that it be shared, that it develop into a tragic culture. This is not merely a secondary phenomenon, something that takes place after the tragic spirit has arisen, but is rather inseparable from the full emergence of that spirit itself. This is because a single tragic soul would not be able to affirm a decadent present in a way that redeems the past, and so would necessarily fall short of the tragic spirit. The emergence of the tragic spirit in any given tragic soul is therefore contingent upon the tragic spirit spreading sufficiently wide and deep that the world becomes affirmable for one healthily infected with it.

Our question can now be refined. What language – what words and what style – could be adequate to both the experience of affirming an impermanent world and the communication of that experience? In what language can the glad tidings of redemption and liberation be offered and received?

Nietzsche emphasizes the connection between style (*Stil*), words, thoughts, and the disposition or attunement (*Stimmung*) that they communicate in "The Wanderer and His Shadow." To choose or develop a style is for Nietzsche at the same time to choose or develop words and thoughts.[7] We can infer that various styles are appropriate to various ways of thinking, to various attunements, dispositions, and spirits.[8]

But, Nietzsche cautions us, we should not infer, as many do, that the best style is the one most suited to whatever spirit we happen to wish to communicate. On the contrary, the best style is the one most suited to communicating the best spirit, the spirit most worthy of communication:[9]

Learning to write well... Always to invent things more worthy of communication and actually to be able to communicate them; to become translatable into the languages of neighbors; to make ourselves accessible (*zugänglich*) to the understanding of those foreigners who learn our language; so that all goods become common-goods, and everything stands free for the free (*den Freien Alles frei stehe*); finally, to prepare that still so distant condition of things, in which good Europeans will come into possession of their great task: the direction and supervision of total earth-culture. – Whoever preaches the opposite, not concerning himself with writing well and reading well – both virtues grow together and decline together – in fact shows peoples a way that they may become ever more national: he augments the sickness of this century and is an enemy of good Europeans, an enemy of free spirits.[10]

The task, that is, is to create the style best suited to the communication of the tragic, Dionysian spirit, and thus to the development of tragic, Dionysian culture.

The question, however, is what general strictures would apply to such a style? First, tragic style must have something in common with the style and language of those who are not yet possessed by the tragic spirit. For if this were not the case it would be incapable of communicating anything to them. Communication requires commonality, and so tragic style must make use of words, concepts, figures, and conventions in common use:

> Three-quarters of Homer is convention; and it is similar with all Greek artists, who had no reason for the modern rage for originality. They lacked all fear of convention; through this indeed they were connected (*sie hingen zusammen*) with their public. Conventions are the *achieved* artistic means, the toilsomely acquired common language, with which the artist can actually *communicate* himself to the understanding of the audience . . . That which the artist invents beyond convention he gives out from his own volition (*aus freien Stücken*) and with it puts himself at risk, in the best case with the result that he *creates* a new convention. The original is often admired, sometimes idolized, but rarely understood; to avoid convention obstinately means: wanting not to be understood. To what, then, does the modern rage for originality point?[11]

As early as the *Meditation* on "Wagner in Bayreuth," Nietzsche attributes to Wagner this understanding that the uncommon tragic spirit, which his music of "infinite melody" aims to express, must somehow be communicated through common means:

> [Wagner] subjects himself to the language of culture and all the laws of its communication, although he has already been the first to discover the profound insufficiency (*Ungenügen*) of this communication. For, if there is something that sets his art apart from all art of modern times, it is this: it no longer speaks the language of the culture of a caste, and in general no longer knows the opposition of cultured and uncultured . . . it must overturn all concepts of education and culture in the spirit of everyone who experiences it; it will appear to him that a curtain has been lifted off of a future, in which there are no more highest goods and happinesses that are not common to all hearts.[12]

But as this passage also indicates, tragic language cannot be *merely* common. The language of common communication is "insufficient" at the same time that it is necessary. It is insufficient because the very feature in virtue of which it is capable of serving as a means of communication – its commonality – consigns it to communicating common feelings and thoughts, the decadent spirit with which it is imbued and which the tragic spirit must overcome. The common language with which one is able to communicate, that is, is not a neutral medium in which any spirit at all can be expressed, but is rather "loaded" with the prevailing spirit of the age.

In Nietzsche's terms, common words are words become petrified, words that have entombed particular views and values and therefore function as prejudices, as invisible boundaries which people using common language can neither think beyond nor even see. In the shortest of the three hundred and fifty aphorisms that comprise "The Wanderer and His Shadow," Nietzsche writes: "*The danger of language for spiritual freedom. –* Every word is a prejudice."[13] In *Dawn*, he elaborates, writing first:

> *Words lie in our way!* – Everywhere the ancients erected a word, they believed they had made a discovery. How different it stood in truth! – They had touched on a problem, and in supposing they had *solved* it they had created a hindrance to its solution. – Now in every act of knowing (*Erkenntniss*) one must stumble over rock-hard, immortalized words, and will thereby sooner break a leg than a word.[14]

And then: "*Words present in us.* – We always express our thoughts with the words we have at hand. Or, to express my whole suspicion: we have at every moment only the thought for which the words we have at hand make possible the approximate expression."[15]

The problem, then, is somehow to use the common words with which one can communicate to communicate something other than the common prejudices that they immortalize. The hope for a solution lies in Nietzsche's view that at the same time that they are stones and stumbling blocks, words are also pockets into which various meanings have been and can be stuffed.[16] The trick is thus to load or stuff these common pockets with tragic rather than decadent contents, and so to transform people's thinking by disrupting the prejudices of the language they already speak.

The tragic content with which language's pockets must be stuffed is itself the knowledge that words are stuffed pockets, that every word is a prejudice. If *this* content can be communicated, it will undermine the tendency of common language to reinforce the metaphysics of being and the morality of enslavement, as it will expose the fact that words do not *refer* to preexisting stable beings and values, but rather temporarily *create* stable beings and values by artificially dividing the chaotic cosmos into unified pieces to which we can henceforth refer: "This has given me and continues to give me the greatest trouble: to realize (*einsehen*) that unspeakably more lies in what things are called than in what they are . . . It suffices to create new names and valuations and probabilities, in order in the long run to create new 'things'."[17]

The communication of this troubling realization can transpire only illustratively, or by example; people must actually see the process by which words and things continually are being and have been constructed.[18] Failing this, people may discover that words have multiple references, or

that their references change over time, but they will not be persuaded
that language itself is not primarily referential. Failing this, that is, people
may be moral or noble, but not tragic, and therefore not free. For freedom
requires us to recognize not just that a particular structure of words and
values is currently dominant, but that the dominant understanding of
linguistic and evaluative structures is misguided.[19]

2. Philosophy as a Source of Tragic Language

Freedom thus depends upon the practice of those activities that are able
to communicate the tragic spirit by illustrating the tragic character of language. And such a liberating illustration, we have seen, requires exposing
the invisible prejudices contained in common words and conventions, as
well as disrupting those prejudices by using common words and conventions in unconventional and transformative ways. Because Nietzsche
considers philosophy, as he understands and practices it, to be one of
the primary sources of linguistic exposition and transformation, he also
considers philosophy to be one of the primary sources of freedom.

The exposition of existing conceptual prejudices as prejudices requires the sort of philosophical work that Nietzsche characterizes as genealogical. Such work is primarily negative, in the sense that it aims to
show that certain concepts, and the social and political institutions that
rest upon them, are not what they seem. Most especially, philosophical
genealogy aims to show that concepts and institutions that seem to be
eternal and necessary are in fact neither; having emerged and evolved in
response to the needs of particular people in particular situations, their
validity is temporal and contingent.

Philosophical genealogy thus has a liberating potential: when successful, it undermines the hegemony of conceptual distinctions and political structures that might once have made sense, but no longer do. By
demonstrating that such distinctions and structures exist not by right of
absolute necessity, but rather in virtue of a cultural forgetfulness that sanctions their continued operation, philosophical genealogy encourages us
to strive to modify or even to dismantle aspects of our world that have
outlived their utility.

Nietzsche's own *Genealogy of Morals* is, of course, the seminal work of
this type. In it, as we have seen throughout Part II, Nietzsche dissects some
of the concepts and values most fundamental to the modern West, and
shows that the very phenomenon of "morality," as traditionally conceived,
is neither necessary nor universally beneficial, but rather the outcome of
millennia of struggle between competing interests, not all of which are
well served by the resulting status quo. Decadence has triumphed over
nobility (not to mention tragedy), and consequently certain interpretations and evaluations of the good, conscience, guilt, and punishment

have come to seem not only true but self-evidently so. The target of Nietzsche's attack is this supposed self-evidence, which prevents us from investigating and transforming the decadent evaluations that inhibit our potential for freedom.

But Nietzschean genealogy is not limited to Nietzsche's own *Genealogy of Morals*, nor did he intend it to be. In an unpublished note from 1884, Nietzsche writes that he offers his philosophical genealogy "not as a dogma, but rather as provisional guidelines for research (*vorläufige Regulative der Forschung*)."[20] And indeed, it is as the founding document of a still-flourishing species of research that Nietzsche's *Genealogy* has had its most profound impact, an impact most notably manifested in, but certainly not limited to, the work of Michel Foucault. In his essay "Nietzsche, Genealogy, History," Foucault articulates the kind of methodological statement for genealogy that Nietzsche himself never did.[21] And in *Discipline and Punish: The Birth of the Prison*, Foucault has produced the classic of contemporary genealogical studies, which not only practices his explicitly Nietzschean method, but also applies it to a concept, that of punishment, that Nietzsche himself raised as a candidate for such analysis in his own *Genealogy*.[22] Elsewhere Foucault examines the emergence and evolution of the concepts of madness, sickness, humanity, and sexuality, and of the institutions that those concepts support.[23] All of this work is indebted to Nietzsche, and an army of current scholars is, in turn, indebted to Foucault. Thus the practice of philosophical genealogy, understood as the potentially liberating exposition of prevailing conceptual and institutional prejudices, is alive and well, more than a century after the appearance of the *Genealogy of Morals*.

Nietzsche has shown us, however, that freedom requires not only the exposition of the prejudices embedded in our language, but also their transformation, and that the success of this transformation depends upon creative linguistic experiments. This creative and experimental work is less easily characterized (and imitated) than is genealogy; by definition there is no one way to go about it. Nietzsche's most elaborate experiment is, of course, *Thus Spoke Zarathustra*, but throughout his productive life he experimented with a variety of styles and forms, including irony, metaphor, polemic, aphorism, dialogue, and autobiography. Perhaps the only thing that these various philosophical experiments can be said to have in common is that they all, in different ways, employ the technique that Nietzsche identifies as *katachresis*: they all, that is, strive to transform common words and conventions by using them in unconventional ways.[24]

Rather than introducing new words, or relying on unusual older words, those who practice the poetic art of *katachresis* succeed by doing more than is customary with the words in common use: "A noble poverty, but a masterly freedom within this inconspicuous possession, distinguishes the Greek artists of speech: they want to have *less* than the people

have – for it is they [the people] who are richest in old and new – but they want to have this less *better*."[25] Instead of shunning traditional conventions, these artists – who are not exclusively either ancient Greeks or poets – transform them through their mastery:

> *Freedom in fetters – a princely freedom* . . . Chopin had the same princely nobility of convention that Raphael shows in the use of the simplest, traditional colors – not in respect to colors, however, but in respect to melodic and rhythmic traditions. He accepted the value of these, as *born to etiquette*, but playing and dancing in these fetters like the freest and most graceful spirit – and without mocking them.[26]

And finally, out of this masterful transformation, they develop new conventions to be taken up by their contemporaries and those to come:

> *Dancing in chains.* – It is to be asked of every Greek artist, poet, and writer: what is the new constraint, which he imposes on himself? . . . For what is called "invention" (in metrics, for example), is always such a self-imposed fetter. "Dancing in chains," making it difficult for oneself and then spreading over it the illusion of ease – that is the artifice they want to show us. Already in Homer an abundance of inherited formulae and epic narrative rules is perceived, within which he had to dance: and he himself created new conventions for those coming afterward. This was the education-school of the Greek poets: firstly to let a manifold constraint be imposed on oneself, through the earlier poets; so as then to invent a new constraint, to impose it on oneself and conquer it gracefully: so that constraint and conquest become noticed and admired.[27]

It is in and through this poetic mastery, transformation, and expansion of conventional forms and words, then, that the pockets of language can be restuffed while also remaining open and accessible to those whose understanding and use of language is more prosaic. Because this is essential to the development and communication of the tragic spirit, and so to freedom, we must now consider in more detail exactly how Nietzsche thinks this poetic restuffing can come about.

We already know that for Nietzsche the activity of poetic transformation cannot be one of will. For the will is measured, defined by its adherence to a fixed set of convictions and values, which themselves rest on a fixed loading of language. The poetic activity of continually unloading and reloading language's pockets, therefore, corresponds not to the will but to the will's continual transgression and reconstitution, undertaken by the tragic soul of great health. It is precisely in and through this poetic activity, that is, that the fixed distinction between the will and its external other is overcome, enabling the more complete liberation characteristic of the tragic soul.

But if the poetic in-formation of language with the tragic spirit is not willed, how does it take place? Nietzsche contends that it is a necessary outcome of the overfullness of tragic souls. Some of these overfull souls who serve as the source of linguistic transformation are artists – Nietzsche describes the essence of beautiful and great art as a gratitude that requires "sublime symbols and practices" because "its heart is too full."[28] And others are philosophers of a certain sort – Nietzsche contends that philosophy can be done out of richness or out of lack, and that in the former cases it comes from a "triumphant gratitude that must write itself in cosmic capital letters on the heaven of concepts."[29]

The overfullness of such tragic philosophers and artists, we have seen, drives them to destroy out of a need to create and, in particular, drives them to destroy their own wills out of a need to create and recreate their own measures. Since we have now linked this cycle of will destruction and reformation with the cycle of linguistic transformation, we can understand Nietzsche's claim that those who must participate in the former cycle must also participate in the latter: the great health characterized by the continual reinfection and convalescence of one's will is also characterized by the continual breaking and relinking of the linguistic chains within which one's will dances. These two cycles – of transforming one's will and one's language – are inseparable, and are perhaps even best understood as being the same.

In continually destroying the measure of her will, in being *unsittlich*, the tragic soul refuses to accept the petrified contents of her language. Whether these are the dominant contents of her age, or contents she herself has managed to develop in constructing a noble will, it is their petrifaction that is unacceptable and incongruous with her tragic disposition. And in striving to love the world, in striving to redeem the past, the tragic soul attempts to provide language with contents that will allow the present to be affirmed. Her continual efforts to redeem the world from within the moment, that is, are primarily linguistic efforts. The tragic soul strives to develop a style and a vocabulary that present the world in such a way that she can affirm it, that she can will both the current world's eternal return and the eternal return of the chaos that ensures the current world's destruction.[30]

This means that just as the tragic soul's will must continually be remeasured, so too must the language in which the convictions and values that form that measure are themselves formed continually be reloaded. The tragic soul must therefore play with her linguistic conventions, transforming both those she has inherited and those she has previously developed, and bequeath them as her gifts to others. She seeks to develop a language that, because its words and styles are never fixed in a way that could lend credence to a metaphysics of being, can do justice to the tragic spirit, its love of chaos, and its continual effort to remake the present in a way that redeems the past in a lovable future.[31]

But we might continue to wonder how this liberating transformation of thought and language is possible. After all, if thought is determined by language, how can thought effect the linguistic change that is necessary to change itself? This would seem to require that thought somehow escape language, at least temporarily, in order to sneak up on it from behind and bring about the alteration.

But on Nietzsche's view, in which thought is not separable from language, this is impossible. No thinking subject can deliberately divest her thought of the language in which it takes place, in order then to use that linguistically purified thought to alter language before quietly slipping back into it.[32]

Instead, the transformation of thought and language must take place precisely through the *suspension* of thinking, because thinking is necessarily linguistically informed. The development of a thinking and a language adequate to the tragic spirit, that is, must come about not through a thoughtful displacement of style, but through a displacement of thought that enables a tragic style to emerge:

> What concerns the making of intimations (*Ahnen-machen*): here our concept "style" takes its point of departure. Above all no thought! Nothing is more compromising than a thought! Rather the condition before thought, the throng of not yet born thoughts, the promise of future thoughts, the world as it was before God created it – a recrudescence of chaos... Chaos makes intimations... Spoken in the language of the master [Wagner]: infinity, but without melody.[33]

In other words, the infinite melody that is the tragic subject, the continual process of self-multiplication and reunification that freedom presupposes, itself presupposes what Nietzsche here calls an infinity without melody. This latter infinity has no melody because it is not the unification of a multiplicity, but rather the continual upsurge of unthought intimations into thought that makes possible both the multiplication and the subsequent reunification of thinking subjects.

But now it seems that that which makes possible the tragic spirit, which in turn makes possible the redemption and liberation of tragic souls, is itself not the doing of those souls themselves. And if this is the case, it seems that those souls can never be fully liberated, for they remain inescapably dependent upon something other than themselves to provide them with the unrequested yet requisite intimations out of chaos. The tragic soul, that is, is overfull with intimations capable of transforming thought and language into a style adequate to tragedy, but does not appear to be responsible for her own overfullness. Indeed, it would seem that she simply could not be responsible for this overfullness, for if she were, she would be full of thoughts rather than intimations. From where, then, does this overfullness arise, and what role does the tragic soul have in its production?

Nietzsche discusses this phenomenon in *Ecce Homo*'s treatment of *Zarathustra*. There, he tells us that in Zarathustra, as well as in himself, language returns to the nature of imagery (*Bildlichkeit*).[34] That is, in the tragic soul intimations rather than thoughts are able to grasp the word. Nietzsche also explains that this must take place through "what poets of stronger ages called inspiration":

> The idea (*Vorstellung*) of being a mere incarnation, mere mouthpiece, mere medium of overpowering forces...The concept of revelation, in the sense that suddenly, with unspeakable certainty and subtlety, something becomes *visible*, audible...One hears, one does not seek; one takes, one does not ask who gives; like a lightning bolt a thought flashes up, with necessity, in form without hesitation – I have never had a choice. A rapture (*Entzückung*) whose tremendous tension occasionally discharges itself in a storm of tears...a complete being-outside-of-oneself (*Ausser-sichsein*)...Everything happens involuntarily to the highest degree, but as in a storm of a feeling of freedom, of being unconditioned, of power, of divinity – The involuntariness of image, of metaphor, is the most curious of all; one has no more concept, what is an image, what is a metaphor, everything offers itself as the nearest, most correct, simplest expression. It actually appears, to recall some words of Zarathustra, as if the things themselves approached and offered themselves as metaphors ("...Here the words and word-shrines of all being burst open to you; here all being wants to become word, all becoming wants to learn to speak from you"). This is my experience of inspiration.[35]

This theme, of the subject surrendering herself as a thinking and speaking subject so that she may be spoken *through* in a way that alters thought, recurs throughout Nietzsche's texts in a number of different guises and vocabularies. Chronologically, we find that: in *The Birth of Tragedy*, "insofar as the subject is the artist...he has already been released (*erlöst*) from his individual will, and has become, as it were, the medium through which the one truly existent subject celebrates its release (*Erlösung*) into appearance";[36] in "Wagner in Bayreuth," "the previously invisible and inward escapes into the sphere of the visible and becomes appearance," "tragedy comes into being," through a "dithyrambic dramatist" whose "wholly heroic-exuberant will" becomes an "ecstatic (*wonnereichen*) going-under and no-more-willing (*Nicht-mehr-Wollens*)";[37] in *Dawn*, those in whom "new and deviant thoughts, valuations, drives again and again broke out" are described as subject to a madness (*Wahnsinn*) "that bore so visibly the sign of complete involuntariness as the convulsions and froth of the epileptic, that seemed to mark the madman as the mask and sound-pipe of a divinity";[38] Zarathustra reports that "a new speech *comes* to me...like a storm come my happiness and my freedom," and describes the earth as "a [gaming] table for gods [that] trembles with creative new words and gods' [dice] throws";[39] *Beyond Good and Evil* defines a philosopher as one "who is struck by his own thoughts as from without, as from above and below . . . who is perhaps himself a storm pregnant with new lightning";[40] the *Genealogy of Morals* understands the artist as "only the precondition of his work, the womb, the soil, sometimes the dung and manure on which, out of which, it grows";[41] finally, *Twilight of the Idols* asserts that intoxication (*Rausch*) is a precondition of all aesthetic doing, perceiving, and transforming, and describes the intoxicated Dionysian as having an "understanding and divining (*erratenden*) instinct" that makes it "impossible *not* to understand a suggestion."[42]

In all of these vocabularies, Nietzsche presents the same insights regarding the conditions of the possibility of freedom: first, that the soul can become tragic and free only by giving up its subjectivity, by giving up the stance from which it is always opposed by an independent and external world of objects, which it opposes with its will, informed by thought and language; and second, that the activities through which this liberating suspension of subjectivity is most likely to transpire are art and philosophy, as he understands and practices it.

Worldly freedom, in other words, ultimately turns not on subjects' willfully conforming the world to the wills that they have constructed for themselves, but on subjects' intermittently letting their own willfulness be overcome. The tragic soul is liberated in virtue of overcoming the distinction between herself and the world that is not-herself, the distinction between what is internal and external to her will. The tragic soul is liberated in virtue of allowing her carefully constructed will to be suspended in order to become the conduit for the emergence of intimations into language, and thus for the emergence of those materials with which she will participate in the always-ongoing reconstruction of herself as willful subject, her culture, and her world.[43]

The tragic soul cannot, however, willfully suspend her own will. She cannot compel intimations to emerge and disrupt her language and thought. She cannot decide, that is, to produce art and philosophy. Of course, she may decide to paint, to undertake genealogical research, or even to write in an experimental fashion, but most such efforts will fail to deliver thought-transforming intimations, and thus will fail to produce art and philosophy in the fullest Nietzschean sense. On the other hand, art and philosophy will not simply happen if she makes no effort at all. The role that the tragic soul must take in pursuit of her own freedom is thus best described neither actively nor passively, but in the middle voice: the tragic soul must let art and philosophy occur through her. Such letting certainly demands willful activity – she must work to develop the talents requisite for these practices and then exercise them – but it also demands passivity – in her artistic and philosophical practices she has no choice but to await being struck from without by transformative intimations. The tragic soul who is able to combine these dispositions, who is able to sustain hard aesthetic and philosophical labor while knowing that such work cannot by itself bring about its desired result, will have at least some hope of serving as a conduit for the tragic language that conditions the freedom of herself and her culture.

The final conclusion to draw from Nietzsche is thus that freedom depends on the success of two philosophical practices: the exposition and disruption of existing conceptual structures through genealogical research, and the ongoing transformation of those structures through linguistic experimentation. These two practices, which are mutually supportive and not always easily distinguished from each other, are perhaps best considered as aspects of a single Nietzschean philosophical endeavor, which I will call "tragic genealogy."

CONCLUSION: PHILOSOPHY AND FREEDOM

The aim of this conclusion is to make explicit the consequences of the work already done by bringing together the insights on freedom developed in the interpretations of Hegel and Nietzsche. Section 1 briefly recapitulates their overlapping analyses of the freedom of willing and its limitations. We have seen that these analyses lead both Hegel and Nietzsche to the conclusion that philosophy must play a crucial role in our liberation, but we have also seen that they understand and practice philosophy very differently. Section 2 therefore reconsiders how Hegel and Nietzsche understand and practice philosophy, and how they understand their own philosophical practice to be liberating. Section 3 suggests that the different philosophical practices of Hegel and Nietzsche are complementary, such that in concert they could yield a more comprehensive freedom than either is able to deliver on its own. Section 4 concludes the book by offering some preliminary indications of the political significance of this most comprehensive philosophical liberation.

1. The Freedom of Willing and Its Limitations

Hegel and Nietzsche are united by their dissatisfaction with the usual ways of thinking about freedom. Each develops his own conception of freedom out of a critique of more conventional understandings, and each bases his critique on the idea that to be free one must be self-determining, one cannot be determined by something external to oneself.

The first conventional understanding of freedom confronted by both Hegel and Nietzsche is that of modern liberalism, in which freedom is understood to be the capacity of an individual person to choose – actions, words, religions, associates – with a minimum of external constraint. Politically, this understanding of freedom leads to an ideal in which government should be as small as possible, yet strong enough to protect its citizens from each other and from foreign threats.

Although liberalism understands freedom as a lack of external constraints on the choosing person, both Hegel and Nietzsche argue that this fails to account for the externality endemic to choice itself. Their critiques turn on the same fundamental point, made before them by Kant: if a person's choices are to be free, not only must she be unconstrained by other persons, but the choices themselves must truly be hers. To the extent that her choices are determined by a source external to herself, a person cannot be said to be responsible for them. In this case, a person does not achieve self-determination, is instead determined by the desires and instincts driving her choices as by an external force, and is not free. Hegel makes this argument in the Introduction to the *Philosophy of Right*, where he contends that to be free the willing subject must be not only capable of choice but also committed to choosing to will its own freedom. Nietzsche advances the same contention in his attacks on modern *laisser aller*, which he understands as a contemporary manifestation of disgregation, the condition of failing to have a will altogether.

For both Hegel and Nietzsche, then, liberalism is inadequate in virtue of its failure to account for the fact that freedom requires not only that a person be allowed to act on her desires, but also that her desires be internally determined by her own willing. Consequently, their analyses of freedom both proceed from critiques of liberal choice to attempts to give an account of the conditions of a freely willing subject.[1] In this they again follow Kant, who thus provides the second conventional understanding of freedom that they explore and ultimately find lacking.

Neither Hegel nor Nietzsche engages Kant's account of autonomous willing directly at length. Hegel's most powerful critique of the Kantian understanding of freedom is implicit in his investigation of the moral will in the second section of the *Philosophy of Right*. Nietzsche includes Kant as one of the targets of his attack on the type of will created by the morality of selflessness. Both Hegel and Nietzsche conclude that the moral will is more liberated than the choosing person, in virtue of its commitment to act in accordance with internally generated purposes. But both also conclude that the moral will cannot fulfill this commitment; for both, the moral will proves to be empty, incapable of generating purposes entirely out of itself, and is thus ultimately reliant on external authorities to provide it with the contents adopted by its conscience as its own. Once again, Hegel and Nietzsche agree that a conventional understanding of freedom fails to account for a significant source of externality to which it is subject.

Their rejection of the Kantian will as empty and therefore subject to external authorities for the source of its contents leads both Hegel and Nietzsche to conclude that a freely willing subject must be one that is able to reconcile itself with, or come to find itself at home in, a world whose contents it has helped to produce and that it understands to be its own. Hegel calls such a willing subject ethical, and considers it to be epitomized by the citizen of the rational state. Nietzsche's freely willing subjects are noble, those whose customs grow out of their own instincts, and who dwell happily in a community made up of others like themselves.

Finally, however, Hegel and Nietzsche agree that even the ethical and the noble fail to be completely liberated by their willing. First, the extent to which such subjects are at home in the world is imperfect; and second, their willing is not entirely responsible for the reconciliation that they do manage to achieve. The liberation that willing can provide is thus doubly incomplete. We will now briefly consider these two limitations of willing, beginning with the latter.

The willing, or purposive activity, of the ethical or noble subject is responsible for transforming the world in such a way that the subject is able to feel at home in it. But the specific contents that the willing subject purposively attempts to build into the world depend on its self-understanding, its conception of its own freedom, for the subject can be at home only in a world that allows it to exist in a way consistent with that understanding. And the subject's understanding of itself as a free being is produced not by willing, but by thinking. The freedom of willing is thus formal, because thinking is ultimately responsible for giving to the willing subject the contents that it strives to translate into objective existence.[2]

Moreover, no matter how thoroughly at home the subject comes to feel in a world that its willing has helped to produce, such reconciliation nonetheless remains imperfect. Hegel and Nietzsche agree about this general point, but they emphasize different kinds of imperfection to which the reconciliation afforded by willing is necessarily subject.

Hegel emphasizes that even for the ethical subject there is an insuperable gap between itself and the world of objective existence. At times this gap is obvious and undeniable – for example, whenever the subject is frustrated in its efforts to transform the world purposively in accordance with its desires, and is therefore unable to find itself at home. More important, however, is that the gap persists even when it is not obvious, even when the intended transformations succeed and the subject truly feels itself to be at home. This is because in such situations the achieved reconciliation with the objective world is attributable solely to the efforts of willing subjects. The world is indifferent to the designs of such subjects, indifferent to their desire to be at home in it, and it is only in virtue of their purposive struggles that this indifferent world can temporarily be made into an unnatural home. The willing subject thus remains alienated from and external to the world, even when it occasionally succeeds in hiding this fact from itself.

Nietzsche emphasizes the particularity of the reconciliation afforded by willing. The noble subject is at home because of its ability to construct a world based on its own values and the thoughts that undergird them.

Success in this endeavor depends precisely upon the noble's avoidance of that to which those values and thoughts cannot be assimilated. This means that the noble, at home in its world, is limited by that which it cannot engage, that for which its categories of appropriation are themselves inappropriate.

Nietzsche, then, insists that the noble is not at home in *the* world, but rather in *its* world, in a partial world to which it is partial. The noble subject's willing enables it to reconcile itself with this partial world, but only by fixing a limit or measure to that which it can encounter. In fixing this limit the noble allows itself to be determined, if only negatively, by that outside its measure, which it can only reject. It has to reject as alien to itself both forms of willing other than its own, and the world itself, for the world is continually becoming and therefore resistant to the establishment of any and all particular forms of being that noble moralities might embrace. Reconciliation with the world thus requires not only embracing a particular form of being, but also embracing becoming, the impermanence to which all forms of being are subject. This embracing of becoming, however, is the activity of the tragic, not the noble.

Nietzsche and Hegel thus agree that the reconciliation forged by the noble or ethical subject is imperfect. Even when successful, willing achieves only a particular and posited reconciliation with the world, one which leaves the subject estranged from the objectivity that confronts it.

Freedom requires that the subject overcome the formality, positedness, and particularity of its reconciliation with the objective world. In Hegel's terms, spiritual beings must achieve the infinite purpose, in which the insuperable limitations and frustrations of willing are overcome through the realization that the subject and the objective world must always already have been reconciled in order for the successful actualization of finite purposes to take place.[3] In Nietzsche's terms, spiritual beings must receive the glad tidings that their liberation does not await the arrival of an external redeemer, but is available in this world at every moment. In these different vocabularies, Hegel and Nietzsche express their agreement that the realization – or actualization – of freedom depends on spiritual beings coming to the realization – or awareness – that they are free. To be free, spiritual beings must achieve a self-understanding through which they discover, and in so doing produce, a liberation that is neither formal, nor subjective, nor particular.

2. Freedom through Philosophy: System and Genealogy

Their analyses of the freedom of willing and its limitations lead both Hegel and Nietzsche to locate the most comprehensive freedom not in the choosing of the person, and not in the purposive action of the will, but rather in the practice of philosophy. For it is philosophy that best enables us to develop the self-understanding necessary to realize our freedom. They differ, however, over what philosophical practice is, and therefore over the precise manner in which it is liberating.

Philosophical practice as Hegel conceives it is able to overcome both the subjectivity of willing, the willing subject's understanding that the world is something from which it remains fundamentally estranged, and its formality, its inability to determine for itself the contents of the freedom that it strives to realize.

In Hegel, the subject's understanding is first transformed through the process by which it arrives at the properly philosophical standpoint, the process that transpires in the *Phenomenology*. The *Phenomenology*, which constitutes an extended attempt to understand what knowledge is, begins with two assumptions that Hegel believes to be constitutive of ordinary consciousness: first, that knowledge is a relationship between a knowing subject and an object that is known; and second, that in this relationship the subject must somehow gain access to the object just as it is, without altering it in any way. In particular, such consciousness assumes that the subject must not gain access to the object by means of concepts, the employment of which would necessarily mediate, and thus alter, its appearance.[4] From this beginning, the entire course of the *Phenomenology* is driven by reflection upon these assumptions: as the characterization of the relationship between knowing subject and known object is found wanting, it is repeatedly revised; ultimately, when no revision proves adequate, the very assumption that knowledge is a relationship between a mutually alienated subject and object must be dropped. The subject finally becomes aware that it cannot maintain a tenable distinction between the determinations of its own concepts and those of the objects it would know, between the determinations of thought and the determinations of being. With this awareness the subject is prepared to begin philosophy proper, which it now understands to be the specification of the conceptual determinations common to thought and being.

As she completes the *Phenomenology* and begins the *Logic*, then, the philosopher no longer suffers the Kantian alienation in which thought is understood to be incapable of determining what things are. The Hegelian logician begins with the simple thought of "being" and understands that in determining what is contained in this thought, she also determines what it is to be.

But the logician knows neither what she herself is, nor the character of her relationship to the natural world, and thus her reconciliation with the latter is incomplete. The subjectivity of willing is fully overcome only when the philosopher determines not only what it is to be, but what it is to be a natural being, and finally what it is to be a spiritual being. In so doing, as we saw in Chapter 4, she becomes a free being by developing the knowledge that she is a free being; the philosopher becomes reconciled with nature by developing the knowledge that she is always already reconciled with the natural world in which her knowing and willing take place.

The reconciliation with nature achieved through philosophy (and art and religion, the other activities that Hegel treats in absolute spirit) is superior to that achieved through knowing (treated in subjective spirit) or willing (treated in objective spirit) because it is not one-sided. The knowing subject, recall, is supposed to be receptive, to conform itself to the content of a given object without imposing any distorting mediation. Conversely, the willing subject aims to make an object conform to its own purposes. In both knowing and willing, then, it is assumed that the spiritual subject and the natural object are mutually alienated, and that their reconciliation involves one side's unilaterally transferring its contents to the other. As we have seen, however, even when such transfers are successful the "reconciliation" they effect is imperfect. But in philosophy the subject neither receives a given content from an object nor imposes her own content upon one. Philosophy is thus best described in the middle voice, for the philosopher *lets* the content of the objects with which her practice is concerned – the categories of thought – develop itself through her thinking. In so doing she allows thought to determine what it is to be natural, and what it is to be spiritual, and thereby realizes that as a spiritual or thinking being she is able to comprehend what nature *is*, that a tenable distinction can no longer be maintained between the determinations of nature and the determinations of her conceptualization of nature. Philosophy thus achieves a more genuine reconciliation of subject and object than either knowing or willing can, because the philosopher serves as a medium for the self-determination of thought, which is at the same time a determination of what it is to be.[5]

The self-determining character of philosophical thinking is also what enables it to overcome the formality of willing. Willing, recall, is formal because it is not capable of determining the contents of the conception of freedom that it strives to realize in the world. Philosophical thinking, however, develops its own categories, without reliance on anything external to it, and freedom is one of the categories it develops. The practice of philosophy therefore enables the philosopher to understand not only the general fact that she is free, but also the specific contents of her freedom. These are the contents that Hegel develops in his philosophy of spirit: to be a free being is to be a knowing, willing, aesthetic, religious, and philosophical being. Moreover, as the *Philosophy of Right* demonstrates, to be a freely willing being is to be a legal, moral, familial, economic, and political being. Freedom thus requires willing, but it is philosophical thinking, and not willing itself, that is able to determine what our freedom requires us to will.

Philosophical practice as Nietzsche conceives it is able to overcome the subjectivity and the particularity of willing. The reconciliation achieved by willing remains subjective for Nietzsche because it cannot affirm the impermanence of the world. The noble, unlike the decadent, is able to affirm her own thoughts and values, and to the extent that she is able to realize them through her willing, she is able to bring into being a world in which she is at home. But any such world that is brought into being must ultimately suffer the destruction of becoming, which the noble is no more able than the decadent to affirm. The noble's commitment to the establishment of a world based on her own thoughts and values thus represents not a reconciliation with, but a flight from, the necessity of the impermanence of any and all worldly establishments.

The affirmation of impermanence, and thus a genuine reconciliation with the world, requires the subject to achieve a tragic rather than a noble stance. The tragic subject can affirm the destruction of the establishments that she loves because, as much as she loves them, she loves even more the possibilities of future creation that only their demise can open. But the achievement of a tragic stance requires, as we also saw, overcoming the metaphysical and moral assumptions built into ordinary language. In turn, this depends on showing that the thoughts and values that language enshrines are made rather than found, through both the genealogical exposition of prevailing conceptual structures and the extraordinary use of ordinary language. When successful, such extraordinary uses of language are poetic – for they literally make new thoughts and values with old words – and Nietzsche thinks that the practice of philosophy is one of their primary sources. Nietzsche thus understands the philosopher, or tragic genealogist, to be one who is able to expose, disrupt, and transform the thoughts and values established and perpetuated by ordinary linguistic usage, and in so doing to achieve a reconciliation with the impermanent world that willing cannot.

Her reconciliation with impermanence enables the tragic genealogist to overcome not only the subjectivity but also the particularity of willing. The particularity of willing resides in the subject's abiding commitment to one set of thoughts and values, which it seeks to establish in the world. Such particularity limits freedom by fixing a horizon of engagement, such that the subject is unable to think, much less to affirm, anything that lies beyond it. The tragic genealogist, however, remains continually open to the possibility of emergent intimations' transforming the horizons of her thought and valuation. She cultivates a resistance to the tendency of categories of thought and value to be imposed upon everything they encounter, a tendency that precludes the possibility of transformation by precluding the possibility of experiencing anything new as new. The tragic genealogist thus resists the will to power of the thinking and willing subject in favor of a love of impermanence that enables her to serve as a medium for the ongoing disruption and reconstruction of thoughts and values, and therefore for the liberating reconciliation of herself and the world.

The works of Hegel and Nietzsche not only discursively present but also dramatically illustrate both their agreement that freedom lies in the practice of philosophy, and the differences in their understandings of philosophy and of the role it must play. They serve this illustrative function by presenting themselves as examples of liberating philosophical practice as they understand it. That is, Hegel and Nietzsche both practice what they preach, because what they preach is that freedom requires philosophical practice.

Hegel's own system represents his best attempt to let the categories of thought determine themselves through him, and to present those categories in the German language; he famously claims that he strives to teach philosophy to speak German.[6] He strives to do so because if philosophy is to realize freedom by enabling thinking subjects to realize that they are free, then the categories of thought, the determination of which constitutes "philosophy" for Hegel, must be educated to be thinkable in the ordinary languages those subjects speak. The task Hegel sets for himself in his system is thus to provide philosophy with such an education in German.[7]

Although Hegel sets himself this task, he nonetheless maintains that its accomplishment – the philosophical determination of the categories of thought – is not truly his, but rather that of thought itself. Having set himself the task of thinking in German, Hegel claims that his own accomplishment is to have *allowed* this to happen through him, and to have observed this happening carefully enough to have written it down. Hegel thus serves thought as its medium and serves others as a guide in their own attempts to let thought think itself through them.[8] If others do follow Hegel, what they are forced to experience, for the sake of their own freedom, is the dialectical and systematic self-determination of the categories of thought, one that is as comprehensive and unified as the German language will allow, while also being as internally differentiated as possible.[9]

Nietzsche's corpus exemplifies his claim that philosophical liberation involves the genealogical disruption and subsequent reconstruction of the thoughts and values embedded in ordinary thought. It also exemplifies Nietzsche's insistence that the work of philosophy is never done, that the philosopher must continually allow her thoughts and values to be undone by the emergence of new intimations, which themselves *become* thoughts as they are brought into relation to, and thus transform, the existing system of thoughts that they have infiltrated.

Nietzsche illustrates these points not only in his explicitly genealogical work, but also through his continual philosophical experimentation.

In the course of such experimentation he develops a new vocabulary for the intimations emerging from him, and shows how these intimations force a revaluation of the older, ordinary thoughts that they infiltrate and transform. The techniques by which he accomplishes this are by now familiar. On the one hand, Nietzsche introduces terms that have no correlates in ordinary German: eternal return, *amor fati*, Zarathustra, *Übermensch*. In doing so, he seconds Hegel's insistence that he is merely a medium for that which he brings to words. As a medium, Nietzsche serves as the site for the unification of subject and object, internal and external, thought and being, which takes place in and through the intimations that come to him to be communicated. On the other hand, he then develops these intimations in such a way that they become thoughts or concepts in virtue of their interrelation with the ordinary German terms whose signification they subsequently revolutionize. In Nietzsche's work, that is, concepts such as redemption, soul, glad tidings – whose use is ordinary and whose genealogy is Biblical – continue to be used, even emphasized, but are turned on their heads, co-opted within a wholly new valuation.[10]

Nietzsche, like Hegel, forces a certain labor on his readers, and also for the sake of freedom, but it is a different kind of labor and it functions in a different way. Whereas Hegel's readers are brought to understand thought's self-determination as they give themselves over to following its development, Nietzsche's are confronted with the particularity of any developed system of thoughts. This inevitably occurs because although Nietzsche's texts provide the reader with a rich stock of concepts, they do so in a deliberately unsystematic fashion. Nietzsche's works do not guide the reader, as do Hegel's, from one concept to the next, from the first and least developed to the last and most comprehensive. Instead, the reader has the experience of being surrounded by concepts – some familiar, some completely foreign – and of having to *make* sense of them, of having to assign meanings to the new and reassign meanings to the old, of having to construct their interrelations as best she can. The result is a strong sense that systems of concepts are manufactured, temporal, fragile, and particular. Nietzsche's reader is forced to conclude that although conceptual systems may well be unified, that unity must always have been *produced*, and that unity can never be closed.[11]

3. The Complementarity of System and Genealogy

Although Hegel and Nietzsche agree that the practice of philosophy is essential to freedom, it is evident that their understandings of philosophical practice and the liberation it affords differ greatly. Moreover, it might seem that their understandings of philosophy and freedom are not only different, but actually incompatible. Hegel understands philosophy as the self-determination of thought: thought's categories must

be *determinate*, or particular, in order to overcome the formality of willing by specifying that which freedom requires us to will; and thought's
categories must be *self*-determining lest the thinking subject's freedom
be compromised by a dependence on something external to itself.
Nietzsche, on the other hand, understands philosophy as the disruption
of thought: conceptual systems must be resistant to closure, because the
establishment of a particular system of thoughts and values limits the subject by making her dependent on what is external to that system; complete
freedom, Nietzsche contends, demands perpetual incompleteness. These
criteria for philosophy and freedom – self-determination and incompleteness – might seem impossible to satisfy simultaneously: a perfectly self-
determining system of categories could not be open to the intermittent
external shocks that Nietzschean incompleteness requires; and a perpetually incomplete system of thoughts and values, intermittently absorbing
external shocks to prevent its own stagnation, could not be perfectly
self-determining.

The self-determination and incompleteness of thought can be reconciled, however, if we distinguish between categories and noncategorial
concepts. Categories are those concepts that are necessary to thought
itself, and which thus make possible all conceptual activity, including the
use of noncategorial concepts. Noncategorial concepts are not necessary to thought itself, but rather develop contingently in response to the
engagements of thinking subjects with the world.

The simplest category is that of "being," which is tacitly employed in
all thinking whatsoever: when we think, for example, that something
is a mosquito, or that some mosquito *is* flying, we use the category of
being. Concepts like "mosquito" and "flying," however, are noncategorial:
if thinking beings had neither encountered mosquitoes nor observed
anything to take flight, then the concepts of "mosquito" and "flying"
would not have developed.

Making the distinction between categories and noncategorial concepts
enables us to see the understandings of philosophical practice offered by
Hegel and Nietzsche as complementary rather than contradictory. For
Hegel's insistence that thought be self-determining can be understood as
applying to categories but not to noncategorial concepts; and Nietzsche's
insistence that systems of thought be perpetually open to transgression
and transformation can be understood, *pace* Nietzsche himself, as applying to noncategorial concepts but not to categories. Understood in
this way, not only does the apparent contradiction between the Hegelian
and Nietzschean philosophies dissolve, but each actually proves to complement the other by emphasizing an important aspect of freedom and
philosophical practice that the other underplays.[12]

Hegel rightly emphasizes that in order to be free, thought must be
self-determining, and that to be self-determining is to be particular.

And Nietzsche rightly emphasizes that in order to be free, thought cannot remain in one particular configuration, because such stagnant particularity threatens thought's self-determination by leaving it negatively dependent upon that which it cannot engage. These apparently contradictory insights can be complementary, but only if we understand the term "thought" in two different senses – to indicate categories in the Hegelian project of allowing thought to determine itself, and to indicate noncategorial concepts in the Nietzschean project of exposing and transforming particular configurations of thought that have become entrenched over time.

Of course, Nietzsche would object to this restriction of his enterprise to noncategorial concepts, for he fully intends the scope of investigation and transformation to be *all* concepts, including those deemed to be categories by Hegel. At times, Nietzsche even asserts that the purported categories have already been exposed as noncategorial.[13] In his more sober moments he only speculates that they *might* be so exposed.[14] But in any case it is clear that Nietzsche takes himself to be in the business of exposing all concepts as noncategorial, and presumably would expect any subsequent "Nietzscheans" to continue the effort.

This means that if Nietzsche's project, as he understands it, were successful, a reconciliation with Hegel would be impossible, since there would be nothing left of Hegel's system. But Nietzsche himself does not even engage, much less successfully undermine, Hegel's account of categorial development. It thus remains to be seen whether some concepts are in fact categories, and whether Hegel's categorial project remains viable in the face of Nietzsche's attack. But to determine the viability of the categorial project we need both to attempt to make a go of it (i.e., to practice Hegelian philosophy), and to be radically suspicious and critical of all such attempts that claim to have succeeded (i.e., to practice Nietzschean philosophy).

My suggestion, therefore, is that we should continue our efforts to refine and complete the Hegelian categorial project, while also heeding Nietzsche's call to be suspicious whenever a concept is accorded categorial status. Moreover, we should take Nietzsche's own genealogical and experimental practices as examples of how to investigate, and potentially transform, those concepts that have come under suspicion. Genealogical scrutiny will both ensure that concepts accorded categorial status are in fact universal structures of thought, rather than determinations inflected by particular linguistic or cultural biases, and destabilize those concepts that prove to be noncategorial but which have become entrenched in a particular culture or language. Experimentation with those destabilized concepts may then transform them, and other concepts with which they are interrelated, in ways that open previously invisible avenues of thinking.

An important corollary to this suggestion is that it is incumbent upon both Hegelians and Nietzscheans to take each other much more seriously than they are often prone to do. Hegelians are too quick to dismiss Nietzschean projects as irrelevant to systematic philosophy, and hence to philosophy *as such*, since the systematic self-determination of thought is often the only project that they recognize as properly philosophical. Conversely, Nietzscheans are too quick to dismiss the systematic Hegelian project as impossible without ever engaging the dialectical developments in any detail. The Nietzschean may suspect that under careful scrutiny *all* purported "categories" will prove to be noncategorial, but rather than asserting this global suspicion as if it were demonstrated fact, she must examine the specific determinations developed by the Hegelian, in order to show exactly where noncategorial concepts have mistakenly been accorded categorial status. And in response, the Hegelian must either show exactly how the Nietzschean critique fails in each particular case, or else revise the account of categorial development accordingly.

In issuing this call for Hegelians and Nietzscheans to engage in a harmonious collaboration that puts the tensions that stand between them to creative use, it is worth reemphasizing that, at the most general level, the project that leads Hegel and Nietzsche to their very different understandings of philosophical practice is the same: both are engaged in determining the ontology of freedom, or what it is to be free. Hegel's ontological conclusion is that to be fully free is to be a systematic ontologist; freedom requires specifying the universal categories necessary to thought and being, and "philosophy" is the name he gives to such specification. And Nietzsche's ontological conclusion is that to be fully free is to be a tragic genealogist; freedom requires illuminating the provenance of our concepts, in order to highlight their contingency and thereby open ourselves to experiment with their transformation, and "philosophy" is the name he gives to such illumination and experimentation.

Moreover, Hegel and Nietzsche themselves demonstrate that systematic ontology and tragic genealogy do not preclude one another, since each of them practices, at least to some degree, what the other preaches. Hegel concentrates on the systematic development of the categories necessary to thought, but at the same time, throughout his remarks and notes he continually uses those categories to comprehend and critique contingent phenomena, including noncategorial concepts. For example, throughout the *Philosophy of Right* (and the philosophy of spirit more generally) he develops the category of freedom in increasing detail. But as he does so he also uses this category, this determination of what freedom *is*, as the basis for trenchant critiques of other philosophers' conceptions of freedom, and of historical developments that have failed to provide the fullest social and political liberation. Nietzsche, on the other hand, implicitly relies on categories in his highly illuminating demonstrations of the contingency of many of the firmly established concepts that structure our culture. For example, Nietzsche never tires of demonstrating that decadent concepts such as "sin" need not have arisen, and should not be retained, and tries to show how we might reconceptualize our actions if they were discarded. But, as I have shown in Part II, he does so on the grounds that such concepts inhibit our freedom, and he never wavers from understanding freedom as self-determination.

Given that Hegelian systematic ontology and Nietzschean tragic genealogy *can* be practiced in concert, the reason that they *should* be is that both are essential if we are to achieve the most comprehensive freedom. We must allow the categories of thought to determine themselves through us, in order to develop both the general knowledge that all thinking beings are free, and the specific knowledge of the requirements of freedom; that is, the continued practice of Hegelian systematic ontology is necessary both to sustain our understanding of ourselves as reconciled with nature in virtue of our ability to think its determinations, and to refine as best we can our understanding of the social and political conditions that freedom requires us to will. Nietzsche can tell us little about the latter, since his critique of all particularity leaves him unable to distinguish between particular conditions genuinely hostile to freedom, and particular conditions that freedom in fact demands.[15] At the same time, however, the continued practice of Nietzschean tragic genealogy is necessary both to sustain our understanding of ourselves as reconciled with nature in virtue of our ability to affirm its destructive impermanence, and to unsettle our belief that any social and political construction we affirm could ever perfectly realize freedom. That is, we must allow the noncategorial concepts that have arisen in the course of our particular history to remain fluid, in order to prevent the establishment of a theoretical and practical closure that excludes those who think and act differently than we do, and that in so doing also threatens our own freedom. If we are to be free, in other words, we need to know that we are free, determine what freedom *is*, and strive to realize it in the world; but we also need to be continually wary of and actively seek to undermine our easy confidence that we have in fact determined what freedom is, and that our worldly strivings either already have brought about, or someday will bring about, such liberation.[16]

4. The Significance of Freedom: From Philosophy back to Politics

We can now conclude by returning to the question of the free subject, with which liberalism, Kant, Hegel, and Nietzsche all begin. Liberalism, recall, understands the subject to be free when she is allowed to pursue her choices without external constraint (assuming, of course, that she respects the right of others to do the same and accepts certain restrictions for the sake of everyone's mutual security). A free society, by liberalism's lights, is then one that protects and maximizes this freedom to choose for its individual subjects. Hegel and Nietzsche, we have seen, criticize liberalism not because the freedom to choose is unimportant, but because it is an incomplete kind of freedom, dependent on the freedom of willing, which is itself dependent on the freedom of philosophical thinking. Freedom of choice, that is, is not to be dismissed, but its conditions must be identified and secured, in order to ensure that "free" choices, subjects, and societies are truly free.

Given the understanding of freedom that we have developed from the complementary work of Hegel and Nietzsche, we can now designate the free subject as one who is genuinely reconciled with the world. Such reconciliation requires the subject to build herself a home by purposively transforming the world. But it also requires more than this, for the subject may well create a home for herself that fails to accord with the conditions of freedom: patriotic allegiance to unjust political arrangements is all too possible, as Hegel, Nietzsche, and history attest. Political subjects must therefore transform the world in such a way that the conditions of freedom are realized, and must transform themselves in such a way that only the realization of those conditions can make them feel at home.

The requisite transformation of political subjects depends upon their coming to know that they are free, for only with such knowledge will they demand to live in a world in which the conditions of their freedom are secured. The best source of such self-knowledge is philosophy: philosophy provides its practitioners with the most explicit and detailed knowledge of their freedom, and does so in the medium most appropriate to the message, that of freely self-determining thought. But philosophy is not the only source of the knowledge that we are free, so the realization of freedom does not require that everyone be a philosopher. The knowledge that we are free, that we are always already reconciled with the world that we strive to know and struggle to transform, is also available through art and religion. Art and religion, we have seen Hegel argue, present us with an awareness of our freedom in the form of sensuous representations and feelings, respectively. The transformation of political subjects can thus be accomplished by means of a combination of aesthetic, religious, and philosophical experiences that educate us to recognize ourselves as free beings.

The requisite transformation of the world, however, does require philosophy. For only philosophy is capable of determining the detailed conditions of freedom. Artistic representations and religious feelings can make us aware of our freedom, but depend on philosophical thinking to provide them with the contents of the freedom that they present. Only philosophy, that is, can determine that our freedom requires us to develop certain legal, economic, and political structures, which are conditions of freedom themselves, and which also secure other conditions of freedom, including the individual's rights to own and exchange property, exercise her moral conscience, enter into family relationships, support herself through her own labor, and be represented in her government. The knowledge that these are the conditions of freedom must be developed by philosophers, and disseminated as broadly and effectively as possible, so that the strivings of those who become aware of their freedom by means other than philosophy do in fact aim at liberation.

Hegel successfully demonstrates that freedom has a particular content, that there are specific conditions that liberation requires. But these conditions, as specified in the *Philosophy of Right*, clearly underdetermine the forms of life appropriate for free beings; various social and political arrangements, that is, are compatible with the general strictures imposed by freedom. And given two or more sets of social and political arrangements that do meet the conditions of freedom, there is no philosophical criterion that can determine one set to be better than the other. The choice between such sets of arrangements can only be a matter of preference, a matter of which way of living enables the members of that society to feel most at home.

Nietzsche reminds us that the social and political arrangements in which we feel most at home depend on the noncategorial thoughts and values we happen to have developed in response to the contingencies of historical tradition and personal experience. And, he emphasizes, our liberation requires not only that we develop social and political arrangements consonant with the determinations of the category of freedom, but also that we not allow the noncategorial arrangements we establish to become overly entrenched.

Avoiding the entrenchment of noncategorial thoughts and values, and of the social and political arrangements that grow from them, involves several things, the first of which is simply understanding that the process of entrenchment is always at work. In order to avoid remaining unwittingly enslaved to unconsciously operative prejudices, that is, the political subject must understand that the aims of all willing are structured by thoughts and values. Moreover, she must also understand the particular thoughts and values that structure her own willing and the world in which she feels at home. And finally, she must understand that these particular noncategorial thoughts and values are particular, and that to allow them to fix the measure of her willing permanently is to allow herself to be limited and unfree.

The achievement of all of these understandings requires the subject who would be free to undertake an examination of the thoughts and values structuring her willing and her world. This examination must investigate both the current interrelations of her thoughts and values, so as to bring to light most clearly their particular function, and the genealogy of their emergence, so as to bring to light that their function is most clearly particular.

But freedom involves more than self-examination and understanding. It also requires that subsequent to the achievement of such understanding the subject attain a resolute openness to the transformation of the self that it reveals, an openness to the transgression of the particular system of thoughts and values that presently structures her willing.[17] And finally, it requires that the subject also retain the energy and means with which to reconstitute and reexamine her willing in the face of such destructive transgressions; the subject must be capable of developing a new system of structuring thoughts and values that incorporate what has emerged and revalue what remains, and in such a way that she is again able to build herself a home.

Because the thoughts and values that structure a subject's willing are not private, but rather are shared by those with whom she forms a linguistic community, and because the building of a home is also a communal affair, the liberation of the individual cannot be independent of the liberation of the larger wholes of which she is a part. Rather, free subjects and free communities – those least subject to external determination – must develop symbiotically.

If this symbiotic development is successful, the result will be subjects and communities that meet the conditions of freedom emphasized by Nietzsche, as well as those emphasized by Hegel. Such subjects and communities, that is, will not only actualize the legal, moral, social, economic, and political structures demanded by freedom, but will also be aware that the particular structures that they actualize are dependent upon noncategorial thoughts and values that have been created, have been produced in history, and must remain open to further historical development. They will therefore be subjects and communities open to transgression and reorganization – within the general limits fixed by the category of freedom – as they will be aware that disruption is the only means to their enrichment, that self-dissolution is the only means to prevent their own loss, and that perpetual incompleteness is the only means to complete freedom. Free subjects and communities, that is, will be free in virtue of being at home with themselves while outside of themselves, of reconciling themselves to the fact that there is no ultimate reconciliation, of achieving the only kind of infinitude available to them precisely through embracing the finite, of internalizing an ongoing engagement with the external, of transcending their limitedness by recognizing it and thus making it their own.

NOTES

Introduction

1. *EG*, §482A.
2. Robert B. Pippin, "Hegel and Institutional Rationality," *The Southern Journal of Philosophy* 39 suppl. (2001): 1–25, at 10. Pippin makes the point in the context of a discussion of Alex Honneth's *Suffering from Indeterminacy: An Attempt at a Reactualization of Hegel's Philosophy of Right* (Amsterdam: Van Gorcum, 2000).
3. Orlando Patterson, *Freedom in the Making of Western Culture* (New York: Basic Books, 1991), and his *Freedom in the Modern World* (New York: Basic Books, 1999); Eric Foner, *The Story of American Freedom* (New York: Norton, 1998).
4. Paul Franco, *Hegel's Philosophy of Freedom* (New Haven, Conn.: Yale University Press, 1999), 156, also characterizes Hegel's conception of freedom as more comprehensive than the liberal alternative: "Hegel's positive conception of freedom ultimately captures more of what we mean by freedom and why we find it valuable than the competing negative conception of doing what we please without hindrance. The latter may be an aspect of the more comprehensive, positive notion of freedom, but it cannot be the ultimate meaning or justification of freedom." I agree with Franco, but I arrived at the terminology of comprehensiveness independently.
5. Thomas Hobbes, *Leviathan* (Cambridge: Cambridge University Press, 1991), 146.
6. This general definition cannot do justice to the variation within the liberal tradition, but as an encapsulation of the liberal understanding of freedom it is hardly idiosyncratic. Both Isaiah Berlin and Allen Wood understand liberalism in a similar way. Wood writes that "in the liberal tradition, 'freedom' usually refers to a sphere of privacy in which individuals may do as they please, immune from the interference of others – especially of the state." Allen W. Wood, *Hegel's Ethical Thought* (Cambridge: Cambridge University Press, 1990), 36. And according to Berlin, who popularized the term "negative liberty," classic liberals all agree that I am free "to the degree to which no man or body of men interferes with my activity." Isaiah Berlin, "Two Concepts of Liberty," in his *Four Essays on Liberty* (Oxford: Oxford University Press, 1969), 122–124.

7. Dick Armey, *The Freedom Revolution: The New Republican House Majority Leader Tells Why Big Government Failed, Why Freedom Works, and How We Will Rebuild America* (Washington, D.C.: Regnery, 1995).

8. Immanuel Kant, *Grundlegung der Metaphysik der Sitten*, in *Kants gesammelte Schriften* (Berlin, 1902), vol. 4, 446–447; Immanuel Kant, *Groundwork of the Metaphysics of Morals*, tr. Mary Gregor (Cambridge: Cambridge University Press, 1997), 52–53.

9. Both Hobbes and Locke, for example, are able to define freedom quite succinctly. See Hobbes, *Leviathan*, Chapter 21; and John Locke, *An Essay Concerning Human Understanding* (New York: Dover, 1959), Book II, Chapter 21. Kant's own discussions of freedom in the *Groundwork* and the *Critique of Practical Reason* are not particularly long, but attempts to make sense of them are. See, for example, Henry Allison, *Kant's Theory of Freedom* (Cambridge: Cambridge University Press, 1990); and Bernard Carnois, *The Coherence of Kant's Doctrine of Freedom*, tr. David Booth (Chicago: University of Chicago Press, 1987).

10. This last consideration places freedom squarely at the center of Kant's entire philosophical system: it is the sine qua non of practical philosophy, as the indispensable precondition of morality; and it is thus the main concern of theoretical philosophy, since the objective application of its concept must be justified in the absence of any possible empirical sanction. Kant says as much in the Preface to the *Second Critique*: "The concept of freedom, insofar as its reality is proved by an apodictic law of practical reason, constitutes the *keystone* of the whole structure of a system of pure reason, even of speculative reason." Immanuel Kant, *Kritik der praktischen Vernunft*, in *Kants gesammelte Schriften* (Berlin, 1902), vol. 5, 3–4; Immanuel Kant, *Critique of Practical Reason*, tr. Mary Gregor (Cambridge: Cambridge University Press, 1997), 3. We might thus label Kant's "Copernican revolution" a "freedom revolution," though in a sense quite different from that employed by Dick Armey.

11. Kant does in fact suggest that some cultures may be more adept than others at teaching their members to *use* the freedom that is their natural gift. But the social and political spheres can have nothing to do with the giving of this gift in the first place. Kant writes that in the social and political spheres, the goal is to balance competing inclinations through a system of competing coercions; the effect of society and politics on individuals is therefore entirely heteronomous. Immanuel Kant, "Zum ewigen Frieden," in *Kants gesammelte Schriften* (Berlin, 1902), vol. 8, 366; Immanuel Kant, "To Perpetual Peace," in *Perpetual Peace and Other Essays*, tr. Ted Humphrey (Indianapolis, Ind.: Hackett, 1983), 124.

12. My project thus responds, although not deliberately, to the recent suggestion of John H. Smith that "the Hegel-Nietzsche connection needs to be more fully developed in terms of their alternative conceptions of will." John H. Smith, "Of Spirit(s) and Will(s)," in *Hegel after Derrida*, ed. Stuart Barnett (New York: Routledge, 1998), 317 n61. I should emphasize that I am not trying to show, nor do I think it is necessary to show, that Nietzsche inherited either his concern for the question of freedom or his response to that question from Hegel. To my knowledge, Nietzsche's understanding of Hegel,

if it could be called that, was minimal, distorted, and based on little or no direct confrontation with the texts – on this point, see Stephen Houlgate, *Hegel, Nietzsche and the Criticism of Metaphysics* (Cambridge: Cambridge University Press, 1986), Chapter 2. But this rules out neither the possibility that Hegel and Nietzsche were both concerned with the question of freedom, nor the possibility that their responses to that question are both importantly similar and complementarily divergent. Raymond Geuss, in "Freedom as an Ideal," *The Aristotelian Society* 69 suppl. (1995): 87–100, and Robert B. Pippin, in "Selbstüberwindung, Versöhnung, und Modernität bei Nietzsche und Hegel," in *Nietzsche und Hegel*, ed. Mihailo Djuric (Würzburg: Königshausen & Neumann, 1992), 130–145, agree that Hegel and Nietzsche are both concerned with developing an adequate grasp of freedom.

13. A recent and notable exception is Elliot L. Jurist, *Beyond Hegel and Nietzsche: Philosophy, Culture, and Agency* (Cambridge: MIT Press, 2000). I share Jurist's "uneasiness with the conception of Hegel and Nietzsche as philosophical opposites," and his belief that we should not "ignore the possibility, where their views seem to be at odds, of finding a way to render their views as complementary," but otherwise our approaches and substantive concerns are rather different. For discussions of the difficulties of bringing Hegel and Nietzsche together, see R. F. Beerling, "Hegel und Nietzsche," *Hegel-Studien* 1 (1961): 229–246; Daniel Breazeale, "The Hegel-Nietzsche Problem," *Nietzsche-Studien* 4 (1975): 146–164; and Houlgate, *Hegel, Nietzsche and the Criticism of Metaphysics*, Chapter 1. Beerling and Houlgate also provide helpful surveys and classifications of the main attempts that have been made. The best-known and most extreme critic of these attempts is Gilles Deleuze, who writes, in *Nietzsche and Philosophy*, tr. Hugh Tomlinson (New York: Columbia University Press, 1983): "Anti-Hegelianism runs through Nietzsche's work as its cutting edge" (8); "we will misunderstand the whole of Nietzsche's work if we do not see 'against whom' its principle [sic] concepts are directed. Hegelian themes are present in this work as the enemy against which it fights" (162); and finally, "there is no possible compromise between Hegel and Nietzsche" (195). Although these claims are unconvincing, Deleuze's interpretation of Nietzsche is itself interesting and helpful.

14. Three recent books, each of which is excellent in its own way, unfortunately perpetuate the tradition of interpreting Hegel's conception of freedom without considering how it develops in his treatments of art, religion, and philosophy: Franco, *Hegel's Philosophy of Freedom*; Alan Patten, *Hegel's Idea of Freedom* (Oxford: Oxford University Press, 1999); and Frederick Neuhouser, *Foundations of Hegel's Social Theory: Actualizing Freedom* (Cambridge, Mass.: Harvard University Press, 2000). The titles of Franco's and Patten's books suggest that they contain full treatments of Hegel's account of freedom, but they are in fact limited in scope to the kind of freedom discussed in the *Philosophy of Right*. Patten does acknowledge that "human beings can achieve a higher form of liberation, according to Hegel, in the *contemplative* spheres of art, religion, and philosophy" (39), but he then proceeds to ignore these spheres while still claiming to provide the first "thorough, full-length

study in the English-language secondary literature of the account of freedom
contained in Hegel's mature work" (6). Franco (xii) stresses the importance
of putting the *Philosophy of Right* in its historical context and in the context
of Hegel's *Phenomenology* and *Logic*, but he does not relate it to Hegel's discussions of art, religion, and philosophy, and even claims that the *Philosophy
of Right* amounts to "a complete elaboration of the meaning and implications of human freedom" (155). Neuhouser recognizes that "Hegel thinks
of [philosophical] contemplation as a form of *freedom*, indeed the highest,
most complete form of self-determination possible" (20), and even grants
in a footnote that there is a sense in which "practical freedom depends on
speculative" (287 n10), but he nonetheless insists that "it is possible to make
sense of the conception of freedom that grounds Hegel's social theory in
abstraction from the rest of his philosophy" (5), and so has very little to say
about art, religion, and philosophy. More sensitive to the interrelation of objective and absolute spirit are Hans Friedrich Fulda, *Das Recht der Philosophie
in Hegels Philosophie des Rechts* (Frankfurt: Klosterman, 1968); Andrew Shanks,
Hegel's Political Theology (Cambridge: Cambridge University Press, 1991); and
Michael Theunissen, *Hegels Lehre vom absoluten Geist als theologisch-politischer
Traktat* (Berlin: de Gruyter, 1970).

15. Despite Hegel's own insistence that the *Logic* is of great importance to understanding the philosophy of spirit, this remains a controversial view, and the
relation between the two continues to be the subject of debate. The extreme
positions are well represented by David Kolb and Allen Wood. Wood claims,
in *Hegel's Ethical Thought*, that to study the logic is to be "in for a difficult
and generally unrewarding time of it, at least from the standpoint of social
and political theory" (xii). Kolb argues that the *Philosophy of Right* cannot be
properly understood without the *Logic*, and he tries to demonstrate exactly
what one misses in the transition from civil society to the state if the *Logic* is
ignored. David Kolb, *The Critique of Pure Modernity: Hegel, Heidegger, and After*
(Chicago: University of Chicago Press, 1986), Chapters 3–5, esp. 38–40. I
employ a method indebted to Kolb's. Other commentators have also made
use of the *Logic* to understand developments in the *Philosophy of Right*, but this
continues to be more common in German scholarship than in English. For
examples, see Lu de Vos, "Die Logik der Hegelschen Rechtsphilosophie: Eine
Vermutung," *Hegel-Studien* 16 (1981): 99–121; Kenley R. Dove, "Logik
und Recht bei Hegel," *Neue hefte für Philosophie* 17 (1979): 89–108; Klaus
Hartmann, "Toward a New Systematic Reading of Hegel's *Philosophy of Right*,"
in *The State and Civil Society: Studies in Hegel's Political Philosophy*, ed. Z. A.
Pelczynski (Cambridge: Cambridge University Press, 1984), 114–136; K. H.
Ilting, "The Dialectic of Civil Society," in *The State and Civil Society*, ed. Pelczynski, 211–226; Udo Rameil, "Sittliches Sein und Subjektivität: zur Genese
des Begriffs der Sittlichkeit in Hegels Rechtsphilosophie," *Hegel-Studien* 16
(1981): 123–162; Ludwig Siep, "Was heisst: 'Aufhebung der Moralität in
Sittlichkeit' in Hegels Rechtsphilosophie?," *Hegel-Studien* 17 (1982): 75–96,
available in English as "The 'Aufhebung' of Morality in Ethical Life," tr.
Thomas Nenon with improvements by Raymond Geuss, in *Hegel's Philosophy
of Action*, ed. Lawrence S. Stepelevich and David Lamb (Atlantic Highlands,
N. J.: Humanities Press, 1983), 137–55; and the collection of essays edited

by Dieter Henrich and Rolf-Peter Horstmann, *Hegels Philosophie des Rechts: Die Theorie der Rechtsformen und ihre Logik* (Stuttgart: Klett-Cotta, 1982), esp. Henning Ottmann, "Hegelsche Logik und Rechtsphilosophie: Unzulängliche Bermerkungen zu einem ungelösten Problem" (382–392), and Michael Theunissen, "Die verdrängte Intersubjektivität in Hegels Philosophie des Rechts" (317–381), available in English as "The Repressed Intersubjectivity in Hegel's Philosophy of Right," tr. Eric Watkins in consultation with Fred Dallmayr, in *Hegel and Legal Theory*, ed. Drucilla Cornell, Michael Rosenfeld, and David Gray Carlson (New York: Routledge, 1991), 3–63.

16. My interpretation of Hegel explicitly excludes his early, presystematic works.
17. The relation between the styles employed in Nietzsche's works and the thoughts those works seek to communicate, especially the thoughts on linguistic style itself, have long been an area of intensive research. For an early consideration of this topic, see Roger Hazelton, "Nietzsche's Contribution to the Theory of Language," *The Philosophical Review* 52.1 (1943): 47–60. For critical surveys of more recent literature on these issues, see Alexander Nehamas, *Nietzsche: Life as Literature* (Cambridge, Mass.: Harvard University Press, 1985), Chapter 1; and Lutz Ellrich, "Rhetorik und Metaphysik: Nietzsche's 'neue' äesthetische Schreibweise," *Nietzsche-Studien* 23 (1994): 241–272. The same issue is also alive in Hegel studies. As Daniel J. Cook correctly notes in *Language in the Philosophy of Hegel* (The Hague: Mouton, 1973), "the problem of philosophical style for Hegel is *a problem that arises from his own system of thought*" (172).

Chapter 1

1. On the *Phenomenology* culminating in the standpoint of the speculative philosopher, see *PhG*, 39/22. On the association of freedom with conceptual thinking, see *PhG*, 156/120.
2. *EL*, §19A. Also see *WL*, I, 44/50.
3. *EL*, §158. Also see *WL*, II, 237–240/569–571.
4. *EN*, §248.
5. *EG*, §382. "Spirit" is my reluctant translation of "*Geist.*" The advantage of the choice is simply that it is one of two ("mind" being the other) to which English-speaking readers are accustomed. The disadvantage, common to both "spirit" and "mind," is that translating "*Geist*" before understanding it begs the question I am trying to answer: how must "*Geist*" be understood if it is to be that in virtue of which free beings are free? "Spirit" suggests something religious and transcendent, with the false implication that Hegelian freedom is to be found in a supernatural flight from the natural world. "Mind" suggests that "*Geist*" is mental as opposed to physical, and again gives the false impression that freedom lies in an escape from the material realm. Since Hegel ultimately shows that the freedom of those beings with "*Geist*" consists precisely in their overcoming distinctions built into the English words "spirit" and "mind," these words not only fail to translate "*Geist*" well but also actively and dramatically alter its sense. Nonetheless, the only alternative – to leave "*Geist*" untranslated – would be unnecessarily tiresome for English-speaking readers. In exchange for this consideration, I hope such readers will attempt to

presume as little as possible about the meaning of "spirit" in Hegel's discussion of freedom.

6. *EG*, §381Z. Although this citation is not from the *Logic*, it expresses the understanding of necessity found there, as will be clear from the citations that follow.

7. *EL*, §158Z.

8. On what is merely internal to a thing being therefore merely external to it, see *EL*, §140+Z.

9. *EG*, §381Z.

10. *EL*, §94Z.

11. Wolfgang Marx thus understands, in "Die Logik des Freiheitsbegriffs," *Hegel-Studien* 11 (1976): 125–147, the transition from necessity to freedom as corresponding to the transition from the logic of essence to the logic of the concept – for, in the latter, a thing and its parts are understood as a self-caused and free whole, whereas in the former things and their parts always remain subject to external causation. Merold Westphal agrees. He notes, in "Hegel's Theory of the Concept," in *Hegel, Freedom, Modernity* (Albany: State University of New York Press, 1992), 8, that only if one as an individual is a genuine unity of the universal and particular, which requires the sort of reciprocity developed in the logic of the concept and not in the logic of essence, can one "remain in control of oneself in giving oneself up to the mediating activity of the other"; and this latter ability he understands to be essential to freedom. For a good discussion of the senses in which social wholes and the agents who are their constituent parts can be said to be free, see Neuhouser, *Foundations of Hegel's Social Theory*, 37–49.

12. As Hegel puts it, in the move from a necessary relation to a free one the content of the relation remains the same (the same elements are subject to the same bonds in each) but changes form, from externality to internality (as the bonds come to be seen as constitutive of the elements bound). See *WL*, II, 179–181/523–526, and *EL*, §§138–141, on the relation of external and internal.

13. *EL*, §158Z. *WL*, I, 114/107, defines a "moment" as that which "has entered into unity with its opposite."

14. *PR*, §158.

15. *PR*, §161. For Hegel's discussion of marriage, see *PR*, §§161–169. Richard Dien Winfield, in *The Just Family* (Albany: State University of New York Press, 1998), emphasizes that traditional marriages are not the only unions in which self-conscious love is enjoyed.

16. *EL*, §28Z.

17. *EL*, §94.

18. *EL*, §94Z. At *EL*, §95, Hegel writes that "in its passing into another, something only comes together *with itself* (*mit sich selbst*); and this relation to itself in the passing and in the other is *genuine infinity*." In the remark to this paragraph he therefore concludes that, just as freedom is the truth of necessity, "the truth of the finite is rather its *ideality*."

19. See *PR*, §158Z. Robert B. Pippin, in "Hegel and Institutional Rationality," *The Southern Journal of Philosophy* 39 suppl. (2001): 1–25, puts Hegel's point

nicely: "he means to highlight an aspect of freedom, independence and so individuality, that is not conceived of as some abstract and unreal absence of all dependence, but a kind of dependence by virtue of which genuine or actual independence could be achieved," 7–8. Frederick Neuhouser's formulation, in *Foundations of Hegel's Social Theory*, is also apt: "Throughout Hegel's philosophy . . . freedom is always thought of as the end point of some process in which a being becomes constituted through its relations to an other and then abolishes the alien character of its other by apprehending it as identical to itself (in a sense in need of further specification), thereby becoming related only to itself" (20). Both Pippin and Neuhouser note that love is one of Hegel's best examples of this phenomenon.

20. *EG*, §381Z.
21. *EG*, §381Z.
22. *EG*, §381Z. An adequate understanding (not to mention a defense) of Hegel's claims and conclusions about natural beings would require a careful reading of his philosophy of nature, which is beyond the scope of this project. Such an understanding, however, is not crucial to the question of the freedom of spiritual beings, which is our concern.
23. *EG*, §381+Z. Also see *WL* I, 127/118.
24. *EG*, §381Z. At *PR*, §343, Hegel writes that "spirit is only what it does, and its deed is to make itself, as spirit, the object of its own consciousness, to apprehend itself interpretively as itself."
25. *EG*, §382Z. Also see *PR*, §42, where Hegel writes that "what is immediately different from free spirit is what is, both for spirit and in itself, on the whole external – the thing."
26. *VPR*, I, 280/384.
27. *EG*, §382Z. Also see *A*, 134/97.
28. Michael Hardimon, in *Hegel's Social Philosophy: The Project of Reconciliation* (Cambridge, Cambridge University Press, 1994), notes that "the project of reconciling people to the social world is one part of the larger project of reconciling them to the world as a whole, which is, in turn, a part of the still larger project of reconciling *Geist* (spirit, mind) to the world as a whole and thereby to itself" (3). Hardimon explicitly limits his own focus, however, to reconciliation within the social sphere (8).
29. *EG*, §382Z. Also see *EG*, §379Z, where Hegel writes that "the entire development of spirit is nothing other than its self-elevation to its truth," truth being understood as the "agreement of the concept with its actuality."
30. There are at least two ways in which the parts of the philosophy of spirit should *not* be understood. First, they are not accounts of three different kinds of being: "subjective spirit," "objective spirit," and "absolute spirit" are not entities. Second, they are not developmental stages through which spiritual beings pass: spiritual beings do not begin in a "subjective" state before becoming "objective" and finally "absolute."
31. *PG*, 69/52. Emphasis added.
32. As does Hegel, I will usually substitute "the will," "the moral will," and "the ethical will" for locutions such as "the willing subject," "the willing subject as conceived in morality," and "the willing subject as conceived in ethical

life." The potential drawback of this procedure is that it runs the risk of hypostatizing "the will" into an entity, when it is more accurate to speak of subjects who engage in the activity of willing. But the advantages of abbreviation, and of faithfulness to Hegel's own phraseology, outweigh this potential drawback.

33. This is to say not that a more general account of the relation between the *Logic* and the philosophy of spirit is impossible, but rather that I think an adequate general account would discover that their relation is not a formal one. In this book, however, I can neither provide such an account, nor even defend my hypotheses about what an adequate one would look like. I aspire here only to provide analyses of the logical structure of a few key sections of the philosophy of spirit, in the hope that the method I employ may serve as a model for other such specific analyses.

Chapter 2

1. Robert B. Pippin, in "Hegel, Freedom, the Will: *The Philosophy of Right:* §§1–33," in *Grundlinien der Philosophie des Rechts*, ed. Ludwig Siep (Berlin: Akademie Verlag, 1997), 31–53, rightly warns that "if we really need a full understanding of Hegel's speculative theory of the concept and conceptual determination (and thereby his theory of the syllogism) to understand, say, how individual freedom can be realized in the universal order of the state rather than sacrificed to it, or to understand the freedom of the will itself as 'the self-reference of negativity', we appear headed into a dangerous and mysterious forest from which few have returned speaking a language anyone else can understand" (36). It is precisely because I think that a full understanding of Hegel's account of the freedom of willing does require entering this speculative forest, and because few people have done so in an illuminating way, that I have developed the approach to Hegel taken in this chapter, and in Part I more generally.

2. For a helpful discussion of individuality, universality, and particularity, see Richard Dien Winfield, "On Individuality," in his *Freedom and Modernity* (Albany: State University of New York Press, 1991), 51–58. Winfield notes that Hegel distinguishes the judgment from the concept, and the different forms of judgment from each other, in virtue of their representing different relations of universal, particular, and individual (55).

3. *EL*, §164.

4. Ibid.

5. *EL*, §166. Also see *WL*, II, 301–304/623–625.

6. *EL*, §171. Also see *WL*, II, 305/626.

7. *WL*, II, 303/624, 307/627. Also see *EL*, §168. For a very helpful discussion of Hegel's conception of judgment, and specifically of the senses in which he does and does not attribute identity to the subject and predicate, see Houlgate, *Hegel, Nietzsche and the Criticism of Metaphysics*, Chapter 6. Houlgate addresses the criticisms of Hegel offered by Bertrand Russell and other analytic philosophers, which suggest that Hegel's treatment of judgment rests on a rather gross misunderstanding, and defends Hegel by showing not only that it is he who has been misunderstood, but also that

his conception of judgment is more sophisticated than those of Frege and Russell.

8. *WL*, II, 304/625.

9. *WL*, II, 309/630.

10. On this point, see Neuhouser, *Foundations of Hegel's Social Theory*, 27–33.

11. For the three moments of choice described in this paragraph and the preceding one, see *PR*, §5, §6, and §7.

12. Hegel uses "universal" here, as he does frequently, to mean one thing containing two or more things: the will is a "universal" with respect to its particular contents. The choosing will is what Hegel calls an abstract universal because it abstracts from the particular contents it happens to have in order to affirm its identity in distinction from them, and as what they have in common. By contrast, a true universal determines for itself the particular contents necessary to its form. See *WL*, II, 297/619, where Hegel describes an abstract universal as one that relates "to itself only as absolute negativity... [which] is a letting go of determinacy." By contrast, at *EL*, §163Z, he says that a true universal is not a "mere commonality," and at *WL*, II, 519/800, says that it must "particularize itself."

13. For helpful discussions of Hegel's treatment of choice, see Stephen Houlgate, *Freedom, Truth and History: An Introduction to Hegel's Philosophy* (London: Routledge, 1991), 79–84; Mark Tunick, *Hegel's Political Philosophy: Interpreting the Legal Practice of Punishment* (Princeton, N.J.: Princeton University Press, 1992), 37–60; and Richard Dien Winfield, "Freedom as Interaction: Hegel's Resolution to the Dilemma of Liberal Theory," in his *Freedom and Modernity*, 89–106.

14. See *PR*, §9–§20, on the immediate identification of the choosing will and its particular contents.

15. *PR*, §11.

16. It is important to avoid confusing these two senses of formality. In what follows, when I use "formal" without further qualification I mean a lack of intrinsic content. I will often use "subjective" in place of Hegel's second sense of "formal," since that conveys more closely what he means. On the formality of the choosing will, see especially *PR*, §§13–15.

17. That the will is free, and that any conception of the will in which it remains limited and externally dependent is therefore inadequate, is presupposed in the philosophy of right. At *PR*, §4, Hegel writes that, "the will is free, so that freedom constitutes its substance and determination." This presupposition is the result of the philosophy of subjective spirit, which we considered briefly in the introduction to Part I.

18. See *PR*, §21–24.

19. For detailed discussions of Hegel's analysis of property as a necessary aspect of freedom, see Richard A. Davis, "Property and Labor in Hegel's Concept of Freedom," in *Hegel on Economics and Freedom*, ed. William Maker (Macon, Ga.: Mercer University Press, 1987), 183–208, esp. 188–193; and Patten, *Hegel's Idea of Freedom*, Chapter 5. Patten attempts to defend Hegel's view, but ultimately faults him for supposedly making a doubtful a priori claim, regarding which Patten would defer to empirical psychologists, about the necessity of private property ownership to the development of a personality with

certain capacities. Such an a priori claim would indeed be doubtful, but Hegel's defense of the necessity of property to freedom does not depend on it. Instead, Hegel argues that property ownership is the first and most immediate way in which a person can will a reconciliation between herself and the natural world.

20. *PR*, §33.

21. *PR*, §73.

22. H. B. Nisbet points out, in a translator's note to *PR*, that "the basic and original meaning of *entäussern* is 'to externalize'" (95). The "alienation" of property is thus the "externalization" of property, and is demanded precisely because property is an "external thing" to which the will cannot be bound if it is to be free.

23. *PR*, §71.

24. It should be noted that on some liberal accounts others can *increase* my freedom by multiplying the number of things and activities from which I can choose. However, this multiplication is not a condition of liberal freedom itself, and therefore even on these accounts others are not strictly necessary to my freedom, as they are for Hegel. On Hegel's argument that freedom requires dependence, see Shaun Gallagher, "Interdependence and Freedom in Hegel's Economics," in *Hegel on Economics and Freedom*, ed. Maker, 159–181, esp. 178.

25. *PR*, §71. On the link between contract and recognition, see Kenley R. Dove, "Logik und Recht bei Hegel," *Neue hefte für Philosophie* 17 (1979): 89–108, esp. 103–104.

26. *PR*, §71+Z. Again, we find Hegel using "universal" to mean one thing containing two or more things: the common will is a "universal" with respect to the particular wills that make it up. Here Hegel points out explicitly that this is not yet a true universal, because the universal will here is *merely* common; it results from the decision of the particular wills to enter into it, rather than determining out of itself what its particular contents must be. Also see *PR*, §75.

27. *PR*, §§71–75, is the basis for the last four paragraphs on the mutual recognition of contracting wills.

28. *PR*, §81.

29. Ibid.

30. *PR*, §81. Wrong (*das Unrecht*) is the third and final main stage of abstract right.

31. *PR*, §82+Z. On *Schein*, see *EL*, §112+Z, and *WL*, II, 19–24/395–399.

32. *PR*, §100. Also see *PR*, §99A+Z, in which Hegel considers and dismisses several of the more common justifications of punishment.

33. *PR*, §103. Lu de Vos, in "Die Logik der Hegelschen Rechtsphilosophie: Eine Vermutung," *Hegel-Studien* 16 (1981): 99–121, notes that contract splits the universal and the particular, and that morality arises because their unification cannot be guaranteed in abstract right (104–107).

34. At *PR*, §145Z, Hegel says that "the contingent is generally what has the ground of its being not within itself but elsewhere." As long as the universal will is external to the individual, the conformity of the latter's particular contents to the universal has "the ground of its being not within itself but elsewhere,"

and is contingent. Thus the logic of contingency demands that the universal will be posited as internal to the individual if the latter is to be free. Also see *WL*, II, 202–207/542–546.

35. See *PR*, §§102–103.
36. *PR*, §104.
37. Also see *PR*, §§105–106.
38. *PR*, §33, identifies the moral will as the particularization of the will. Udo Rameil, in "Sittliches Sein und Subjektivität: zur Genese des Begriffs der Sittlichkeit in Hegels Rechtsphilosophie," *Hegel-Studien* 16 (1981): 123–162, notes that the universal and particular aspects of freedom are divided in morality and reunified in ethical life (139). He understands this transition, however, as being structured by the move from the logic of essence to the logic of the concept, rather than by that from judgment to syllogism.
39. *PR*, §104.
40. *PR*, §104A, §33. We might say that although the will has internalized this externality, it still remains as an internal externality, which must yet be internalized. At *PR*, 34Z, Hegel says that in the sphere of morality there is "an opposition, for therein I am as individual will, whereas the good is the universal, even though it is within me."
41. *PR*, §§106–108, §108Z.
42. *PR*, §108.
43. *PR*, §106A.
44. *WL*, II, 309/629. Also see *WL*, II, 272/599, and *EL*, §171.
45. *EL*, §168.
46. *WL*, II, 307/627, 309–310/630.
47. *EL*, §180; *WL*, II, 309/629.
48. *WL*, II, 306–307/627. It is not important for our purposes to work through the details of the stages of judgment. What is important are the reasons for judgment's ultimate failure to overcome its own finitude, which we have just seen, and the manifestation of this failure in the moral will, which we are about to examine.
49. This shows that judgment is also finite in a third sense: it relies on something other than itself to overcome its limitations. See *WL*, I, 139/129, and *WL*, II, 79–80/442–443, for Hegel's discussion of this sense of finitude.
50. *PR*, §108.
51. *PR*, §§108–109. We might say that the moral will must internalize the world by externalizing itself.
52. *PR*, §§110–112.
53. *PR*, §112A. In other words, the moral will is ultimately unable to overcome all of the externalities to which it is subject.
54. *PR*, §113. This is another place where the *Logic* sheds light on the *Philosophy of Right*. See *EL*, §140, which shows that an essence must appear externally. In *EL*, §140Z, Hegel explicitly links this point to the fact that morality must be expressed in action, and illustrates his point by saying that "a man is nothing but the series of his acts." Also see *PR*, §124. Kenley Dove, in "Logik und Recht bei Hegel," emphasizes that the moral subject is what it is through action (105).

55. *PR*, §114+Z.
56. *PR*, §123.
57. *PR*, §123+A+Z.
58. *PR*, §125.
59. *PR*, §124A. On the contrast between ancient and modern freedom, also see Hegel's discussions of Plato and Aristotle at *GP*, II, 129–130/114–115, 226–228/208–210.
60. *PR*, §126+A+Z. Hegel's example is St. Crispin, who stole leather to make shoes for the poor, an act Hegel describes as "both moral and wrong."
61. *PR*, §127+A.
62. *PR*, §128, §130.
63. Ludwig Siep, in "Was heisst: 'Aufhebung der Moralität in Sittlichkeit' in Hegels Rechtsphilosophie?," *Hegel-Studien* 17 (1982): 75–96, is especially sensitive to the fact that the conception of the will undergoes development *within* morality.
64. *PR*, §131, §133.
65. This is confirmed in the *Logic* itself, where Hegel makes reference in the sections on finitude and infinity to the "ought" that characterizes the moral standpoint. See *WL*, I, 142–165/131–149; *EL*, §94.
66. See *WL*, I, 148–166/136–150. Stephen Houlgate has a brief but helpful discussion of this point in *Freedom, Truth and History*, 68.
67. Looked at in another way, such a "solution" to the problem of the external relation between the universal and the individual is obviously not a solution, since it proposes not to determine an internal identity of the two, but rather to accept their mutual externality as an insuperable condition.
68. *PR*, §132.
69. *PR*, §§134–135.
70. *WL*, II, 96–109/456–466. These are the first two moments of determinate ground (*bestimmte Grund*). In determinate ground, generally, a determinate content is posited as being the same in both the ground and the grounded elements, which are understood to differ only in form.
71. *PR*, §135.
72. Hegel describes the moral will as reflected into itself at *PR*, §33A.
73. By contrast, a truly or positively infinite subject would, as we saw earlier, find itself in its others, internalizing them, rather than identifying itself only in distinction from them.
74. *PR*, §135A.
75. It is in the just-cited remark that Hegel brings his analysis of the moral will to bear on Kant, and concludes that the Kantian will is formal and empty. It is not possible to pursue this issue here, but readers interested in a concise and helpful exposition of Hegel's reading and critique of Kant's categorical imperative should see Houlgate, *Freedom, Truth and History*, 96–97.
76. *PR*, §138.
77. In fact, Hegel's own example of a judgment of the concept is that of subsuming an action under the good. *EL*, §171Z, §172Z.
78. *WL*, II, 344/657.

79. *WL*, II, 344–351/657–663; *EL*, §§178–180.
80. *WL*, II, 346–347/659–660.
81. *EL*, §179.
82. In Hegel's terms, the problematic judgment explicitly posits the subjectivity that is merely implicit in the assertoric judgment.
83. *PR*, §137A.
84. Ibid.
85. Ibid. Among others, Kenley Dove, in "Logik und Recht bei Hegel," 105–106, and Ludwig Siep, in "Was heisst: 'Aufhebung der Moralität in Sittlichkeit' in Hegels Rechtsphilosophie?," 81/142, note the subjectivity of conscience's determination of the good.
86. *PR*, §139A.
87. In *PR*, §140+A, Hegel goes on to discuss at great length the specific stages of evil that arise from the commitment to conscience. This passage is among the most interesting and insightful in the *Philosophy of Right* (among other things, it perfectly describes those who kill with a serenity bred of the certainty that their cause is morally justified), but examination of its details is not directly relevant to the task at hand.
88. This would be the point of departure for a Hegelian critique of Kant's notion of a "kingdom of ends." Such a critique, however, lies beyond this study.
89. It should be emphasized that Hegel does not advocate responding to this failure of the moral will by obeying the standards of just any community one happens to find oneself in. In *PR*, §138Z, he writes that "in ages when the actual world is a hollow, spiritless, and unsettled existence the individual may be permitted to flee from actuality and retreat into his inner [that is, moral] life." Of course, in order to determine when one's age is incongruent with an ethical life based on freedom (that is, hollow and spiritless) one has to know what genuine ethical life entails, which Hegel goes on to think through.
90. See *PR*, §110, on the moral will being an unresolved contradiction.
91. With the help of the *Logic*, we have been able to understand Hegel's claim that the moral will is formal and empty, and therefore unfree and self-contradictory. This demonstrates the *necessity* of the move to ethical life: the will simply must be reconceived, understood to have a different logical structure, if it is to be adequate to the freedom implicit in its concept. To Allen Wood, and to others who neglect the *Logic* when interpreting the *Philosophy of Right*, Hegel's formality claim appears to be less well justified, and they are therefore tempted to invent alternative explanations for the move to ethical life. Wood argues that Hegel fails to show that the moral will is totally empty, but does show that it has a hard time accounting for the values of groups, as opposed to those of individuals. He suggests that ethical life can thus be understood as supplementing morality with a community-based ethics. Although Wood notes that Hegel does not pursue "this promising line of thought," he does not seem to see that this is because to Hegel it does not appear at all promising, since it is inconsistent with his actual critique of the moral will, which is based on an analysis of its logical structure. See Wood,

Hegel's Ethical Thought, 172–173. I thus agree with Robert Pippin, in "Hegel, Freedom, The Will," 35–36, who responds to Wood and to others who approach Hegel in a similar vein that "without some attempt to understand [Hegel's] speculative reformulation of the basic issues presupposed in ethical and political life, his full case against liberal individualism, and conscience and duty based moralism (as opposed to interesting *ad hoc* arguments against particular claims) cannot be defended, and, especially, the implications of that critique for the possibility of a just, modern, secular, free society and constitutional regime cannot be drawn." For other interpretations of Hegel's formality claim and of the motivation for the transition to ethical life that also neglect the *Logic*, see H. B. Acton, Introduction to G. W. F. Hegel, *Natural Law* (Philadelphia: University of Pennsylvania Press, 1975), 26; and M. J. Petry, "Hegel's Criticism of the Ethics of Kant and Fichte," in *Hegel's Philosophy of Action*, ed. Lawrence S. Stepelevich and David Lamb (Atlantic Highlands, N.J.: Humanities Press, 1983), 125–136, esp. 135.

92. *WL*, II, 309–310/630.

93. See *PR*, §33 and §141Z, on the ethical will overcoming the particularization of the will found in morality. Also see *PR*, §24, which points to the need to understand the sections on judgment in the *Logic* (*EL*, §§168–179) in order to understand that the free will must be a true or concrete universal (that is, a syllogism) as opposed to a mere commonality that leaves the individual, particular, and universal external to each other (as in judgment). Robert B. Pippin, in *Idealism as Modernism: Hegelian Variations* (Cambridge: Cambridge University Press, 1997), 127, notes the importance of the "notion of a 'concrete universal'" to Hegel's critique of morality and account of ethical life, and he offers a helpful interpretation of that logical notion in *Hegel's Idealism: The Satisfactions of Self-Consciousness* (Cambridge: Cambridge University Press, 1989), Chapter 10.

94. *PR*, §141.

95. *PR*, §144Z.

96. *PR*, §141. The fact that ethical life unites subjective and objective freedom is important enough that Frederick Neuhouser uses it as an organizing principle for his *Foundations of Hegel's Social Theory*; Chapter 3 is devoted to the former, Chapters 4 and 5 to the latter.

97. A thorough discussion of ethical life, or even of any of its major parts, would require a book unto itself. But my aim here is not to investigate ethical life in all of its rich detail. Rather, it is to understand the freedom that ethical willing provides, in order ultimately to understand the limitations to which even the ethical will is subject, and which therefore drive the concept of freedom beyond willing altogether, beyond objective spirit to absolute spirit.

98. *PR*, §158Z.

99. *PR*, §162.

100. *PR*, §176. On the fragility of marriage being due to its reliance on feeling, and on Hegel's view of divorce, see Hardimon, *Hegel's Social Philosophy*, 228–230.

101. *PR,* §177.
102. *PR,* §181.
103. For an interpretation of Hegel's account of why the system of needs is necessary to the objectification of freedom, see Davis, "Property and Labor in Hegel's Concept of Freedom," 193–200.
104. §182Z.
105. *PR,* §183. Emphasis added.
106. *PR,* §193.
107. See *PR,* §§190–195, on the proliferation of needs.
108. *PR,* §198.
109. *PR,* §199.
110. Note that for Hegel poverty is a disposition, not simply a financial condition. See *PR,* §244, Remark.
111. *PR,* §243, §244.
112. Note that this is a contrast with contract, in which wrong was only a *possibility.* In the system of needs, poverty, the analogue of wrong, is *necessary,* according to Hegel. Michael Hardimon notes in *Hegel's Social Philosophy,* 236–250, that Hegel diagnoses poverty as a structural feature of civil society, but mistakenly believes that "Hegel is not... committed to the doctrine that it must be possible for *everyone* to come to be at home in order for anyone to be" (248). For an in-depth account of Hegel's analysis of poverty, from which I have learned a great deal, see Houlgate, *Freedom, Truth and History,* 104–119. Also see Davis, "Property and Labor in Hegel's Concept of Freedom," 201–206.
113. In fact, it might not be too much of a stretch to say that the poverty of the unemployed is the "crime" of the successful in civil society, even though it is a wrong committed in the legitimate pursuit of welfare and property. See *PR,* §232, and an extended passage in the lecture notes from Hegel's 1819–20 course on the philosophy of right, *PdR,* 195–196. For an excellent discussion of Hegel's claim that economic relations are matters of right, justice, and freedom, see Richard Dien Winfield, "Hegel's Challenge to the Modern Economy," in his *Freedom and Modernity,* 227–259. Also see Wilfried Ver Eecke, "Hegel on Freedom, Economics, and the State," in *Hegel on Economics and Freedom,* ed. Maker, 127–157. For helpful discussions of the passage from the lecture notes, see Tunick, *Hegel's Political Philosophy,* 116–119, and Henrich's introduction (entitled "Vernunft in Verwirklichung") to *PdR,* 9–39, esp. 20.
114. *PR,* §230.
115. See *PR,* §188, where Hegel calls the public authority and the corporations "provisions against the contingency which remains present in [the system of need and the administration of justice]." Following Allen Wood, I use "public authority" for Hegel's "*Polizei.*" See Wood's note in *PR,* 450, explaining Hegel's use of this term. Also see his note on Hegel's use of the term "*Korporation*" (*PR,* 454). Generally, it means a society officially recognized by the government, though not a part of it, usually representing a particular trade or profession. For a thorough discussion of the historical tradition from which Hegel draws his understanding of this term, see G. Heiman,

"The Sources and Significance of Hegel's Corporate Doctrine," in *Hegel's Political Philosophy: Problems and Perspectives*, ed. Z. A. Pelczynski (Cambridge: Cambridge University Press, 1971), 111–135.

116. *PR*, §230.
117. *PR*, §235. On Hegel's analysis of externalities, see Ver Eecke, "Hegel on Freedom, Economics, and the State," 152–154.
118. *PR*, §237–239.
119. *PR*, §240.
120. *PR*, §245. Two commentators who note this point are Raymond Plant, "Hegel and the Political Economy," in *Hegel on Economics and Freedom*, ed. Maker, 95–126, esp. 120; and Davis, "Property and Labor in Hegel's Concept of Freedom," 203–204.
121. *PR*, §246. Another alternative for the public authority that Hegel does not seem to consider might be the creation of "make-work" jobs that do not contribute to overproduction. But these jobs might well amount to charity, which creates a different problem that Hegel does recognize: it violates the ability of the recipient to respect herself as a self-determining being, and is thus equally destructive of her freedom. See *PR*, §245. Commentators noting Hegel's objection to charity include Plant, "Hegel and the Political Economy," 120–121; Ver Eecke, "Hegel on Freedom, Economics, and the State," 156; and Davis, "Property and Labor in Hegel's Concept of Freedom,"203.
122. *PR*, §255.
123. *PR*, §253.
124. Henning Ottmann has noted that the role of the corporation is to guarantee right and welfare by transforming our self-understanding and thereby reducing our need to achieve recognition by seeking individual prestige. Henning Ottmann, "Hegelsche Logik und Rechtsphilosophie: Unzulängliche Bemerkungen zu einem ungelösten Problem," in *Hegels Philosophie des Rechts*, ed. Henrich and Horstman, 389–390. Also see Gallagher, "Interdependence and Freedom in Hegel's Economics," 174–175; Davis, "Property and Labor in Hegel's Concept of Freedom," 205; and Heiman, "The Sources and Significance of Hegel's Corporate Doctrine,"121, 125, 129.
125. *PR*, §253.
126. Stephen Houlgate, in *Freedom, Truth and History*, 115–119, agrees with me that Hegel sees in the corporations the key to overcoming the poverty that he considers necessary to the unfettered free market or system of needs. Many commentators, however, conclude that Hegel thinks poverty can never be overcome, and is as necessary in the state as it is in civil society. See Kolb, *Critique of Pure Modernity*, 108; Plant, "Hegel and the Political Economy," 118–119; and Davis, "Property and Labor in Hegel's Concept of Freedom," 204.
127. *PR*, §249. Note that this is exactly how liberal individualism understands government: it is necessary, yet its presence in our lives and the economy should be minimized, since by definition anything the government does must be an interference and a restriction of our freedom.

128. Others who emphasize that the corporations succeed because people understand the restrictions they impose to be *self*-imposed are Peter G. Stillman, "Partiality and Wholeness: Economic Freedom, Individual Development, and Ethical Institutions in Hegel's Political Thought," in *Hegel on Economics and Freedom*, ed. Maker, 65–93, esp. 87; and Houlgate, *Freedom, Truth and History*, 115–119.

129. See *PR*, §255+A+Z.

130. *PR*, §256. For an especially helpful discussion of the transition from civil society to the state, see Kolb, *Critique of Pure Modernity*, Chapters 3–5.

131. Alan Patten draws the basic distinction between civil society and the state in a similar fashion in *Hegel's Idea of Freedom*, Chapter 6, esp. 170–172.

132. *PR*, §268.

133. *PR*, §158Z.

134. *PR*, §268.

135. *PR*, §268Z. Hans Friedrich Fulda, in *Das Recht der Philosophie in Hegels Philosophie des Rechts*, 31–32, also notes that in modern states the patriotic disposition is conditional upon the existence of rational laws and institutions.

136. For a clear and insightful discussion of the central elements of Hegel's rational state, see Franco, *Hegel's Philosophy of Freedom*, Chapter 8, esp. 306–337.

137. *PR*, §141Z.

138. *PR*, §144, §145.

139. *PR*, §145+Z, §146, §156A.

140. *PR*, §145.

141. *PR*, §147.

142. *PR*, §149+Z.

143. *PR*, §151+Z, §257, §339.

144. See *PR*, §147+A, where Hegel says that the individual's relationship to ethical universals is "closer to identity than even faith or trust."

145. *PR*, §151. See Adriaan Peperzak, "'Second Nature': Place and Significance of the Objective Spirit in Hegel's *Encyclopedia*," *The Owl of Minerva* 27.1 (Fall 1995): 51–66.

146. *PR*, §156, §257.

147. On adequate conceptual cognition not being the same thing as reflective awareness, see *PR*, §147A. On such cognition not being provided in the political (*weltlich*) realm, which remains within representational thinking, see *PR*, §359. On philosophy providing adequate conceptual cognition, see *PR*, §258A, §360.

148. Frederick Neuhouser, in *Foundations of Hegel's Social Theory*, 117, also notes that the objective freedom realized in ethical life must be objective in three distinct senses.

149. *PR*, §156, §157.

150. *PR*, §143, §258+A; *EG*, §515.

151. *VPR*, III, 264/341–342. On *Sittlichkeit* being an adequate realization of the freedom of the will, see Adriaan Peperzak, "Hegel's Pflichten und Tugendlehre: Eine Analyse und Interpretation der 'Grundlinien der Philosophie des Rechts' §§142–156," *Hegel-Studien* 17 (1982): 97–117.

Chapter 3

1. Commentators who have paid attention to the fact that the *Philosophy of Right* as a whole represents but one moment in the larger development of spirit, which suggests that the freedom it explores – freedom of the will – is a limited and incomplete form of freedom, include: Lu de Vos, "Die Logik der Hegelschen Rechtsphilosophie: Eine Vermutung," *Hegel-Studien* 16 (1981): 99–121, esp. 120; Houlgate, *Freedom, Truth and History*, 124–125; Kolb, *Critique of Pure Modernity*, 108; John McCumber, *Poetic Interaction: Language, Freedom, Reason* (Chicago: University of Chicago Press, 1989), 86–99; John McCumber, "Contradiction and Resolution in the State: Hegel's Covert View," *Clio* 15.4 (1986): 379–390; Adriaan Peperzak, "'Second Nature': Place and Significance of the Objective Spirit in Hegel's *Encyclopedia*," *The Owl of Minerva* 27.1 (Fall 1995): 51–66; Stanley Rosen, "Theory and Practice in Hegel: Union or Disunion?," in *Hegel's Social and Political Thought: The Philosophy of Objective Spirit*, ed. Donald Phillip Verene (Atlantic Highlands, N. J.: Humanities Press, 1980), 35–45; and Theunissen, *Hegels Lehre vom absoluten Geist als theologisch-politischer Traktat*, 109ff. Zbigniew Pelczynski, in "Freedom in Hegel," in *Conceptions of Liberty in Political Philosophy*, ed. Zbigniew Pelczynski and John Gray (London: Athlone, 1984), 177, acknowledges that the activities of absolute spirit have an essential role to play in "providing the intellectual basis" of the freedom of willing, but nonetheless insists that "the highest stage in the dialectic of freedom results from the rational necessity of reconciling the objective and subjective will." Pelczynski thus fails to acknowledge the more comprehensive freedom available in the activities of absolute spirit alone.

2. For a graphical representation of the location of the elements of Hegel's system treated in Chapters 2 and 3, refer back to the figure on page 26.

3. *A*, 152–154/112–113. Also see *EG*, §384Z and §381Z.

4. At *WL*, II, 465/757, Hegel writes, "Finite things are finite insofar as they do not have the reality of their concept completely within themselves...That actual things are not congruent with the idea is the side of their *finitude* and *untruth*."

5. See *EG*, §441Z and §381Z.

6. *EL*, §224.

7. He also discusses knowing and willing at the end of the *Logic*, in the sections on the theoretical idea and the practical idea. For a helpful discussion of the practical idea, see Friedrich Hogemann, "Die 'Idee des Guten' in Hegels 'Wissenschaft der Logik'," *Hegel-Studien* 29 (1994): 79–102.

8. *EG*, §441Z.

9. *EG*, §445. Also see *VPR*, I, 280/384: "Nature is cognized as a rational system: the final peak of its rationality is that nature itself exhibits the existence of reason...But this law is only in the inner being of things; in space and time it exists only in an external manner, for nature knows nothing of the law."

10. Conceptual representation is not the only spiritual form into which spiritual beings put natural contents. In earlier sections of subjective spirit, Hegel also discusses feeling and perception. My discussion of subjective spirit is limited

to its treatment of knowing, however, because this provides the transition to willing that signals the emergence of objective spirit, which is our concern.

11. *EG*, §387Z.
12. *PR*, §11. Also see *PR*, §10, and *EG*, §469+Z.
13. See *EG*, §§476–477, and *PR*, §14.
14. On this double obligation of the will, see *EG*, §470, and *PR*, §27.
15. *EG*, §443Z. Also see *PR*, §4Z; *EL*, §11, §225, §232+Z; and *A*, 235/179.
16. *EL*, §233.
17. See *EG*, §444Z, §482; and *PR*, §§21–23. In order for this to occur, for the willing subject to be able to will itself, it must be able not only to will but also to think or know what it itself truly is. Since this latter task is a theoretical one, freedom of the will involves the unification of theoretical and practical spirit. For an excellent discussion of this, see Stephen Houlgate, "The Unity of Theoretical and Practical Spirit in Hegel's Concept of Freedom," *Review of Metaphysics* 48 (June 1995): 859–881.
18. See *WL*, II, 543–544/819–820.
19. *EG*, §483.
20. *PR*, §25.
21. *EG*, §484. Also see *EG*, §482; *PR*, §28, §353; and *WL*, II, 541–542/818–819. The language Hegel uses here shows that the freedom of the willing subject, like the logical freedom that we considered in the introduction to Part I, depends upon becoming *bei sich selbst* in an other. Mark Tunick notes that the will's freedom involves becoming *bei sich selbst*, or at home in the world, and links it to Hegel's point, made in the *Phenomenology of Spirit* and elsewhere, that freedom involves a feeling of satisfaction (*Befriedigung*). But Tunick does not note the connection to Hegel's explication of logical freedom. See *Hegel's Political Philosophy*, 50–51.
22. See *EG*, §486, and *PR*, §§29–30.
23. *EG*, §513.
24. *EL*, §233; *WL*, II, 542/818–819.
25. *EL*, §234.
26. Hegel confirms directly, in several places, that the willing subject is externally purposive. At *WL*, II, 463–465/755–758, he writes that the state, the highest form of the will, gets translated into reality in the form of external purposiveness. And at *WL*, II, 543/819, he writes that the activity of willing, which he refers to as the syllogism of immediate realization, is identical to the syllogism of external purposiveness, save for a single difference (which is that whereas the content of the will is determinate, the content of external purposiveness itself is indeterminate).
27. For a helpful account of Hegel's discussion of teleology, which also identifies interesting connections between it and current work in the analytic philosophy of mind, see Willem A. deVries, "The Dialectic of Teleology," *Philosophical Topics* 19.2 (Fall 1991): 51–70.
28. *EL*, §204; *WL*, II, 443–444/739–740.
29. *EL*, §205+Z.
30. *EL*, §205; *WL*, II, 439–440/736–737.
31. *EL*, §205+Z; *WL*, II, 446–448/741–743.
32. *EL*, §204. Also see *WL*, II, 445/740–741.

33. *EL*, §204+A. Also see *WL*, II, 444/739.
34. *EL*, §206. Also see *WL*, II, 448–451/743–745.
35. *EL*, §206Z. The second stage is referred to as the means (*das Mittel*) at *WL*, II, 448/743.
36. *EL*, §207. Also see *WL*, II, 443/739, 445–448/740–743.
37. *EL*, §208A. Also see *EL*, §208+Z, and *WL*, II, 448/743.
38. The subject cannot communicate its own purpose directly to the world, because that purpose has the form of a thought, and the world to which it must be communicated has the form of objective existence. This communication can take place, therefore, only through a mediation that translates the purposive content between these two forms.
39. *EL*, §209+Z.
40. *EL*, §209Z.
41. *WL*, II, 456/749.
42. The formal syllogism is also known as the qualitative syllogism, the syllogism of existence, the immediate syllogism, and the syllogism of the understanding. See *EL*, §182; *WL*, II, 353–355/665–666.
43. *WL*, II, 351–353/664–665.
44. *EL*, §182; *WL*, II, 353/665.
45. *WL*, II, 456/749.
46. There are actually three subtypes of formal syllogism, distinguished by whether the middle term has the form of individuality, particularity, or universality. But consideration of the first of these will be sufficient to illuminate formal syllogism's finitude. See *EL*, §183–§187; *WL*, II, 355–371/666–679. Readers interested in the subtypes of formal syllogism might see Clark Butler, *Hegel's Logic: Between Dialectic and History* (Evanston, Ill.: Northwestern University Press, 1996), 246–249; John Burbidge, *On Hegel's Logic: Fragments of a Commentary* (Atlantic Highlands, N. J.: Humanities Press, 1981), 158–173; and Errol E. Harris, *An Interpretation of the Logic of Hegel* (New York: University Press of America, 1983), 242–246.
47. *EL*, §185; *WL*, II, 362/672.
48. *EL*, §184; *WL*, II, 359–360/670.
49. *EL*, §185; *WL*, II, 359–362/670–672, 369/677–678.
50. *EL*, §185A; *WL*, II, 362–363/672–673.
51. *EL*, §182.
52. *EL*, §184Z and §185; *WL*, II, 362–363/672–673.
53. *EL*, §210.
54. *WL*, II, 449/473–744.
55. *WL*, II, 456/749.
56. *WL*, II, 456/749–750. Also see *WL*, II, 451/745, 455–458/748–750.
57. *EL*, §211.
58. This contingency of the object's form means that "such a determinateness is already through the sphere of necessity, through being, at the mercy of becoming and alteration and must pass away," *WL*, II, 457/750.
59. *WL*, II, 463/755.
60. That the subject cannot achieve genuine infinitude by performing an infinite number of acts in which it fails to produce a genuine identity with the finite material of the objective world can also be understood from Hegel's

discussion of infinity and finitude in the *Logic*. At *WL*, I, 157/143–144, he points out, as we noted in Chapter 2, that an infinite that is merely other than the finite is not truly infinite at all, for such an infinite is limited by the finite that it is not, and to be limited is not to be infinite. The truly infinite, Hegel argues at *WL*, I, 163/148, can only be "the process in which it is deposed to being only *one* of its determinations, the opposite of the finite, and so to being itself only one of the finites, and then raising this its difference from itself into the affirmation of itself and through this mediation becoming the *true* infinite." Here, the purposive subject has made itself the opposite of the finite, objective world, thereby reducing itself "to being itself only one of the finites," but has proved unable to mediate this difference by producing a genuine identity with the finite object in which it would be truly infinite.

61. *WL*, II, 440/736–737.

62. This illustrates one meaning of something being only a posit – that it is merely a subjective result. That the posited unity of subject and object accomplished by purposiveness is only posited thus signifies that the purposive subject understands its unity with the object to be something that it has forged, rather than the true character of the object itself. See *WL*, II, 32–33/406.

63. Hegel writes at *WL*, II, 544/820, that "in respect of its content the good is restricted, there are several kinds of good; good in its concrete existence is not only subject to destruction by external contingency and by evil, but by the collision and conflict of the good itself." Also see *WL*, II, 543–548/819–823.

64. It is interesting to recall that this is also the fate of the moral will, which internalizes the external and contingent content of abstract right, but only to discover that the contingency persists within itself.

65. *EG*, §385Z. *VPR*, III, 234/310–311, also makes the point that a merely posited reconciliation is in fact no reconciliation at all.

66. At *PR*, §8, Hegel writes that the will "is the process of translating its subjective goal into objectivity through the mediation of its own activity and some external means." And at *PR*, §122, he claims that "insofar as any such aim is finite, it may in its turn be reduced to a means for some further intention, and so on *ad infinitum*."

67. The externality of the willing subject to the natural world in which it actualizes itself also means that its actualizations are doomed to decay, because they represent a form imposed upon nature, rather than its own shape. In other words, the rational state is an historical creation, bound to fall apart over time. See *WL*, II, 542–544/818–820, where Hegel writes that in the practical idea "the formerly objective world, on the contrary, is now only something posited, something *immediately* determined in various ways, but because it is only immediately determined, the unity of the concept is lacking in it and it is, by itself, a nullity . . . [The realization of the good] gives [the good] an external existence; but since this existence is determined merely as an intrinsically worthless externality, in it the good has only attained a contingent, destructible existence, not a realization corresponding to its idea." At *PR*, §258Z, §340 and §347A, Hegel discusses the contingency of the state. This contingency has recently been emphasized by de Vos, "Die Logik der Hegelschen Rechtsphilosophie," 120; Houlgate, *Freedom, Truth and History*, 124–125; and

Peperzak, "'Second Nature': Place and Significance of the Objective Spirit in Hegel's *Encyclopedia*," 58–62. Also see Stephen Houlgate, "Necessity and Contingency in Hegel's *Science of Logic*," *The Owl of Minerva* 27.1 (Fall 1995): 37–49, esp. 49, where he writes that "one of the sobering, but overlooked lessons of Hegel's philosophy of history is indeed that, far from being absolutely necessary, self-conscious freedom in the state and civil society is itself ultimately subject to the *absolute necessity* of destruction."

68. *WL*, II, 458/750.

69. *EL*, §234+Z. Also see *WL*, II, 544/820.

70. *WL*, II, 544/820. In his *Critique of Pure Modernity*, David Kolb points out that in the second moment of any dialectic, "the unifying bond shows only as external necessity or as the failure of the parts, taken on their own, to account for their own status and togetherness" (59). We have just seen that willing, as the second moment of the dialectic of spirit, is unable to account for the unity of spiritual beings with nature, and is therefore one manifestation of this general pattern. John McCumber emphasizes that willing is always in need of an external reality or alien world upon which it can work, in both "Contradiction and Resolution in the State," 384–385, and "Hegel's Anarchistic Utopia: The Politics of His *Aesthetics*," *Southern Journal of Philosophy* 22.2 (1984): 203–210, esp. 204–205.

71. *WL*, II, 547/822.

72. *PR*, §26A.

73. *A*, I, 129/93. Also see *VRP*, IV, 751–752, where Hegel says that in the state "subjective spirit has its satisfaction."

74. See especially, *WL*, II, 468–469/760, 496–497/782–783, 541–544/818–820. Also see Hogemann, "Die 'Idee des Guten' in Hegels 'Wissenschaft der Logik'," 94–99.

75. See *PR*, §112, where Hegel distinguishes three corresponding senses of objectivity and subjectivity, two of which are important in what follows here.

76. Hegel makes this point, explicitly and implicitly, many times in the *Philosophy of Right*. See, for example, §150A, §156, §258A+Z, §336, §337, §339, §340, §341, §§346–352.

77. As McCumber puts the point in "Hegel's Anarchistic Utopia," the state cannot justify itself and therefore requires a "higher confirmation and sanction," which only absolute spirit can provide (207). See also *EG*, §552, on the content of a particular state's ethical substance being made up of unreflective natural customs; *PR*, §26, on one sense of the objective will implying that the will is unreflectively immersed in its object, so that its actions are guided by an alien authority; *VRP*, IV, 146, and *VRP*, III, 161, on this making unethical content possible for an ethical will; *PR*, §270A, on the "bad state" being finite; and *VRP*, IV, 751–752, on the goal of the *philosophy* of right being "to come to know which contents spirit must have in objectifying itself."

78. See *EG*, §484.

79. *A*, I, 129–130/93.

80. *WL*, II, 393–394/697.

81. *WL*, II, 391–392/695–696, 398/701, 354/666. This explains how the syllogism of necessity gets its name – the relation between its terms is necessary, since one is the nature of the other two, which are the necessary forms of

existence of that nature. Likewise, the terms in the syllogism of reflection are related reflectively, and the terms in the formal syllogism are related formally.

82. *WL*, II, 398/701.
83. *WL*, II, 399/702.
84. *WL*, II, 399/702.
85. *WL*, II, 397–398/700–701; *EL*, §192.
86. *WL*, II, 400/702–703, 393–394/697; *EL*, §192Z.
87. *WL*, II, 401/703–704, 392/696; *EL*, §193.
88. *EL*, §212.
89. *WL*, II, 458/751.
90. Ibid.; *EL*, §212+Z.
91. It should be evident here that the self-overcoming of external purposiveness has produced the same features as those identified earlier as the result of the transformation of the formal syllogism into the syllogism of necessity.
92. But neither is the identity of subject and object merely immediate – it is also mediated by the subject. This is important, because if the identity is merely immediate, as in judgment, the subject and object remain mutually external. On the other hand, if it is merely mediated, as in syllogism, the subject and object also remain mutually external. The self-overcoming of external purposiveness shows that the true mutual internality of subject and object requires that their identity be both immediate and mediated. (See *WL*, II, 461/753–754.) In the *Philosophy of Right*, the moral will provides a merely immediate connection of subject and object, while ethical life provides a merely posited or mediated connection. Both of these connections, therefore, leave subject and object mutually external, driving the transition beyond willing to absolute spirit, which we will consider shortly.
93. *EL*, §212Z.
94. *WL*, II, 461/754.
95. On the finitude of the actualizations of the ethical will – nations – and their interactions giving rise to the infinite self-knowledge of absolute spirit, see *PR*, §340, §352.
96. Hegel confirms that the two overcomings are analogous at *EL*, §204A, where he writes that the negation of the externality of subject and object performed by the syllogism that realizes purpose is "the same negation that is put into practice in the elevation of spirit to God, above the contingent things of the world as well as above our own subjectivity." On the willing subject overcoming itself by reflecting on what its own activity says about its conception of itself, Hegel writes at *WL*, II, 547/822, that "what still *limits* the objective concept is its own *view* of itself, which vanishes by reflection on what its actualization is *in itself*. Through this view it is only standing in its own way, and thus what it has to do is to turn, not against an outer actuality, but against itself."
97. *WL*, II, 545–546/821–822.
98. *WL*, II, 547–548/822–823.
99. At *EL*, §234A, Hegel writes that "it is through the process of willing itself that [its] finitude is sublated, together with the contradiction that it contains." The state thus plays a key role in enabling the spiritual subject to achieve the freedom it cannot find in the political arena. George Armstrong Kelly, in "Politics and Philosophy in Hegel," in his *Hegel's Retreat from Eleusis*

(Princeton, N.J.: Princeton University Press, 1978), 8–28, makes this point, emphasizing that the state is not an end in itself but a means to the truth that is found in art, religion, and philosophy, and claiming that the first root issue of Hegel's political philosophy is precisely the consideration of how objective spirit helps to produce the achievement of absolute spirit.

100. *WL*, II, 545/821. Also see *PR*, §13A: "[It] is in the will that the intelligence's own finitude begins... [the] will is thinking reason resolving itself to finitude." And see *VPR*, I, 331/442: "limitation first begins with the practical domain ... In willing I exist for myself; other objects stand over against me and so they are my limit. The will has an end and moves toward this end; it is the activity of sublating this finitude, this contradiction, the fact that this object is a limit for me."

101. *EL*, §234+A; *WL*, II, 547–548/822–823. At *EL*, §234A, Hegel writes that the self-overcoming of willing produces a reconciliation that "consists in the will's returning – in its result – to the presupposition of cognition; hence the reconciliation consists in the unity of the theoretical and practical idea. The will knows the purpose as what is its own, and intelligence interprets the world as the concept in its actuality. This is the genuine position of rational cognition."

102. *EL*, §193A.

103. *EL*, §234.

104. *WL*, II, 546/821–822.

105. *EG*, §386Z. See James P. Kow, "Hegel, Kolb, and Flay: Foundationalism or Anti-Foundationalism?," *International Philosophical Quarterly* 33.2 (1993): 203–218. Kow writes that "for Hegel, we fall necessarily, in order to rise freely. We suffer self-division necessarily, in order to be unified in freedom ... We go under in order to go over" (217). He also writes that "logically, freedom is self-determining reflection, or positing the presupposed as presupposed" (214 n42). This is consistent with the liberation of spirit just described, since spirit becomes free by discovering that the will's presupposition of the externality of nature is just that – a presupposition – and as such imposes on spirit an unnecessary finitude.

106. Daniel J. Cook, in *Language in the Philosophy of Hegel*, writes that "self-consciousness enters the realm of absolute spirit when it becomes aware that its experience of alienation from the outside, object world has been transcended" (101).

107. See *EL*, §234+A+Z, §235; and *WL*, II, 547–548/822–823. At *EL*, §234Z, Hegel writes that "unsatisfied striving vanishes when we [re]cognize that the final purpose (*Endzweck*) of the world is just as much accomplished (*vollbracht*) as it is eternally accomplishing itself (*sich ewig vollbringt*)." Also see *EL*, §212+Z, and *WL*, II, 458–461/751–754, where we can see clearly that this result of the willing subject's self-overcoming is analogous to that of the self-overcoming of external purposiveness. That overcoming, he concludes at *WL*, II, 461/753, demonstrates that "the end is not merely an *ought-to-be* and a *striving* to realize itself, but as a concrete totality is identical with the immediate objectivity." *VPR*, I, 332–333/443–444, expresses the point in the language of religious representation.

108. *PR*, §27.

109. *EG*, §564.
110. On the self-overcoming of willing and its implications, see *EL*, §234+Z, §235, §236; and *WL*, II, 545–548/821–823.
111. In logical terms, the idea (the identity of subjectivity and objectivity) now has itself for its object (i.e., it is aware of itself as this identity). As Hegel puts it at *WL*, II, 546/822, "the concept is posited as identical with itself, not with an other, and thus alone is posited as the free concept." In absolute spirit the spiritual subject has thus taken on the logical form of the absolute idea, the idea that is infinite because it is aware of its own infinitude. On absolute spirit being the actuality of the absolute idea, see *A*, I, 128/92. On beauty (the first form of absolute spirit) being "the absolute idea in its appearance in a way adequate to itself," see *A*, I, 128/92.
112. See *A*, I, 139/101, and *EG*, §385Z.
113. *PG*, 69/52. Emphasis added.

Chapter 4

1. *WL*, II, 549/824. Also see *A*, I, 139/101; *PR*, §270A, §341, §360; and Hegel's note to *PR*, §140A (f), in which he says that the ethical order (the pinnacle of finite spirit) has an infinite content, but that this content exists in a limited and finite form.
2. At *A*, I, 21/8, 155/114, Hegel describes art as the first reconciling middle term between thought and existence. John McCumber argues, in "Hegel's Anarchistic Utopia: The Politics of His *Aesthetics*," *Southern Journal of Philosophy* 22.2 (1984): 203–210, that art frees us from the externalities to which the will always remains subject by reconciling us to them.
3. A full treatment of absolute spirit, one that carefully explicated Hegel's analyses of art, religion, and philosophy, would require a study unto itself. Here my remarks on art and religion will be limited to those necessary to understand the freedom distinctive to philosophy. For an extensive discussion of absolute spirit, and of the interrelations among art, religion, and philosophy, see Theunissen, *Hegels Lehre vom absoluten Geist als theologisch-politischer Traktat*, 103–221, 291–322.
4. *VGP*, 81/54.
5. *VGP*, 88/59. Stephen Houlgate, in *Freedom, Truth and History*, 65, writes that "Hegel's logic disturbs that 'freedom' to think for *oneself*. It disturbs our 'freedom' to stand above a topic and think 'about' it as seems rational to us. It requires of us, rather, that we exercise 'restraint' (*Enthaltsamkeit*) and let ourselves be guided by the immanent self-development of the matter at hand."
6. *VGP*, 118/87.
7. *VGP*, 101/70–71.
8. *VGP*, 42/28.
9. *VGP*, 41–42/27.
10. *VGP*, 34/21–22.
11. At *VGP*, 81/54, Hegel writes that "there is an old assumption that it is thinking which distinguishes man from animals. We will abide by it. Whatever makes a man nobler than an animal he possesses in virtue of his thinking.

Whatever is human is so only so far as thought is effective in it; however it
may look, it is human only because thought makes it so. This is the one thing
that distinguishes man from an animal."

12. *GP*, III, 460/552. At *VGP*, 104/74, Hegel writes that "man knows what he
is, and only then is he actual." See *EG*, §377+A, and *PR*, §343A, on "know
thyself" being the law of spiritual beings. Also see *VGP*, 149/112.

13. *VGP*, 106/76. At *PR*, §352, Hegel writes that the spiritual being is "simply
the movement of its own activity in gaining absolute knowledge of itself and
thereby freeing its consciousness from the form of natural immediacy and so
coming to itself." Also see *VGP*, 175–176/131, 233–234/172–173.

14. *A*, I, 139/101. Also see *VGP*, 47–48/31–33, and *PR*, §341.

15. See *VGP*, 82–84/55–57, 92/63.

16. *EG*, §444Z. On language being the most appropriate manifestation of spirit,
also see *PR*, §78, §164. Daniel J. Cook, in *Language in the Philosophy of Hegel*,
writes that "because language is the least corporeal mode of expression, it is
best capable of representing man's inner thoughts and of reproducing his
knowledge of the outer world" (105). John McCumber, in *The Company of
Words: Hegel, Language, and Systematic Philosophy* (Evanston, Ill.: Northwestern
University Press, 1993), 56, describes language as the only "exteriorization *of*
spirit which remains *within* spirit."

17. On feeling not determining its content out of its own form, see *EG*, §400+Z,
§472+Z. Also see *VPR*, I, 336/449: "Faith is of course still not free in itself in
regard to the content, and it is only thought that seeks to be free with regard
to the content too . . . The ultimate analysis, in which there are no longer any
assumed principles, arrives only in the advance to philosophy."

18. At *A*, I, 28/13, Hegel writes that it is only through philosophy that art receives
its real ratification (*echte Bewährung*); and at *VPR*, III, 268/487, he makes the
same point regarding religion: "[Philosophy] is the justification of religion,
especially of the Christian religion, the true religion; it knows the *content* [of
religion] in accord with its necessity and reason." At *VGP*, 192/141, he adds
that "by thinking in terms of the concept and grasping this content in thought,
philosophy has this advantage over the pictorial thinking of religion, that it
understands both, for it understands religion and can do justice to it . . . but
the reverse is not true." Also see *PR*, §270A.

19. Hegel writes at *EL*, §133Z, that we should recall "the distinction between philosophy and the other sciences. The finitude of the latter consists altogether
in the fact that thinking, which is a merely formal activity in them, adopts its
content as something given from outside, and the content is not known to
be determined from within by the underlying thought, so that the form and
content do not completely permeate one another." Also see *EG*, §442+Z, and
EL, §3+A, §160Z.

20. *PG*, 69/52.

21. See *EG*, 404, on freedom being realized only through the grasping of the idea
(the unity of thought and being, subject and object), which spiritual beings
do in philosophy. This reference is to the Appendix of *EG*, the "Einleitung
zur Enzyklopädie-Vorlesung, 22 October 1818," which is not translated by
Miller.

22. *EL*, §11. On thinking being the determination of humanity, see *WL*, I, 132/123. At *VGP*, 153/110, Hegel says that "from the point of view of the thinking spirit ... philosophy must be regarded as the most necessary thing of all." Also see *VG*, 56/48, 74/64.
23. *EG*, §384Z.
24. *PhG*, 29/14, 39/22, 156/120.
25. My response here to the hypothetical critic of Hegel has strong affinities with those offered by Franco, *Hegel's Philosophy of Freedom*, 179–187; Patten, *Hegel's Idea of Freedom*, Chapter 2, esp. 73–75; and Wood, *Hegel's Ethical Thought*, 52. Patten's response, like mine, relies on the strategy of first pointing out that Hegel and his critics agree "that freedom and authority are opposed to one another" (63), and then arguing that "agreeing with Hegel about this relationship commits one to accepting at least a central part of his much more ambitious idea of freedom as rational self-determination" (63–64). Although Wood rightly notes that liberals such as Isaiah Berlin beg the question, I am not convinced that his own interpretation of Hegel is actually immune to Berlin's point. Wood writes that one "Hegelian response" to Berlin is "that unless we view freedom in the ordinary sense as subordinate to other goals, we cannot properly estimate its value, or have full insight into its importance, since that is best appreciated when it is seen in light of the larger human good it serves" (52). He adds that in Hegel "subjective freedom is subordinated to the end of self-actualization" (258). Not only is this not a Hegelian response to Berlin, it is precisely Berlin's objection to Hegel! – namely, that freedom is "freedom in the ordinary sense" (that is, subjective freedom or choice), even if such freedom is not valuable in itself but only for the sake of "the larger human good it serves" (that is, self-actualization). Just as Berlin fails to respond adequately to Hegel because he fails to grasp the dialectical nature of Hegel's critique of choice, Wood fails to defend Hegel adequately because, in his own words, he resists the conclusion that "speculative logic is a propaedeutic to Hegel's theory of modern society" (6). I concur with David Kolb, who contends that Hegel's argument for the developments in his *Philosophy of Right* lies in their logical progression, and that those who do not attend to the logical progression can never be convinced of the necessity of those developments. Kolb thus agrees with me that it is only in virtue of this logical progression that the structures developed in *PR* do not merely represent Hegel's preference for "positive" freedom as opposed to Berlin's preference for the "negative" variety, but can instead claim the status of necessary structures of freedom. See Kolb, *Critique of Pure Modernity*, esp. 69 and 90.
26. This type of objection was made famous by Marx, and variations on it have been advanced ever since.
27. Michael Hardimon, in *Hegel's Social Philosophy*, points out that "the negative connotations of the English word 'reconciliation' (e.g., the suggestion of resignation) are not shared by *Versöhnung*, the German world Hegel uses, which is far more positive than the English and essentially involves an element of affirmation" (2 n3). For an elaboration on the meaning of *Versöhnung*, see Hardimon, Chapter 3.

28. *R*, 74–75/69–70. Hegel makes this contention throughout his lectures on absolute spirit. See, in particular, *R*, 237/247, and *VGP*, 199–200/148, 225–226/165–166, 229/169.

29. I do not think that Hegel believes this development to be either necessary or straightforwardly progressive. Rather, it occurs in fits and starts, and is subject to contingencies that always make regression a real possibility. An account of Hegel's philosophy of history, however, is well beyond the scope of this study.

30. *PG*, 31/21.

31. *PG*, 31–32/21.

32. On the practical potential of religion, see Michael Theunissen, *Hegels Lehre vom absoluten Geist als theologisch-politischer Traktat*, 10–11, 387–403. Andrew Shanks, in *Hegel's Political Theology*, writes that "one might perhaps define the central concern of Hegel's philosophy of religion as being with the pre-political preconditions of freedom" (183).

33. *PR*, Preface, 14/11. Also see *PR*, §270A+Z, and *K*, 265–6/124–5.

34. *PR*, Preface, 27/22.

35. *VPR*, I, 339–347/451–460.

36. *VPR*, I, 339–341/452–453.

37. *VPR*, I, 340–341/453.

38. *VPR*, I, 341/453.

39. Ibid. Hegel offers late seventeenth-century England as an example of a Protestant country in which oppression and tyranny resulted from a religious demand for passive obedience to the law. Of course, as early as the *Phenomenology* he diagnosed the terror that followed the French Revolution as a consequence of adherence to an abstract or formal conception of freedom. He repeats this diagnosis here at *VPR*, I, 347/460.

40. *VPR*, I, 342/454.

41. *VPR*, I, 345/458. Earlier in the section, at *VPR*, I, 341/454, Hegel notes that "what the rational is, and the cognition of it, is a matter for the cultivation of thought and particularly for philosophy, which can well be called worldly wisdom in this sense." Also see *VGP*, 201/150: "[P]hilosophy brings into consciousness the substance of the state's constitution," and *VGP*, 226/166.

42. Hans Friedrich Fulda, in *Das Recht der Philosophie in Hegels Philosophie des Rechts*, 27, also notes that the advantage of philosophy in comparison to religion lies in its ability to develop adequate knowledge of the ethical.

43. *PR*, 28/23.

44. *EN*, §246Z. This passage is cited by Michael Theunissen, in *Hegels Lehre vom absoluten Geist als theologisch-politischer Traktat*, 404–405, in the midst of a helpful account of the relations among philosophy, religion, and politics (403–419). Theunissen offers a nice distillation of his own view (408), in which he describes Hegelian philosophy as mediating between the subjective representation of freedom developed in religion and the objective actualization of freedom in the state. Hans Friedrich Fulda, in *Das Recht der Philosophie in Hegels Philosophie des Rechts*, 33, rightly emphasizes that philosophical education must not devolve into ideological indoctrination, and that the only way to prevent this is for philosophy to be truly scientific in Hegel's sense.

Fulda even suggests (33–34, 39) that Hegel's attempt to develop a scientific philosophical method may well have originated from a desire to find the basis for a fully legitimate social and political critique.

45. Robert B. Pippin, in "Hegel and Institutional Rationality," *The Southern Journal of Philosophy* 39 suppl. (2001): 1–25, at 16, is absolutely right when he claims that "philosophy does not do better what persons at the level of 'objective spirit' do poorly; it does something else"; but I believe he is wrong to conclude from this that philosophy "is not relevant to objective spirit." Pippin is correct that philosophy can offer neither "instructions about how the world ought to be" (29), nor "the sort of account that might be practically relevant in generating allegiance and forestalling defections" (28). But philosophy can determine what freedom is, and it can thus be relevant to objective spirit by communicating this knowledge to those who already have an allegiance to the project of liberation. It is Hegel's commitment to philosophy's ability to determine the requirements of freedom in concrete detail that heads off the relativistic and deflationary worries that Pippin acknowledges are raised by his own interpretation. For a more extensive consideration of Pippin's interpretation, and of the worries that it raises, see Patten, *Hegel's Idea of Freedom*, 27–34. Paul Franco shares Pippin's view that the admonition that philosophy cannot issue instructions about how the world ought to be reflects "Hegel's belief that (*pace* Marx) philosophy cannot change the world but only interpret it" (*Hegel's Philosophy of Freedom*, 138–139). Closer to my own view is Frederick Neuhouser, in *Foundations of Hegel's Social Theory*, 287 n10: "Though speculative and practical freedom can be distinguished, they are not wholly independent of one another. For a modern individual who is subjectively alienated from his society, speculative philosophy can reveal the essential goodness of his social order, enabling him to embrace it and hence participate in it freely (with a free will). In such a case, practical freedom depends on speculative." Closer still is Hans Friedrich Fulda, whose entire elegant essay, *Das Recht der Philosophie in Hegels Philosophie des Rechts,* is devoted to the argument that philosophy has a dual political function, serving not only to preserve but also to improve the state through a rational critique of its institutions. For statements of his thesis, see 22 and 38.

Chapter 5

1. This effort cannot be avoided simply by assuming that Nietzsche is in fact an aphorist whose insights are unrelated to each other. For such an assumption itself bears powerfully on the interpretation of those insights and therefore requires a justification that, if possible at all, could only be provided by doing the work of demonstrating that the relations between Nietzsche's discussions of different topics are insignificant.

2. For an extended and exemplary consideration of Nietzsche's political thinking and its evolution, see Henning Ottmann, *Philosophie und Politik bei Nietzsche,* 2nd ed. (Berlin: de Gruyter, 1999). Ottmann (7–8) identifies one important stage in Nietzsche's thought as the working out of the dialectic

of an *Emanzipationsphilosophie*, which is precisely the object of my concern. Ottmann, however, sees in Nietzsche's late writings and the concepts that they contain a turn away from this project, whereas I, as will become clear in what follows, see its continuation and further development.

3. I thus agree to a significant extent with Werner Hamacher, who argues in "'Disgregation of the Will': Nietzsche on the Individual and Individuality," in his *Premises*, tr. Peter Fenves (Cambridge: Harvard University Press, 1996), 143–180, that the central category of Nietzsche's late work is that of the will (164). I disagree, however, with Hamacher's claim, in "The Promise of Interpretation: Remarks on the Hermeneutic Imperative in Kant and Nietzsche" (*Premises*, 81–142), that "Nietzsche does not inquire, as Kant does, into the structure of free will but into its history" (110). In my view, one of the most valuable by-products of Nietzsche's quasi-historical inquiries is the illumination that they shed on the structure of free willing. Richard White, in "Nietzsche contra Kant and the Problem of Autonomy," *International Studies in Philosophy* (1990): 3–11, also understands Nietzsche to be concerned with the Kantian question of the meaning and structure of autonomous willing. On Nietzsche's combining this structural question with a concern for the historical and social questions of how such a structure could develop, see Mark Warren, *Nietzsche and Political Thought* (Cambridge, Mass.: MIT Press, 1988), 115, 120, 123; and Volker Gerhardt, "Selbstbegründung: Nietzsche's Moral der Individualität," *Nietzsche-Studien* 21 (1992): 28–49, esp. 30.

Chapter 6

1. *EH*, II, 8. In this passage, "freedom" appears in quotation marks, suggesting that although Nietzsche wants to distinguish freedom as self-initiated activity from reactivity, he also wants to distance himself from the conception of freedom as self-initiated activity at the same time that he is putting it forward. The reasons for this will become clear at the beginning of the next chapter, and we will return to the issue then.

2. *GD*, II, 11. It is misleading to suggest that "the decadent" has a single referent for Nietzsche; on the contrary, there are multiple varieties of decadence. This complexity will emerge in the course of what follows.

3. *GD*, II, 4, 9, 10.

4. *FWag*, 7, Second Postscript. On the will being that which appoints a direction and measure to the drives, see *WM*, 84.

5. *GD*, II, 11.

6. *A*, 24. The word "decadent" itself (from the Latin, *de-cadere*) signifies that which has fallen, presumably from a prior state of superior health or excellence.

7. *GD*, V, 2.

8. At *WM*, 45, Nietzsche understands strength as the ability to postpone response, in contrast to the weakness of the decadents, who react immediately to external stimuli. And at *WM*, 46–47, he defines a strong will as one that systematically orders the impulses under a single predominant one.

9. *A*, 15. Such mendacious flight is thus necessary for the sick and weak, whereas honesty and affirmation of the actual world are necessary outgrowths of health and strength. See *EH*, IV, 2.

10. Nietzsche discusses and criticizes the mendacious invention of the "true" world by those too weak to affirm the actual world in many places. See, for example, *EH*, Preface, 2; *EH*, IV, 2; *FW*, Second Preface, 2; and, *A*, 29.

11. *A*, 43.

12. *GM*, I, 13.

13. *GM*, I, 13. Also see *GD*, VI, 3. Nietzsche castigates this postulation of free will as a "hangman's metaphysics," because on his view it attributes freedom to humans only in order to be able to judge them and hold them responsible. It thus comes from a will to find guilty and a will to punish, and deprives becoming of its innocence (*Unschuld* – literally, lack of guilt). See *GD*, VI, 7. Also see *A*, 25; and *M*, I, 13.

14. On the central elements of the metaphysics of weakness, see Richard Schacht, *Nietzsche* (New York: Routledge, 1983), Chapter 3.

15. *A*, 9. Nietzsche takes this to be an example of a general phenomenon: the intellect produces many errors, and those conducive to self-preservation survive. See *FW*, 110, 151. He thus concludes that belief in free will is necessary for the weak (as we saw him conclude about belief in the "true" world earlier), a part of their fate. See *MA*, II, 2: 61.

16. Nietzsche devotes the entire second essay of *GM* to guilt and bad conscience. For the points discussed in this paragraph and the one preceding it, see especially *GM*, II, 16, 18. As will be seen later, Nietzsche does not consider the development of bad conscience to be wholly undesirable. On the contrary, he contends that bad conscience is necessary to the achievement of a greater kind of health than would be possible had humanity never suffered from this disease. On this point, see David Lindstedt, "The Progression of Slave Morality in Nietzsche's *Genealogy*: The Moralization of Bad Conscience and Indebtedness," *Man and World* 30 (1997): 83–105, esp. 100.

17. For the points discussed in this paragraph and the one preceding it, see especially *GM*, II, 4, 14, 15.

18. Actually, to distinguish only three kinds of nihilism oversimplifies matters. Alan White, in *Within Nietzsche's Labyrinth* (New York: Routledge, 1990), 15–25, identifies no less than nineteen varieties of nihilism discussed by Nietzsche (which White then classifies into three levels). But for our purposes it is important only to have a general understanding of what Nietzsche means by nihilism, and of how it grows out of decadence and the metaphysics of weakness. For a thorough discussion of nihilism and its political implications, see Warren, *Nietzsche and Political Thought*, Chapter 1.

19. Nietzsche uses this and similar terms in many places; one in particular, where he connects it with nihilism (using both to describe Wagner's art), is *FWag*, Postscript.

20. For Nietzsche, the decadent is thus characterized by avoiding the honest conclusion that "I am worth nothing anymore" and instead drawing the false conclusion that "nothing is worth anything," or "life is worth nothing." Nietzsche therefore understands the decadent's postulation of the "beyond"

as an attempt to find not only herself but the whole of actuality guilty, as an attempt to take revenge on the actuality she considers worthless. See *GD*, IX, 34; *GD*, II, 1; and *EH*, Preface, 2.

21. Although nihilism is primarily associated with decadence and weakness, it should be noted that this does not preclude the possibility that those who are not decadent will occasionally suffer from a sense of meaninglessness as well.

22. For the purposes of discussion in this chapter, I am distinguishing between the metaphysics of weakness (as a set of *beliefs* about the ultimate reality of the "true" world, the soul, free will, and God) and the morality of self-lessness (as a set of *purposes* and *practices* designed to achieve those purposes, whose specifics we are about to explore). However, since Nietzsche thinks that the beliefs, purposes, and practices are all necessary and mutually reinforcing offshoots of weakness, he often does not distinguish among them, and frequently uses the term "morality" to cover the entire package of decadent theory and practice. See *GD*, IX, 5, where he contends that Christian belief and morality are a system and cannot successfully be separated.

23. Nietzsche compares this approach to that of a dentist who pulls teeth to make them stop hurting. See *GD*, V, 1.

24. *GD*, II, 4–10; *A*, 21. Reason thus serves as something akin to an executive power, repressing certain instincts in favor of others, in the hope of producing a unity of the self that is preferable to the chaos of disgregation. This distinguishes the subjection to reason from forms of asceticism (about to be discussed) that attack all of the instincts indiscriminately. Both, however, are attempts to alleviate suffering through selflessness.

25. *GD*, II, 10. Nietzsche also explains Socratic morality and dialectic as decadent efforts to avoid the truth that one's instincts are dissolute in *GT*, SK, 1, 4. There he further suggests that modern science and democracy might also be understood as similar efforts. We will have more to say about Nietzsche's estimation of their decadent character later.

26. *EH*, VII, 2; *GM*, Preface, 5.

27. *EH*, I, 4. The morality of selflessness thus understands "egoistic" and "unegoistic" to be opposites. It understands all self-directed behavior to be at the expense of others, and is unable to envision the possibility that one might best help others by developing oneself. See *GM*, I, 2.

28. Nietzsche identifies the goals of morality and Christianity as nothingness, rest, and an end to all aspects of the world from which their adherents suffer at *GT*, SK, 5, concluding the passage by suggesting that morality is a "will to negate life." He criticizes all ways of thinking that measure the value of things by how much pleasure or suffering they cause, on the grounds that well-being understood as the lack of suffering is no goal, and thus by implication criticizes the morality of selflessness, at *JGB*, 225.

29. Nietzsche identifies morality's self-described attempt to "improve" humanity as the attempt to tame humanity, an attempt he considers to be driven by *ressentiment* and to result in a regression rather than an improvement, at *GD*, VII, 2, and at *GM*, I, 11. He links this to the ascetic ideal throughout the third essay of *GM*, entitled "What Is the Meaning of Ascetic Ideals?," and

also in the second essay, at *GM*, II, 3. He describes this ascetic taming, one of the "blessings" of Christianity, as evincing contempt for good and honest instincts, as the art of self-violation, as the creation of a self-contradiction out of humanity, and as the burdening of ourselves with antinature – for example, by linking sex with impurity. See *A*, 62; *KSA*, 6: 254, not translated in *A*; and *GD*, V, 4. Such ready acceptance of burdens suggests that adherents of the morality of selflessness are at the stage of the camel in *Zarathustra*. See *Z*, I, 1. For a discussion of asceticism, and of the morality of selflessness in general, see Nehamas, *Nietzsche*, Chapters 4 and 7.

30. At *GM*, III, 28, Nietzsche says that the curse lying over decadent humanity, prior to the morality of selflessness, was not suffering itself but meaningless suffering.

31. Nietzsche describes this interpretation of suffering as punishment for sin as part of the imaginary explanatory apparatus of Christianity and morality at *A*, 15, and at *GD*, VI, 5, 6. In general, he thinks the doctrine that a supersensible free will is exercised to cause good or bad actions, which make a person well- or ill-constituted and consequently rewarded or punished, is misguided, mistaking the true cause and effect for each other. In Nietzsche's view, being well- or ill-constituted, being happy or suffering from oneself, is the *cause* of good or bad actions, virtue or vice, *not* their effect. See *GD*, VI, 2.

32. The moral adherent thus takes pride in her morality as that which exalts her, and is therefore willing to suffer on account of her morality for the sake of this exaltation. Nietzsche complains that this pride prevents a new and better understanding of morality, which he suggests might require our taking pride in ourselves on account of something else. See *M*, I, 32.

33. The morality of selflessness thus overcomes the third type of nihilism only by reinforcing the other two: it makes suffering in this world meaningful and therefore bearable only for those who accept the existence of the "true" world and find the value of all earthly experience, including suffering, in its relation to the ultimate goal of attaining that world.

34. Judeo-Christian morality, of course, does this quite literally, giving us the very phrase "forbidden fruit." Nietzsche emphasizes this in *The Antichristian*, pointing out that knowledge of good and evil is the *original* sin in the Bible, causing the expulsion from the Garden of Eden, in which humanity had enjoyed blissful ignorance. See *A*, 48.

35. Nietzsche notes that it also makes the people and institutions empowered by the metaphysical lie – the priests and churches that, for as long as the lie is believed, are needed by the adherents of the metaphysics to alleviate their suffering and make possible their achievement of the true world – impervious to attack. These moral authorities of the metaphysics of weakness therefore have a strong incentive to secure their own position of earthly power by making doubt, reflection, and knowledge sins. See *M*, I, 89; *M*, Preface, 3; and *GD*, VI, 7. At *A*, 9, Nietzsche claims that in all of these people with "theologian blood" the "nihilistic will wills to power."

36. *A*, 49. Moreover, the precondition for loving actuality has been destroyed, so that moral adherents can have reverence, pride, gratitude, and love only for the "true" world. See *M*, I, 33.

37. Humanity thus becomes instinctively mendacious, because faith is the habit of closing one's eyes and allowing the resulting blindness to drown reason. See *EH*, Preface, 2; *A*, 9; and *M*, I, 89.

38. Thus allowing the persistence of all of its false causes, which are "known" not through investigation but as "inner facts" or by "intuition." See *A*, 15, and *GD*, VI, 3–7.

39. Morality thus eternalizes itself by reinforcing and intensifying the very need to which it responds. See *A*, 62.

40. Nietzsche points out that morality thus preserves the sufferer through a hope that can be neither fulfilled nor contradicted by any actuality, and that this suspension of the unhappy was considered the evil of all evils by the Greeks. See *A*, 23.

41. *GM*, III, 28.

42. See *A*, 18, where Nietzsche says that in the Christian God "the nothing is deified, the will to nothing called holy!"

43. *MA*, II, 1: 349. Nietzsche contends that this will to nothing, to the achievement of immortality by serving God through the denial of all earthly purposes, constitutes an implicit attack on public life, since denying the value of this world eliminates all reasons for communal-sense (*Gemeinsinn*), cooperation, trust, and furthering of the total-welfare (*Gesammt-Wohl*). See *KSA*, 6: 254, not translated in *A*; and *A*, 43. He finds the same thing in any philosophy that proposes an "ethical world order," which Nietsche thinks also denies value in itself to customs and institutions that he considers natural, including the state, the order of justice, marriage, and tending to the sick and the poor. See *A*, 26, and *WM*, 245.

44. *GM*, I, 11.

45. We have already seen that one symptom of decadence is its imitation (*Nachbildung*) of organization and form where there truly is none. At *FWag*, Second Postscript, Nietzsche attributes these faults to Wagner.

46. *GD*, II, 11.

47. In making this point, at *A*, 29, Nietzsche refers to the biblical injunction to "resist not evil."

48. *GD*, IX, 37.

49. *FW*, 76.

50. On moral judgment being based on conscience, without asking why conscience should be trusted, see *FW*, 335. On conscience having no content but that put into it by authority, see *MA*, II, 2: 52; *WM*, 294; and *JGB*, 199, where Nietzsche equates "formal conscience" with unconditional obedience and claims that it can incorporate any content. This suggests an obvious comparison to Hegel's moral will, which is also purely formal and ultimately reducible to whatever contents its conscience happens to have.

51. At *WM*, 319, Nietzsche writes: "A virtuous man is a lower species because he is not a 'person' but acquires his value by conforming to a pattern of man that is fixed once and for all . . . he *must* not be an individual." As will be seen later, noble cultures, although healthier than decadent cultures, are also herdlike in certain respects. This will help to explain, in Chapter 7, why the nobles are themselves incompletely free. In what follows, however, I will use herd morality as a synonym for the morality of selflessness.

52. In *MA*, II, 1, Nietzsche associates fanaticism with an overreliance on feeling due to an inability to think clearly, and contrasts this with a model in which reason moderates and guides feeling (but without lapsing into a decadent submission of instinct to reason). See maxims 133, 180, 196, 230, 279, and 326.

53. Nietzsche makes a variety of comments in many works relevant to the main points of this paragraph. For example, in *Dawn* he suggests that the lasting dissimulation of those subjecting themselves to the ban on knowledge becomes like second nature to them, that the mastery of community morality, or *Sittlichkeit*, increases as more and more individuals draw unscientific conclusions about cause and effect, and that knowledge and small deviances are therefore important counterweights to these tendencies (*M*, 248, 10, 149); in *Beyond Good and Evil*, he notes that herd morality experiences individual independence as evil and judges moderate drives that do not threaten it to be moral, and that it insists that it alone is morality, denying that any other or higher moralities are possible (*BGE*, 201, 202); in The *Genealogy of Morals*, *The Antichristian*, and *The Joyful Science*, he contends that herd morality wages a death-war on higher types, banning their instincts and passion for knowledge, which herd morality calls evil and irrational, and subordinates to purpose (*Zweck*) and advantage (*A*, 5, 6; *GM*, I, 11; *FW*, 3); in *The Antichristian* he claims that herd morality requires that a certain optic be highest in value, which links good conscience with false seeing (*A*, 9); and in *Twilight of the Idols* he concludes that all means of making humanity moral are lies, and therefore immoral (*GD*, VII, 3).

54. *MA*, II, 2: 40, 44, 57.

55. *MA*, II, 2: 22, 26, 31. This is so even if it is the case that the rule of law originates with the nobles, and thus initially represents the interests of a nonegalitarian kind of herd. The decadents succeed in coopting legal and communal institutions, thereby giving them a new meaning and purpose.

56. *FW*, 21.

57. *FW*, 116; *MA*, II, 1: 89.

58. He calls this freedom of the heart, *MA*, II, 1: 209. It might well be compared to Hegelian patriotism, which is also a feeling of freedom that one gets from identifying with one's community.

59. *FW*, 296.

60. Nietzsche emphasizes that the free will is without goal or motive at *MA*, II, 2: 23. There he does not explicitly identify the free will with the moral will, but the section is part of a longer discussion of punishment, and in the preceding section, part of same discussion, Nietzsche discusses both morality and weakness. Thus for Nietzsche, as for Hegel, the moral will is empty, unable to determine its own ends out of itself, and dependent upon external sources to provide it with content.

61. *EH*, VII, 2; *EH*, XIV, 7. Hollingdale translates "*Entselbstung*" as "selflessness," but this is seriously misleading, since Nietzsche uses "*Selbstlosigkeit*" for "selflessness" and clearly means something distinct by "*Entselbstung*." According to Kaufmann (*BW*, 748 n1), "*Entselbstung*" is Nietzsche's own coinage, and Kaufmann's translation of it as "unselfing" seems appropriate.

62. *A*, 54.

63. This explains why Nietzsche also calls decadent morality "slave" morality. It is not exclusively the morality of those physically enslaved (although they are perhaps especially likely to need the metaphysics of a true world without struggle and suffering), but rather the morality of all with weak wills, and thus in need of "slavery in a higher sense," slavery to conviction or faith. See Michel Haar, "Nietzsche and Metaphysical Language," tr. Cyril and Liliane Welch, *Man and World* 4.4 (1971): 359-395. As Haar puts it, "The slave is enslaved to himself" (380).

64. We have also seen, of course, that this cycle from decadence to metaphysics to morality and back to decadence is further reinforced by several subcycles. The metaphysics of weakness not only leads to morality, but also directly reinforces decadence through the exacerbation of bad conscience; and morality reinforces decadence not only directly but also indirectly, since its success depends on continued faith in the metaphysics, which it therefore reinforces with its ban on knowledge. In the end, then, all three nodes of the cycle – decadence, the metaphysics of weakness, and the morality of selflessness – are mutually reinforcing, and once entrenched all become increasingly hard to displace.

65. Nietzsche famously and repeatedly castigates morality for this inversion of values, for calling "good" all that is sick in humanity and "evil" all that is healthy, thus pretending that our flaws and incapacities were deliberately and rightly chosen because of their inherent virtue, and inhibiting efforts truly to improve ourselves. See, for example, *EH*, XIV, 8; *GM*, I, 7; *GD*, IX, 35; *A*, 2–6; *FW*, 352.

66. *EH*, I, 4; *FW*, 120.

67. *JGB*, 270.

68. *EH*, I, 4. In *Twilight of the Idols*, Nietzsche writes that the nihilism of morality – the conviction that nothing in this world is worth anything – is contagious when it takes the form of religion or philosophy (i.e., of a doctrine taken on faith), and as such it can poison life for thousands of years (*GD*, IX, 35).

69. *A*, 7. Note that, as in English, in German "sympathy" or *Mitleid* is literally "suffering-with."

70. Nietzsche claims that the morality of selflessness worships values that are the opposite of those required to guarantee that humanity will flourish in the future, calling "true" what is harmful (for example, the lie of personal immortality) and "false" what is elevating. See *EH*, Preface, 2; and *A*, 9, 43.

71. *JGB*, 225.

72. *A*, 49. Christianity is thus opposed to, and warns us away from as a dangerous temptation, the very condition that Nietzsche considers essential to spiritual well-constitutedness and health – namely, the honest and scientific pursuit of knowledge. See *A*, 52, 25. Nietzsche concludes that those with the courage for health will have contempt for the Christian perspective and ideals, and that those who adopt them must be sick and cowardly. See *A*, 51; and *GD*, IX, 32.

73. So Nietzsche concludes that the morality of selflessness is a great danger to humanity because it is a seduction to nothing, a will to turn against life, a nihilistic will (*GM*, Preface, 5). In other words, it is a regression in which we

become ill-constituted, dwarfed, atrophied, and poisoned, instead of feared and admired (*GM*, I, 11).

74. At *MA*, II, 1: 320, Nietzsche identifies schools and armies as two primary means by which states keep people dependent and obedient.

75. *GD*, VIII, 6. Again, however, nobility too will ultimately prove to be conventional.

76. At *GD*, VI, 5, Nietzsche writes that "the first idea which explains that the unknown is in fact the known does [one] so much good that one 'holds it for true,... The new, the unexperienced, the strange is excluded from being the cause. – Thus there is sought not only some kind of explanation as cause, but a *selected* and *preferred* kind of explanation... Consequence: a particular kind of cause-ascription comes to preponderate more and more, becomes concentrated into a system... The banker thinks at once of 'business', the Christian of 'sin'." At *WM*, 479, he says that "'to understand' means merely: to be able to express something new in the language of something old and familiar."

77. *GD*, VIII, 6. One of Nietzsche's many criticisms of modernity is precisely what it praises as its "objectivity," which Nietzsche sees as a misguided attempt to treat all objects of experience equally and impartially, i.e., from the same perspective. For more extended treatments of Nietzsche's perspectivism than I can give here, see Nehamas, *Nietzsche*, Chapters 1 and 2; Alan D. Schrift, *Nietzsche and the Question of Interpretation* (New York: Routledge, 1990), Chapter 6; and Tracy B. Strong, "Reflections on Perspectivism in Nietzsche," *Political Theory* 13 (1985): 164–182.

78. *A*, 50; *M*, 101.

79. *A*, 50, 59; *FW*, 2. Note that Nietzsche thinks this struggle of intellectual conscience against herd conviction is bound to be difficult, as our instinct against separating ourselves from our community is powerful. See *FW*, 50.

80. *GD*, IX, 18. Nietzsche's critique of this lack of intellectual conscience provides a strong reason to reject the central thrust of James J. Winchester's *Nietzsche's Aesthetic Turn: Reading Nietzsche after Heidegger, Deleuze, Derrida* (Albany: State University of New York Press, 1994), which is that "if two of his views do not fit with one another, Nietzsche does not feel the need to reject one or to rework both of them in order to bring them into line" (xi). Winchester attempts to demonstrate this thesis by showing that no single interpretation can account for the various things Nietzsche says about, for example, the eternal return (Chapter 1) or the will to power (Chapter 2).

81. On thinkers needing to be just to things, and on our failing to see things because we ourselves have concealed them, see *M*, 43, 438.

82. See Jean-Luc Nancy, "'Our Probity!' On Truth in the Moral Sense in Nietzsche," tr. Peter Connor, in *Looking After Nietzsche*, ed. Laurence A. Rickels (Albany: State University of New York Press, 1990), 67–87.

83. *M*, Preface, 4. The commitment to truth thus amounts to a "declaration of war" on "all old concepts of 'true' and 'untrue'" (*A*, 13). To take a famous example of an old truth against which this war has supposedly been victorious, Nietzsche believes that morality's commitment to truth has killed its own God, in whom belief is no longer possible. See *FW*, 357, 343. As Werner

Hamacher puts it in "'Disgregation of the Will': Nietzsche on the Individual and Individuality," in his *Premises*, 143–180, the old morality outlives itself, and "the 'individual' is the survivor and decomposer of itself and society" (158).

84. *JGB*, 192. One way in which Nietzsche distinguishes "higher" humans from "lower" is in virtue of the former's ability to see and hear *more* than the latter, and more thoughtfully. See *FW*, 301.

85. *FW*, 355.

86. *FW*, 305. In a similar vein, Nietzsche contends that only things of our own kind make an impression on us, that we are only in our own company (*FW*, 166), and that we can take from things only what belongs to us (*FW*, 242). The conclusion to be drawn from these remarks is, again, that if we are to experience anything other than ourselves we must lose ourselves.

87. *FW*, 214. He also writes that "[w]hoever has greatness is cruel to his virtues" (*FW*, 266).

88. Nietzsche claims that all versions of monotheistic religion and *Sittlichkeit*, or custom-based morality, insist that there is only one norm for humanity, one eternal horizon or perspective. Polytheism, in his view, prefigures the shedding of this belief, the development of what he calls the "free-spiritedness" and "many-spiritedness" of humanity (*FW*, 143).

89. In fact, Nietzsche claims, herd morality *must* not justify itself to its adherents on utilitarian grounds, since ultimately it does not serve the utility of these individuals but rather that of the community as a whole and of religious leaders. Instead, it must become sacred through the forgetting of its actual origins. See *MA*, II, 2: 40.

90. Indeed, morality may even interpret such periods as *opportunities* for its adherents to demonstrate the strength of their faith by refusing to question it. At *M*, 196, Nietzsche argues that this failure to ask, "What am I really *doing*? And why am *I* doing it?" is indicative of a lack of pride.

91. Nietzsche contends that one cannot observe or consider that to which one is still too close. One must achieve distance, and even opposition, in order to see the old as new. See *MA*, II, Preface: 1; *MA*, II, 1: 200.

92. At *EH*, XIV, 1, Nietzsche says that "revaluation of all values" is his "formula" for the "highest self-reflection of humanity" and connects the latter with opposing the "mendacity of millennia."

93. At *EH*, VII, 2, Nietzsche describes the highest self-reflection of humanity as a great midday, in which humanity looks back on its past and out on its future, asking why it has been moral, and whether it should remain so.

94. *GD*, VII, 1; *A*, 20. In this passage in *The Antichristian* Nietzsche suggests that Buddhism is beyond good and evil, with the deception of moral concepts behind it, because it struggles against suffering but without interpreting suffering in terms of sin. Also see *GT*, SK, 5. At *WM*, 259, he equates "comprehension beyond esteeming things good and evil" with justice.

95. At *GD*, Preface, Nietzsche links the revaluation of all values with the questioning of venerable idols and their subsequent twilight.

96. In the Preface to *the Genealogy of Morals*, Nietzsche identifies these questions as being at the heart of his own task: "[M]y problem . . . under what conditions

did man devise these value judgments good and evil? *and what value do they themselves possess?* Have they hitherto hindered or furthered human prosperity? Are they a sign of distress, of impoverishment, of the degeneration of life?" (*GM*, Preface, 3), Also see *GM*, Preface, 5; *GM*, I, 17; *FW*, 345; and *WM*, 260, where Nietzsche writes: "'Willing' means willing an end. 'An end' includes an evaluation. Whence come evaluations?"

97. *EH*, XIV, 1.

98. *M*, 95.

99. *GD*, III, 2–5. Also see *M*, 1, where Nietzsche claims that reason is added to things until eventually their irrational origins have been forgotten; and *M*, 210, where he writes that we take predicates to apply to things in themselves, having forgotten that it is we who lend things their predicates. On these points, see Lawrence M. Hinman, "Nietzsche, Metaphor, and Truth," *Philosophy and Phenomenological Research* 43.2 (1982): 179–199, esp. 180, 182, 191; Sarah Kofman, *Nietzsche and Metaphor*, tr. Duncan Large (Stanford, Calif.: Stanford University Press, 1993), Chapter 3; Allan Megill, "Nietzsche as Aestheticist," *Philosophy and Literature* 5.2 (1981): 204–225, esp. 210–212; Nehamas, *Nietzsche*, 86; Alan D. Schrift, "Language, Metaphor, Rhetoric: Nietzsche's Deconstruction of Epistemology," *Journal of the History of Philosophy* 23.3 (1985): 371–395, esp. 373; and George Stack, "Nietzsche and the Correspondence Theory of Truth," *Dialogos* 16 (1981): 93–117, esp. 97–98.

100. *MA*, II, 2: 11. At *JGB*, 21, Nietzsche writes, "It is *we* alone who have fabricated causes, succession, reciprocity, relativity, compulsion, number, law, freedom, motive, purpose; and when we falsely introduce this world of symbols into things and mingle it with them as though this symbol-world were an 'in itself', we once more behave as we have always behaved, namely *mythologically*." Also see *JGB*, 20, 24; *GM*, I, 13; and *WM*, 482, 548.

101. *JGB*, 19. At *MA*, II, 2: 11, Nietzsche writes, "Belief in freedom of will – that is to say in *identical* facts and in *isolated* facts – has in language its constant evangelist and advocate." Also see *A*, 14, and *FW*, 127.

102. *JGB*, 12. At *GD*, VI, 3, Nietzsche writes that the "I" is a fable, fiction, and word-play. And at *M*, 120, he claims that we are acted on at every moment, but that our grammar confuses active and passive. On Nietzsche's understanding of the constructions of "thinking," "thing," "motion," "cause and effect," and "natural law," see Schrift, "Language, Metaphor, Rhetoric," 391–392.

103. *FW*, 111. Nietzsche suggests that this logical tendency developed because the capacity to perceive stability and similarity are crucial to survival.

104. *GD*, III, 1, 2. For Nietzsche's account of how "reason" and grammar support belief in God, see *GD*, III, 5.

105. *GD*, IV. Also see *GD*, III, 5, 6.

106. *JGB*, 187.

107. *FW*, 354.

108. *JGB*, 268. At *GM*, I, 2, Nietzsche writes that "only with the decline of aristocratic value judgments... did the herd instinct finally get its word (and its *words*) (*zu Worte* [*auch zu Worten*] kommt)."

109. Conversely, what is harmful to the decadents comes to be understood as evil in itself. See *M*, 102. Also see *FW*, 115, 116.

110. He distinguishes decadent morality, which, as we have already noted, he also calls slave morality, from noble moralities most famously in the first essay of *the Genealogy of Morals*. See especially *GM*, I, 2-4, 7, 10-11.

111. See *A*, 24.

112. At *JGB*, 221, Nietzsche argues that the values of self-abnegation are inappropriate for those capable of commanding.

113. On morality sacrificing the future to itself, see *Z*, III, 12: 26. On this being the meaning behind Nietzsche's dubbing the moral adherent the "last man," see *EH*, XIV, 4. On noble valuations doing the opposite – encouraging the present to live in a way that guarantees a flourishing future – see *EH*, XIII, 2, and *MA*, II, 2: 229. On states preventing the taking of such a long view by generating instabilities that force people to concentrate on short-term goals, see *SE*, 4, 5.

114. *EH*, VII, 2. Also see *FW*, 294, where Nietzsche blames these slanderers of nature for our injustice to both our nature and nature in general, and blames that injustice for the lack of noble people.

115. *EH*, VII, 2.

116. Thus the priests of slave morality are themselves masters – over both others and themselves – in a way that members of their flock cannot be.

117. *A*, 4. I have chosen not to translate *Übermensch*. Rendering it as "superman" cannot help but turn a subtle and complicated figure into a comic book hero with otherworldly powers. "Overman" is better, but not particularly helpful, since it is a neologism; and it is still potentially pernicious because it emphasizes the connotation of one who stands over others in a position of dominance. Although that connotation is not always absent from Nietzsche's works, on the interpretation I will offer it is not central. It is therefore best, I think, to leave *Übermensch* in the German, minimizing the preconceptions that leap to English ears, and allowing a careful consideration of Nietzsche's uses of the term to determine its meaning.

118. *A*, 3. Also see *WM*, 898. We can see from the cited passage that Nietzsche's talk of "breeding" has nothing to do with eugenics. For he claims that the decadent man has been "bred," and this was certainly no genetic accomplishment. Rather, it was, according to Nietzsche, an achievement that resulted from a deliberate cultural response to a particular crisis. This, then, is what he means by "breeding" and "willing" in this context, and this is how we should understand his calls to breed and will the *Übermensch*: as exhortations to adopt a particular, deliberate cultural response to the crisis of decadence. At *WM*, 398, Nietzsche defines breeding as "a means of storing up the tremendous forces of mankind so that the generations can build upon the work of their forefathers"; and at *GM*, III, 11, he writes that the priest does not "breed and propagate his mode of valuation through heredity." Also see *SE*, 5, 7, where Nietzsche claims that nature shoots artists and philosophers at culture to make it intelligible to itself, but that it scores too few hits and none with enough force, so that our communal duty must be to produce artists and philosophers for ourselves. For a very helpful discussion of Nietzsche's concept of "breeding," see Ottmann, *Philosophie und Politik bei Nietzsche*, 245-270. Ottmann argues that Nietzsche means by "breeding" something very close to what the Greeks meant by *paideia*.

119. See Z, I, 3, where Zarathustra proclaims, "A new will I teach men: to *will* this way which man has walked blindly."
120. *M*, 575.
121. *FW*, 124.
122. Citations in this paragraph are all from *FW*, 227. It is instructive to note that this section of *The Joyful Science*, the second section of Book IV, immediately follows the section in which Nietzsche introduces his concept of *amor fati* for the first time and vows to become one who makes things beautiful by learning to see as beautiful what is necessary. We will not discuss *amor fati* until later, but for now we can be certain that Nietzsche wants to distinguish it from interpretations of the world that superficially conclude, as those believing in a personal providence do, that "all is for the best." This is further confirmed at *WM*, 243, where Nietzsche blames these modern variants on divine Providence for "the absurd trust in the course of things . . . as if what happens were no responsibility of ours – as though it were permissible to let things take their course"; and at *WM*, 585(A), where he writes that "the belief that the world as it ought to be is, really exists, is a belief of the unproductive who do *not desire to create a world* as it ought to be."
123. *FW*, 344.
124. *FW*, 121.
125. *FW*, 344.
126. *FW*, 373. This section is headed '*Science*' as a prejudice.
127. *FW*, 344. Note that this remark makes it clear that Nietzsche's critique is not of truthfulness per se, but only of the "ultimate and audacious" truthfulness that characterizes the will to truth. The same can be said of his critique of the will to system. A will to system indicates a refusal to affirm a world that is not systematic, and an insistence on presenting the world as systematic. Nietzsche is certainly critical of this, but this does not mean that he must repudiate all systematicity. Like truth, systematicity is to be valued when properly understood and appropriately pursued. For critical comments on the will to system and systematizers, see *GD*, I, 26, and *M*, 318. For comments suggesting sympathy for some kinds of systematicity, see *GM*, Preface, 2, where Nietzsche writes that philosophers, among which he here includes himself, have no right to singular thoughts, but instead all of their thoughts must be related and grow with necessity out of a single will to knowledge; and *SE*, 8, where he distinguishes neo-Kantians, who build systems serving science, from "real philosophers," who are admirable system builders. We will have more to say later about the character of Nietzsche's own works, and the senses in which they are and are not systematic.
128. Nietzsche understands democracy to be the political manifestation of this phenomenon. Democracy, for him, rests on a false metaphysical conviction in the equality of souls, which leads to social conventions likely to produce and reinforce cultural mediocrity and uniformity. For a thorough exploration of Nietzsche's critique of democracy (as well as an argument that Nietzsche's thought actually provides us with the basis for an alternative reconception and *justification* of democracy), see Lawrence J. Hatab, *A Nietzschean Defense of Democracy: An Experiment in Postmodern Politics* (Chicago: Open Court, 1995). For my evaluation of Hatab's book, see my review essay,

"Should Nietzsche Have Been a Democrat?" *Philosophy & Social Criticism* 24.4 (1998): 113–119. Also see *FW*, 377, where Nietzsche is careful to point out, after criticizing democracy, that he is also an opponent of nationalism and especially of German "race hatred" and "mendacious racial self-admiration." He describes himself and those like him as "good Europeans," who, through inheriting the manifold bequests of thousands of years of European spirit, have outgrown Christianity, democracy, and nationalism.

129. *FWag*, 7.
130. *GD*, IX, 39. For Nietzsche's critique of the modern understanding of freedom, also see *WM*, 62, 65, 67, 86, 93.
131. *GD*, IX, 41. *Laisser aller* is also linked to decadence at *WM*, 122. And at *Z*, I, 17, Zarathustra challenges his audience: "You call yourself free? Your dominant thought I want to hear, and not that you have escaped from a yoke. Are you one of those who had the *right* to escape from a yoke? There are some who threw away their last value when they threw away their servitude. Free *from* what? As if that mattered to Zarathustra! But your eyes should tell me brightly: free *for* what?"
132. We have already seen Nietzsche explain decadence as a condition in which the whole is no longer genuine. In *The Case of Wagner*, he suggests that there are two possible modes or styles of this affliction: the decadent "whole" is subject to either "paralysis" or "chaos." The two ways in which the escape from morality fails to achieve liberation can be understood as representing these two styles of decadence: adopting an externally directed will that extirpates one's instincts is a kind of "paralysis"; failing to have a will at all and turning oneself over to one's instincts is a kind of "chaos." See *FWag*, 7.
133. See *M*, 9, where Nietzsche writes that the free human is *unsittlich* not only in the sense that he does not want to depend on tradition, but also in the sense that he wants to depend on himself, wants to create customs and give laws to himself. At *WM*, 269, Nietzsche writes that "goals are lacking and these must be *individuals*'!"
134. *EH*, VI, 4. Also see *SE*, 3, where Nietzsche writes that being free requires being wholly oneself, and thus requires fighting that in one's time which inhibits one, fighting that part of oneself that is not truly oneself.
135. *WB*, 2. Also see *SE*, 1. Helmut Rehder suggests that Nietzsche may have derived his conception of the naïve from Schiller. Helmut Rehder, "The Reluctant Disciple: Nietzsche and Schiller," in *Studies in Nietzsche and the Classical Tradition*, ed. James C. O'Flaherty, Timothy F. Sellner, and Robert M. Helm (Chapel Hill: University of North Carolina Press, 1976), 156–164, esp. 159–160. Also see Friedrich Schiller, *Über Naïve Und Sentimentalische Dichtung*, ed. William F. Mainland (Oxford: Basil Blackwell, 1951), and his "On Naïve and Sentimental Poetry," tr. Daniel O. Dahlstrom, in his *Essays* (New York: Continuum, 1993), 179–260.
136. *NN*, 7.
137. *WB*, 3.
138. Ibid.
139. Ibid.

140. *WB*, 5.
141. *WB*, 4.
142. *JGB*, 248. At *GM*, III, 4, Nietzsche describes the artist as the womb of his work.
143. At *M*, 548, Nietzsche writes that "perhaps the most beautiful thing . . . [is] the spectacle of that force which employs genius *not on works* but on *itself as a work*; that is, on its own constraint, on the purification of its imagination, on the ordering and selection of the influx of tasks and impressions." Also see *JGB*, 206, and *MA*, II, 1: 177, where Nietzsche writes that the "ultimate human" is "at the same time the simplest and most complete."
144. *EH*, II, 9. Note that the subtitle of *Ecce Homo* is *How One Becomes What One Is*.
145. *WB*, 11. In *Ecce Homo*, Nietzsche says that his *Untimely Meditations* present Schopenhauer and Wagner as "two pictures of the hardest selfishness, self-breeding (*Selbstzucht*)," and he also identifies himself with them. See *EH*, V, 1.
146. *M*, 552. A few pages before, at *M*, 547, Nietzsche writes that "'What do I matter!' stands over the door of future thinkers."
147. At *M*, 146, Nietzsche writes: "Is the essence of the truly moral to lie in our keeping in view the nearest and most immediate consequences of our actions for others and deciding in accordance with them? . . . It appears to me higher and freer to *look beyond* (*hinwegzusehen*) these nearest consequences for others and under certain conditions to pursue more distant goals *even at the cost of the suffering of others*."
148. *EH*, III, 5. Also see *GD*, IX, 33, where Nietzsche writes that egoism and selfishness can be worth much or be contemptible, depending on the individual in whom they are found, and that they are valuable in those capable of helping the total-life (*Gesammt-Lebens*) take a step further. This idea also occurs in *Zarathustra*: Zarathustra is described as a raiser (*Zieher*), cultivator (*Züchter*), and disciplinarian (*Zuchtmeister*), who counsels himself to become who he is (IV, 1), but this selfishness is wholesome and healthy (III, 10) because Zarathustra must perfect himself, become the master of a long will, in order to create companions capable of doing the same and contributing to the greater perfection of all things (III, 3). At *M*, 174, Nietzsche asks "whether one is *more useful* to another by immediately leaping to his side and helping him . . . or by *creating* (*formt*) something out of oneself which the other sees with pleasure."
149. *EH*, II, 8.
150. *EH*, II, 3. At *GM*, III, 8, Nietzsche writes that "every artist knows what a harmful effect intercourse has in states of great spiritual tension and preparation." Presumably this is not to be taken literally, but rather is to serve as another metaphor for the necessity of self-walling.
151. *EH*, II, 1. The sense of virtue Nietzsche is after is that of virtuosity, excellence, or proficiency in the sense of *arete*, which he is trying to distinguish both from virtue in the moral sense of selflessly obeying the code of the herd, and from the profligacy of *laisser aller*. With respect to the latter he writes, at *WM*, 871, that "*the virtuosi* of life" have an autonomy that offers "the sharpest antithesis to the vicious and unbridled."

152. *EH*, II, 3. At *JGB*, 276, Nietzsche claims that the nobler a soul is the more susceptible it is to perishing from injury, since its conditions of life are so manifold.

153. In *Dawn*, Nietzsche puts this solution as that of being not only the soil out of which one's thoughts and drives grow, but also the gardener of that soil, and as that of improving one's soul by giving oneself an environment conducive to the development of better habits. See *M*, 382, 560, 462.

154. *EH*, I, 2. Nietzsche adds that he has just described himself. Also see *WM*, 705, where Nietzsche writes that being fortunately organized produces fitness, which produces freedom in the sense of "facility in self-direction."

155. *GM*, II, 1.

156. *NN*, 1. Recall that Nietzsche praises Wagner for being able to encounter and incorporate a tremendous amount of material without this stifling his will to act. Here we see that this ability depends crucially on the capacity to forget. At *GM*, I, 10, Nietzsche emphasizes the importance of forgetting to the active nobles. By contrast, the reactivity and *ressentiment* of the decadent adherents of slave morality signal precisely their inability to forget their enemies and their injuries.

157. *GM*, II, 1. At *M*, 112, Nietzsche understands "freedom of the will" as the ability "to promise determinate things and obligate ourselves to them." At *NN*, 1, Nietzsche understands memory as the ability to overstep the moment and live historically, which he identifies with thinking and being human. On the links between willing, promising, and memory, see Werner Hamacher, "The Promise of Interpretation: Remarks on the Hermeneutic Imperative in Kant and Nietzsche," in his *Premises*, 81–142, esp. 112.

158. For a helpful discussion of Nietzsche's account of the conditions for achieving agency, which recognizes the importance of both memory and forgetting, see Jurist, *Beyond Hegel and Nietzsche*, Chapter 10, esp. 212–225.

159. At *EH*, II, 1, Nietzsche writes, "Everybody has his own measure, often between the narrowest and most delicate limits."

160. See *NN*, 1. In the vocabulary of *The Birth of Tragedy*, this person who knows the measure appropriate to herself is Apollinian, obeying the command: "Nothing in excess." See *GT*, 4.

161. *GM*, II, 2.

162. *GM*, II, 3.

163. *GM*, II, 15.

164. *GM*, II, 17; *GM*, I, 10.

165. *GM*, II, 18. Also see *GM*, I, 9.

166. *GM*, II, 2. At *M*, 484, Nietzsche writes that sovereignty begins when "we take the decisive step and set upon the way that one calls his 'own way' ('*eigenen Weg*')." Of course, on Nietzsche's account the immediate need that gave rise to bad conscience and memory was the formation not of sovereign individuals, but rather of individuals capable of keeping their promises and paying their debts to the social whole. Nietzsche's point is that sovereign individuals, the antithesis of these desired herd men, were themselves a necessary by-product of this development. This suggests that for Nietzsche, as for Hegel, ethical structures are a necessary condition for the possibility of individual autonomy.

167. *GM*, II, 3. Thus Nietzsche writes at *FWag*, Epilogue, that "noble morality, master morality, has its root in a triumphant Yes-saying to oneself – it is self-affirmation, self-mastery of life" (*KSA*, VI, SO).

168. *GM*, II, 16. This, I believe, is the significance of Nietzsche's remark, cited earlier, that the sovereign individual is *again* liberated from the ethics of custom. Prior to being enslaved by such herd morality, humanity was "liberated" from it, but only in the sense that animals are: animals have no customs that require them to suppress their instincts, and so may act on all of their instincts without reprisal. But at that stage, like animals, humans were unable to will, instead merely responding immediately to their instincts' commands. To avoid this condition, as we have seen, humanity became *dependent* on herd morality to give it a will. It is only now that this will has been destroyed, and bad conscience has enabled the forging of a new and truly independent will, that humanity is again independent of the ethics of custom, and this time in a sense more significant than that in which the animals are.

169. *GM*, II, 19.

170. *MA*, II, 2: 350. Nietzsche credits our adopted moral, religious, and metaphysical chains with making us more mild, spiritual, joyful, and reflective than other animals, but concludes that they have now outlived this usefulness and become burdensome. They must therefore be taken off, but carefully, for only the noble will know what to do with this freedom of spirit.

171. *JGB*, 282.

172. *JGB*, 224.

173. On noble cultures (which are also identified as strong ages) exhibiting a will to be oneself, to lift oneself apart (*sich abheben*), see *GD*, IX, 37. Nietzsche also writes that nobles have an agonal instinct for the polis (*GD*, X, 3), that the strong are as inclined to separate as the weak are to congregate (*GM*, III, 18), and that superior humans seek a citadel free from the crowd (*JGB*, 26). At *GM*, III, 14, he argues that such setting apart is increasingly important as the increasing normalcy of sickness makes it especially important that the healthy few be protected so that they may eventually deliver their promise for the future. On freedom as having the will to self-responsibility, see *GD*, IX, 38. On this will diminishing in a society based on 'freedom' and 'equality', see *WM*, 936.

174. *FW*, 117. Also see *M*, 104.

175. On noble commanding also being an obeying, see *Z*, I, 10. On living requiring obeying, and on those who cannot obey themselves being commanded, see *Z*, II, 12. Such throwing off of externally imposed burdens, and taking on of self-imposed ones, turning the "thou shalt" of morality into the "I will" of sovereign responsibility, suggests that the noble individual is at the stage of the lion in *Zarathustra*. See *Z*, I, 1.

176. *WB*, 2.

177. *M*, 9, 19, 20. Note, however, that Nietzsche emphasizes that he is not suggesting that all actions formerly considered *sittlich* should be forsworn. Nobles may indeed retain some established customs, but they will do so out of new motives and on new grounds. See *M*, 103.

178. On the pluralism that follows from Nietzsche's critique of morality, see Ottmann, *Philosophie und Politik bei Nietzsche*, 210–213.

179. Historically, of course, there has been more than one manifestation of decadent morality. But Nietzsche's point is that each of these manifestations is fundamentally the same in certain respects, and that this deep similarity is much more important than their superficial differences. Nietzsche thus inverts the famous lines with which Tolstoi opens *Anna Karenina*: "Happy families are all alike; every unhappy family is unhappy in its own way."

180. On virtue being devalued by being made common, see *FW*, 292. Also see *Z*, IV, 12, where Zarathustra announces, "I am a law only for my kind, I am no law for all."

181. See, respectively, *JGB*, 221, 228, 198. At *MA*, II, 2: 21, Nietzsche suggests that such morality attempts to measure the unmeasurable.

182. *FW*, 120. Also see *MA*, II, 2: 188, where Nietzsche describes different cultures as offering different spiritual climates, each of which is conducive to the flourishing of certain kinds of people but not of others.

183. Morality's immorality is therefore not static over time but proportional to the degree to which its adherents are aware that it is not best for everyone, just as a doctor's immorality in prescribing medicine that makes a patient sick is greater if the doctor *knows* in advance that this will happen. For this reason Nietzsche thinks contemporary advocates of the morality of selflessness are completely indefensible, as he thinks it is now impossible *not* to know that such morality is not for everyone. See *A*, 38; KSA, 6: 254, not translated in *A*.

184. *FW*, 143.

185. On the conclusions drawn in this sentence and the one preceding, see *Z*, II, 4, and *Z*, III, 12: 11. Also see *MA*, II, 1: 19, 359, where Nietzsche claims that, although the Bible tries, it is impossible to paint *the* picture of life, and rhetorically asks us to consider if our view of the world is so beautiful that we do not want to allow others or even ourselves to see another.

186. On free spirits fighting the antiperspectivism and "good-in-itself" of Christianity and Platonism, see *JGB*, Preface. At *JGB*, 186, Nietzsche suggests that the traditional project of grounding or justifying a single moral perspective needs to be replaced with a "collection of material, a conceptual grasping and ordering of a monstrous realm of tender value-feelings and value-distinctions... as preparation for a typology of morality." On valuations having to be judged by means of a lived comparison, since there is no absolute moral measure, see *M*, 61, 139, 195. On every good law book summarizing a long period of moral experimentation, see *A*, 57.

187. Nietzsche discusses these relationships between morality, tyranny (*Tyrannei*), *laisser aller*, and freedom at length at *JGB*, 188. He claims that necessity and freedom of will are one for artists and philosophers at *JGB*, 213, and has Zarathustra describe his will as "my *own* necessity" at *Z*, III, 12: 30. Alexander Nehamas, in *Nietzsche*, 48, also notes that Nietzsche is not critical of tyranny per se.

188. At *A*, 57, Nietzsche claims that the goal of law books is to enable those living under them to achieve a kind of unconscious automatism, and that this achievement is the precondition of mastery and perfection in any art. On

the equation of perfection with unconsciousness, also see *WM*, 289. Much earlier, at *SE*, 3, he understands freedom of spirit to consist in manifesting self-imposed limitations in everyday life.

189. See *A*, 11.

190. See *Z*, II, 5.

191. See *FW*, 304; *GD*, V, 4; and *MA*, II, 2: 318. This conception of the process of becoming virtuous as habituating oneself to performing acts of virtue is recognizably Aristotelian. Nietzsche describes it as early as *Schopenhauer as Educator*, 1. There he calls it following the ladder of your loves to your true self. This is in contrast to the morality of selflessness, whose list of "shall nots" determines its "shalls." Noble morality thus creates its values out of richness, while decadent morality is creative only out of lack. See *FW*, Second Preface, 2; *FW*, 370.

192. See *GD*, IX, 48. Noble moralities thus manage to master the instincts without extirpating them or putting them to sleep (as the morality of selflessness does). In Nietzsche's terms, nobilities "spiritualize" and "beautify" the desires, "giving them a new rank." See *GD*, V, 1, and *M*, 27, 76.

193. See *GM*, II, 23, 24, and *FW*, 297. At *EH*, VI, 1, Nietzsche claims that *Human, All Too Human* represents his own achievement of freeing himself from that not belonging to his nature and retaking possession of himself. At *WM*, 384, Nietzsche writes: "*Overcoming of the affects?* – No, if what is implied is their weakening and extirpation. But putting them into service: which may also mean subjecting them to a protracted tyranny . . . At last they are confidently granted freedom again: they love us as good servants and go voluntarily wherever our best interests lie."

194. At *FW*, Second Preface, 3, Nietzsche attributes these processes of transformation and self-mastery to philosophers, even claiming that they are what philosophy itself truly is.

195. *FW*, 290. Also see *FW*, 18, on being able to dispose of oneself as the opposite of slavishness.

196. *FW*, 320.

197. *FW*, 99. The words that still sound the same to Nietzsche he first wrote in "Richard Wagner in Bayreuth." See *WB*, 11.

Chapter 7

1. This explains the fact, touched on in note 1 to the preceding chapter, that Nietzsche wants to distance himself from the noble conception of freedom as self-initiated activity at the same time that he offers it as an improvement on decadence and morality.

2. At *A*, 57, Nietzsche contends that, although noble moralities are the products of experimental revaluation, ultimately they also depend upon bringing an arbitrary end to such experimenting, so that their valuations may become instinctive and automatic. At *M*, 255, in a discussion of music, he associates nobility with having forgotten everything outside of oneself. At *MA*, II, 2: 337, he writes that the hero carries the "holy, inviolable borderline" wherever he goes. And at *GM*, I, 11, he says that the nobles are beasts to that which is outside (*Aussen*) or strange (*Fremde*). It is for these reasons that

noble cultures are ultimately as conventional and conformist as decadent ones.

3. At *MA*, II, 1: 36, Nietzsche writes, "Our character is determined even more by the lack of certain experiences than by that which we experience."

4. See *MA*, II, 1: 60, headed *Open contradiction often reconciliatory*, and *MA*, II, 1: 233, where Nietzsche writes, in a sentence reminiscent of Hegel, "He who regards men as a herd and flees from them as fast as he can will certainly be overtaken by them and gored by their horns." At *JGB*, 26, he claims that although superior individuals instinctively seek separation from the masses of average people, they must voluntarily overcome such separation if they are to achieve knowledge.

5. At *FW*, 55, Nietzsche begins a section headed *Ultimate noblemindedness* by asking, "What makes noble?" He goes on to answer that it involves "self-sufficiency" and "the use of a rare and singular standard (*Masstab*) and almost a madness." At *WM*, 943, he writes that the noble care for external things, but only "insofar as this care forms a boundary, keeps distant, guards against confusion."

6. The noble is thus clearly distinct from the wise man or sage, as presented at *MA*, II, 2: 339: "The sage will involuntarily circulate affably with other people, like a prince, and will easily treat them as equals, despite all differences of talent, standing, and ethos (*Gesittung*)."

7. *JGB*, 224. In *Ecce Homo*, Nietzsche points out that as early as the *Untimely Meditations* he identified the "historical sense" as a disease and a symptom of decay (*EH*, V, 1).

8. At *JGB*, 260, Nietzsche claims that "in all the higher and more mixed cultures there also appear attempts at mediation between [master morality and slave morality]," and that the same thing is true "even in the same human being, within a *single* soul." Also see *FWag*, Epilogue, where he writes that the opposed optics of Christianity and master morality are both necessary. Joan Stambaugh, in "Nietzsche on Creativity and Decadence," *Philosophy Today* (1977): 162–167, is thus surely wrong to conclude that "creativity and decadence . . . are diametrically opposed in the way that Nietzsche conceives them" (167). On the contrary, Werner Hamacher is correct, in "'Disgregation of the Will,'" to conclude that "the will does not experience . . . freedom through itself and does not therefore even experience it as a will; it is experienced only in the passivity of a disgregation that, itself without a subject, suspends the law of the will and the will as law and subject" (167). Hamacher also associates disgregation with the will's overcoming of its submission to the herd (166), which in this case would be the herdlike tyranny of its noble culture.

9. In the previous chapter it was suggested that the construction of the measured, noble will is an Apollinian activity, and now it is instructive to understand the undoing in which its measure is eluded and exceeded as Dionysian. An adequate exposition of this idea cannot be attempted here, but certain parallels are obvious. In *The Birth of Tragedy*, sections 1 and 3, the Apollinian is associated with an individuation that is not ascetic but rather exults in and justifies its life by living it, achieving a kind of naïveté. Apollo is the ethical deity, and the god of political structure, who exacts measure from his disciples and whose commands are "know thyself" and "nothing in excess" (section 4). By contrast,

the Dionysian is associated with a collapse of individuation, self-forgetfulness, and vanishing subjectivity (section 1). Dionysus is the god who celebrates excess and eludes measure. For an extensive treatment of the Apollinian, the Dionysian, and tragedy in *The Birth of Tragedy*, see John Sallis, *Crossings: Nietzsche and the Space of Tragedy* (Chicago: University of Chicago Press, 1991).

10. *EH*, II, 9.

11. Nietzsche acknowledges in this passage that forgetting oneself and one's goal sounds suspiciously like a retreat from his insistence that independence requires selfishness. But he claims that, far from representing a repudiation of selfishness, in this exceptional case such "selflessness" is actually "a protective measure for preserving the hardest self-concern," and works "in the service of selfishness, self-breeding (*Selbstzucht*)." At *EH*, I, 4, he adds, "I have to be unprepared to be master of myself."

12. At *GM*, II, 1, Nietzsche writes that forgetfulness is useful in making room for the new. At *MA*, II, 1: 350, he contends that in exceptional cases achieving the highest requires disavowing one's ideal, and at *MA*, II, 1: 122, he claims that "many a person fails to become a thinker only because his memory is too good."

13. *JGB*, 248.

14. *MA*, II, Preface, 4, 5. Also see *MA*, II, Preface, 2, where Nietzsche describes the contents of this second volume of *Human, All Too Human* as "a doctrine of health, which may be recommended as a *disciplina voluntatis* to the more spiritual natures of the rising generation."

15. *EH*, Preface, 3.

16. At *FW*, 380, in a section headed *The wanderer speaks*, Nietzsche relates that one who wants to achieve "a freedom from everything 'European . . . must first 'overcome' this time in himself (*diese Zeit in sich selbst zu 'überwinden'*) . . . and consequently not only his time, but also his previous aversion and opposition to this time (*Widerwillen und Widerspruch gegen diese Zeit*), his suffering from this time, his untimeliness (*Zeit-Ungemässheit*)."

17. At *GM*, Preface, 1, Nietzsche writes that knowers are unknown to themselves. One reason he gives is that they never seek themselves, for they are too busy seeking knowledge of what is beyond themselves. But another reason, implied in his claim that they are *necessarily* unknown to themselves, is that *as* knowers they are not the kind of self that could be known. Their self *is* the transformative process of knowing, which means the contents and measure of the self are continually in flux. To "know" this continually self-transforming self is thus to falsify it, to freeze it and know it as something that it is not. The only way such a self can "know" itself is therefore not to attempt to know itself, but rather to continue being what it is and doing what it does, transforming itself through seeking knowledge of things other than itself. Related passages include *JGB*, 281, where Nietzsche expresses his mistrust of the possibility of self-knowledge understood as "immediate knowledge"; *MA*, II, 1: 223, where he explains that this is because we are what we have experienced of the past, so "we" cannot be observed, except by acquiring universal knowledge of the past; *MA*, II, 1: 37, where he concludes that this last kind of "self"-knowledge protects us from having a selective self-image based on forgetting or excluding

what we take to be outside ourselves; and *SE*, 3, where Nietzsche writes that philosophers challenge convention to obtain knowledge, but out of a desire not for "pure knowledge" but for practical transformation.

18. In the Preface to *The Antichristian*, Nietzsche writes that to understand him one must ask questions for which no one today has sufficient courage, have courage for the forbidden, be predestined for the labyrinth, and have unconditional freedom with respect to oneself. At JGB, 29, he says that whoever attempts independence, even if strong enough for it, is probably daring to the point of madness (*Ausgelassenheit*), multiplying the dangers of life, risking being cut off from others by venturing into the labyrinth. And, at JGB, 205, he claims that the genuine philosopher risks himself constantly.

19. At *GM*, III, 1, Nietzsche points out that in philosophers ascetic ideals can indicate an instinct for the most favorable preconditions of higher spirituality. In section 7 of the same essay, he writes, "Ascetic ideals reveal so many bridges to *independence* that a philosopher is bound to rejoice and clap his hands when he hears the story of all those resolute men who one day said No to all servitude and went into some *desert*," but he tempers this enthusiasm by pointing out that some who go into the desert are strong asses, the opposite of strong spirits. Also see section 5 of this essay (*WM*, 915), and A, 57, where he writes that "the most spiritual human beings, as the *strongest*, find their happiness where others would find their destruction: in the labyrinth, in severity towards themselves and others, in attempting; their joy lies in self-constraint: with them asceticism becomes nature, need, instinct. They consider the hard task a privilege, to play with vices which overwhelm others a *recreation*... Knowledge – a form of asceticism."

20. At *A*, 54, Nietzsche describes great spirits as skeptics. He writes that the strength and freedom of a spirit proves itself as skepticism; that convictions are prisons; that to be allowed to speak of value one must have five hundred convictions under and behind oneself; and that freedom from every kind of conviction, the capacity to view freely, belongs to strength. At *JGB*, 227, he calls honesty the virtue of free spirits, and associates it with the courage of an adventurer. At *Z*, IV, 9, he cautions against being imprisoned by the temptations of a narrow and solid faith. And at *MA*, II, 1: 86, he says that we can get stuck in our proficiencies, and that these virtues can prevent us from attaining spiritual-ethical freedom.

21. *JGB*, 41. In other words, one must preserve oneself from becoming preserved; one can only preserve oneself by refusing to cling to what one currently is. This helps to explain Nietzsche's comments suggesting that the drive for self-preservation or existence is itself only a single and limited mode of the more basic drive for continual self-expansion or self-overcoming. See *FW*, 349, and *Z*, II, 12.

22. *MA*, II, 1: 323.

23. See *EH*, IV, 2; *EH*, Preface, 3; *JGB*, 39; and *FW*, 110.

24. On the self being its overcomings, see *MA*, II, Preface: 1.

25. See *M*, 9. In *Dawn*, Nietzsche is discussing primarily those releasing themselves from decadent, moral *Sittlichkeit*; but many of his comments are appropriate to those releasing themselves from *Sittlichkeit* in general, with whom we are

concerned. On *Sitte* originating in the thought that "the lasting advantage is to be preferred to the fleeting," see *MA*, II, 1: 89.

26. *M*, 56.

27. *MA*, II, 2: 333.

28. *FW*, 347.

29. *MA*, II, 1: 211. In German, the tension between free spirits being pulled toward freedom by freedom itself is displayed more directly, in the etymological connection between *freizügig* and *Zug*. The root *Zug*, which appears in both words, suggests directed movement (a train, for example, is a *Zug*). So by calling the spirits *freizügig* Nietzsche emphasizes that they direct their own movement, but by immediately relating that they feel the *Zug* of freedom, he also emphasizes that this self-directed movement is, at the same time, being drawn in a certain direction.

30. We have already compared the empty Nietzschean moral will to the Hegelian, and now we can see that the former, like the latter, is able to adopt any content precisely because no content is truly its own.

31. *MA*, II, 1: 325. It is difficult to capture in English the nuances of the German in this paragraph. Several word choices are significant, however. In the phrase "clothes make the man," the word *Leute*, translated "man," normally has the meaning "people." This signifies both that the "man" made thereby is a *common* or *herd* man, and that he is made into a "man" in virtue of the impression his attire makes on the public. Specifically, by wearing what the culture expects him to wear (e.g., business suits and Christian opinions), he becomes recognized as a "man" by that culture. But as the words in the last sentence make clear, he is *not* this "man." His manhood is a mask, a disguise, *Putz* – Sunday best, which he puts on in order to put people on. In the contrasting phrase, applied to exceptional people, *Träger* connotes not only one who wears clothes, but also one who carries, bears, upholds, or supports something; and *Tracht* can mean the load supported, as in *Traglast*. So these exceptions support their own opinions, which thus reflect the self bearing the load.

32. At *GM*, III, 9, Nietzsche writes that we moderns "experiment with ourselves in a way we would never permit ourselves to experiment with animals"; and at *JGB*, 242, he claims that the modern, democratic age both enables and requires people to engage and adapt to a variety of valuations and customs. But, he contends, consistent with our current discussion, that the reactions of strong and weak to this opportunity and obligation are vastly different.

33. *GM*, III, 13.

34. *JGB*, 211.

35. *M*, 164.

36. *M*, 45.

37. *M*, 164. Also see *SE*, 6, where Nietzsche makes a plea for cultural institutions that protect the genius by not banishing the oddball.

38. Nietzsche describes himself with this phrase, in the course of describing how one becomes what one is, at *EH*, II, 9. Also see *EH*, V, 3, where he writes that "it is my cleverness, many and many places to have been, in order to be able to become one."

39. At *FW*, 23, Nietzsche emphasizes that the work of these experimenters, which is disruptive and therefore considered evil by the herd, is for the benefit of humanity as a whole. He writes that these people have done the most to advance humanity and calls them "seed-carriers of the future" and "initiators... of the new building of political and social associations." Also see *MA*, II, 1: 223, where he suggests that the "self-determination and self-education of the freest and widest-sighted spirits could someday become all-determination with respect to all future humanity."

40. Note that the decadent moral adherent also loses herself by clinging to her established perspective. So again we can see that the noble, although more free than the decadent in virtue of developing her own perspective internally, is not entirely free from the problems that plague morality. We might say that both the decadent and the noble desire an immaculate conception: they want to give birth to a will without being impregnated from outside.

41. The spirit seeking freedom is thus always faced with the question that Nietzsche asks at *EH*, III, 3: "Should I allow a *strange* thought to scale the wall secretly?" Refusing the strange thought risks noble stagnation, but allowing it entrance risks a return to decadence. It is perhaps this that leads Nietzsche to conclude, at *GD*, IX, 38, that "one would have to seek the highest type of free human where the highest resistance is continually being overcome: five steps from tyranny, near the threshold of the danger of servitude."

42. *JGB*, 211. Also see *WM*, 736, where Nietzsche says that freedom from tradition and duty is only a means to great goals, not the goal itself. L. Nathan Oaklander, in "Nietzsche on Freedom," *Southern Journal of Philosophy* 22.2 (1984): 211–222, notes that "a fully developed freedom does not stop, but continues to create new values over and over again, opening oneself up to new and different challenges" (221).

43. *JGB*, 210.

44. *JGB*, 212.

45. Nietzsche makes the link between freedom and unifying the manifold that results from experimenting with oneself, and the distinction between philosophers who do this and scholars who do not, as early as the *Untimely Meditations*. In *Schopenhauer as Educator*, especially in sections 1 and 2, he identifies liberation with being oneself, but insists that one is none of the things that one now does, thinks, or desires. Thus conceived, liberation therefore requires, first, unfettering from one's current self, the "nature" and limitations one has been given, and second, finding one's more genuine self, giving oneself a new nature with its own limits. Nietzsche considers scholars to be capable of the former, but not of the latter, which he says is like being capable of *laissez-faire* but not of *Sittlichkeit*. In the terms of our current discussion, it is being capable of skepticism without being capable of nobility, being capable of multiplicity without being capable of wholeness. True philosophers, educators, and teachers, however, enable students to find their own center in their talents and passions, and to find the circumference around that center within which they can be at home with themselves, and therefore whole and free. In *On the Uses and Disadvantages of History for Life*, especially in sections 4 and 5, he distinguishes between the modern (scholarly) pursuit of philosophy and the more genuine practice of the ancients, and again connects this distinction to

the inability of moderns to be free. The moderns have developed a distinction between form and content, between inner and outer, between their activity of knowing and the objects known. This gives them a kind of freedom, because they can roam over a vast field of study without restraint or concern, secure in the knowledge that the activity of knowing will not affect who or what they are as knowers. But, as we have already seen, Nietzsche argues that such lack of restraint and self-discipline, such "free personality," is a poor kind of freedom. In this essay, he characterizes freedom as requiring that one have a character and style of one's own, which requires precisely that one overcome the distinctions between content and form, inner and outer, and incorporate the material that is initially external, transforming it and oneself into a larger whole.

46. *MA*, II, 2: 306. Also see *FW*, 371, where, in a section headed *We incomprehensible ones (Unverständlichen)*, Nietzsche writes: "One mistakes us – because we ourselves continually grow, change . . . We are no longer free to do any one particular thing, to *be* any one particular thing (*etwas Einzelnes*)."

47. At *JGB*, 44, Nietzsche writes that free spirits are "occasionally proud of tables of categories," but are also "grateful even to need and vacillating sickness because they always rid us from some rule and its 'prejudice'." At *EH*, I, 1, Nietzsche says, with respect to himself, that the years signify the "periodicity of a kind of decadence."

48. The phrase appears at only one other place in Nietzsche's published writings, in the first paragraph of the section of *Nietzsche contra Wagner* headed *Wagner as a dancer*, which is a reprinting, with some revisions, of section 134 of "Opinions and Maxims." It appears a further half-dozen times in the *Nachlass*, in notes ranging from 1872 to 1887, virtually the entirety of Nietzsche's productive life.

49. *MA*, II, 1: 113. Note that *geschlossen* is the past participle of *schliessen*, which normally means to close or conclude. But what is *geschlossen*, that which has achieved *Geschlossenheit*, is often not only closed but unified. These words thus emphasize the formative process in which disparate parts have been brought together to form a whole which en-closes them, and excludes everything else. In English, perhaps the best phrase for this process is that of "closing ranks," which aims at forming an "enclosure" that brings together and protects everything within it from what remains outside.

50. *MA*, II, 1: 134. Note that *Besonnenheit* is the nominative form of the past participle of *besinnen*, which shares the root of *die Sinne*, the senses. *Besonnenheit* thus indicates roughly what we mean in English by "being in possession of our senses," namely, a state of composed awareness. Also see KSA, 8: 379, for a note from 1877 in which Nietzsche describes infinite melody as "losing the shore, giving oneself over to the waves." Nietzsche's discussion of groundless infinite melody in these passages on Sterne and Wagner evokes what Werner Hamacher, in "Disgregation of the Will," calls the "individual": "the undecidability between determination and indeterminacy . . . a self out of the difference from the self, a self out of de-stancing, the undoing of stances and distances, the self out of *Ent-fernung*. Still to come, individuality is always only promised . . . It 'is' not – and is nothing that 'is' – but it comes" (179; also see 178–180).

51. I have chosen to pursue the metaphorics of swimming and the sea, rather than music, for the benefit of readers who (like myself) do not have the requisite background to appreciate the nuances of Nietzsche's musicology. For more detailed and technical considerations of music in Nietzsche, see Eric Blondel, "Philosophy and Music in Nietzsche," *International Studies in Philosophy* 18 (1986): 87–95; Michael Allen Gillespie, "Nietzsche's Musical Politics," in *Nietzsche's New Seas*, ed. Michael Allen Gillespie (Chicago: University of Chicago Press, 1988), 117–149; and Curt Paul Janz, "The Form-Content Problem in Friedrich Nietzsche's Conception of Music," tr. Thomas Heilke, in *Nietzsche's New Seas*, ed. Gillespie, 97–116.

52. One such pair of ears belongs to Claudia Crawford, who claims in "Nietzsche's Great Style: Educator of the Ears and of the Heart," *Nietzsche-Studien* 20 (1991): 210–237, that Nietzsche considers Wagner's "infinite melody" an extreme of decadence because it is "unmarked," by which she means that it does not "exhibit a strong rhythmic sense of movement and dance" (230–231). But Nietzsche's point, as we have just seen, is that Wagner's music succeeds (as that of his imitators usually does not) in being rhythmic without relying on traditional rhythms, and precisely in virtue of this succeeds in being neither decadent nor noble (or a combination of both).

53. Later we will examine the role that swimming art plays in producing swimming individuals and cultures, but for now we will treat them as distinct phenomena.

54. This swimmer is reminiscent of what Zarathustra calls "the highest species of all being," at Z, III, 12, 19: "the most comprehensive soul, which can run and stray and roam farthest within itself; the most necessary soul, which out of sheer joy plunges itself into chance; the soul which, having being, dives into becoming; the soul which *has*, but *wants* to want and will."

55. On being a cycle that generates a series of temporary perspectives, see the following related passages from *The Joyful Science*: at *FW*, 143, in a discussion of polytheism, Nietzsche writes that in it "the free-spiritedness and many-spiritedness of humanity lay prefigured" in "the force to create for ourselves our own new eyes, and ever again new eyes that are even more our own, so that for man alone among all the animals there are no eternal horizons and perspectives." At *FW*, 253, Nietzsche claims that we travel far by being unaware that we are traveling, imagining ourselves to be at home at each stage of the journey. And at *FW*, 295, Nietzsche says that he loves short habits, as a means to know many things and conditions, hates long habits, which prevent such learning and experimenting, and finds most intolerable living completely without habits, through continual improvisation. On the possible return from moral skepticism being either weakness or a repossession of instinct that can affirm again, see *M*, 477. On those returning to their instincts, who enjoy this struggle with multiplicity as a stimulus to self-mastery, being magical, incomprehensible (*Unfassbar* – literally, ungraspable), and unimaginable (*Unausdenklich*), in contradistinction to the common and weak-willed, who want the struggle that they are to come to an end, see *JGB*, 200, 208.

56. In our aquatic language, these herds might better be thought of as schools of fish.

57. Christoph Menke, in "Tragedy and the Free Spirits: On Nietzsche's Theory of Aesthetic Freedom," *Philosophy and Social Criticism* 22.1 (1996): 1–12, calls such a culture "artistic," and writes that it "is characterized by the ability to expose itself to the Dionysian experience of art and its pleasure and its freedom, whereas the Socratic culture is characterized by its weakness that forces it to exclude the same experience" (8). Below we will have more to say about art, the Dionysian, and their relations.

58. *MA*, II, 2: 189.

59. Ibid. Nietzsche concludes the passage by exclaiming that this is a task "of reason and for reason!" Also see *Ecce Homo*, where Nietzsche insists, at *EH*, XII, 2, that only with him are there again "hopes, tasks, prescribed ways to culture," and reflects, at *EH*, V, 1, that the *Untimely Meditation* on history attacked scholars for forgetting that their purpose ought to be culture.

60. As we will see, spirit's *Grundwille* is a *Wille* to *Grund*, its basic will is a will to have a base, and it is this will that must be overcome in order to actualize the perpetual cycle of experimentation.

61. Like the English word, the German word for "assimilate" contains the root of "similar," and thus signifies a transformation in which what is other is made to be the same so that it can be incorporated.

62. *JGB*, 230. Note Nietzsche's use of three words sharing the root "to close" in the final sentence of this paragraph. The German word *Entschluss* shows that the very decision to close one's horizon is itself a closing: having decided, one is no longer open to the possibility of an open horizon. The English "decision" is connected to the verb "to cut" (as in "in-cision"), and so also reflects the fact that a decision cuts one off from possibilities that were available before it was made; but the German is more evocative of Nietzsche's discussion of measures being opened and closed. The English "con-clusion" is perhaps more closely related to *Entschluss*, while the German *Ent-scheiden* is more akin to "decision."

63. *JGB*, 230. The link between the German words for habituation and dwelling (*Wohnung*) preserves the connection between having habits and being at home in them, as do the English words habit and habitat.

64. For descriptions of the will to power in these terms, see *JGB*, 259; *GM*, II, 18; and *WM*, 511, 552, 644, 660, 675, 681. In *WM*, 499, 501, 503, 510, Nietzsche discusses the growth of crystals, single-celled animals' nutrition, and "thinking" as manifestations of this phenomenon of a thing extending its boundary by taking possession of the external and simplifying it to fit the thing's own preexisting form. In *WM*, 488, he treats the subject like a crystal or an amoeba, writing that its sphere is "constantly growing or decreasing, the center of the system constantly shifting; in cases where it cannot organize the appropriate mass, it breaks in two parts." George Stack, in "Nietzsche and the Correspondence Theory of Truth," *Dialogos* 16 (1981): 93–117, notes this connection between our imposition of conceptual schemes on the world and the most basic organic and inorganic processes (111–112). Eugene G. Newman, in "Truth as Art – Art as Truth," *International Studies in Philosophy* 15 (1983): 25–33, identifies the artist and the metaphysician as representatives of the will to power because they have the ability "to place a definite

segment of the stream of existence under the stamp of a single constructive schema" (32). Also see Paul Evans Holbrook, Jr., "Metaphor and the Will to Power," *International Studies in Philosophy* 20 (1988): 19–28; and Alan D. Schrift, "Language, Metaphor, Rhetoric: Nietzsche's Deconstruction of Epistemology," *Journal of the History of Philosophy* 23.3 (1985): 371–395, esp. 388. For a critical survey of several extant interpretations of the will to power, see Ofelia Schutte, *Beyond Nihilism* (Chicago: University of Chicago Press, 1984), Chapter 4. Elliot L. Jurist, in *Beyond Hegel and Nietzsche*, Chapter 11, offers an account of the relationship between the will to power and agency in Nietzsche, but I disagree with his conclusion that "Nietzsche's idea of the will to power is meant to be a rebuke to the emphasis on freedom that one finds in the tradition of German Idealism" (243).

65. Christoph Menke, in "Tragedy and the Free Spirits," identifies the free spirit as one who "no longer tries to appropriate the world and to secure this appropriation" and is thus liberated "from the perspective of the 'individual'" (5). Werner Hamacher, in "The Promise of Interpretation: Remarks on the Hermeneutic Imperative in Kant and Nietzsche," in his *Premises*, 81–142, writes that "the condition for the independence of the will thus lies in whatever in the will desists from willing...The will is its release from itself, and this release occurs when the will lays itself out in the direction of something else – something independent from it – and when it reclaims for itself precisely what it never was: the unrepeatable, the unappropriable, its 'own' alteration" (139–140). Volker Gerhardt, in "Selbstbegründung: Nietzsche's Moral der Individualität," *Nietzsche-Studien* 21 (1992): 28–49, contends that Nietzsche continually emphasizes a countermovement to the will to power, a temporary unharnessing (*Ausspannen*) of the concentrated will (37). Walter A. Brogan, in "The Central Significance of Suffering in Nietzsche's Thought," *International Studies in Philosophy* 20 (1988): 53–62, suggests that in the *Übermensch*, creative willing gives way to letting be. Stephen Houlgate, in "Power, Egoism, and the 'Open' Self in Nietzsche and Hegel," *Journal of the British Society for Phenomenology* 22.3 (1991): 120–138, builds an interesting but ultimately unpersuasive case that the Nietzschean subject never genuinely achieves such openness; Houlgate argues that the Nietzschean subject is never able to let go of itself and its insistence on the primacy of its own will, and is thus never able to encounter an other on its own terms, but must always willfully interpret it. Michel Haar, in "Nietzsche and Metaphysical Language," tr. Cyril and Liliane Welch, *Man and World* 4.4 (1971): 359–395, rightly concludes that to will is to will one's own growth, to will the appropriation of an ever-larger field of action, but he is incorrect both to identify "Dionysus" as "another world for the will to power" (362), and to describe the *Übermensch* as the "master" of his own "inward chaos" (379). As we will see, the Dionysian and the *übermenschlich* are open to otherness and the chaotic in precisely the way that the appropriative will to power is not.

66. Nietzsche does not always distinguish the senses in which he uses the terms "health" and "nobility." On my interpretation, sometimes he uses them to indicate the state that must be overcome (which I refer to simply as "health" or "nobility"), and sometimes to indicate the state in which this overcoming

has transpired (which I call "great health" or "tragedy"). Commentators also employ these terms in various ways. Gilles Deleuze, in *Nietzsche and Philosophy*, for example, clearly uses "noble" in the latter sense, since he writes that it is that "which is capable of transforming itself... the power of transformation, the Dionysian power" (42).

67. The difference between the old health and this new health can also be put in terms of the drive for self-expansion, which we have seen that Nietzsche considers fundamental. The noble seeks self-expansion in the sense of making herself larger without changing; she wants to assimilate what she can to her existing measure and to distance herself from what she cannot. By contrast, the freer spirit of new health seeks self-expansion in the sense that she pursues an engagement with the other that is mutually transformative of both of their previous measures. It is thus the latter spirit who engages in a genuine overcoming that, as Gilles Deleuze, in *Nietzsche and Philosophy*, characterizes it, "is opposed to preserving, but also to appropriating and reappropriating" (163).

68. Note that, as in English, the German for "Mediterranean," *Mittelmeer*, literally means a sea surrounded by various coasts and lands. This is significant, given our earlier discussions about freedom requiring that one leave one's land for the water and not succumb to the temptation to settle on alternative ground.

69. *FW*, 382. Also see *EH*, IX, 2. Mark Letteri, in "The Theme of Health in Nietzsche's Thought," *Man and World* (1990): 405–417, correctly notes that sickness is always essential to great health, because to have great health is to lose oneself in repeated struggles with sickness yet endure in transfigured form. On this point see *WM*, 864, 1013. Michel Haar, in "Nietzsche and Metaphysical Language," 385, and George de Huszar, in "Nietzsche's Theory of Decadence and the Transvaluation of All Values," *Journal of the History of Ideas* 6.3 (1945): 259–272, esp. 270, both mistakenly claim that *übermenschlich* great health consists in eliminating all weakness and decadence. James P. Cadello, in "Nietzsche and the Living Body, Late- and Post-Modern Readings of Nietzsche on Health," *International Studies in Philosophy* 25 (1993): 97–107, is also mistaken to claim that "Nietzsche never undercuts his own opposition between health and disease" (100). Cadello is explicitly following the position of Bernd Magnus, as expressed in his "Deification of the Commonplace: *Twilight of the Idols*," in *Reading Nietzsche*, ed. Robert C. Solomon and Kathleen Higgins (New York: Oxford University Press, 1988), 152–181.

70. *EH*, III, 1.

71. *Orgiasmus* appears to be a neologism, combining *Orgie* and *Orgasmus*, "orgy" and "orgasm."

72. *GD*, X, 5.

73. Of course, Nietzsche's explicit reference in the passage to *The Birth of Tragedy*, and his decision to reiterate the passage in the discussion of *The Birth of Tragedy* in *Ecce Homo*, forge a strong link between these "late" concepts and his earliest work.

74. *EH*, IV, 3.

75. *EH*, IX, 6. The passage is too long to repeat here, but we will have cause to return to portions of it later. Also see *EH*, IX, 1, the first numbered paragraph of the discussion of *Zarathustra*.

76. These two senses of "affirmation" are perhaps more naturally associated with the English word "belief." When I ask, "Do you believe in ghosts?," I want to know if you think ghosts exist, regardless of whether you would like them to. But when I ask, "Do you believe in the death penalty?," I want to know if you think the death penalty is a good idea, regardless of whether it happens to exist in your country or not.

77. George de Huszar, in "Nietzsche's Theory of Decadence and the Transvaluation of All Values," notes this point (265). At *FW*, 12, Nietzsche asks us: "What if pleasure and displeasure were so tied together that whoever *wanted* to have as much as possible of one *must* also have as much as possible of the other?" He goes on to note that the Stoic reaction to this possibility is to strive for as little as possible of both, but holds out hope that we might yet pursue the other path. Also see *FW*, 268, where Nietzsche defines the heroic as "going out to meet one's highest suffering and one's highest hope at the same time."

78. On the tragic spirit's affirmation of the world of becoming growing out of her overfullness, see *EH*, IV, 2.

79. Her naïve playfulness suggests that the tragic soul has reached the stage of the child, the last of the three stages presented at *Z*, I, 1. Also see *Z*, I, 20. At *WM*, 940, Nietzsche writes, "Higher than 'thou shalt' is 'I will' (the heroes); higher than 'I will' stands: 'I am' (the gods of the Greeks)." I would suggest, without being able to defend the suggestion here, that these stages correspond to those of camel, lion, and child in *Zarathustra*, and to those of moral, noble, and tragic in my own interpretation of Nietzsche's work.

80. At *WM*, 1049, Nietzsche contrasts *"Apollo's* deception: the *eternity* of beautiful form; the aristocratic legislation, *'thus shall it be forever!'"* with *"Dionysus*: sensuality and cruelty. Transitoriness could be interpreted as enjoyment of productive and destructive force, as *continual creation.*" Also see the next section, *WM*, 1050.

81. She thus recognizes "that which is most strictly confirmed and born out by truth and science. Nothing that is may be reckoned away, nothing is dispensable" (*EH*, IV, 2). Also see *EH*, XIV, 4.

82. *MA*, II, 1: 332.

83. *MA*, II, 2: opening dialogue.

84. *GD*, V, 6. Note that *Aberwitz*, the "lunacy" of the priest, is a complete lack of *Witz*. *Witz* can mean the capacity for understanding, the capacity for humor, and even a piece of humor itself (connections preserved in English phrases employing "wit" – "to have one's wits about one," "to be witty, to be a wit," "a piece of wit"). To lack *Witz*, "to lose one's wits," is thus to be a lunatic, to lose one's capacity for understanding. But it is also connected to losing one's capacity to get a joke, to losing one's sense of humor. The degenerate priest is thus morbidly serious, unable to play, unable to laugh, unable to enjoy the childlike levity of creation because he is obsessed with the weight of destruction.

85. *A*, 57.

86. *GD*, X, 4. At *EH*, IX, 8, and *EH*, XIV, 2, Nietzsche writes that the Dionysian task of creation requires as its precondition that one take pleasure in destruction. At *GT*, SK, 1, he calls the Dionysian that out of which tragedy was born, and associates it with "an intellectual predilection for the hard, gruesome, evil,

and problematic things of existence, out of well-being, out of overflowing health, out of *fullness* of existence."

87. *EH*, XIV, 5.

88. *EH*, II, 10.

89. Also see *EH*, XIII, 4, where Nietzsche writes, "The necessary does not injure me; *amor fati* is my innermost nature." Yirmiyahu Yovel, in "Nietzsche and Spinoza: *Amor Fati* and *Amor Dei*," in *Nietzsche as Affirmative Thinker*, ed. Yirmiyahu Yovel (Dordrecht: Martinus Nijhoff, 1986): 183–203, writes that "whatever liberation [Nietzsche and Spinoza] foresee involves in both the rejoicing acceptance of necessity" (201).

90. *FW*, 276.

91. *FW*, 341.

92. This distinction between metaphysical and psychological, or objective and subjective, readings of the eternal return is at least as old as Karl Löwith's work on the subject. For a compact presentation of his views, see "Nietzsche's Doctrine of Eternal Recurrence," *Journal of the History of Ideas* 6.3 (1945): 273–284. For a more expansive presentation of his interpretation, see *Nietzsches Philosophie der ewigen Wiederkehr des Gleichen* (Stuttgart: Kohlhammer, 1956), recently translated by J. Harvey Lomax as *Nietzsche's Philosophy of the Eternal Recurrence of the Same* (Berkeley: University of California, 1997). Henning Ottmann employs a similar distinction in *Philosophie und Politik bei Nietzsche*, 361–382. Perhaps the best-known advocate of the metaphysical reading is Arthur Danto; see his "The Eternal Recurrence," in *Nietzsche: A Collection of Critical Essays*, ed. Robert Solomon (New York: Doubleday, 1973): 316–321. Maudemarie Clark, in *Nietzsche on Truth and Philosophy* (Cambridge: Cambridge University Press, 1990), Chapter 8, points out that recent scholarship has tended to reject the metaphysical reading entirely as indefensible. She identifies the beginning of this trend with Ivan Soll, "Reflections on Recurrence: A Re-examination of Nietzsche's Doctrine, *die ewige Wiederkehr des Gleichen*," in *Nietzsche: A Collection of Critical Essays*, ed. Solomon, 322–342. She follows Soll, as do Bernd Magnus, in *Nietzsche's Existential Imperative* (Bloomington: Indiana University Press, 1978), esp. 111–154, and Richard Schacht, in *Nietzsche*, 253–266.

93. *FW*, 109. Also see *FW*, 322, and *MA*, II, 1: 9, where Nietzsche emphasizes that nature's necessity is not to be understood as lawfulness. Alexander Nehamas, in *Nietzsche: Life as Literature*, suggests that in interpreting Nietzsche's claim that *alle Dinge* return "we would be wrong . . . to assume without question that the expression *alle Dinge* refers to each and every individual occurrence in the history of the world, for Nietzsche connects the recurrence with Dionysianism, a religion that emphasizes the infinite repetition of the cycles of nature, not the individual events that constitute world history" (146). Nonetheless, Nehamas concludes that it is the psychological consequences of the eternal return that are "the most serious and valuable aspects" of Nietzsche's teaching (150). See Nehamas, Chapter 5, for a detailed discussion of the eternal return and its possible interpretations.

94. Nietzsche provides support for this interpretation, at least in his early work, when he writes at *SE*, 1: "At bottom every man knows quite well that, being something unique (*ein Unicum*), he will be in the world only once, and that

no peculiar chance will shake together for a second time such a fantastically variegated assortment (*Mancherlei*) as he is into a unity (*Einerlei*)." George de Huszar, in "Nietzsche's Theory of Decadence and the Transvaluation of All Values," 263, notes that the tragic take delight in cosmic disorder and do not yearn for changelessness, certainty, or uniformity. In "Nietzsche and Metaphysical Language," Michel Haar points out that in affirming passing away, the tragic affirm time itself (387). Yirmiyahu Yovel, in "Nietzsche and Spinoza," writes that in affirming eternal recurrence, "I recognize and accept the mode of being in which transience is the rule" (198). And Gilles Deleuze, in *Nietzsche and Philosophy*, goes so far as to claim that "the sense of Nietzsche's philosophy is that multiplicity, becoming and chance are objects of pure affirmation. The affirmation of multiplicity is the speculative proposition, just as the joy of diversity is the practical proposition" (197).

95. *FW*, 341.

96. This is not to deny that at times Nietzsche may have entertained the possibility of such a metaphysics. It is rather to suggest that we can produce an interpretation of the text that is more fruitful and defensible if we leave these metaphysical speculations aside.

97. *EH*, IX, 1.

98. See *GD*, VI, 8; *GD*, V, 6; and *JGB*, 56. This would include, of course, willing the eternal return of even our greatest enemies and those things most hateful to us, as preconditions of ourselves. At *GD*, V, 3, Nietzsche calls this the spiritualization of enmity, the realization that only through one's enemies has one come to be what one is. Considering his own situation, Nietzsche writes, in a discarded draft for the section in *Ecce Homo* on *The Case of Wagner*, "even Christianity becomes necessary: only the highest form, the most dangerous, the one that was most seductive in its No to life, provokes its highest affirmation – me," included by Kaufmann in *BW* as an appendix (799).

99. My interpretation of the eternal return is perhaps closest to that of Gilles Deleuze, in *Nietzsche and Philosophy*, who characterizes the thought of the eternal return as involving a "double selection": an ethical selection, in which one is encouraged to will only that which one could will to return eternally (xi, 68), and an ontological selection, in which "only becoming has being," so that what is repeated is diversity and difference (xi, 46, 49). Deleuze thus shares my view that the eternal return is *both* a metaphysical and a psychological doctrine, and further agrees with me that metaphysical recurrence cannot be extended to detailed configurations of the universe: "Every time we understand the eternal return as the return of a particular arrangement of things after all the other arrangements have been realized . . . we replace Nietzsche's thought with childish hypotheses. No one extended the critique of all forms of identity further than Nietzsche" (xi). James Winchester, in *Nietzsche's Aesthetic Turn*, points out that Deleuze's interpretation attempts to solve the standard problem of how to reconcile the eternal return (understood as a metaphysical doctrine) with the will to power (understood as a doctrine of irreducible plurality and differentiation) (76). Winchester thinks that Deleuze fails, but I believe that he succeeds (and that I join him in doing so) by claiming that, as a metaphysical doctrine, the eternal return itself asserts precisely the irreducibility of plurality, differentiation, and chaos,

so that there is nothing to reconcile. For another interpretation with affinities to mine, see Haar, "Nietzsche and Metaphysical Language," 388–389, 391, 393.

100. On this characterization of Stoicism, see *FW*, 306.

101. See, for example, *EH*, I, 6, where Nietzsche criticizes "Russian fatalism" as "a kind of will to hibernate" in the "sick person" who is no longer capable of any reaction. The *amor fati* of the person of great health is clearly distinct from this passive stance. Michel Haar agrees with me when he contends, in "Nietzsche and Metaphysical Language," that *amor fati* does not signal a blind fatalism, but rather an elimination of the opposition between active willing and passive acceptance of destiny (391–392). For an opposing view, see Bernd Magnus, "Deconstruction Site: The 'Problem of Style' in Nietzsche's Philosophy," *Philosophical Topics* 19.2 (1991): 215–243, esp. 233–237. Magnus notes the distinction between the metaphysical and psychological versions of eternal recurrence, but insists that the latter leads to fatalism and Stoicism and therefore concludes that it can have no imperative effect.

102. At *MA*, II, 1: 201, Nietzsche suggests that the value of a philosophy lies in what the future can build out of the materials with which it has been constructed, rather than in the present construction itself. At *Z*, I, Prologue: 4, he makes the same point with respect to humanity itself – namely, that its greatness lies not in the end that it currently is, but in being a bridge to something else.

103. See Alan White, *Within Nietzsche's Labyrinth*, who interprets willing the eternal return as willing life's temporality by affirming the double fact that one's past will always be retained, in all its concreteness, but at the same time will always remain open to future transformations (101–104).

104. *WB*, 3. He also characterizes the first task, the determination of necessity, as one of physics at *FW*, 335, and characterizes the second task, the making-lovable of oneself and the present, as an artistic activity. For example, at *FW*, 107, in a section headed *Our ultimate gratitude to art*, he writes: "We do not always keep our eyes from rounding off, from finishing the poem (*zu Ende zu dichten*); and then it is no longer eternal imperfection that we carry over the river of becoming – then we believe ourselves to carry a goddess... As an aesthetic phenomenon existence is still *bearable* for us, and art gives us the eyes and the hands and above all the good conscience to be *able* to make such a phenomenon out of ourselves."

105. *M*, 19.

106. See *Z*, IV, 10, which reports "Zarathustra's proverb" to be "one thing is more necessary than another," and *WB*, 4, where Nietzsche says that the tragic artwork struggles precisely against the injustice of political and social arrangements that oppose it with "*apparently* invincible necessity" (emphasis added).

107. See *FW*, 7. At *FW*, 306, 375, Nietzsche suggests that this gives the tragic soul more affinity with the Epicureans than with the Stoics.

108. *MA*, II, 2: 86. That affirmation of the past requires improvement of the future through experiment and struggle in the present allows us to understand Nietzsche's comment that tragic affirmation is both wholesale and yet

not the affirmation of the ass, who says yes to everything, at *Z*, IV, 17–18. This is therefore the solution to the riddle of how a yes-saying, affirmative spirit can say no to so many things, which Nietzsche designates "the psychological problem in the type of Zarathustra... how he who says No and *does* No to an unheard of degree, to everything to which one previously said Yes, can nonetheless be the opposite of a no-saying spirit" (*EH*, IX, 6). For example, Nietzsche may have to affirm Christianity as having been necessary to the emergence of tragic affirmation and himself, but that precludes him neither from denouncing the consequences of its continued existence nor from desiring and struggling for a future in which Christianity has been overcome. This also explains, therefore, how Zarathustra can say "the great despisers are the great reverers" (*Z*, IV, 13), and conclude that the "last man," who cannot despise himself, is the most despicable man (*Z*, I, Prologue: 5). On this distinction between Nietzschean affirmation and that of the ass, see Deleuze, *Nietzsche and Philosophy*, 3, 178–179, 184.

109. The figure of the pale criminal in *Zarathustra* represents, I believe, one who has indeed been crushed and paralyzed by the realization that he has performed an act that he will never be able to affirm. Zarathustra says of him: "An image made this pale man pale. He was equal to his deed when he did it; but he could not bear its image after it was done. Now he always saw himself as the doer of one deed. Madness I call this: the exception now became the essence for him. A chalk streak stops a hen; the stroke that he himself struck stopped his poor reason: madness *after* the deed I call this" (*Z*, I, 6). Also see *WM*, 235, and White, *Within Nietzsche's Labyrinth*, 78–80.

110. At *FWag*, Epilogue, Nietzsche calls "the need for redemption" the "epitome (*Inbegriff*) of all Christian needs." From the Christian perspective, only Jesus is capable of redeeming the infinite debt to God we have incurred through our sins. Such an infinite debt is, by definition, incapable of expiation through finite human action. See *GM*, II, 20–22.

111. At *M*, 96, Nietzsche suggests that Europe must follow India in arriving at a religion of self-redemption. At *JGB*, 262, he writes that where "life *lives beyond* the old morality, the 'individual' stands there, reduced to his own law-giving, to his own arts and stratagems for self-preservation, self-enhancement, self-redemption." See Ted Sadler, *Nietzsche: Truth and Redemption* (London: Athlone, 1995), esp. Chapter 3, entitled "Redemption and Life Affirmation." Sadler agrees with me that Nietzsche is trying to give redemption a meaning without religious assumptions (122), and that this involves no longer seeking a justification of life from outside (155–156).

112. *EH*, IX, 8. Zarathustra's speech within this passage comes from *Z*, II, 20. Also see *GM*, I, 12, where Nietzsche calls the sight of such a man who can justify humanity his last hope. In "Nietzsche's Doctrine of Eternal Recurrence," Karl Löwith points out that Zarathustra accepts "voluntarily what cannot be otherwise, thus transforming an alien fate into his proper destiny" (279).

113. On the links between redemption and liberation, see *Z*, II, 20. The German word for redemption, *Erlösung*, preserves some of these links, since a *Lösung* is both a solution and a severance, and the verb *lösen* means to cut something loose. As traditionally conceived, then, redemption solves humanity's

problem, understood as its being bound to this fallen actual world, by cutting it loose, by freeing it from this bond. In Nietzsche's reconception, tragic redemption continues to signal humanity's liberation, but a liberation that takes place *in* the world rather than through a severance from it.

114. *GD*, IX, 49. In the very next section, *GD*, IX, 50, Nietzsche suggests that the entire nineteenth century strove for what Goethe did, but was not up to the task. It placed itself in the world, seeking knowledge, but did not have the strength to reunify the various perspectives it adopted and the result was not liberating redemption but chaos and a nihilistic sigh. At *WM*, 95, Nietzsche writes that "Hegel's way of thinking is not far different from *Goethe's.*"

115. See *Z*, II, 2, where Zarathustra proclaims: "Creation – that is the great redemption from suffering, and life's growing light. But that the creator may be, suffering is needed and much change. Indeed, there must be much bitter dying in your life, you creators. Thus are you advocates and justifiers of all impermanence. To be the child who is newly born, the creator must also want to be the mother who gives birth and the pains of the birth-giver." In "Nietzsche and Metaphysical Language," Michel Haar comments that tragic affirmation vindicates and redeems both the deepest suffering and all becoming (386–388).

116. Actually, she needs to perform the redemption herself if she is to be free at all, for it is impossible to be completely free if one is "liberated" by someone else, since one is then dependent on that other person.

117. *Z*, IV, 13.

118. *FW*, 343.

119. *EH*, IX, 6.

120. *Z*, III, 2: 1.

121. *EH*, IX, 6. Note that for Zarathustra and the tragic soul the sight of the *Abgrund* becomes a *Grund* of their affirmation of the world, whereas if the world itself had a *Grund* they would have one less *Grund* for affirming it. Also note Nietzsche's deliberate use of the biblical term "Amen" to designate affirmation of precisely that abyssal state of the world that the Bible's Christian interpreters either refuse to acknowledge or struggle mightily against.

122. It also signifies that we are no longer required to think of life as a duty to God, but can instead think of it as an experiment of knowledge, a "joyful science" that luxuriates in the infinity of interpretations now open to it. See *FW*, 343, 374.

123. *Z*, IV, 6.

124. Nietzsche says of himself, "I am a bringer of glad tidings (*ein froher Botschafter*) like there has never been," at *EH*, XIV, 1.

125. Becoming regains its innocence, which it had prior to morality's judgment that it is necessarily evil and in need of being transcended, when it is recognized that becoming is all there is (so no transcendence is possible) and that therefore no judgment can be passed upon it as a whole, since there is no perspective external to it from which it could be judged (so no transcendence is necessary). See *GD*, VI, 7, 8 and *Z*, III, 4. The judgment by which morality condemns life and becoming is thus exposed as both impossible and decadent. See *GD*, II, 2, and *GD*, V, 5.

126. Note that Nietzsche considers taking on guilt to be nobler than accepting punishment. He attributes the former function to the Greek gods, as distinct from the Christian God, who does the latter, at *GM*, II, 23.

127. *A*, 33. Also see the paragraph preceding it (*A*, 32), where Nietzsche writes that the 'glad tidings' is just that there are no more oppositions."

128. *A*, 34.

129. In addition to the passages just cited at length, see *A*, 35–42. Leon Rosenstein, in "Metaphysical Foundations of the Theories of Tragedy in Hegel and Nietzsche," *Journal of Aesthetics and Art Criticism* 28.4 (1970): 521–533, suggests that tragedy is best understood as a new way of seeing, acting, and living. In "Nietzsche and Metaphysical Language," Michel Haar argues that for Nietzsche divinity signifies an affirmation that embraces imperfection itself (389). This is supported by *WM*, 416, where Nietzsche writes that the significance of Hegel was "to evolve a pantheism through which evil, error, and suffering are not felt as arguments against divinity." Unfortunately, Nietzsche continues, this project "has been misused by the existing powers (state, etc.), as if it sanctioned the rationality of whoever happened to be ruling."

130. *GM*, II, 24. Nietzsche's late concern with preparing the conditions in which redemptive tragic souls can emerge and communicate the tragic spirit might profitably be compared to his early concern, expressed at *SE*, 7, 8, with preparing the conditions in which philosophers can arise, educate other philosophers, and ultimately develop into a force that will impact the whole.

Chapter 8

1. The following commentators identify the development of a new kind of language and conceptualization as crucial to Nietzsche's project of overcoming the status quo and enabling a new kind of experience (although each understands the details of that project somewhat differently): J. Daniel Breazeale, "The Word, the World, and Nietzsche," *Philosophical Forum* 6 (1974–75): 301–320; Deborah Cook, "Nietzsche, Foucault, Tragedy," *Philosophy and Literature* 13.1 (1989): 140–150, esp. 144; Deleuze, *Nietzsche and Philosophy*, 35; Douglas A. Gilmour, "On Language, Writing, and the Restoration of Sight: Nietzsche's Philosophical Palinode," *Philosophy and Rhetoric* 27.3 (1994): 245–269, esp. 253; Michel Haar, *Nietzsche and Metaphysics*, tr. and ed. Michael Gendre (Albany: State University of New York Press, 1996), Chapters 4 and 8; Allan Megill, "Nietzsche as Aestheticist," *Philosophy and Literature* 5.2 (1981): 204–225, esp. 220–221; Kelly Oliver, "Revolutionary Horror: Nietzsche and Kristeva on the Politics of Poetry," *Social Theory and Practice* 15.3 (1989): 305–320, esp. 309, 313; Brigitte Scheer, "Die Bedeutung der Sprache im Verhältnis von Kunst und Wissenschaft bei Nietzsche," *Kunst und Wissenschaft bei Nietzsche*, ed. Mihailo Djuric and Josef Simon (Würzburg: Königshausen & Neumann, 1986), 101–111; George Stack, "Nietzsche as Structuralist," *Philosophy Today* 27.1 (1983): 31–51, esp. 43–46, 49. Breazeale (311), Oliver (315), and Stack (116), conclude that the project is necessarily a failure, on the grounds that Nietzsche himself

famously claims (*WM*, 517, 715) that no language can be adequate to becoming. Alan Schrift, in "Language, Metaphor, Rhetoric: Nietzsche's Deconstruction of Epistemology," *Journal of the History of Philosophy* 23.3 (1985):
371–395, agrees with Breazeale, Oliver, and Stack on this point (385), but
suggests that Nietzsche's project of transvaluation requires only the "dis-
mantling of metaphysical language" (392) through the "recognition of the
universal scope of the activity of interpretation" (394), rather than the
development of its own nonmetaphysical means of speaking and writing.
Gilmour attempts to rescue Nietzsche by interpreting his point that language is inadequate to becoming as being directed only at ordinary language, and therefore as not applying to Nietzsche's own language to the
extent that it departs significantly from such ordinariness (246, 253–254,
258–259). Alexander Nehamas, in *Nietzsche: Life as Literature*, not only claims
that the project of linguistic transformation is a failure, but also denies that
Nietzsche even undertakes it (93–96). In his view, "linguistic reform is not
part of the revaluation of all values" (93), and Nietzsche's claim is "not that
our language is wrong but that we are wrong in taking it too seriously" (96).
I agree that part of Nietzsche's point is that we should take language less seriously, but I also believe that Nietzsche thinks the chief means to this goal is the
development of a different kind of linguistic practice. Nietzsche supports this
interpretation both at *EH*, III, 1, where he describes his books as containing
"the first language for a new series of experiences," and in section 4 of the
Preface to *GM*, where he remarks that in his earlier works he lacked his own
language for his own things.

2. Sarah Kofman, in *Nietzsche and Metaphor*, 58, points out that morality is the
natural ally of linguistic reification and universalization. Also see Warren,
Nietzsche and Political Thought, 50–58, on the role of language in structuring
and reifying cultures.

3. George Stack, in "Nietzsche as Structuralist," 38, identifies Nietzsche's concern
about the entrenchment of such patterns of dominant thinking, speaking, and
writing with Foucault's concern about *epistemes*. Deborah Cook, in "Nietzsche,
Foucault, and Tragedy," 144–145, compares Nietzsche's tragic language to
Foucault's language of transgression, which she believes Foucault hoped, at
least in his early works, could subvert the modern *episteme* by enabling a tragic
experience precluded by referential language.

4. On language being sick and an enslaving carrier of nihilism and reactive
forces, see Brigitte Scheer, "Die Bedeutung der Sprache im Verhältnis von
Kunst und Wissenschaft bei Nietzsche," 108–109, and Michel Haar, *Nietzsche
and Metaphysics*, 70.

5. *EH*, IX, 7.

6. See Nietzsche's description of the future heralded by Wagner's art at *WB*, 11.

7. *MA*, II, 2: 135.

8. At *EH*, III, 4, Nietzsche writes that "*good* is any style that really communicates an
inward state." He makes this connection between particular linguistic styles and
particular spirits or modes of thinking as early as "David Strauss, the Confessor
and the Writer": "he who has sinned against the German language has profaned
the mystery of all that is German: through all the confusion and changes of
nations and customs, it alone has, as by a metaphysical magic, preserved itself

and therewith the German spirit" (*DS*, 12). This passage, of course, leaves open the question of what the "German spirit" is. Earlier in this *Untimely Meditation*, at *DS*, 2, Nietzsche explains that it is characterized by seeking rather than finding, which is consistent with the passage from "Opinions and Maxims" considered earlier, *MA*, II, 1: 323, in which he claims that the best Germans are those who continually degermanize themselves.

9. *MA*, II, 2: 88. Nietzsche suggests this as early as *WB*, 5, where he laments that language is sick, stuck in conventional thoughts and concepts, and therefore unable to teach right feeling to people.

10. *MA*, II, 2: 87. The potentially ominous talk of "good Europeans" directing and supervising a "total earth-culture" is attenuated both by the fact that this passage is explicitly directed against nationalism in general and German nationalism in particular, and by recollection of our earlier discussion of the tree of a billion blossoms. That discussion made clear that the "total earth-culture" Nietzsche advocates is not at all homogenous, not at all "European" in any standard sense of the term, but rather precisely a culture in which the strange and the foreign are *not* sacrificed but rather nourished. This passage, with its exhortation to become open to the foreign and to make ourselves available to those foreigners who are open to us, for our mutual benefit, reinforces that interpretation. For other passages in which Nietzsche discusses the responsibility of thinkers, writers, and artists for the development and elevation of culture, see *JGB*, 61, 211; *MA*, II, 1: 99; and *WB*, 5, 10. These passages obviously bear on the issue, which we deferred earlier, of how swimming, tragic art is productive of swimming, tragic culture. On such culture's being an end in itself, and being "unpolitical, even anti-political," see *GD*, VIII, 1–5.

11. *MA*, II, 2: 122. Also see *MA*, II, 2: 135.

12. *WB*, 10. At *GD*, IX, 24, Nietzsche defines an artist as a "genius of communication," and at *WB*, 9, he suggests that art is "only the capacity to communicate to others what one has experienced" and that Wagner's greatness lies in a "demonic communicability." Also see *WM*, 809.

13. *MA*, II, 2: 55.

14. *M*, 47. Also see *MA*, II, 2: 135.

15. *M*, 257.

16. See *MA*, II, 2: 33. His most famous expansion on this view, of course, is found in the *Genealogy*, where Nietzsche treats the many meanings that have been associated over time with the word "punishment."

17. *FW*, 58. Also see the preceding section, headed *To the realists*, as well as *M*, 210, and *GM*, I, 2, where Nietzsche writes that "one should allow himself to grasp the origin of language itself as an expression of power of the masterful (*Herrschenden*): they say 'that *is* that and that', they seal every thing and happening with a sound and thereby take it, as it were, into their possession." Allan Megill, in "Nietzsche as Aestheticist," describes this process of linguistic creation as an aesthetic act of world-making that liberates us, through a displacement and disarrangement (*Verstellung*) of reality, from the oppressiveness of the established and determined (213–214, 216, 222). In "The Word, the World, and Nietzsche," Daniel Breazeale describes Nietzsche's theory of language as "transcendental," because he understands language to be

constitutive of both consciousness and the world that is its object (303–304). Jochem Hennigfeld, in "Sprache als Weltansicht: Humboldt – Nietzsche – Whorf," *Zeitung für philosophische Forschung* 30.3 (1976): 435–451, contends that in Nietzsche linguistically fixed worldviews are bound up with determinate ontological presuppositions (435).

18. The trick, that is, as Daniel Breazeale has pointed out in "The Word, the World, and Nietzsche," is to "*use* language in such a way that its semblance of total descriptive adequacy breaks down and shows itself to be but a semblance" (314).

19. On liberation being furthered by recognizing that our particular conceptual structure has come to dominate us, see Stack, "Nietzsche as Structuralist," 37, 43. In "Nietzsche and the Correspondence Theory of Truth," *Dialogos* 16 (1981): 93–117, Stack draws the further conclusion that liberation requires not only a transition to a new conceptual structure, but also the more fundamental transition to a new *kind* of conceptualization (117). Allan Megill, in "Nietzsche as Aestheticist," 213, also notes this latter point, as do Jean Graybeal, in *Language and 'The Feminine' in Nietzsche and Heidegger* (Bloomington: Indiana University Press, 1990), 3, and Josef Simon, in "Ein Geflecht praktischer Begriffe Nietzsches Kritik am Freiheitsbegriff der philosophischen Tradition," in *Nietzsche und die philosophische Tradition*, ed. Josef Simon (Würzburg: Königshausen & Neumann, 1985), 106–122, esp. 116–117. Lawrence M. Hinman, in "Nietzsche, Metaphor, and Truth," *Philosophy and Phenomenological Research* (1982): 179–199, suggests that what results is an "aesthetic model of reference," in which words continue to refer in a rule-governed way, but it "simply [does] not make sense to ask whether they succeeded in dividing things up according to the way in which they are in themselves" (197).

20. *KSA*, 11:266.

21. Michel Foucault, "Nietzsche, Genealogy, History," tr. Donald F. Bouchard and Sherry Simon, in *Language, Counter-Memory, Practice: Selected Essays and Interviews*, ed. Bouchard (Ithaca, N.Y.: Cornell University Press, 1977), 139–164.

22. Michel Foucault, *Discipline and Punish: The Birth of the Prison*, tr. Alan Sheridan (New York: Pantheon, 1978).

23. Foucault classifies his various studies into three types, which he calls archaeological, genealogical, and ethical. These distinctions are unimportant for our purposes, however, since all three types of study are genealogical in the broader, less technical, Nietzschean sense. For a helpful discussion of Foucault's distinctions, see Arnold I. Davidson, "Archaeology, Genealogy, Ethics," in *Foucault: A Critical Reader*, ed. David Couzens Hoy (New York: Basil Blackwell, 1986), 221–233.

24. On *katachresis*, see the discussion of Quintilian in Nietzsche's lecture notes on ancient rhetoric (1872–3) at *RL*, 50/51. Richard Schacht, in "Philosophy as Linguistic Analysis: A Nietzschean Critique," *Philosophical Studies* 25 (1973): 153–171, also suggests that Nietzsche's own practice exemplifies this technique of making use of the old but transforming it with the new: "Through what might be called a process of imaginative intellection, [Nietzsche] lifts certain terms *out of* 'the language games which are their original homes'

(in Wittgenstein's phrase, and counter to his admonition); and, by linking them with other notions and suggesting new uses for them, while at the same time drawing upon certain of their original connotations, he employs these terms to work out new ways of thinking about things" (164). Kathleen Higgins, in "Nietzsche's View of Philosophical Style," *International Studies in Philosophy* 18 (1986): 67–81, seconds the thought, claiming that Nietzsche's own style directly reflects his goal of communicating the uncommon by helping his readers to liberate themselves from an externally imposed set of categories but without imposing a new and equally external set.

25. *MA*, II, 2: 127. Also see *MA*, II, 2: 113, and *GD*, X, 1.

26. *MA*, II, 2: 159. Here we see most clearly the link that Nietzsche identifies between the liberating process of opening oneself to the new and the deliberate simplification and impoverishment of one's style. Such impoverishment may have this effect because it responds to and highlights the inevitable inadequacy of any current term to express what is to be expressed, yet without lapsing into silence.

27. *MA*, II, 2: 140. Also see *MA*, II, 1: 134, where Nietzsche discusses Wagner's attempt to avoid petrifaction in the old even-measured rhythms while at the same time seeking to prevent the decay of rhythm altogether. Kelly Oliver, in "Revolutionary Horror," argues that poetry can create new grammatical conventions through the employment of rhythm, and that in so doing it highlights the arbitrariness of grammar and thus undermines the symbolic order (308). Mark Warren, in "Nietzsche and the Political," *New Nietzsche Studies* 2.1/2 (1997): 37–57, esp. 48, suggests that poetry is a use of language that resists linguistic reification. At *WM*, 809, Nietzsche calls the aesthetic state "the source of languages," and at *WM*, 812, describes "inartistic states" as those of "objectivity" and "mirroring."

28. *FWag*, Epilogue.

29. *FW*, Second Preface, 2.

30. See *GD*, VIII, 7–9. There, Nietzsche emphasizes that artists do not take from nature but rather give to it, out of an overloaded will that *must* spill over, resulting in a transformation of things that enriches and perfects them. Also see *GD*, III, 6, where Nietzsche writes that tragic artists select, strengthen, and correct reality in a way that enables their Dionysian affirmation of it. As noted before, Nietzsche does not limit such artistry to poets, so we must take "linguistic" broadly, in a sense that includes "conceptual" transformations of which philosophers, painters, and musicians are also capable. Indeed, in Nietzsche's early work he seems to think that music is the best of all the arts for effecting these transformations. See, for example, *WB*, 5.

31. Such tragic philosophers and poets are thus aware that language forms a bridge over becoming, and that the great danger to humanity is not that the bridge should collapse, but rather that it should be built *too well*, so well that those travelling over it lose all sense of the becoming that flows beneath it. In these terms, their task is to continually rebuild the bridge, out of the materials it already contains, and in such a way that its continual reconstruction is evident to travelers but does not pose an impassable barrier to their journeys. See *NN*, 9, where Nietzsche speaks of man as a bridge spanning becoming.

32. At *WM*, 522, Nietzsche writes, "We think *only* in the form of language ... *We cease to think when we refuse to do so under the constraint of language.*" Daniel Breazeale, in "The Word, the World, and Nietzsche," considers Nietzsche's most original contribution to the philosophy of language to be combining the awareness that language is essential to thought with the attempt to liberate us from the limits and coercions of language (301). Breazeale also notes that the two options one might consider in the latter attempt are the development of a linguistically unmediated knowing (which we have just seen Nietzsche reject) and the development of a new, philosophically adequate language (309) (the possibility of which we are currently examining). On these points also see Hennigfeld, "Sprache als Weltansicht," 443, 445.

33. *FWag*, 6.

34. Also see *GT*, 5, where Nietzsche says that Dionysian art is nonimagistic precisely because its images *are* its reality.

35. *EH*, IX, 3. Zarathustra's words come from *Z*, III, 9. It is significant that being only wants to become word through Zarathustra when he is at his home, which he calls solitude. This suggests that being becomes new, imagistic words only when the soul serving as its mouthpiece is sufficiently removed from the common use of words that normally constrain thought to think being in habitual ways. On this point also see *EH*, IX, 6, and A. M. Frazier, "Nietzsche on Inspiration and Language," *Journal of Thought* 9 (1974): 142–152, esp. 149. J. Hillis Miller, in "*Gleichnis* in Nietzsche's *Also Sprach Zarathustra*," *International Studies in Philosophy* 17 (1985): 3–15, esp. 10–12, understands this involuntary emergence of being into word, in which the inspired poet must first be transported so that she can later perform her own linguistic transportation beyond the ordinary, as the essence of parable or metaphor. Paul Evans Holbrook, Jr., in "Metaphor and the Will to Power," *International Studies in Philosophy* 20 (1988): 19–28, also links metaphor with revelation, divination, and inspiration (22, 26). James C. O'Flaherty, in "The Intuitive Mode of Reasoning in 'Zarathustra'," *International Studies in Philosophy* 15 (1983): 57–66, describes Nietzsche's practice in the writing of *Zarathustra* as the employment of various modes of "intuitive reasoning," the origins of which O'Flaherty locates in the work of Johann Georg Hamann. Mihailo Djuric, in "Denken und Dichten in 'Zarathustra'," 86, writes: "In 'Zarathustra' Nietzsche has superceded (*aufgehoben*) the previous meaning of thinking and poetizing (*Dichten*), conquered their abstract opposition (*Entzweiung*), discovered the original possibility of thinking, an original configuration (*Urgestalt*) that preceded both of these modes of saying which later became independent. For that which comes to language in 'Zarathustra' ... is equally poetic thinking or thinking poetry."

36. *GT*, 5. In *The Birth of Tragedy*, the Dionysian represents the collapse of individuation and the vanishing of subjectivity, the state in which we cease to be artists in the usual sense and instead become ourselves a work of art produced by and for the primordial unity. See *GT*, 1, 7, 8, 10, 16. Greek tragedy is then understood to balance this Dionysian state with the Apollinian, enabling each to speak the language of the other, so that in it the whole is perceived without destroying the individual. See *GT*, 21.

37. *WB*, 7. In this same section, Nietzsche says of Wagner, whom he considered such a dramatist, that his highest accomplishment is a "demonic communicability... whose greatness consists in its capacity both to surrender and to receive," and that his music serves as a "bridge between the self and the non-self" because "primordially determined nature" speaks through it. Also see *WB*, 9, where Nietzsche understands "the poetic" in Wagner to lie in the fact that he "thinks in visible and palpable events (*Vorgängen*), not in concepts."

38. *M*, 14. It is further suggested, at *M*, 500, that a thinker may fight these thoughts that offer themselves only at the cost of eventually making herself sick.

39. *Z*, II, 1, emphasis added; *Z*, III, 16. Gilles Deleuze, in *Nietzsche and Philosophy*, claims that this throwing of the dice – "an unreasonable and irrational, absurd and superhuman act" – "constitutes the tragic attempt and the tragic thought *par excellence*" (32). "The sense of the dicethrow," he continues, is to demonstrate that "thought" is opposed to "reason" (93); "Nietzsche proposes a new image of thought," which, unlike reason, "is never the natural exercise of a faculty... Thinking depends on forces which take hold of thought" (108).

40. *JGB*, 292.

41. *GM*, III, 4.

42. *GD*, IX, 8-10. Heidegger is perhaps the commentator who has made the most of Nietzsche's use of *Rausch*, but an adequate treatment of Heidegger's relation to Nietzsche, on this topic or in general, would require a study unto itself. See Martin Heidegger, *Nietzsche* (Pfullingen: Neske, 1961), esp. "*Der Rausch als ästhetischer Zustand*," vol. 1, 109-126, and "*Der Rausch als formschaffende Kraft*," vol. 1, 135-145. This has been translated by David Farrell Krell as *Nietzsche* (San Francisco: Harper & Row, 1979-1987); see esp. "Rapture as Aesthetic State," vol. 1, 92-106, and "Rapture as Form-engendering Force," vol. 1, 115-123. Mark P. Drost, in "Nietzsche and Mimesis," *Philosophy and Literature* 10.2 (1986): 309-317, esp. 314-316, describes Dionysian *Rausch* as the "state of being outside of oneself in such a way that the limits which constitute an interior self-space are disrupted... [The] subjective element vanishes into forgetfulness. The boundaries separating man from man and man from nature erode." Consequently, he continues, the artist in such a state "is not so much the creator of a work of art as he is himself a product of nature's impulses." Such an artist experiences "the essence of ecstasy" in being subject to "the movement of one impulse as it transgresses the other." Note, however, that Nietzsche explicitly distances himself from those who, with what he calls "faith in intoxication," consider only their intoxicated self to be their true self. Nietzsche thinks this is all too often merely one more mask for a decadent hostility to one's actual self and the actual world. See *M*, 50.

43. As Werner Hamacher puts it in "The Promise of Interpretation," Nietzsche carries out "a Copernican turn whose center is no longer the will but, as it were, the turn itself, alteration and decentering" (131). He goes on to draw the conclusion that as a result of this Copernican turn "it is no longer

possible to decide whether knowledge forces its forms onto the 'things in themselves' or whether the forms of things – which may be completely heterogeneous with respect to one another – force themselves onto human knowledge" (135). In "'Disgregation of the Will'," Hamacher adds: "The hyposemantic exuberance of the 'word' and the 'thing' 'outliving' is also the abyssal condition for every conventional employment of language and for every life that performs its functions according to the forms of consistent social codes" (163). Deborah Cook, in "Nietzsche, Foucault, Tragedy," concurs in her comparison of Nietzsche's new language to Foucault's, concluding that no subject speaks the language of transgression. She finds an affinity between the madness which serves for Foucault as the "empty space from which work and writing come" and Nietzsche's Dionysian frenzy; both, on her account, contest the limits that constitute us and our perceptions of the world, and at the same time make possible the discursive language through which those limits are then reconstituted (146–148). Also see Gary Shapiro, "*Übersehen*: Nietzsche and Tragic Vision," *Research in Phenomenology* 25 (1995): 27–44, who notes that as early as *The Birth of Tragedy* Nietzsche understood tragedy as a new kind of seeing or framing that subverts individuality. Allan Megill, in "Nietzsche as Aestheticist," offers an opposed and, in my opinion, mistaken interpretation, writing that Nietzsche portrays the process of imposing new categories on the world as a "totally free and individual matter" (213–214).

Conclusion

1. Mark Warren, *Nietzsche and Political Thought*, 152–158, points out that much of modern political theory fails to make even this move, taking free agency for granted without inquiring into its conditions.
2. Nietzsche asks "whether we know of any other method of acting well than always thinking well; the latter *is* an action, and the former presupposes thought" (*WM*, 458).
3. On this reciprocal unification of the spiritual subject and the natural object that willing presupposes, see McCumber, *The Company of Words*, 146–147. McCumber describes the relation between philosophy's systematic dialectics (in our terms, the subjective, or spiritual, pole) and that which is outside it (the objective, or natural, pole) as "one of mutual transformation."
4. At *PhG*, 76/53, Hegel writes that in the *Phenomenology* "we are asking what knowledge is." On the first assumption, see *PhG*, 76/52: "consciousness simultaneously *distinguishes* itself from something, and at the same time *relates* to it, or, as it is said, this something exists *for* consciousness; and the determinate aspect of this *relating*, or of the *being* of something *for a consciousness*, is *knowing*." On the second assumption, see *PhG*, 82/58: "approach to the object must be *immediate* or *receptive*; we must alter nothing in the object as it presents itself. In apprehending (*Auffassen*) it, we must refrain from trying to comprehend (*Begreifen*) *it*."
5. Hegel thus agrees with Kant that thought constitutes its own objects, but takes a step beyond him in arguing that it also constitutes the very means by which

it constitutes those objects, its own categories (which for Kant remain a fixed given, not produced by thought itself).

6. Hegel makes this claim in a letter to Voss (the German translator of Homer) written in March 1805, which can be found in *Hegel: The Letters*, tr. Clark Butler and Christine Seiler (Bloomington: Indiana University Press, 1984), 106-108.

7. On the relation between ordinary languages and philosophical thought in Hegel, see McCumber, *The Company of Words*, Chapters 4, 7, and 10. McCumber distinguishes between what he calls historical and systematic dialectics. In the former, ordinary representational terms (of German, for example) develop in response to new experiences of the linguistic community. In the latter, philosophical concepts develop in an attempt to maintain their systematic integrity while also incorporating new terms that have arisen through historical dialectics. Ideally, the two processes work together, so that the meanings of representational terms and philosophical concepts converge and whatever disparities remain between the two can be clearly stated. McCumber characterizes this double process as one in which philosophy is taught to speak German and German is taught to speak philosophy. Also see Daniel J. Cook, *Language in the Philosophy of Hegel*, esp. 66-73, 118-119, 139-140, 161-169, 173; and Houlgate, *Hegel, Nietzsche and the Criticism of Metaphysics*, 272-273 n31.

8. See, for example, the poem Hegel wrote just before his death, to his student Heinrich Stieglitz, which can be found in *Hegel: The Letters*, tr. Butler and Seiler, 680. There Hegel describes it as a "crime" that each individual "wants to hear himself, to do the talking, too." Distinguishing himself from such individuals, Hegel claims to have been driven by the word (rather than the other way around). He hopes that this word will at last escape from him, "that to this word other spirits [will] reciprocate," and "that these spirits may bear it to the people and put it to work!"

9. We have not, of course, followed Hegel through the entirety of his system, but in Chapters 2 and 3 we have been witness to substantial portions of his efforts to articulate the categories of will and spirit.

10. Nietzsche thus takes his own advice, which he presents to philosophers in *WM*, 409: "No longer accept concepts as a gift, nor merely purify and polish them, but first *make* and *create* them, present them and make them convincing... What is needed above all is an absolute skepticism toward all inherited concepts." In a related vein, at *WM*, 767, Nietzsche writes that to be an individual one "has to interpret in a quite individual way even the words he has inherited... even if he does not create a formula: as an interpreter he is still creative." Sarah Kofman, in *Nietzsche and Metaphor*, writes that Nietzsche "attaches novel and unheard of metaphors to habitual ones, [which] enables the latter to be enlivened and revaluated, their inadequacies to be highlighted" (60).

11. There have been many noteworthy contributions to the issue of the relation between Nietzsche's styles and the thoughts they seek to communicate: Daniel Conway, in "Parastrategesis, or: Rhetoric for Decadents," *Philosophy and Rhetoric* 27.3 (1994): 179-201, emphasizes that Nietzsche needs readers capable of bringing his work to fruition, and argues that he therefore

employs a "parastrategic" rhetorical method – "neither fully strategic nor purely accidental" (189) – designed to create such readers; Babette E. Babich, in "On Nietzsche's Concinnity: An Analysis of Style," *Nietzsche-Studien* 19 (1990): 59–80, and Alan D. Schrift, in "Reading, Writing, Text: Nietzsche's Deconstruction of Author-ity," *International Studies in Philosophy* 17 (1985): 55–63, make similar points, contending that Nietzsche's style invokes the reader's response to project a completion of the text; Douglas A. Gilmour, in "On Language, Writing, and the Restoration of Sight: Nietzsche's Philosophical Palinode," *Philosophy and Rhetoric* 27.3 (1994): 245–269, notes not only that the inconclusiveness of Nietzsche's aphorisms requires an aesthetic effort on the part of the reader, but also that Nietzsche's unfamiliar gestures of communication disrupt the process of linguistic familiarization against which he wants his readers to struggle; Paul de Man, in *Allegories, of Reading: Figural Language in Rousseau, Nietzsche, Rilke, and Proust* (New Haven, Conn.: Yale University Press, 1979), makes both of these points, and concludes that Nietzsche shakes our "ontological confidence" (123) by forcing us always to interpret his residual meaning by means of "nonauthoritative secondary statements" (99); Gary Shapiro, in *Nietzschean Narratives* (Bloomington: Indiana University Press, 1989), contends that Nietzsche describes and exemplifies "a battery of narrative forms and styles" in an attempt to escape both the quest for absolute certainty (2) and the certain fixation on any particular errors (29); Alexander Nehamas, in *Nietzsche: Life as Language*, emphasizes that Nietzsche employs stylistic pluralism in an "effort to present views without presenting them as more than views of his own" (20–21); Michel Haar, in "Nietzsche and Metaphysical Language," tr. Cyril and Liliane Welch, *Man and World* 4.4 (1971): 359–395, argues that Nietzsche employs concepts with pluralistic, incompatible meanings in order to undermine language's tendency to fabricate false identities. Haar insists, however, that "language cannot smash the principle of identity without smashing itself," and thus concludes that Nietzsche "deprives himself of both speech and writing" and is cast back "into the dissociated and inexpressible clutches of Chaos" (395). Haar thus betrays himself to be one of those readers we saw Nietzsche chastise in Chapter 7, one who cannot perceive, because he cannot conceive, unity without closure, meaning without monosemy. Closer to my own position is Bernd Magnus, "Deconstruction Site: The 'Problem of Style' in Nietzsche's Philosophy," *Philosophical Topics* 19.2 (1991): 215–243. Magnus agrees with Haar that Nietzsche's style, by resisting closure and forcing the reader to provide connections that unify the text, embodies the thesis that meaning is undecidable. But, contrary to Haar, Magnus does not think that this leaves Nietzsche mute. Magnus refers to Nietzsche's "polysemantic metaphors" as "self-consuming concepts." Such a concept "requires as a condition of its intelligibility (or even its iteration) the very contrast it wishes to set aside," and Magnus contends that these concepts "remain perennially fresh and plausible in an important sense, even *after* it has been pointed out that their intelligibility and force are purchased at the cost of presupposing the very concepts to be displaced" (230–231). Magnus concludes that such polysemantic self-consumption – which he considers equivalent to Hegelian *Aufhebungen* without the optimistic elevation that he attributes to the latter – is Nietzsche's response to the problem of thinking about language nonrepresentationally. Also see Magnus's more extensive discussion, coauthored with Stanley Stewart and Jean-Pierre Mileur, *Nietzsche's Case: Philosophy As/And Literature* (New York: Routledge, 1993), esp. Chapters 1 and 4.

12. Whether Hegel's own system is actually or potentially open to the development of new conceptual categories is the subject of ongoing debate. For a helpful consideration of this topic, see David Kolb, "What Is Open and What Is Closed in the Philosophy of Hegel," *Philosophical Topics* 19.2 (1991): 29–50. Kolb argues that "an open thinking would have difficulty comprehending and reconciling in the strong sense Hegel has in mind," 34. In *The Company of Words*, John McCumber contends, to the contrary, that "the System is much more supple than has previously been thought. Not only could Hegel have developed it in directions other than those it actually takes in his writings, but it has enormous capacities for revision" (127–128). For a further development of Kolb's position, and a direct response by John W. Burbidge, see their contributions to *Hegel and the Tradition: Essays in Honour of H. S. Harris*, ed. Michael Baur and John Russon (Toronto: University of Toronto Press, 1997). I have offered a brief summary and interpretation of the debate between Kolb and Burbidge in my review of *Hegel and the Tradition* in the *Bulletin of the Hegel Society of Great Britain* 43/44 (2001): 72–79.

13. Typical is a note from 1888 or 1889, *KSA*, 13:333: "The categories are 'truths' only in the sense that they are life-conditioning for us."

14. Another note from 1888 or 1889, *KSA*, 13:282: "The categories of reason *could* have become established, after a lot of rummaging around and trial and error, on the basis of relative utility. There came a point where they were assembled, and brought to consciousness as a whole – and where they were 'ordered,' that is, where they came to work as providing order. From then on they counted as a priori, as beyond experience, as undismissable. And yet, *perhaps* they expressed nothing but a purposiveness of a specific race or species their only 'truth' is their usefulness."

15. A variety of commentators have made similar points. Kelly Oliver, in "Revolutionary Horror: Nietzsche and Kristeva on the Politics of Poetry," *Social Theory and Practice* 15.3 (1989): 305–320, notes that Nietzsche's poetry cannot discriminate between goals that liberate and goals that oppress (316–317). Werner Hamacher, in "'Disgregation of the Will'," writes that "by virtue of its specific inconclusiveness, incompleteness, and defenselessness . . . disgregation remains open onto other ideologies of freedom, other moralities of undifferentiated equality, and a politics of authoritarian leveling that needs violence to establish a common measure where no measure is to be found" (167). David Kolb argues in *The Critique of Pure Modernity* that although Hegel is wrong to claim that "all importantly constitutive difference can be thought through determinate negation and mediation" (43), it is still the case that "if we need to do more than point out the self-undermining of closures and totalities, and if we need to say more about the particulars of our age, Hegel can be of great use" (48). He also rightly points out that "to criticize closure and totality should not mean simply to avoid it. That would be to remain dependent on it as the negative pole of our efforts" (46). Alexander Nehamas, in *Nietzsche*, points out that Nietzsche

does not make this mistake, since he criticizes not unity per se, but rather unities that are *given* rather than *achieved*, and unities that are permanently closed to future change (182, 189).

16. John McCumber, in *Poetic Interaction*, identifies a complementarity between Hegel and Heidegger similar to that which I find between Hegel and Nietzsche. In McCumber's view, Heidegger complements Hegel by providing an account of the ways in which aesthetic language and dialogue open individuals and cultures to new contexts of shared significance, while Hegel complements Heidegger by providing an account of how language enables individuals and cultures to be unified within and reconciled to these contexts. McCumber thus concludes that "freedom as unification of the self and as improvisation ... must come into play together ... I cannot have Hegel without Heidegger" (425). See Chapters 6, 7, 18, 23, and the introduction to Part 3. David Kolb also explores the possibility of our taking something from both Hegel and Heidegger in *The Critique of Pure Modernity*, Chapters 10–12, esp. 213–230. He emphasizes that we need to do this while resisting the temptation to reconcile the two into a harmonious whole, which he believes would be to remain too closely allied with Hegel.

17. In "The Promise of Interpretation," Werner Hamacher describes "the only freedom this side of the autonomy of the subject" as an opening of the self to others, an opening in which both self and other are altered in their co-action and communication, and in which the will's self-projection toward its destination or goal is suspended and disrupted (128, 131). He thus concludes that the will is "autonomous only in being heteronomous" (128). Also see his "Disgregation of the Will," where he writes: "If there is individual autonomy, it is only by virtue of that which exceeds this autonomy" (156); "at the moment of departure, which language marks – and only at that moment, nowhere else – individuals contact one another and make a stab, in their division, at co-division, at communication, at *Mit-teilung*. The mobile site of society, like that of the individual, is this departure in which the two never stop separating from each other and from themselves" (173); "communication is therefore not the mediation between various already constituted positions but is the constitution of these very portions from the distribution of difference that holds them apart ... Communication ... denies [the] claim that it is an autonomous positing" (177–178); "the art of socializing the individual ... shows itself here as an art of tangential touching: not a differential unfolding of a single thought that must constantly demonstrate its formal necessity but an art of contingency" (178). Hamacher finally concludes that "what remains for the individual – without further consolation – is its freedom: the freedom to assume that under the law of disgregation and the law of 'outliving' and thus under the law of exposition, it is indeterminate, unsent-for, undefined. Finite, without end" (180).

INDEX

absolute spirit, 10, 23–5, 69–70, 74–5, 87, 91, 99–100, 101–2, 105–6, 108, 110–11, 115, 126, 232, 245–6, 249, 256, 260, 264, 265, 266, 267, 270

abstract right, 24, 28, 31–2, 34–6, 39, 40–2, 44–5, 49, 52, 56–8, 65–6, 69, 126, 252, 263

abyss: dancing by, 184; seeing with pride, 209–10

Acton, H. B., 256

administration of justice, 61

Allison, Henry, 244

ancient freedom, 46, 254

ancient linguistic prejudices, 218

ancient philosophers, 294–5

Apollo (Apollinian), 286, 290–1, 300, 311

Aristotle, 104, 113, 254

Armey, Dick, 244

asceticism, 136–8, 140–4; as a bridge to freedom for philosophers, 292; as a condition of destroying noble will, 182; as creating memory, 167–8

authority, modern rejection of, 114–5

autonomy, 109, 126; and *arête*, 285; heteronomy as a condition of, 317; Kantian, 4–6, 7–9, 25, 28, 228; moral, 56, 109–10; Nietzsche's concern with the structure and history of, 272; noble, 10; *Sittlichkeit* as a condition of, for both Hegel and Nietzsche, 286; of the sovereign individual, 168

Babich, Babette E., 315

becoming: conditioned by pain, 200; eternal return of, 202–3, 215; innocence of, 210, 273, 305; joy of, 196; obscured by linguistic mythology of being, 150–2,

214, 310; subjection of contingent objects to, 262; subjection of world to, 209, 230, 233; tragic affirmation of, 197–8, 204, 210, 215, 230, 233; wants to learn to speak through the tragic soul, 224; what one is, 106, 163, 166, 169–70, 179–80

Beerling, R. F., 245

Berlin, Isaiah, 243, 269

Bible (biblical), 206, 235, 275, 276, 288, 305

Blondel, Eric, 296

Breazeale, Daniel, 245, 306, 307, 308, 309, 311

Brogan, Walter A., 298

Buddhism, 280

Burbidge, John, 262, 316

Butler, Clark, 262

Cadello, James P., 299

Carnois, Bernard, 244

categories: inappropriate use of, by herd morality, 146–8; inappropriate use of, by nobility, 230; and noncategorial concepts, 236–9, 241–2; of ordinary consciousness, 118; of pure thought, 104–5, 232, 234–9, 241–2; relationship of free spirits to, 295; revolutionary changes of, 118

Catholicism, 114

chaos: beautiful, 157; as a condition of creation, 145; of decadent instincts, 161–2, 274, 284; eternal return of, 203; flight from, 159; forging a will out of, by simplifying and mastering, 162, 176; of *laisser aller*, 172; of modern souls, 177–8; as a result of destroying the moral will,

319